Seascape Gardening

From New England to the Carolinas

Seascape Gardening

ANNE HALPIN
Photography by ROGER FOLEY

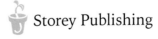 Storey Publishing

The mission of Storey Publishing is to serve our customers by publishing practical information that encourages personal independence in harmony with the environment.

Edited by Carleen Madigan Perkins
Cover design by Kent Lew
Text design by Kent Lew and Vicky Vaughn
Production by Vicky Vaughn and
    Jennifer Jepson Smith
Indexed by Christine R. Lindemer,
    Boston Road Communications
Illustrations copyright © Janet Fredericks

Printed in China by Regent Publishing Services
10 9 8 7 6 5 4 3 2 1

Text copyright © 2006 by Anne Halpin
Cover and interior photographs copyright © Roger Foley
    with the exception of those listed on page 215

The information in this book is true and complete to the best of our knowledge. All recommendations are made without guarantee on the part of the author or Storey Publishing. The author and publisher disclaim any liability in connection with the use of this information. For additional information please contact Storey Publishing, 210 MASS MoCA Way, North Adams, MA 01247.

Storey books are available for special premium and promotional uses and for customized editions. For further information, please call 1-800-793-9396.

LIBRARY OF CONGRESS CATALOGING-IN-PUBLICATION DATA

Halpin, Anne Moyer.
    Seascape gardening / by Anne Halpin ; photographs by Roger Foley.
        p. cm.
    Includes index.
    ISBN-13: 978-1-58017-533-1; ISBN-10: 1-58017-533-3 (jacketed hardcover : alk. paper)
    ISBN-13: 978-1-58017-531-1; ISBN-10: 1-58017-531-7 (pbk. : alk. paper)
    1. Seaside gardening. 2. Seaside gardening—Atlantic Coast (U.S.) I. Title.

SB460.H35 2006
635.9'0914'6—dc22
                                                        2005021732

For all the intrepid gardeners who nurture plants near the sea

Contents

CHAPTER 1

Coastal
Conditions

WHO DOESN'T LOVE THE SEASHORE? The sparkling water, the soft summer breezes, and the rhythmic crashing of waves on the beach have a way of drawing the tension right out of us. The climate at the seashore is so congenial because it is modified by the ocean. Look at the USDA Hardiness Zone Map (see page 216) and you will notice that coastal areas are designated as warmer zones than places not far inland. In summer and early autumn, the seaside is indeed a pleasant place.

ABOVE: Purple wands of anise hyssop (*Agastache* sp.) and pink cosmos sway in the coastal breezes in this seaside garden.

RIGHT: A quiet cove at sunset along the dramatic, rocky shoreline of Massachusetts becomes a very different place when storm winds blow.

But for plants, as for year-round residents, the seashore can be a tough place to live. There is a lot of wind, for one thing; at the beach it blows almost constantly, carrying with it abrasive sand and drying salt. The soil is sandy — almost entirely sand close to the beach — and sand is a harsh growing medium for plants. Sand is low in the nutrients plants need to grow, and it is usually dry, because rainwater passes through it quickly, ending up in the water table far below.

Autumn weather is mild along the coast, because the sea cools more slowly than do the landmasses inland. But in spring the weather is cool because the ocean warms more slowly than land, and spring weather can be unpredictable at the seashore, with chilly rains and late cold snaps alternating with spells of mild, sunny conditions. Fall brings hurricanes; winter offers the coastal storms called nor'easters that can be as devastating as hurricanes. Plants can be flattened by the strong storm winds, trees can be uprooted, and high tides can wash over the dunes and flood gardens with icy saltwater.

To survive at the seashore without help from humans, a plant has to be able to stand up to winds and abrasive blasting from wind-driven sand and salt. It can demand little in the way of nourishment from the soil, and it must be able to survive with little water or to send its roots deep underground to tap into the nearest aquifer. In addition, the plant has to endure the salty fogs that settle over it when the wind is still. But plants can, and do, survive at the shore. When you grow plants adapted to seashore conditions, and create sheltered places for other kinds of plants, seaside gardens can be dazzling and full of color from spring well into fall, or even winter in the southernmost regions.

To succeed with a garden at the seashore, you first have to understand the sort of environment you're dealing with. That's where we'll begin.

Goldenrod is one tough plant — it grows happily among rocks near the water's edge and withstands salt spray and wind.

A Snapshot of the Seashore, from North to South

THE COASTLINE IS CONSTANTLY changing in response to climatic cycles. During the ice ages, the polar ice caps expanded and glaciers formed, locking up more water, so the overall sea level dropped. More land was exposed and the beaches were broader. During warmer periods, the polar ice caps shrank, glaciers melted and retreated farther and farther north, and the sea level rose. In our own time, global warming is widely believed to be causing shrinkage of the polar ice and a corresponding rise in sea level. As the shoreline moves, coastal plants and animals move along with it.

Rivers also influence the coastline. Bays, estuaries, and salt marshes all formed as a result of the action of rivers. Rivers flowing into the sea carry with them sediments and dissolved materials that are deposited on the ocean floor when the river meets the sea. The sediments build up over time — they cover the continental shelf, which was created as sea level rose after the last ice age and now underlies the fairly shallow water close to the coast.

Ocean waves and currents help to shape the coastline too. The waves pound away relentlessly. Waves in winter are bigger and stronger than summer waves, which are gentler. Winter waves tend to erode and wear down beaches, while in summer the beach can be naturally replenished when the waves are less intense.

THE ROCKY NORTH

The Atlantic seacoast looks different depending on where you are. The northernmost part of the coast, from Maine south to Connecticut, is the edge of the North American continent itself; it is rocky, with wooded bluffs and stony shores. There are high cliffs and headlands, rocky bluffs that were once part of ancient mountains, ledges and caves, bays and coves. The coastline changes continuously, but these rocky shores have changed little

Along the coast of the northeastern United States, rocky ledges and bluffs drop right to the edge of the sea, and where beaches do exist, they are usually stony.

From Cape Cod southward, Atlantic beaches are sandy and lined with dunes, an ecosystem undergoing a continual process of change as beaches are eroded and rebuilt.

since ancient times. Rock seems hard and permanent to us, but it is slowly, constantly weathering. Waves wear away at the base of rocky cliffs, rainwater seeps into cracks and causes fractures when it freezes, and eventually pieces of the rock break off and fall. The rock pieces break into smaller stones, and eventually are ground into sand. In the Northeast, the coastline drops steeply toward the ocean and the strong tides and high-energy wave action carry away any sand that forms — there's no place for it to collect. Instead of being flat and sandy, many of the beaches there are covered with stones.

There are islands, capes, and peninsulas in the Northeast, surrounded by bays and coves. Around some of the edges of these bodies of water are marshes. Long Island Sound, which lies between Long Island and Connecticut, protects both southern Connecticut and northern Long Island from the effects of the ocean.

From Massachusetts to Long Island, the seashore was formed by debris left behind by glaciers as they retreated after the last ice age. As you travel down the coast, from Cape Cod southward, you can find salt marshes and sandy beaches. From Long Island to South Carolina, the seashore is lined mostly with beaches and dunes. These beaches are in a process of continuous change; they shrink, then are replenished in response to natural seasonal cycles

and the effect of storms. As the beach and dunes reestablish themselves, their position is often a bit farther landward than their previous position. Human interventions — bulkheads, jetties, and other coastal structures — also alter the coastline. These structures cause sand to erode in one place and deposit in another.

SANDY SHORES

From Long Island south to Virginia Beach, in northern Virginia, the Atlantic coastline is a low, flat plain. The Delmarva Peninsula, made up of Delaware and parts of Maryland and Virginia, lies between the ocean and the Chesapeake Bay. The Delaware Bay turns southern New Jersey into a sort of peninsula, too. A string of low-lying, sandy barrier islands runs along this stretch of the coast, with bays separating them from the mainland.

Barrier islands are created by the action of waves and currents that deposit sand that builds up high enough to rise out of the ocean. The islands begin as sandbars that get bigger and bigger and then act as buffers for the mainland coast, dissipating the force of surging ocean waves during storms and absorbing the energy generated by tides and ocean currents to ameliorate the impact of floods and winds. The Atlantic barrier islands are not isolated entities but are connected to one another by common winds, water currents, and, in

Freshwater rivers deposit sediment where they flow into the salty sea, and estuaries form around the junction of river and ocean.

turn, the movement of sand along the coast. What happens to one of the barrier islands affects the rest. The seaward sides of the barrier islands are lined with dunes. The back sides have salt marshes and, in some cases, more dunes.

Beaches and barrier islands are ephemeral, in geological terms. They change all the time, from year to year and even day by day. The chain of barrier islands ends with North Carolina's Outer Banks. Farther south is Cape Hatteras, the most northerly of a series of capes that extends into South Carolina. At Cape Hatteras, the warm Gulf Stream flowing north meets cold offshore currents flowing south, and the climate can be stormy. The North Carolina coast represents the limit of the growing range for a variety of plants. Some, such as palms, can grow no farther north. For others, like beach heather, North Carolina is the southern limit of their range.

THE LOW COUNTRY

The coast of South Carolina is generally calmer than that of North Carolina. A number of islands, called sea islands, lie off the coast. These islands are wider than the Outer Banks and the barrier islands farther north. Dunes lie along the oceanfront, with flatlands and swales around them. Farther into the interior of the islands the natural vegetation is pine and oak wood-

lands. The western boundary of the sea islands and the eastern edge of the mainland are dotted with marshes, with creeks cutting through them. The Ashley and Cooper Rivers run into the ocean and deposit sediment at their mouths.

RIVERS, ESTUARIES, AND BAYS

Rivers affect the ocean wherever they empty into it. They deposit sediment into the sea that can change the coastline. Estuaries, salt marshes, and bays all can form because of the action of rivers. Estuaries, which are really tidal rivers, are a unique environment, a mix of freshwater and saltwater. The freshwater flowing into an estuary from a river is lighter and less dense than saltwater and tends to float on top of the saltwater where it flows into the bay.

Salinity varies in an estuary. Closer to the river, the water is brackish, lower in salt. Approaching the bay, the water becomes increasingly salty. Sea creatures living in estuaries must adapt to fluctuating salt levels caused by tidal currents and flooding caused by storms.

Bays are parts of the ocean protected by arms of land extending into the sea. The tide rises and falls in a bay as it does in the ocean, but large waves do not break onto the shoreline as they do on ocean beaches. Although waterfront conditions on the bay are often less severe than those on the oceanfront, storms can still cause damage.

THE COMPOSITION OF SAND

The composition of beach sand varies along the length of the coast. Northern and mid-Atlantic beaches contain a high percentage of quartz particles, which offer little in the way of mineral nutrients for plants. The sand provides a medium in which plants can anchor their roots, but it offers little else for them. Farther down the coast, in South Carolina, the sand contains calcium carbonate, which comes from the decomposition of seashells. But no matter what its composition, beach sand doesn't stay in one place — it blows around almost constantly. Over time, entire dunes can move and re-form.

Changes in the Land

On eastern Long Island, Montauk daisies (*Nipponan-themum nipponicum*) bloom lavishly in October. Tolerant of salt and wind, these are growing right on the dunes.

Not all seashore places are the same. Although this book deals with only the temperate parts of the Atlantic coast of the United States (the subtropical climates of Florida and the Deep South are a very different environment), there's a lot of variation from one end to the other, and sometimes even within a five-mile stretch. The rocky coast of Maine is a whole lot different from the Outer Banks of North Carolina. The back side of the primary dune is different from the plain a mile behind it.

BARRIER BEACHES AND PRIMARY DUNES

Beaches form when ocean waves and currents deposit sand, or rock weathers over time, on an unobstructed coastline. An important thing to remember about beaches is that they change all the time. The sand is constantly on the move. Along the Atlantic Coast, winter storms tear away at the beach and the dunes. In summer, the ocean is quieter and the beach rebuilds. As described on pages 11 to 13, the beach surface may be sandy or stony (in which case it is called shingle).

Dunes are simply mounds of sand that form where something stops the flow of wind inland from off the sea, in turn causing the wind to drop the sand it is carrying to the lee side of the obstruction. The obstruction need not be large — it could be

as small as a clump of grass or a piece of driftwood. Sand begins to pile up around the obstruction as the wind dumps more of it, always to the lee side. Over time, a dune is built. Then pioneer plants, notably American beach grass (*Ammophila breviligulata*) and sea oats (*Uniola paniculata*), begin to colonize the dune and hold the sand in place. American beach grass is adept at stabilizing moving sand because its rhizomes grow both horizontally and vertically, providing good anchorage. We usually think of dunes in relation to barrier beaches, but dunes can be found in other places where there's a lot of wind and enough sand for it to blow around. Near the coast, dunes can form along shores at the back of barrier islands as well as at the front, and along the shores of the mainland, too. The dunes develop when the wind blowing across the beach picks up sand and carries it along until it meets with plants, fences, or other impediments that slow it down enough to cause it to drop the sand.

Dunes protect the land behind them from the ravages of the sea. Naturally formed dunes have breaks in them through which ocean surges can flow and release their considerable energy. Where these gaps don't exist, such as in artificially constructed dunes or hard structures like seawalls, wave energy doesn't dissipate and the waves are more likely to erode the

Only the most resilient plants can survive in sand dunes, even secondary dunes set back from the beach. Most dune plants are low growing, and the few trees that can adapt, like these pines, will not be tall.

beach and cut away at the dunes. Eventually the sea will break through somewhere.

Even naturally occurring dunes change. The wind that forms the dunes can also destroy them. The breakdown process often starts when the dunes are disturbed by people or animals walking on them, vehicles driving over them, natural vegetation being damaged or removed during construction, recreational activities, or storms or other forces of nature.

Sometimes referred to as the "pioneer zone," the beach and primary dunes are the toughest places for plants to grow. The primary dunes are those closest to the sea. Not many plants can survive on the beach on a long-term basis, and almost none of the ones that can are woody. You won't find trees growing on the barrier beaches of the Atlantic Coast, at least not on their own. In fact, the first plants of any kind are found from the high-tide line into the dunes. It's almost always windy at the beach, with abrasive sand and drying salt carried on the breezes and gusts. Sand can be carried in the air when the wind blows 12 to 15 miles per hour or faster — a very common occurrence. The system of dunes above the high-tide line on the beach protects the flatlands behind them. But occasionally a storm will send the tide surging into the dunes, flooding inland areas.

Plants play a critical role in the ecosystem of beach and dune. American beach

Bluffs, being raised above the highest wind and salt concentrations, can support a greater variety of plants than can dune environments.

Dunes form where beach grass and other barrier plants obstruct the wind blowing inland from the ocean and cause it to drop the sand it carries.

Behind the dunes lies a somewhat protected "scrub zone." It can support a good variety of plants, though it is sometimes inundated with seawater.

grass, for example, helps to stabilize the dunes on which it grows along the Middle Atlantic beaches. Farther south, sea oats are an important dune stabilizer. The plants' leaves trap sand being blown inland and slow the speed of the wind as it passes over the tops of the dunes. The wide-ranging roots of the grass plants help to keep the sand in place on the dunes and prevent them from eroding.

Many communities actively plant beach grass to protect their dunes. Some put up snow fencing, which also reduces the degree of erosion on primary dunes.

COASTAL BLUFFS

When you think about the rocky coast of Maine, you're thinking of coastal bluffs. Ocean bluffs are found farther down the coastline as well, such as in Montauk, at the very eastern tip of Long Island. But they are most closely associated with New England. The bluffs are raised above sea level — in some places by more than 100 feet — and don't get hit with as much salt spray as barrier beaches and primary dunes. The northern shore of Long Island has coastal sound bluffs — sandy bluffs that border Long Island Sound, which separates Long Island from Connecticut.

Long Island's bluffs are sandy, but along the northern Atlantic coast the underlying rock contains less quartz, and the soil that results is less sandy and more moist. Where the bluffs are wooded the soil contains more organic matter and nutrients than beach sand. In some parts of New England, the woods come almost to the edges of bays. Flooding from high tides isn't an issue on the bluffs. These environments are altogether more congenial places for plants — and easier places to garden — than beachside locations. Still, they are not without challenges. The soil on

Much of the seaside landscape in South Carolina — often called the Low Country — is dominated by low-lying saltwater marshes.

New England bluffs is rocky. Fogs rolling in off the ocean bring moisture, but they also carry salt, which is drying to plants. And the wind can be severe.

COASTAL PLAINS

A coastal plain, sometimes referred to as the "scrub zone" (which for our purpose here is not quite the same as the broader coastal plain defined by geologists), we will consider to be the flat landmass that lies behind primary dunes or coastal bluffs. The coastal plain gets some protection from salt spray and wind from the dunes or bluffs, and the soil, while sandy, generally has at least a thin layer of organic matter on top. But storms can still send saltwater flooding inland, and strong winds blow. Planting or building windbreaks makes the coastal plain a better place for gardening.

In some places there are depressions in the coastal plain, between the primary and secondary dunes, called swales. A variety of plants grows naturally in these low pockets — bearberry (*Arctostaphylos uva-ursi*), bayberry (*Myrica pensylvanica*), beach plum (*Prunus maritima*), and eastern red cedar (*Juniperus virginiana*), for instance. If the water table is close enough to the surface, ponds may form in these depressions; if the ocean does not flood into them, these ponds can contain freshwater. When seawater mixes in they become brackish, and marsh habitats — supporting plants like

cordgrass (*Spartina pectinata*) and sea lavender (*Limonium carolinianum*) — may develop around their edges.

The size of our coastal plain varies a great deal. In Maine there really is no coastal plain, but in North Carolina it extends inland for about 150 miles.

BARRIER ISLANDS AND SALT MARSHES

Barrier islands are narrow islands separated from the mainland by saltwater bays or lagoons. They lie parallel to the coastline, close to sea level, and are subject to plenty of wind and salt spray. Storms can bring saltwater flooding to barrier islands, and in severe storms the sea can cross the entire island to meet the lagoon. The soil is mostly sand, with perhaps a thin layer of organic matter on top. Even with regular rainfall, plants must have deep roots and be able to tolerate drought if they are going to survive.

Barrier islands may have secondary dunes behind the coastal plain, on the north or west side (depending on which part of the coast they are near). The lee (landward) side of secondary dunes can be home to an assortment of plants in different microclimates.

The two big limiting factors for plants growing on barrier beaches are how exposed they are to the briny sea breezes and how far above sea level they sit. At lower elevations, plants must endure occasional flooding, but they are also closer to the water table, so more moisture is available on a regular basis.

Farther up the back of a dune, the surface of the sand becomes hot and dry in summer. Only plants that have deep roots can access the water table. The only other plants that can grow here without human intervention are desert plants that can survive for long periods without water.

Salt Spray and Gale-force Winds

Wind is a constant at the seashore, and plants must be able to bend before it without breaking. Ornamental grasses are flexible enough to sway and dance in the breeze.

THE WEATHER AT THE SEASHORE IS often dramatic, and it can change quickly. But no matter where you live along the coast, your plants will have to contend with wind, salt, sand, and intense sun. It's important to choose plants that can handle the stressful conditions, of course. But gardeners can take steps to moderate the climate in their garden, to give plants a more hospitable environment and to broaden the range of plants likely to thrive in it.

Plants native to seashores have developed special adaptations that enable them to withstand the environmental stresses. Many are especially strong structurally, with sturdy but flexible trunks and branches able to withstand strong winds. Some plants (grasses, for instance) bend and sway before the wind so their stems do not snap. Deep root systems provide good anchors against the wind, and can travel far underground to tap into natural water sources. Some plants, such as beach plum, are smaller when they grow near the beach and grow larger in more protected locations farther back. See "How Plants Protect Themselves" (page 19) for more on plants' protective measures.

Here are some of the major challenges the seashore environment presents, and how to work with them in the garden. When you understand what combination of conditions exists right on your property,

you can figure out which plants are good candidates for your landscape and garden, and how you can modify the existing conditions to better suit their needs.

WIND

It's usually windy at the seashore. The wind is sometimes continuous, at other times intermittent, but it doesn't ever stop for long. Its speed can vary from a gentle breeze to a stiff gale to hurricane force of 80 miles per hour and up. The direction of the prevailing wind can change with the seasons. On Long Island, where I live, summer winds loaded with salt blow out of the south or south-southwest, and winter brings the fierce storms called nor'easters, which are driven by icy northeast winds. If the southwest corner of a beachfront property, or the northeast corner of a property fronting on Long Island Sound or a north-facing bay, is exposed, the wind will just bulldoze right through and chew up the landscape. Not all of the East Coast is subject to nor'easters, but they can occur in places as far apart and as different in climate as Maine and the Outer Banks of North Carolina.

It is especially important to understand wind direction if you live right along the beach. If the beach lies perpendicular to the direction of the prevailing winds, as in much of North Carolina, your property will be hit with stronger winds that will carry more salt across the beach and farther inland than if you live where the beach lies parallel to the prevailing winds, as is the case in much of South Carolina. There will be heavier salt spray on a perpendicularly positioned beach, too.

Wind affects seashore gardens in a number of ways. Strong winds can do plenty of damage in and of themselves. But at the seashore, the wind carries sand and salt with it, which causes even more trouble. Windblown sand is abrasive, scouring leaves and blasting stems. Salt blown onto leaves is very drying, drawing out moisture and sometimes causing burning of the foliage. The closer you are to the beach, the more extreme will be the effects that are produced by the wind.

HOW PLANTS PROTECT THEMSELVES

Seashore plants have developed a variety of adaptations that enable them to withstand salt spray, sand blasting, drying winds, and intense sun. Many plants, such as bayberry (*Myrica pensylvanica*) and yaupon holly (*Ilex vomitoria*), have tough, leathery leaves that resist damage from salt and dry out more slowly than thin leaves.

Some plants, such as sea grape and southern magnolia (*Magnolia virginiana*), have smooth, glossy leaves that repel saltwater. Others, like wax myrtle (*Myrica cerifera*) and most blue-toned conifers, have a waxy protective coating on their leaves that fends off salt and slows the evaporation of moisture.

Still other plants, such as sea buckthorn (*Hippophäe rhamnoides*) and Russian olive (*Elaeagnus angustifolius*), have very narrow or small leaves that offer less surface area to be battered by windblown sand and salt, and also less space for salt to cling to. Other leaves curl their edges inward to reduce transpiration and conserve moisture. Gray and silver leaves such as those of artemisias are covered with fine hairs that hold salt off the leaf surface and also reflect back some of the fierce sunlight, keeping the plants' internal temperature from rising to damaging levels. In addition, these leaf hairs protect the stomates, the pores from which leaves excrete moisture and gases.

Some plants conserve moisture by opening their stomates at night, when it's cooler, and closing them during the hot daytime, when evaporation is greatest.

Some plants, such as seashore elder (*Iva imbricata*) and glassworts (*Salicornia* spp.), are succulent and can store water in their stems or leaves. Some plants have even developed special glands that filter salt from the water the plants take in to fuel their growth (photosynthesis requires freshwater) and expel it from the plant. Some species of *Limonium* (sea lavender) contain these salt glands, as do salt hay and smooth cordgrass.

Some plants have more than one of these special adaptations.

Trees along a driveway or road, and the dunes at the back of the beach, can funnel wind like tall buildings in cities do. The wind can speed along these avenues faster than it blows over surrounding areas. These channeled winds can be very destructive to plants. If you have this problem on your property, you may need to either move some of the affected plants to different locations or install additional windbreaks.

If you are building a house or making other improvements on a property that has significant wind exposure, be very wary of removing the existing native vegetation. Remove as few plants as you possibly can, and replant the area as soon as the construction project is complete.

The best defense against the wind is a good windbreak. For waterfront properties, a windbreak is essential if you want to be able to grow any plants other than the toughest native species. See chapter 3 for information on creating a windbreak for your garden.

SALT

Salt gets into seashore gardens both from the air and from floodwaters. Windborne salt can cause serious damage to plants over time, and here's how: As waves break upon the shore, they throw droplets of seawater into the air. The saltwater droplets then travel inland on the wind, and some

The narrow, feathery foliage of tamarisk is especially salt tolerant. Here, its fall color catches the evening sun.

of the water evaporates along the way, making the salt more concentrated. Eventually the salt drops down to land on the plants (or anything else) below. Unless washed away by rain or a spray from a hose or sprinkler, the salt builds up on the plants, with the heaviest accumulation on the side of the plant nearest the sea. Growth on that side of the plant slows down, as the salt draws moisture from the leaves and interferes with transpiration and the normal growth processes of the plant tissues. The side of the plant facing away from the sea develops less of a salty cover, and continues to grow more or less normally. After a while, the lopsided growth produces a plant that appears to lean away from the water — the windswept look that is so typical of trees, especially, growing near the beach.

A hedge or other windbreak between the sea and the garden can protect plants from the worst effects of wind and salt spray. See chapter 3 for information on how to create a windbreak for your garden. When planning a beachfront garden, it's a good idea to put the most salt-tolerant plants in the most exposed spots.

Salt spray is most damaging to plants within 1,000 feet of the shoreline, and to new growth and tender young leaves early in the growing season. Salt-damaged leaves will turn brown and may die off if the damage is severe enough. Luckily for Atlantic shore gardeners, the worst storms come in late summer and fall, when the current year's growth has matured and gotten tougher. Surprisingly, in some cases salt appears actually to be *good* for plants. Some gardeners swear that salt spray rids their roses and hollies of insect infestations, and helps to control fungal diseases. Salt spray has also been reported to benefit lilacs and zinnias, which are notoriously prone to mildew.

Salt can also land on plants when fog envelops the garden when the air is still. Fog-borne salt just sits on the plants until the mist clears and rain or the gardener washes it off.

Salt can also come into contact with plants through water. This can happen in a couple of ways. First, during a storm, high tides can flood the beach and flow through gaps in the dunes or, in extreme circumstances, pour right over them, flooding inland areas beyond. Even the best-protected gardens can experience occasional storm-surge flooding if they are located near the beach in low-lying areas. The second way saltwater can get into the garden is during times of drought, when the water table drops so low that saltwater gets into the groundwater. Saltwater infiltration is becoming especially problematic as unrelenting development in seashore towns puts more and more pressure on finite water supplies.

When groundwater becomes salty, plants draw up the saltwater through their roots. But too much salt begins to pull moisture out of the leaves, in a process called exosmosis. The plants start to wilt, and eventually they'll die from lack of water. The gardener's natural response is to water the drooping plants. But if the water coming from the hose or sprinkler is salty, watering only exacerbates the problem.

Plants native to the seashore have developed varying degrees of tolerance to salt, and some other kinds of plants are naturally tolerant, too. See "Salt-Tolerant Plants" (right) for listings of plants and their level of salt tolerance.

Some plants will withstand occasional saltwater flooding without undue harm, especially if the flooding occurs while the plants are dormant. See "Plants That Tolerate Flooding," (page 22). Still, it is far better for plants not to have to cope with saltwater around their roots. If drought and resulting saltwater infiltration are an ongoing or increasingly frequent problem where you live, you would be wise to rely on salt-tolerant plants for your property, especially when choosing trees and shrubs. This is particularly true if you get your water from a well rather than from a municipal source. Grow intolerant flowers, herbs, and vegetables in containers, where you can control the water source.

SALT-TOLERANT PLANTS

Plants with High Salt Tolerance

Agave spp., century plant (drought tolerant)

Arundo donax, giant reed

Chamaecyparis obtusa, Hinoki falsecypress

×*Cupressocyparis leylandii*, Leyland cypress

Euonymus fortunei, wintercreeper

Gaillardia, blanketflower

Hedera helix, English ivy

Ilex vomitoria, yaupon holly (drought tolerant)

Ipomoea pes-caprae, beach morning glory

Juniperus conferta, shore juniper (drought tolerant)

Juniperus horizontalis, creeping juniper (drought tolerant)

Juniperus virginiana, eastern red cedar (drought tolerant); may show some burning when very exposed; best used along with other plants

Lantana camara, lantana

Liriope spicata, lilyturf

Magnolia grandiflora, southern magnolia

Myrica cerifera, wax myrtle

Nerium oleander, oleander

Ophiopogon japonicus, mondo grass

Panicum amarulum, bitter panic grass

Parthenocissus quinquefolia, Virginia creeper

Pittosporum tobira, Japanese pittosporum

Portulaca grandiflora, rose moss (drought tolerant)

Quercus virginiana, live oak

Schizachyrium scoparium, bluestem

Tamarix ramosissima, tamarisk, salt cedar

Trachelospermum jasminoides, Confederate jasmine

Thymus spp., thyme

Uniola paniculata, sea oats

Viburnum tinus, laurustinus

Plants with Moderate Salt Tolerance*

Acer rubrum, red maple

Agapanthus spp., lily of the Nile

Ageratum houstonianum, flossflower

Artemisia 'Silver King'

Asclepias tuberosa, butterfly weed

Begonia semperflorens, wax begonia

Calendula officinalis, pot marigold

Canna spp., canna

Catharanthus roseus, Madagascar periwinkle

Centaurea cyanus, bachelor's button

Cosmos spp., cosmos

Cycas revoluta, sago palm

Helianthus annuus, sunflower

Hemerocallis spp., daylily

Ilex cornuta, Chinese holly

Juniperus chinensis, Chinese juniper

Ligustrum spp., privet

Liriope muscari, lilyturf

Lobularia maritima, sweet alyssum

Mahonia aquifolium, holly grape

Nyssa sylvatica, tupelo

Ophiopogon japonicus, mondo grass

Pentas lanceolata, star-cluster

Persea borbonica, redbay

Phlox drummondii, annual phlox

Podocarpus macrophyllus, yew pine

Pyracantha coccinea, firethorn

Rosmarinus officinalis, rosemary

Salvia spp., sage

Santolina chamaecyparissus, lavender cotton

Sedum acre, goldmoss sedum

Senecio cineraria, dusty miller

Serenoa repens, saw palmetto

Thuja orientalis, arborvitae

Verbena spp., verbena

Vitex agnus-castus, chastetree

*These plants do best when planted in sheltered areas behind windbreaks.

Sedum is hardy and drought tolerant. It can also withstand occasional saltwater flooding, especially during winter dormancy.

If parts of your property flood regularly and are poorly drained (if, for instance, your land is marshy or near an estuary or wetland), think long and hard before you put in garden beds and borders there. Examine existing vegetation for clues. If you find the groundsel bush (*Baccharis halimifolia*) in residence, for example, there is likely saltwater, too. This shrub is native to coastal wetlands and can tolerate a high degree of salt around its roots.

If you nonetheless want to explore landscape possibilities, first consult your local building codes for ordinances that specify what homeowners may or may not do to wetlands and estuaries on their property, or parts of the property adjoining natural wetlands. Wetlands are important wildlife habitats and water-recharge areas, and are closely regulated in many coastal communities, even when they are located on private property. If you are allowed to plant in your wet spots, work with an experienced, well-qualified environmental engineer, landscape architect, or garden designer to plan the garden.

SAND

Sand is a helpful ingredient in soil; its large particles and loose texture help to lighten and aerate heavy, fine-textured clay soils into which it is incorporated. But as a main component of soil, sand leaves a lot to be desired. The beach sand found along the East Coast is made up almost entirely of quartz particles, which contain few of the nutrients plants need to grow. It has no organic matter to nourish beneficial soil microbes. The problem of poor nutritional value is compounded by the sand's inability to hold water.

Water is one of the main vehicles for transporting nutrients from soil to plants via their roots. Water powers plants' growth processes, and fine-textured beach sand repels water at first. Watering it is like trying to moisten peat moss or talcum powder. But when the sand does become wet, the moisture drains through it quickly, and plant roots have little time to absorb what they need. On top of that, the constant winds cause plants to lose what moisture they do have through rapid transpiration from their leaves. Salt deposited on leaves also draws out moisture. Without frequent watering in summer, seaside gardens can be full of stressed-out plants.

There are a few ways to reduce the amount of water a seaside garden is likely to swallow. Using drought-tolerant plants is one option. Working lots of organic matter into the soil is another (see chapter 3). Laying mulch after the garden has been planted also helps conserve soil moisture (see chapter 4). Many seaside homeowners install automatic watering systems for lawns and gardens. Overhead sprinklers, although less efficient than underground

Beach sand is a difficult growing medium for plants; it contains few nutrients for them and practically no organic matter, and moisture passes quickly through it.

systems, can be beneficial at the shore because they help rinse salt deposits from plant leaves. But any watering system should be carefully calibrated to provide thorough, deep watering and not just a quick daily spritz.

One additional problem with beach sand is that the carbonate in the seawater and the lack of humic acid formed by decaying plant material usually means the pH is alkaline, which makes some nutrients unavailable to plants even when they are present in the root zone. You can't, however, automatically assume that your soil is alkaline if you live at the shore. Seacoast soils away from the beach can be acidic. My own garden is about 1,000 yards from a bay and the soil is quite acid. Trailing arbutus, wintergreen, and huckleberry bushes grow wild in my backyard along with pine and oak trees — remnants of the pine/oak woodland that once covered this area. A soil test is always a good idea for seashore gardens.

Another problem with sand is that it blows around so easily. Carried on a strong wind, sand particles can scour leaves, bury young plants, and blanket lawns. It flies into woodlands; piles up against walls, fences, and rocks; and gets into equipment and machinery. Windbreaks will help trap blowing sand and keep it out of the garden.

STRONG SUN

Sunlight near the sea is especially intense because it bounces off the water and reflects off the light-colored sand. The beating sun heats up the sand on the beach — as you know if you've ever tried to walk barefoot on the beach up near the dunes in July. The sand can be 50 degrees hotter than the air temperature. The same effect, to a lesser degree, occurs away from the beach. Mulching the garden will help moderate soil temperatures for plants.

The strong sun near the sea can heat sandy soil to lethal levels for plants. Mulching the garden can help moderate soil temperatures.

Seeking Shelter

IF YOU OWN BEACHFRONT PROPERTY, you won't want to garden on the beach or the primary dunes. Primary dunes are off-limits for planting in many communities because they are so important in protecting the land behind them from flooding and erosion during storms. The ecosystem is too delicate to support landscaping even if you were permitted to install any. And not much grows on the dunes, anyway.

But the somewhat sheltered land *behind* the dunes — on the coastal plain, in swales, atop bluffs — offers plenty of opportunity for gardening, and the ecosystem is more stable in these places.

If you can plant on the lee side of the dunes, put in drought- and salt-tolerant ground covers to stabilize them. Bearberry and shore juniper are two of the best. It might be tempting to use beach grass, too, but beach grass does better on the windward side of the dunes (as explained in the entry on beach grass in chapter 5). Vines are also helpful for stabilizing dunes. Virginia creeper (*Parthenocissus quinquefolia*) and muscadine grape (*Vitis rotundifolia*) both do well behind the dunes and may creep right over the top.

If you live in an exposed location, plant windbreaks or hedges as described in chapter 3 to create sheltered areas for gardening, and also be sure to take advantage of the protected area that exists behind your

The dunes are essential for protecting the shoreline, and they provide shelter for beachfront gardens planted behind them. Planting drought- and salt-tolerant plants on the lee side of dunes helps stabilize the sand.

house. You'll have the greatest choice of plants for gardens in these sheltered places. If your house is higher than one story, you can even include some shade trees in the landscape if you site them behind the house.

If you live along a rocky coastline where the soil is thin, consider a rock garden. You might be able to make some of the natural outcrops part of your garden by tucking plants into soil-filled pockets and crevices in the rock.

CHAPTER 2

Planning and Design

ABOVE: A straight path, a mortared brick wall with pillars framing a view, and topiary standards in elegant urns give this seaside garden a serene, formal look.

RIGHT: This informal perennial garden blends loose drifts of yellow-orange black-eyed Susan (*Rudbeckia hirta*), red and yellow daylilies (*Hemerocallis* cvs.), lavender mallows (*Malva* sp.), and deep red coreopsis.

ONCE YOU HAVE A GOOD UNDERSTANDING OF THE GROWING conditions available on your seashore property, you can start to plan your garden. You'll probably want to start by thinking about what kinds of plants you'd like to grow — this is the most enjoyable part of garden design for many of us. But those decisions should also fit with your lifestyle and the kind of house you have. And you also need to find the best places on your property for the plants you want to grow. Depending upon your location and the kind of garden you want, you may need to modify the environment to create more congenial growing conditions for your plants.

Finding the Best Site

A sheltered spot behind the house can accommodate tropicals like canna, coleus, and sweet potato vine, whose leaves would be battered by wind in an exposed beachfront location.

ALL GARDENERS WITHIN A FEW MILES of the sea have to contend with wind and salt to some degree, but specific conditions vary widely. Salt, wind, and sand are most intense on waterfront properties, and oceanfront properties have the toughest conditions of all. If your house is on an ocean beach, you will be able to grow a variety of salt-tolerant plants in the lee of the dunes. Ornamental plants with less resistance to salt and wind will need to be behind a windbreak or shelterbelt. Hedges or informal screens of plants can provide a secondary line of protection or, farther away from the water, they may be all the protection necessary. See "Creating Sheltered Places" on page 41 for information on windbreaks and hedges.

The area behind your house can also be a good place for plants, as can low spots over which the wind passes easily. If your house is more than one story high, the protected area behind it will be higher too, and you may be able to include some trees in the garden to create shade and add structure to the landscape. Take advantage of any protected spots you can find. But be wary of planting along the sides of the house, where salty winds can whip by and prove very damaging to plants.

It's important to know the direction from which the prevailing winds blow on your property, both in summer and in winter. Even if you only use your seashore house in summer, the plants are there year-round. To create a sheltered spot, you need to have something sizable — whether it be plants or structures — between the garden and the wind. For example, on eastern Long Island, where I live, the prevailing winds blow out of the north to northeast in winter and from the south-southwest (right off the ocean) in summer, so windbreaks should be placed on those sides of properties to protect garden plantings from wind damage.

Another strategy for seaside gardeners is to grow plants in containers, especially on decks and patios and around swimming pools. In the event of a storm, the containers can be moved under cover, or replanted afterward if they are too big to move.

Most salt-tolerant plants are sun lovers used to growing in somewhat exposed locations. But a sheltered position in full sun will afford you the broadest choice of shrubs, perennials, annuals, and ornamental grasses, including some without a lot of tolerance to salt. Roses, too, need plenty of sun to thrive. Southern gardeners will have more choices, because many plants that prefer full sun in the North need some shade in the afternoon in torrid southern landscapes, especially in seaside areas where the sun is especially intense. (The plant profiles in chapter 5 contain information about each plant's degree of salt tolerance and sun/shade requirements.)

This garden on the lee side of a seaside house is full of color from dahlias, coreopsis, cosmos, and geraniums in a lively mix of pinks, reds, and yellows.

What Kind of Garden?

An Indian bench backed by tall rosemary plants that are overwintered in a greenhouse strikes an exotic note in a Long Island garden.

WHEN YOU'VE GOT POTENTIAL garden sites figured out, you can turn your attention to how you want the garden to look and what you might like to grow there. Here is where your lifestyle figures in. For instance, if your seashore house is a second home that you use only in summer, you will probably want to showcase shrubs and flowers that bloom in summer. If you use the house primarily on weekends, you might opt for a low-maintenance landscape of shrubs, ornamental grasses, and ground covers, especially if you will be taking care of the garden yourself. Weekenders who want more demanding plants, such as perennials and annuals that need deadheading, can hire a local nursery or landscaping company to maintain the garden.

If your seaside house is your permanent home, you will want to think about providing interest in your landscape year round. The structural elements of the garden — trees and shrubs, fences and walls, paths and driveways, arbors and trellises — play a more prominent role in winter, when the summer flowers have died back. Evergreens offer year-round color and structure.

If you enjoy watching birds, plan to include in your landscape some plants they can use for food, cover, and nesting sites. Find likely spots for feeders and a birdbath. You can also plant a garden to attract butterflies or hummingbirds. Using environmentally friendly techniques and materials in your garden will make it especially supportive of wildlife.

The garden profiles in chapter 4 provide some fine examples of successful seaside gardens up and down the East Coast. Perhaps they will inspire you as you set out to create your own little piece of paradise. If you study the photos, you will find a variety of ingenious solutions to the challenges posed by seaside sites. Let these examples point you toward paths you might take in your own thinking about the kind of garden you want to create.

WHAT'S YOUR STYLE?

Garden designs are as diverse as the people who create them, and you will derive the greatest satisfaction from your garden when it expresses your own personal sense of style. The best gardens are the ones that express the personalities of their owners. In figuring out what kind of garden you want, you don't need to be a slave to the rules of garden design.

That said, you do need to investigate whether your community has ordinances governing things like setbacks and hedge heights, whether you can have a meadow if you want one or if a mowed lawn is mandated, and whether there are utility easements and rights-of-way on your property that must be maintained. Also, it takes time and experience to learn how to work with plants to express your style and create different effects. You can certainly rely on established design traditions to guide you. If you are new to gardening, or new to gardening at the shore, one of the best ways to learn what works is to look at other gardens in the area.

Basically, garden styles fall into three broad categories: informal, formal, and naturalistic. Each style tends to work best with particular kinds of houses and lifestyles.

A garden's formality or informality is determined by the way it is laid out, the plants that grow in it, the colors used, and how the plants are maintained.

HOW TO HIRE LANDSCAPING HELP

Because most seashore towns include second homes and seasonal rental properties, there are also a lot of local landscaping companies. If you want to hire someone to create or maintain your seascape garden, how can you find good help? Here are some tips.

First, think about what kind of help you need. Do you want someone to plant pots on your deck? To pull the weeds and deadhead the flowers? To renovate an existing garden that does not meet your needs? To create a comprehensive landscape design for the entire property?

Next, think about how you use, or would like to use, your outdoor space. Do you want space for outdoor dining or recreational activities? An arbor or gazebo, or other quiet space where you can relax and read? A private place to sunbathe?

Then think about what you'd like to see in your landscape. Think first in general terms — do you want lots of color? Low maintenance? Support for wildlife?

When you have an idea of what you're looking for, investigate local companies. Ask friends and neigh-bors for recommendations. Drive around your town and look for gardens you like, then find out who created them (many companies place signs on newly finished projects to advertise their work).

When you talk with potential landscaping contractors, ask to see their portfolio of work, and then go look at some actual properties. If possible, talk to clients to find out whether they were satisfied with the company's work.

Most companies will provide free estimates for work you want done. Once you agree on the work to be done, unless the job is quite small, get a written proposal or contract that spells out the work and projected costs for site preparation, labor, and plants.

Some companies will guarantee their plants for an added cost and provide replacements for plants that fail to thrive; others do not. You must decide how important this is to you. And bear in mind that seashore environments are difficult for plants, so you have to be willing to accept the fact that gardening by the sea, however well planned the garden, involves a certain element of risk.

Informal. Many seashore homes are informal cottages and bungalows that are well served by casual, relaxed gardens. Informal gardens typically employ curves and diagonals, which make them feel lively and dynamic. Beds and borders are laid out in sweeping curves and softly undulating shapes, with plants spilling over the edges and onto pathways. Informal gardens generally have curved edges, and the beds are ovals or soft-edged free-form shapes. Within the garden, plants are allowed to assume their natural forms, growing together in flowing drifts and intermin-

These plants have a loose, open, or rambling habit, and work well in informal gardens.

Achillea, yarrow

Arctotis × hybrida, African daisy

Artemisia spp., artemisia

Aster spp., aster

Astilbe spp., false spirea

Buddleia spp., butterfly bush

Campsis radicans, trumpet creeper

Clethra alnifolia, sweet pepperbush

Coreopsis spp., tickseed

Cosmos spp., cosmos

Cytisus scoparius, Scotch broom

Gaillardia × grandiflora, blanketflower

Hemerocallis spp., daylily

Hibiscus spp., rose mallow, rose of Sharon

Ilex glabra, inkberry

Ilex verticillata, winterberry

Ilex vomitoria, yaupon holly

Juniperus spp., juniper

Lantana camara, lantana

Lonicera spp., honeysuckle

Monarda didyma, bee balm

Nepeta × faassenii, catmint

Oenothera spp., evening primrose

Ornamental grasses

Perovskia atriplicifolia, Russian sage

Petunia × hybrida, petunia

Philadelphus spp., mock orange (pictured)

Pittosporum tobira, Japanese pittosporum

Rudbeckia spp., black-eyed Susan

Rosa spp., rambler rose, rugosa rose, shrub rose

Salvia spp., sage

Sedum spp., stonecrop

Solidago spp., goldenrod

Spiraea spp., spirea

Thalictrum spp., meadow rue

Tropaeolum majus, nasturtium

Viburnum spp., viburnum

Vitex agnus-castus, chastetree

Wisteria spp., wisteria

Zinnia angustifolia, narrow-leaved zinnia

Mock orange is a classic choice for cottage gardens.

gling their colors where two drifts meet. Paths and walkways wind and curve, and they are surfaced with loose materials such as gravel, crushed bluestone, pebbles, and wood chips. Stepping-stones might be made with irregular fieldstone or wood rounds sawn from logs and sunk into the soil with their top surface at ground level.

In an informal garden you can mix and match colors in any combination you like, although there are traditional ways to create pleasing color schemes. See "Working with Color" on page 36 for information on mixing colors.

Saltboxes, cottages and bungalows, capes and ranch houses are all examples of house styles that usually work well with informal gardens. If you are unsure whether or not you have an informally styled house, consider its architectural features. Is the front door off to one side of the façade, with unequal numbers of windows on either side? That's one clue that you have an informal house. What is the house built of? If the construction is wood shingles, siding, or logs, for example, the house is probably informal.

There are many kinds of informal gardens. Cottage gardens of old-fashioned plants and plants chosen for their particular qualities and personal associations represent one style. The garden described in "A Secret Garden by the Sea," in chapter 4, is a charming example of a cottage-style

Neatly sheared shrubs and topiaries make an elegant formal statement in this seashore garden.

garden. Although many plants can be at home in both formal and informal gardens, some plants are just inherently less formal than others. Ornamental grasses, for instance, are by nature informal, with their fountainy, billowy forms and their constant swaying and dancing as their leaves are ruffled by passing breezes. See "Informal Plants" (page 32) for more examples.

Formal. Some seashore houses, particularly in traditionally upper-class enclaves like Newport and the Hamptons, are grandly formal and often complemented by formally designed gardens. Formal homes are built of solid, traditional materials such as stone and brick, often with classic columns and broad staircases. The façade of a formal house is typically symmetrical, with the front door in the center and equal numbers of windows on either side of it.

The formal gardens that suit such homes are laid out in precise geometric shapes — squares, rectangles, and circles — with beds and borders arranged around straight axes (lines of sight) that lead directly to prominent features of the property, such as the house itself, or important ornaments, such as fountains and works of art. The axes are often paths, with the main axis path being widest and bisected at a 90-degree angle by a narrower, secondary axis. Formal gardens have neat,

sharp edges, and the plants are meticulously groomed and shaped. Topiaries are classic components of formal gardens, as are neatly clipped hedges. The overall feeling in a formal garden is one of serenity and calm. Colors are restrained, and the color scheme is usually simple — cool blues and crisp whites, for example.

Many seaside communities are populated by contemporary homes constructed of simple geometric forms. These kinds of houses can be well served by updated formal gardens of bold, sculptural plants. Spare, weeping junipers and large, spiky yuccas are at home in these modernistic settings. Another way to landscape a contemporary home, depending on its setting and design, is with the third kind of garden: the naturalistic garden.

Naturalistic. Naturalistic gardens aim to evoke the look of particular natural environments — woodlands, deserts, prairies, beaches, and marshes — and they can beautifully integrate a home with its site. Naturalistic gardens also call for plants that are naturally adapted to the growing conditions present in the garden environment. The best of them are native plants,

FORMAL PLANTS

These plants have a neat growing habit and work well in formal gardens.

Catharanthus roseus, Madagascar periwinkle
Clematis spp., large-flowered clematis
Cryptomeria japonica, Japanese cedar
Dahlia spp., dahlia
Euonymus japonicus, evergreen euonymus
Hosta spp., plantain lily
Hydrangea macrophylla, bigleaf hydrangea
Ilex crenata, Japanese holly
Ilex opaca, American holly
Ilex pedunculosa, longstalk holly
Ligustrum spp., privet
Liriope muscari, lilyturf
Nerium oleander, oleander
Pelargonium ×hortorum, geranium
Phormium tenax, New Zealand flax
Picea spp., spruce
Prunus caroliniana, Carolina cherry laurel
Rosa cvs., hybrid tea roses
Santolina chamaecyparissus, lavender cotton
Stachys byzantina, lamb's ears
Tagetes spp., marigold
Taxus cuspidata, Japanese yew
Teucrium chamaedrys, germander
Yucca filamentosa, Adam's needle

NATURALISTIC GARDEN PLANTS

These plants are well suited to naturalistic gardens — beach gardens, meadow gardens, and native plant gardens. The letter following each plant, B, M, or N, indicates whether it is best suited to a beach, meadow, or other native plant garden.

Ammophila breviligulata, American beach grass, B

Arctostaphylos uva-ursi, bearberry, N

Aronia spp., chokeberry, N

Artemisia stelleriana, beach wormwood, B

Asclepias tuberosa, butterfly weed, M, N

Aster spp., aster

Baccharis halimifolia, groundsel bush, B, N

Campsis radicans, trumpet creeper, B

Caragana arborescens, Siberian pea tree, B

Elymus arenarius 'Glauca', blue lyme grass, B

Eryngium maritimum, sea holly, B

Gaillardia pulchella, Indian blanket, N

Gelsemium sempervirens, Carolina jessamine, N

Hippophäe rhamnoides, sea buckthorn, B

Ilex glabra, inkberry, N

Ilex opaca, American holly, N

Ilex verticillata, winterberry, N

Ilex vomitoria, yaupon holly, B, N

Juniperus chinensis 'Torulosa', Hollywood juniper, B

Juniperus conferta, shore juniper, B

Juniperus virginiana, eastern red cedar, B, N

Monarda didyma, bee balm, N, M

Myrica spp., bayberry, wax myrtle, B, N

Pinus mugo, mugo pine, B

Pinus rigida, pitch pine, B, N

Pinus taeda, loblolly pine, B, N

Pittosporum tobira, Japanese pittosporum, B

Prunus maritima, beach plum, B, N

Rhus spp., sumac, N

Rosa rugosa, saltspray rose, B

Sabal palmetto, cabbage palmetto, B, N

Solidago spp., goldenrod, N, M

Spartina pectinata, cordgrass, B, N

Tamarix ramosissima, tamarisk, B

Thuja occidentalis, American arborvitae, N, B

Trachelospermum jasminoides, Confederate jasmine, N

Uniola paniculata, sea oats, B

Vaccinium spp., blueberry, N

Viburnum dentatum, arrowwood viburnum, N

Zinnia angustifolia, narrow-leaved zinnia, B

or plants from other parts of the world where growing conditions are similar. For instance, a house situated on the beach, just behind the dunes, looks great with plantings of bayberry, seaside goldenrod, and beach grass in garden areas closest to the dunes. If the house is set near a marsh or estuary, and parts of the property are wet, a pond edged with wetland plants can provide an ideal landscape solution. Along a rocky coast, a rock garden might be the best option. For a house in a wooded area, a woodland garden of shade-tolerant plants would nicely fill the bill.

Knautia macedonica seems to float on tall, slender stems in this meadow garden, like balloons tethered to the ground.

A Sense of Place

IN ADDITION TO CREATING A GARDEN that works with your house, you might give some thought to making a garden that "fits" the seashore environment. The seaside is a beautiful place to be, and having a landscape around your house that captures the essence of the surroundings can enhance your experience of and appreciation for it.

IN PRAISE OF NATIVE PLANTS

One good way to create a garden with a sense of place is to feature native plants. Whether you simply build garden beds and borders with native species or opt for a truly naturalistic garden that evokes the look of dune and swale, woodland, marsh and wetland, or coastal plain, your garden will look like it belongs at the shore. Take a look at James van Sweden's garden on page 120 to see how beautifully a garden of primarily native plants integrates into its setting.

There are many good reasons to grow native plants. For one thing, they are adapted to the climate and conditions, and will thrive with less fussing than a lot of imports. Natives will be less likely than exotic species and flashy hybrids to suffer pest and disease problems. You won't need as much fertilizer or supplemental water — native plants are far less demanding of our dwindling natural resources.

Native plants tend to be less dramatic and showy than traditional commercial plant varieties, and for that reason many people turn up their noses at them, considering them little better than weeds. But don't sell native plants short. Natives have a quieter, subtler beauty that can be just as appealing as those grand English perennials, precisely because they are better suited to the environment. It's a different sensibility, a matter of seeing the garden in a new way. And natives can be richly colorful, too. Consider, for example, New England aster (*Aster novae-angliae*), which bears masses of yellow-centered daisy flowers in shades of rose, pink, purple, and white in late summer and fall. Or bee balm's (*Monarda didyma*) heads of brilliant scarlet, soft purple, or fresh pink flowers in summer.

As more and more homeowners are discovering the positive attributes of native plants, breeders are putting more energy into developing improved cultivars. New England aster is just one native that is available in many cultivar forms. There are new varieties of bee balm, butterfly weed (*Asclepias tuberosa*), sweet pepperbush (*Clethra alnifolia*), and many other plants as well. And more landscape designers are discovering the virtues of natives and using them in creative ways.

If you don't think you would be happy with an all-native garden, how about a compromise? Create a basic framework with natives and add plants — such as ornamental grasses — with a similar spirit. Inject extra shots of color by adding some more-traditional perennials. Grow flowering annuals in containers to use around the house and outdoor living areas or as accents right in the garden. Create a separate garden "room" enclosed by hedges or fences for a flower garden bursting with color and texture.

Using native plants ties a garden to the natural landscape beyond its borders and enhances the sense of place. The windmill palm places this garden unmistakably in the Southeast.

Working with Color

In this perennial garden, shades of green blend with silvers, whites, and pale pastels for a peaceful, cooling effect near the sea, where the summer sun glows hot.

Displaying a single type of flower, such as this purple coneflower (*Echinacea purpurea*), against green foliage is a simple, effective way to work with color.

I F YOU ARE GOING TO HAVE A FLOWER garden, it goes without saying that color will be an important part of the design. Here are some guidelines to use, and some issues to ponder, in choosing colors for your garden.

First, think about the basic kinds of colors you like in other areas of your life — your home and its furnishings, your clothes and accessories. Do you generally prefer bright, warm colors (reds, oranges, and yellows) or cool, peaceful colors (blues, greens, and violets)? Are you drawn to subtle, harmonious blends of colors or to contrasting colors? Rich, deep tones, brights, or pale pastels? Do you like the serenity of white instead of other colors?

What are the colors on the exterior of your house? You might consider trying to echo a trim color from the home in the landscape to create a visual link between house and garden.

If you have a good sense of the colors you like, you can mix them in whatever combination you want in the garden. Your garden should please you above all. Don't feel you have to be a slave to the laws of garden design. Nothing is written in stone. But if you feel at a loss about where to start, you may find it helpful to learn a bit about how designers have traditionally used color. Very basically, there are four ways to work with color in the garden: you can combine harmonious or analogous colors; you can use contrasting or complementary colors; you can rely on a single flower color contrasted against green foliage; or you can plant in an assortment of mixed colors.

HARMONIOUS COLOR SCHEMES

Harmonious, or analogous, colors are related; they are located near one another on an artist's color wheel and blend smoothly with one another. Examples of harmonious colors are red, orange, and gold, or blue, purple, and cool pink. Analogous color schemes are often quiet and subtle, as in the case of a pot full of pastel shades of pink, rose, and lilac petunias. But they can also be surprisingly dramatic, as in the case of a bed of chrysanthemums in brilliant gold, rich orange, russet, and

crimson. These combinations of closely related colors are most appealing to the eyes of some people. For others, more contrast is needed to bring more life to the composition.

CONTRASTING COLOR SCHEMES

Contrasting colors are farther apart on a color wheel, and placing them next to each other emphasizes their different qualities. Complementary colors lie opposite one another on the color wheel and contrast more intensely than any other juxtaposition of colors. Examples of complementary colors are blue and orange, purple and yellow, and red and green. The nineteenth-century English landscape painter John Constable placed in his paintings small strokes of red amid expanses of foliage to make the greens look greener. If you look closely, you may perceive the same effect in a garden.

If you want to plant a garden of complementary colors, you will probably find the most pleasing results by planting the softer of the two colors over a larger portion of the garden and using the brighter color sparingly, as an accent. For example, if you want to combine blue salvia with orange marigolds, plant lots more salvia than marigolds. If you plant more marigolds and fewer salvia, the orange will overwhelm the blue.

Another way to tone down a contrasting scheme is to soften the shade of the brighter color. Instead of using orange marigolds with the salvia, you could plant salmon-colored geraniums.

A third way to soften intensely contrasting colors is to introduce some neutral tones — white flowers or silver foliage, for example — to blend the colors, or to surround the contrasting hues with lots of green foliage to absorb some of the color.

Monochromatic gardens need not be boring. This juxtaposition of clear pink roses with the raspberry-hued flower clusters of Japanese spirea is lovely and long blooming.

SINGLE-COLOR GARDENS

The simplest color scheme of all is built on a single color, perhaps expressed in several different shades and tints, and perhaps with just a small amount of a second color added as an accent. Monochromatic gardens can be quite soothing to the eye, and their simplicity can work extremely well in a formal setting. You might like a garden of all white flowers, or pink, or blue. Or you could combine soft pale yellows with rich deep golds. A single-color garden need not be boring; you can vary the types of flowers; plant heights, shapes, and textures; flower sizes; and tones of color (pale, bright, or dark). Or you can mix in some variegated foliage for added interest.

MULTICOLORED GARDENS

In a mixed-color, or polychromatic, garden, the variety of colors included depends entirely on the gardener's preference. Multicolored gardens can be blindingly brilliant, if all strong colors are used, or they can be cheerful and festive, if you mix pastels and soft shades. You can create a multicolored garden by planting a favorite flower, such as daylily or iris, in mixed colors or by planting a selection of plants, each in a different color, for a rainbow of blossoms.

A polychromatic garden generally works best if one color is dominant, to bring a sense of cohesiveness to the overall scheme. And don't spread the plants of each color throughout the garden like so many polka dots; you will lose the visual impact, and your garden will look like just a motley collection of plants. Instead, plant in color groups, in bands, or in drifts or clumps. Don't plant one yellow coreopsis; plant five or nine or fifteen.

To get the best effect from a polychromatic garden, surround it with lots of green to provide some visual relief and give the viewer's eye some rest. Set your flowers of many colors in front of evergreens, or a hedge, or in a bed in the middle of a lawn.

If you are not sure what sort of color scheme would most please you in your garden, start with a simple blend and add to it in subsequent years if you feel you need more color. It is easier and more satisfying to add color than to subtract it.

plan to grow plants with some tolerance for salt and wind, the windbreak could be 20 feet away. You will notice that I said "the inside edge" here. That's because a shelterbelt of several rows of trees and shrubs can be quite wide. You have to allow enough room for the depth of the windbreak. Hedges and fences, of course, are much narrower than shelterbelts.

Alternatively, you could design a windbreak by determining the best height for the windbreak based on the size of the garden. The windbreak should be one-fifth to one-tenth as high as the depth of the area you need to protect.

Another factor to take into account is how long the windbreak will be. The rule of thumb for this is that it should extend 50 feet past the sides of the area to be protected. If the windbreak is too short — say, the same length as the garden's width — strong wind gusts can swirl around the windbreak's ends right into the garden and wreak havoc with the plants.

If your beachfront property is flat and quite large, you may need to have a series of windbreaks to adequately protect the plantings. In such a case, you might make the outermost windbreak a good shelterbelt, and for the inner windbreaks use a

series of hedges incorporated into the landscape design to serve as the walls of garden rooms or otherwise act as space dividers. Place the windbreaks a distance apart that is equal to 10 times their height. For example, 10-foot hedges would go 100 feet apart from one another.

Properties that are near the ocean but are not flat are a lot harder to protect with windbreaks. Wind does not flow straight across hilly land, and the wind patterns are complicated to figure out. In this case it would be wise to consult an experienced professional landscape architect or engineer to plan the necessary windbreaks.

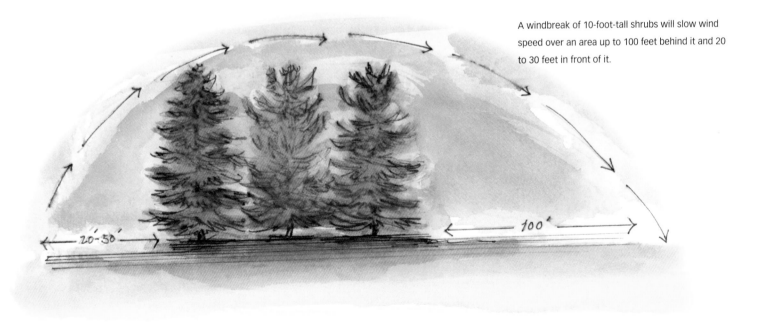

A windbreak of 10-foot-tall shrubs will slow wind speed over an area up to 100 feet behind it and 20 to 30 feet in front of it.

20'-50'   100'

SHAPING A WINDBREAK

Near the sea, a windbreak or shelterbelt must do more than simply slow the force of the wind in order to be effective. You need the windbreak to deflect the wind up and over the garden to carry its cargo of salt past your garden plants. The best way to direct the wind is to design the windbreak of plants in a gradation of heights. Viewed from the side, the windbreak is shaped like a wedge. Each row of plants protects the plants behind it. The lowest and most salt-resistant plants — such as beach grass (*Ammophila breviligulata*), sea oats (*Uniola paniculata*), and Adam's needle (*Yucca filamentosa*) — go closest to the beach. Behind them go shrubs of increasing height, and behind them, on the inner side of the windbreak, go taller evergreen trees.

This layered construction will draw the wind up and over the tallest trees in the barrier and allow it to flow above the garden. If the windbreak is made of only shorter plants, the wind will pass lower over the garden and will likely be slowed enough to drop its load of salt right on the plants in the garden, just where you don't want it to go.

PLANTING WINDBREAKS

When planning a shelterbelt of plants, start with the toughest ones on the ocean side, or on the outside facing into the prevailing winds. It is best to put in young plants, even if it means delaying the rest of your garden for several years — younger plants will adapt better to the harsh conditions than larger, more mature specimens. It's worth the wait. While you wait for the windbreak to grow tall enough to be effective, you can grow some plants in containers in protected spots, such as behind the house. You could also put up a fence and grow behind it plants with some degree of salt tolerance.

Be aware that trees and shrubs in seaside windbreaks and other very exposed locations will probably not grow as large as

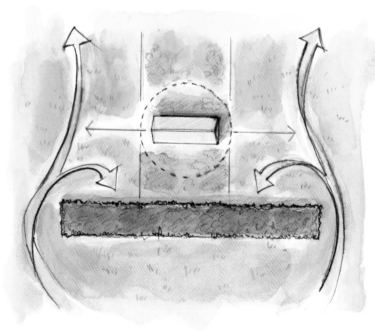

A windbreak meant to protect a house needs to extend 50 feet beyond the sides of the house so that wind currents sweeping around the edges will not blast the building.

they would farther inland. Seaside trees and shrubs are also likely to take on a gnarled, windswept look over time as the fierce salt winds stunt their growth on the seaward side.

Another point to keep in mind is that trees and shrubs growing in exposed seashore locations often appear to grow very slowly, if at all, during their first few years. That's because in dry, sandy conditions, they first put their energy into sending roots deep into the sand to find a source of water and to provide a secure anchor. When the roots reach the water table, the aboveground parts of the plant will start to grow faster.

When the windbreak is established and you begin to plant inside it, you may want to choose shade-tolerant ground covers for the area immediately to the lee of the windbreak. This space will tend to be shady and dry, especially if the windbreak is to the south, because the trees and shrubs will block much of the sunlight and rain from reaching the ground there. This area will also be cooler than sunnier locations.

One final caveat: If your windbreak will be located close to your property line, be sure to set the plants far enough back from the boundary that they will have room to fully mature without encroaching on your neighbor's property. Remember to consider the spread, as well as the height, of each tree or shrub.

To deflect salty winds up and over your house or garden, plant a windbreak with several layers of plants of increasing height. From the side, the windbreak appears wedge-shaped.

PLANTS FOR WINDBREAKS

Acer pseudoplatanus, sycamore maple

Agave spp., century plant

Baccharis halimifolia, groundsel bush

Caragana arborescens, Siberian peashrub

Chamaecyparis obtusa, Hinoki falsecypress

Crateagus spp. (deciduous, but will filter the worst of the wind in summer; fairly small but very tough)

×*Cupressocyparis leylandii,* Leyland cypress

Cytisus scoparius, Scotch broom

Elaeagnus commutata, silverberry

Euonymus japonicus, evergreen euonymus

Hippophäe rhamnoides, sea buckthorn

Ilex vomitoria, yaupon holly

Iva imbricata, marsh elder

Juniperus conferta, shore juniper

Juniperus horizontalis, creeping juniper

Juniperus virginiana, eastern red cedar

Magnolia grandiflora, southern magnolia

Myrica cerifera, southern wax myrtle

Myrica pensylvanica, bayberry

Nerium oleander, oleander

Ornamental grasses (*Schizachyrium scoparium, Panicum amarulum*)

Pinus mugo, mugo pine

Pinus nigra, Austrian pine

Pinus rigida, pitch pine

Pittosporum tobira, Japanese pittosporum

Prunus maritima, beach plum

Quercus virginiana, live oak

Rosa rugosa, saltspray rose

Sabal palmetto, palmetto

Tamarix gallica, French tamarisk, saltcedar

Tamarix ramosissima, tamarisk

Uniola paniculata, sea oats

Vitis rotundifolia, muscadine grape (use on lee side of dunes to help stabilize)

Yucca filamentosa, Adam's needle

A board-on-board fence like this one allows air and light to flow between the boards but still provides privacy.

OTHER WINDBREAK OPTIONS

While a shelterbelt of mixed trees and shrubs is probably the best kind of windbreak for properties along ocean beaches, homeowners a bit farther inland have other options to consider.

For a property away from the beach, or as a second line of defense for beachfront locations, a tall clipped hedge or an informal screen of unsheared evergreens can be a good option. Hedges and screens afford welcome privacy and are also useful for delineating space in the landscape. Hedges can mark property boundaries, enclose swimming pools and tennis courts, and separate the driveway from the garden. Privet (*Ligustrum* spp.) is by far the most popular hedge plant, and most types have some degree of salt tolerance. But you can also make hedges or screens of arborvitae or juniper, and southern gardeners can use pittosporum or oleander.

Fences also make good windbreaks if they are of permeable construction. Picket styles, board-on-board, stockade fences, woven panel and louver designs, even snow fencing, all can work. In fact, snow fencing, though not much to look at in terms of aesthetics, will slow the wind speed by as much as 80 percent. Do not use a solid-panel or closed-board fence as a windbreak. Stucco and cinderblock walls are also poor choices. A brick wall could serve, however, if it is made with screening brick, or if holes are left between bricks at regular intervals to permit airflow. In the Delaware garden described in chapter 4 ("A Secret Garden by the Sea"), the brick wall surrounding the courtyard is a fine example of this kind of permeable yet solid wall.

This brick wall at an oceanfront home in Delaware includes spaces for air to pass through, making it a most effective — and sturdy — windbreak.

It's not a good idea to clear all the vegetation from an oceanfront lot when building a house, but some developers still do it. If you have purchased a beachfront home on an empty, bulldozed lot, here is a basic plan of attack that might work for you.

First, take photos of the property from various angles. Make sure you photograph the view of the water, and also the street and neighboring properties. You can use these photos later in planning for your landscaping.

The next order of business is to create some protection for the house and grounds. First, you need to create sand dunes if none currently exist. Probably the best way to encourage dune formation is to erect a line of snow fencing at the front edge of your property, well back from the high-water mark and running parallel to the beach. Put up a second line of fencing 30 to 40 feet behind the first one. (If you want to stabilize existing dunes on your property, run the first line of fencing at the base of the dunes.) The fencing should run at a right angle to the prevailing winds. If the prevailing winds do not come off the water, run a fence that is at the proper angle in relation to the wind and 30 feet away from the first fence.

The snow fencing will trap and hold sand. When the dune is high enough to provide reasonable protection, plant American beach grass (*Ammophila breviligulata*) to stabilize it. Southern gardeners can use beach grass or sea oats (*Uniola paniculata*) to help stabilize dunes. Beach grass spreads readily by means of underground stems. Local nurseries sell small clumps of beach grass ready for planting. The best planting time ranges from October 1 to April 30; ask the nursery about the best time for your area. Set the clumps 8 inches deep and about 18 inches apart, in a staggered pattern like you'd use for planting other ground covers.

Water thoroughly after planting, so the water soaks down to the roots of the grass. Keep the grass watered so it stays as evenly moist as you can manage until it becomes established and sends out new roots. Fertilize heavily in spring with a balanced fertilizer such as 10-10-10, applied at a rate of 100 pounds per quarter acre. Fertilize again at the same rate in midsummer.

After a couple of years when the beach grass has stabilized the dune, it will start to lose its vigor. At that time you can begin putting in more permanent plants, such as seaside goldenrod (*Solidago sempervirens*), beach plum (*Prunus maritima*), sea oats (*Uniola paniculata*), beach wormwood (*Artemisia stelleriana*), and groundsel bush (*Baccharis halimifolia*), to hold the dune in place.

When more permanent dune plantings are in place, you can start working to improve the soil so you can plant shelterbelts and, eventually, gardens. See "Improving the Soil," on page 48, for information. The next step is to form windbreaks to create sheltered locations for gardening and to help protect the house. You might also decide to build a berm, with shrubs along the top, to help deflect wind.

With windbreaks in place, get out the photos you took of the property. If you can have a local copy shop make blowups for you, you can use tissue paper overlays or paper cutouts of tree, shrub, and hedge shapes to play around with different locations for ornamental plantings. Lay the cutouts on the photo enlargements to try out different arrangements of plants. Think about using groups of trees and shrubs to frame views; provide shade; and screen decks, patios, and other outdoor living areas from view. When planning windbreaks, be sure to place them between the prevailing winds (in winter or summer or both, if necessary) and the future garden.

Improving the Soil

Pure sand is a difficult growing medium for plants. If you want a garden, you will need to add lots of organic matter.

As explained in chapter 1, pure sand is not a good growing medium for most plants. Even if you don't live right on the beach, if you live at the seashore, your soil is probably very sandy. There are exceptions to the rule, of course. In my area, rich, beautiful, loamy soil can be found in the village of Bridgehampton within sight of the dunes.

Bridgehampton loam is some of the best farmland in the country (although now, alas, it is sprouting more and more houses instead of vegetables). On the other hand, my garden 15 miles away is a few thousand feet from a bay, and my soil is sandy but poorly drained in spots, low in fertility, and highly acidic. My neighborhood was once a pine-oak coastal forest, a tiny remnant of which remains in my backyard. But often, sandy seashore soil is alkaline because of the salt it contains. The pH of beach sand can range from a mildly acid 6.5 to a decidedly alkaline 8.0. If you don't manage to have the soil tested, a general improvement strategy is to work in 50 pounds of ground limestone per thousand square feet.

But it's always a good idea to have your soil tested before beginning a new garden. Most USDA county Cooperative Extension offices do soil testing, and along with your test results they provide recommendations on how to amend your soil to create a better growing environment for plants. There are also private soil-testing labs, and various sorts of do-it-yourself test kits. If you choose this last option, purchase a good kit — one that tests more than just the soil's pH.

ADDING ORGANIC MATTER

Whether or not you garden organically, the best thing you can do for your seashore soil is to add copious amounts of organic matter to it. Organic matter — compost, leaf mold, livestock manure, and other natural materials — improves the soil's texture and the ability of sandy soil to retain moisture. It aerates and improves drainage in compacted soils, and improves nutrient content as well. Seashore gardeners can take advantage of local materials, particularly seaweed. Some gardeners prefer to rinse or soak seaweed gathered from the beach in freshwater before digging it into the garden or tossing it onto the compost pile. Other gardeners do not rinse and do not find the salt problematic. It is a good idea, though, to add a nitrogen source such as dried blood or cottonseed meal at the same time to help the seaweed decompose more quickly. In very poor sandy soil, you could add as much as three parts by volume of compost to one part of the existing soil. Or use two parts compost and one part good topsoil to one part existing soil.

A more useful guideline is to spread the compost and/or topsoil over the entire garden area before making beds and borders

BELOW: Seaweed that washes up on the beach can be an excellent soil amendment. Add a nitrogen-rich material to the soil along with seaweed to speed its decomposition.

or other planting areas. This is easiest to do if nothing is currently growing on the site. If there are any existing indigenous trees you want to keep, you will need to build individual retaining walls around them to keep the soil around the trunk at the same level it is now. If these measures aren't taken, the tree could die.

You will need lots of compost and/or topsoil to make an appreciable improvement in the soil. Plan on at least a three- to four-inch layer for an area where you will have a lawn; six to eight inches would be even better. For beds and borders, foundation plants, and trees and shrubs, 8 to 12 inches of compost and/or topsoil is the goal.

After spreading the compost/topsoil, work it into the top few inches of the existing sand. You could also spread 15 pounds per 1,000 square feet of a fertilizer high in phosphorus and potassium, such as a 5-10-10 or a 6-12-12 formula, and work it in.

An alternative to spreading compost and topsoil over the entire garden area is to create a series of raised beds in which to garden and simply amend the soil in the beds. The spaces between the beds become paths. Working in raised beds reduces the amount of compost and topsoil you will need, and the design and layout of the beds can become the basis of an elegant formal flower garden or a charming herb garden.

To hold the compost, buy some bins (available at most garden centers) or make simple enclosures of hardware cloth or turkey wire. Or you can dig a pit in the ground six to eight inches deep and line the bottom with hardware cloth or heavy-duty plastic into which you will punch lots of holes, which will keep roots from growing into the compost pile from nearby trees while still allowing for drainage.

In the bottom of the enclosure, spread a six-inch layer of shredded leaves, weeds pulled from the garden that have *not* gone to seed, or upside-down chunks of sod. Next, add a four-inch layer of kitchen waste (excluding fats, oils, and meat remains) and/or manure. If you have fresh grass clippings, spread a *thin* (no more than ½ inch deep) layer on top. Then sprinkle with ground limestone, dried blood, or other organic fertilizer.

Repeat the layers as you acquire more materials. Turn the pile with a pitchfork or garden fork once a week, moving the ingredients from the outside to the inside of the pile. Water the compost thoroughly once a week in dry weather. The compost is ready to use when it has become dark and crumbly and you can't distinguish the different materials that went into it.

For a homemade fertilizer that's especially useful for container plants, you might try your hand at making compost tea. Put a couple of shovelfuls of finished compost into a burlap sack or other similarly porous container and place the bag in a tub of water (outdoors). Let it steep like a tea bag until the water turns dark brown. Then toss the compost into the garden and use the "tea" to water plants. If the tea is very dark colored, dilute it with water until it is the color of weak coffee. You can also fill the bag with manure instead of compost and make manure tea.

Deciding What to Grow

Petunias, ageratum, and marguerites thrive in full sun in northern gardens but prefer some shade in the afternoon farther south.

Even in the sheltered places behind windbreaks and in gardens not right at the beach, some plants just do better at the seashore than others. In chapter 5 you'll find profiles of 100 of the best plants for Atlantic coastal gardens. But you still need to consider the usual particulars of the growing environment when you set out to select plants for your garden. Before you go shopping at local nurseries, assess the planting sites you will be using so you will be able to make wise choices.

GROWING CONDITIONS

To choose the best plants for any garden, you need to have a good understanding of the growing conditions present in the garden site. Seashore climates vary, and different locations come with different sets of challenges. On eastern Long Island, where I live, spring weather is cool and rainy, and late cold snaps and even frosts are not uncommon. Hydrangeas and other sensitive plants that begin to emerge from dormancy when the weather warms in spring can have their flower buds blasted by a late frost, and the hoped-for display of summer color will be cut off for the year. Planting of potatoes and other commercial crops may have to be delayed, pushing back the harvest at the end of the season.

For southern gardeners, winter can be difficult when a spell of warm weather is followed by a sudden, steep drop in temperature that chills plants before they have had time to harden their growth.

A problem in both northern and southern regions is that so many seashore plants that are drought tolerant in summer need good drainage year-round. Prolonged rainy weather in the South and snowpack in the North can lead to soggy soil in winter that is deadly to these plants.

Temperature. The average temperature range is an important factor in where plants will thrive. Most gardeners are aware that it's important to know the cold hardiness of a plant — the lowest winter temperatures at which it is likely to survive — to determine whether or not they can grow it. But for southern gardeners, especially, a plant's heat tolerance is just as important. See the appendix for the USDA Hardiness Zone Map and visit www.ahs.org to see the the AHS Heat Zone Map.

Sunlight. The amount of light your garden receives is another critical component of the growing environment. Full, unobstructed sunlight can be very intense at the seashore, and it can be amplified near the beach, where it bounces off white sand and reflects off the water. In understanding how much sun your garden gets, the duration of the sunlight is as important as the quality. Full sun is defined as unobstructed sunlight directly striking the

garden for at least six hours a day. Partial shade is a location that receives two to six hours of sunlight a day, in either the morning or the afternoon, or dappled sunlight all day long. Light or thin shade, sometimes called medium shade, can be found under trees with a high, lacy canopy; such a location may receive a couple of hours of sun a day but is brightly, though indirectly, lit the rest of the day. Full shade is found under mature trees with dense canopies, and deep shade is cast by large evergreens and nearby buildings. Deep shade is dim and cool all day, and very difficult for gardening.

How much sun or shade a plant can take depends in part on where it is growing. Many plants that need full sun in northern gardens do better with some shade, especially in the afternoon, in the South. The quality of light affects colors in the garden, too. Bright colors stand up better under the strong southern sun, where lighter, softer tones would wash out in the glare. Pastels often work better in the cool, misty air of New England, where bright, hot colors can sometimes seem too strident.

Precipitation. Rainfall and humidity are also important factors. The East Coast generally receives adequate rainfall to support a wide variety of plants. But sandy seashore soils drain quickly, and the wind and salt are also drying, so many plants need to be drought tolerant in order to survive. Supplemental watering is helpful, indeed a must for many gardens, but a watering system should be installed before the garden is planted. High humidity levels can also be problematic, especially in southern gardens. Not all plants that thrive in high temperatures can also withstand very humid conditions. In addition, when temperatures soar above 90°F and the atmosphere is very humid, garden soil that heats up during the day cannot cool down during torrid southern nights, stressing plants and encouraging the growth of pathogens.

Finally, the soil itself is all-important. Seashore soils are usually — but not always — sandy, and it is important to understand your soil type, how well it drains, its pH level, and its fertility. See "Improving the Soil," on page 48, for information on building good soil for your plants.

For a flourishing garden like this one, the first step is to understand the growing conditions present on your site. Fences or other windbreaks provide shelter, but can also shade the garden.

Along a sunny driveway, naturalistic drifts of purple Russian sage (*Perovskia atriplicifolia*), golden rudbeckia, grasses, and other perennials flourish in the coastal conditions.

CHOOSING PLANTS

The universe of plants is vast indeed, but some plants are undeniably better suited than others to life near the sea. Plants native to seashore environments, such as bayberry (*Myrica pensylvanica*), sea oats (*Uniola paniculata*), and seaside goldenrod (*Solidago sempervirens*), are some obvious choices. So are halophytes like sea pink (*Armeria maritima*) and sea lavender (*Limonium*). Plant names can offer clues to species that might be well suited to seashore gardens. If you see a word like *beach, coast, sea,* or *seaside* in a plant's common name, it is probably worth checking out. Botanical names containing such words as *maritima* and *littoralis* (of the seacoast) also tip off likely candidates.

Traits to Look For. When you begin to seek out other likely candidates, you can look for some particular characteristics. Low-growing, mat-forming plants such as thymes (*Thymus* spp.) and ceratostigma (*Ceratostigma plumbaginoides*) allow the wind to pass easily over them. Plants with small or narrow leaves, like tamarisk (*Tamarix ramosissima*), are also resistant to wind. Silver-leaved plants like artemisias and curry plant (*Helichrysum italicum*) are able to withstand intense sun, dry soil, and salt. Blue-toned conifers have a waxy coating on their needles that protects them from the effects of salt winds and spray.

Trees are essential for providing shade from the strong summer sun. Removing lower limbs allows sunlight to reach the ground and light up the space beneath.

Plants native to the Mediterranean region and other hot, dry places, such as lavender, rosemary, and santolina, stand up well to hot sun and drought. Deep-rooted plants like sea buckthorn are also very resistant to drought.

Attributes to Avoid. At the other end of the plant spectrum, there are those that are generally *not* good choices for seaside gardens. Tall, top-heavy perennials, such as delphiniums, whose stems need staking even in calmer conditions, may snap and topple under seashore gusts. Plants with large leaves can look ragged in exposed, windy sites. Trees with brittle wood or narrow crotch angles, such as are common in Bradford pear, would be at risk of damage from the wind.

It is also the wise and responsible course to refrain from planting invasive species. This is a difficult issue, since many of these tough plants are favorites along the coast because they can tolerate the harsh environment and grow where little else will. But even at the seashore these plants can get out of bounds and spread into natural environments and habitats, where they crowd out native plants and, in so doing, eliminate some of the food sources relied upon by local wildlife. Other popular and widely planted imported species are at risk from pests and diseases. Where I live, for example, Japanese black

pines that were planted for their tolerance to salt, wind, and drought are now being killed off by beetles and bacterial disease. See "Plants to Avoid" (page 54) for a list of undesirables.

TREES AND SHRUBS

Trees and shrubs are invaluable in seaside gardens. Although a rarity down on the beach, trees and shrubs are important in windbreaks, for hedges and screening, to provide cooling shade, to bring order to the landscape, to help support wildlife, and for ornamental purposes. Evergreens offer year-round color, protection, and structure. Some of the best conifers for seaside gardens are those with a bluish coloration. The blue color comes from a waxy coating on the needles, which protects them from salt damage near the beach. The best broad-leaved evergreens are those with thick, leathery leaves; some also carry a glossy, waxy surface on the leaves that has a protective effect. Many broad-leaved evergreens have ornamental flowers, too.

Deciduous trees may offer ornamental flowers, welcome shade, colorful autumn foliage, attractive bark, or fruit that is edible to people or wildlife or simply decorative.

Deciduous trees and shrubs for seascape gardens need a sturdy framework with wide crotch angles and well-spaced scaffold branches. Both evergreen and deciduous trees need enough flexibility to bend before the wind without snapping.

TRIAL AND ERROR

As in gardening anyplace else, learning what will grow best in your seashore garden is a process of experimentation, trial, and error. It takes time. You can obtain guidance on what generally grows well in your area by talking to your neighbors, joining a local garden club, and taking tours of public and private gardens when they are offered. You can visit good local nurseries and ask questions of knowledgeable staff. But experience is still the best teacher. Take time to get to know your particular property and its growing conditions. If there's already a garden in place from previous owners, wait a season to see what does well before making changes. Spend time in the garden and on the grounds. Watch and learn.

When you do start gardening on your own, keeping a garden journal is an invaluable aid. Jot down when trees leaf out, when roses and perennials bloom, what thrives and what languishes, which plants suffer from pests or disease. Note weather conditions: dates of major storms, periods of drought, floods, first and last frosts. As the years pass, your journal will become an ever-more-detailed portrait of the climate and your landscape, a better guide than even the best reference book.

An ancient copper beech (*Fagus sylvatica* var. *purpurea*) lends a sense of history to this Massachusetts harbor.

Gardening in Containers

CONTAINERS OFFER GREAT FLEXIbility for seashore gardeners. Where the soil is poor, or during the time you are building better soil for gardening or waiting for a protective windbreak to grow in, containers can be the focus of your gardening efforts. You might set large tubs holding small shrubs, perennials, trellised vines, or topiaries in sheltered locations behind the house, on a patio protected by a fence or hedge, or in low spots in the lee of the dunes.

In more established gardens, containers of plants can accent beds and borders, porches, decks, patios, and swimming pools. Colorful combinations of well-chosen annuals will bloom all summer, many until frost shuts them down. Neatly clipped evergreens in containers can add elegant touches to formal gardens. Tubs of bold tropicals inject a dramatic note to foliage beds and outdoor living spaces.

When choosing places for pots and plants to put in them, it is important to carefully assess sun and shade conditions and wind exposure. And be honest: a spot that gets a few hours of morning sun and is shaded by the house the rest of the day is not a "sunny" spot. For pots in a shady location, use shade-tolerant plants.

In a windy location it is a good idea to rely mostly on plants that stay reasonably compact. Tall plants in narrow pots will be blown over. Large leaves can become

tattered. Brittle stems can snap. Smaller-leaved plants with flexible stems are better able to bend with the wind.

Try to use heavy, sturdy pots rather than small, lightweight plastic ones. Fewer, larger pots will be more stable than lots of smaller ones. Water the pots well to keep them heavy. If the pots are in garden areas, you can sink them partway into the ground to hold them in place.

Hanging baskets overflowing with cascading and trailing plants are delightful additions to summer landscapes. But be sure they are well anchored, with sturdy hangers. Keep them out of the most exposed locations and place them instead in more protected places — on the lee side of the house rather than on the windward side, or under an arbor, perhaps. Take down hanging baskets (and wind chimes and other dangling ornaments) when you expect a storm or higher-than-usual winds.

Remember that plants in containers need plenty of water, especially in sunny, windy seashore locations. See chapter 3 for information on watering.

Finally, if you are a weekend resident, you may want to have a local nursery or gardener plant and maintain your pots for you.

Container plantings can enhance the garden and outdoor living space in myriad ways, offering an easy way to add color to porches and decks.

Planting and Maintenance

WHEN THE DESIGN IS IN PLACE AND THE SITE PREPARED, it's time to get growing. This chapter provides a summary of the best gardening techniques for seaside gardens. You'll find guidelines for planting, watering, fertilizing and maintaining good soil quality, mulching, deadheading and pruning, preventing and controlling pests and diseases, and getting ready for winter. There's also information on what to do after a storm.

Bear in mind that you will need to adapt these techniques to fit the particular microclimates in your garden. Weather conditions also will vary from year to year and may necessitate adjustments in planting dates, amount of watering, and other aspects of plant care. Watch your garden and be sensitive to its needs.

ABOVE: Drought-tolerant yucca provides an architectural presence in the seaside garden.

RIGHT: This well-maintained garden benefits from the protection of a stone wall. A greenhouse can expand your plant palette by offering a warm site to overwinter tender species.

Planting Guidelines

Before you plant a tree or shrub, find out what its mature size is likely to be, and be sure to allow enough space for it to reach its full height and spread.

Planting techniques for sea-shore gardens are basically the same as those used in other gardens, although, as I will explain in a minute, you do need to be aware of the effects of wind and intense sun. Before you plant anything, make sure the plant you are putting in will have enough space to reach its full mature size without crowding. Space considerations are especially important along property lines, the street, driveways and paths, and alongside the house. Large shrubs such as hollies and false cypress can easily grow to six or more feet wide, and evergreen trees can be even wider.

Investigate the best planting times in your area. Trees and shrubs can be planted in either spring or fall in many seashore areas. In the South, woody plants can go into the ground in February, while they are still dormant. Farther north, you have to wait until the soil thaws and becomes workable.

It's best to plant on a cloudy day, or in the morning if the weather is hot and sunny. First, water the soil deeply before planting. If you are planting bare-root nursery stock, it's important to prevent the roots from drying out before you get the plants in the ground. Many mail-order plants are shipped in bare-root form in a loose, light packing material; roses are also sold this way. If you cannot plant as soon as the stock arrives, unwrap the plants to inspect them and moisten the roots if they are very shriveled and dry. Pull a plastic bag over the roots to hold in moisture until you can plant (which will be, hopefully, in 24 hours or so). A few hours before planting, set the roots in a bucket of water and let them soak to rehydrate them. When you are ready to plant, carry the bucket to the planting site, or put each plant's roots into a plastic bag to hold in the moisture. If you're working in the sun, cover the bag with a cloth to keep it from heating up and damaging the plants.

PLANTING TREES AND SHRUBS

For trees and shrubs, dig a planting hole as deep as the root-ball is high and twice as wide. There is one exception to the rule: If you are planting in sand rather than soil, set plants an inch or two deeper than they were growing at the nursery. Also, if you are planting on or very near the beach, it's not a bad idea to scrape away the top few inches of dry sand before you dig the hole. Fine, dry sand is hard to moisten — it sheds water like dry peat moss does. Removing the top layer of it decreases the chance that some of the sand will fall into the planting hole and create a dry spot around plant roots.

Excavate two bucketfuls of sand or existing soil from the bottom of the hole and mix it with two bucketfuls of compost or good-quality topsoil. Mix some of the amended soil with the soil in the hole, and set the plant in the hole to check the depth. Remove more soil as needed to correct the depth. An alternative method is to dig the hole a little deeper and work some compost or leaf mold into the bottom before planting. In any case, the plant should sit at the same level it was growing in the nursery, which you can see by a difference in color at the bottom of the trunk. The part that grew below the soil line should appear darker than the rest of the trunk. If you aren't sure about the planting depth, it is better to err by planting too high than too deep, because the plant will settle after it is in the ground. Make sure all the roots are covered, but don't cover the trunk. If the plant has a long taproot, make sure the hole is deep enough to accommodate it.

When the planting hole is ready, if the soil is mostly sand or otherwise of very poor quality, make two slits in the bottom of the hole with a trowel and put about a tablespoon of all-purpose fertilizer into each one. Or you can pour a liquid fertilizer solution, such as compost tea, a fish/seaweed product, or a synthetic all-purpose liquid fertilizer diluted to half strength, into the hole. Or add an organic fertilizer to the amended soil that will go into the hole around the plant.

If the tree or shrub is in a container, remove it (cut off the container if you need to). Lay the plant on its side and gently

PLANTING A TREE OR SHRUB

When planting in sand, set a tree or shrub one to two inches deeper than usual (1). Remove some sand from the planting hole, mix with compost, and return some to the hole (2). Set the plant in the hole and partially fill with soil (3). Check to make sure the plant is at the proper depth (4). Make a saucerlike depression around the stem to catch and hold water for the roots (5).

untangle the roots as best you can. If the root-ball is very tight, try to tease out a few of the bigger roots without breaking them. If the plant has a taproot, handle it carefully to avoid breaking it. Fill the hole halfway with amended soil, working it

PLANTING A PERENNIAL

To remove a perennial from its nursery pot, support the top growth with one hand as you turn over the pot with your other hand, and slide out the root-ball.

around the roots with your fingers. Water well to settle the soil and get rid of air pockets. Fill the hole the rest of the way, gently rock the plant a bit, water again, and firm the soil around the base of the plant with your hand or, for a larger specimen, with your foot. Make a depression in the soil around the trunk to catch water and channel it down to the root system.

Staking is not generally recommended for trees and large shrubs anymore, but you may need to stake them in exposed seaside locations. If you do need to stake, thread the wires through pieces of garden hose where they touch the trunk. Leave just enough slack in the wires for the trunk to be able to flex a bit in the wind — it makes for a stronger trunk and better anchorage in the roots.

PLANTING PERENNIALS AND ANNUALS

When planting a perennial or annual, you will probably be planting in soil that already has been improved (such as in a prepared bed). Dig a hole just deep enough for the plant and fill it partway with water. While the water drains away, remove the plant from its pot. To do this, tap the bottom of the pot with the handle of a trowel to loosen the plant. Turn the pot over and support the top of the soil ball with one hand, placing a finger on either side of the stem for support. With your other hand,

slide the pot off the root-ball. If the root-ball does not slide out easily, lay the pot on its side and roll it back and forth while pressing on it to loosen the soil ball. If it still doesn't come out easily, cut away the pot with shears.

If the plant is severely root-bound, make two or three vertical cuts a few inches up into the root-ball from the bottom and gently spread apart the root-ball.

Set the plant gently into the planting hole. Make sure the plant sits at the correct depth in the hole, and proceed as directed above for trees and shrubs. If the plant grows as a rosette of leaves close to the ground, be sure you do not cover the crown of the plant (where roots meet the stem) or the plant could rot. Bushy, branched plants generally can be set a bit deeper in the soil without harm.

Water to settle the soil around the plant and ensure good root contact, then fill in any holes that remain.

To remove a plant from a market pack or cell pack, tap or lightly press on the bottom of a cell to loosen the plant. If the plant does not slide easily out of the cell, cut the plastic with scissors and tear it away from the soil ball. Grasp the plant *very gently* by two upper leaves (but not the growing tip, or you could damage the plant) and slip it out of the cell. When the plant is out, support it underneath and plant as described above.

Watering

Unless you are growing only tough native plants that are highly drought resistant, your garden is going to need supplemental watering. Many seashore residents install automatic watering systems; if you're not a full-time resident, that's probably the best course of action. There are several different kinds of watering systems, and each has its own benefits and disadvantages.

OVERHEAD SPRINKLERS

Overhead sprinklers are the least efficient means of watering; some of the water evaporates into the air before it gets to plants, and some runs off before it can soak into the ground. Overhead watering can cause soil to splash up onto plant leaves, which can lead to the transfer of disease organisms from soil onto susceptible plants. And drought-tolerant plants do not always fare well under overhead watering — the crowns may rot if they get wet on a regular basis, and the plants will eventually die.

On the other hand, overhead sprinkling can be beneficial because it rinses salt off plant foliage and dilutes salts that have settled on lawns and ground covers. This is especially important for gardeners who aren't at their seaside homes every day to keep an eye on plantings and rinse them as needed. Despite its detractions, therefore, you may decide that an overhead sprinkler system is right for you.

SOAKER HOSES

Soaker hoses are a very efficient means of watering. They deliver water directly to the soil, where it can reach the roots, and little water is lost to evaporation. Soaker hoses emit water in a slow trickle, so it doesn't run off before soaking in, and they don't cause soil to splash onto plants. They are easy to install — you simply lay out the hoses on top of the soil near plants, and you can cover them with mulch to hide them. And many soaker hoses are made from recycled tires, making them environmentally helpful.

The downside is that soaker hoses have to run for a pretty long time in order to deliver enough water. Depending on the quality of your soil and the plants you are growing, you may need to run soaker hoses for several hours at a time.

HOW LONG TO WATER

Timing is important where sprinklers are concerned. You need the system to run long enough that the water it puts out can soak deep enough to reach the root zone. It is generally better to water longer and less often than to let the system run 10 or 15 minutes every day. Many municipalities have regulations that forbid overhead watering during daylight hours. In such a case (or even when no watering restrictions are in place, for that matter), it is better to have the system run early in the

SOAKER HOSES

Soaker hoses are a very efficient way to water, trickling moisture slowly onto the soil where it is readily absorbed. Lay the hoses on top of the soil, snaking them among plants in a pattern that allows all the plants to get water.

USING DRIP IRRIGATION IN SANDY SOIL

Drip irrigation is the most efficient way to water; its slender plastic tubes deliver water directly to the root zone, where plants can best use it. However, drip systems don't always work well in very sandy soils, because the water lines can clog. Robert Kourik, author of *Drip Irrigation for Every Landscape and All Climates* (Metamorphic Press, 1992), offers the following tips for using a drip system in sandy soil:

• Don't install the system underground. Instead, keep the emitters on top of the soil and cover them with mulch.

• Use tubing that does not have built-in pressure compensation (as some do); the higher water pressure will help to flush the lines.

• Use tubing with one-foot intervals, and place the lines a foot apart in the garden.

To revive a wilted plant in a pot, submerge the pot in a bucket of water. When the bubbling stops, remove the pot and let the excess water drain away.

day so foliage will dry in the morning sun, rather than in the evening, when moisture sitting on leaves overnight could promote the growth of disease organisms. It is also important to adjust the watering schedule according to the weather so you are not watering when it rains.

The other way to water is with a hand-held hose. It's a time-consuming chore if you've got more than a few plants, and there's a tendency not to water long enough to allow the water to soak deep into the ground.

Many localities have ordinances governing watering. Become familiar with regulations where you live and abide by them: they are for everyone's good.

WHEN TO WATER

Be sure to water new plants thoroughly after planting. Thereafter, water as needed to keep the soil moist until the plants can send out new roots and establish themselves in the soil. How long this process takes depends upon the plant. Annuals and perennials will settle in in a couple of weeks, but trees and shrubs will take longer. Trees in exposed locations should be watered during dry weather for the first year after planting.

The old gardener's rule of thumb for watering — that plants need one inch of water per week — does not necessarily apply to seashore gardens. Sandy soil

drains so quickly that an inch of water a week might not be enough. On the other hand, it might be too much moisture for drought-tolerant plants like arctotis and prickly pear. A better general guideline for seashore gardens is to make sure gardens of nonnative plants that are not highly drought tolerant receive one deep watering, thorough enough to send water 1 to 1½ feet down into the soil, once a week if no rain falls.

More sensitive perennials and other plants that thrive in soil that is "moist but well drained" would probably fare best in soil amended with lots of organic matter where they receive water two or three times a week. Drought-tolerant plants should need water only during prolonged periods of dry weather. If you want to grow plants with different needs, try to group like-minded ones together in separate beds or even in different parts of the garden. Water each group according to its needs.

WATERING CONTAINERS

Containers need watering much more frequently than gardens in the ground. In hot, windy seashore conditions, plants in containers may need watering every day or even more than once a day. How often your containers will require watering depends in part on the moisture needs of the plants growing in them. But a number of other factors also come into play.

Ask yourself these questions:

- Is it hot? The higher the temperature, the more water plants need.
- Is the humidity high or low? On dry days, pots need water more frequently.
- Is the container in sun or shade? Plants in the shade need less water than plants in full, blazing sun.
- Is it windy? Pots dry out faster on windy days.
- What kind of soil mix is in the pot? Lightweight, soilless, peat-based planting mixes dry out faster than potting mixes containing a larger amount of soil and/or compost.
- How big is the pot? The smaller the pot, the smaller the volume of soil it holds and the faster it dries out.

To help reduce watering frequency, mix a polymer gel into the potting mix before planting. These polymers come in the form of crystals that can absorb many times their volume in water, turning into blobs of gel. They release their moisture gradually, so the potting mix dries out more slowly. Follow package directions; if you use too much polymer, the expanding gel will cause the potting mix to overflow the container.

Don't wait until your plants look wilted before watering — wilted plants are stressed, and their growth can be adversely affected. The best way to tell when plants need water is to poke a finger into the soil. When it feels dry an inch below the surface, it's time to water. To judge if a hanging basket needs water, place your hand under the basket and let the basket rest on your palm until you can feel its weight. If the pot feels heavy, it is probably still moist; if it feels very light, it's in need of water.

When you do water, do it thoroughly. Water enough for some excess to drain from the holes in the bottom of the pot. The goal is to moisten the potting mix all the way to the bottom. Use a watering can or a hose. A long-handled watering wand makes it easy to reach hanging baskets. If you have an automatic drip system in your pots, make sure it runs long enough to provide a thorough watering. A drip system will emit water far more slowly than a hose and will need to run for a much longer time. Experiment by connecting the drip line to just one pot and water until the potting mix is moist throughout. Keep track of the time so you know how long to run the system in the future.

TOP: Drought-tolerant plants like these sedums, echeverias, and aeoniums are a good choice for weekend gardeners.

BOTTOM: Pots may need watering daily — or more than once a day — in hot, windy summer weather.

Fertilizing and Soil Care

Soil building is an important, continuous process for seashore gardens, especially if you want to grow heavy-feeding flowers like these lilies.

Building good soil is not a one-time proposition. When you've spent time and money to improve your soil, you will want to keep it in good condition so your garden will continue to thrive. Organic matter, as we saw in chapter 3, is tremendously valuable for improving the quality of sandy soil. But it doesn't last forever. Organic matter breaks down and disappears quickly at the seashore; the sandier the soil and the hotter the weather, the faster organic materials get used up in the soil. It's important to replenish the supply every year.

Try to add an inch or two of compost to your garden each year. That's easy to do if you're growing annual flowers or vegetables — you simply spread the compost over the empty garden in spring and till it in before you plant. In a perennial garden, drop the compost in between plants and spread it around and among them with your hands or a hoe. But be careful not to cover the plant crowns. For shrubs, a more feasible method of application is to spread the compost around the base of each plant, keeping it a few inches away from the main stems. For trees, the layer of compost should, ideally, cover an area from a foot or so away from the trunk outward to the drip line (an imaginary line on the ground beneath the limit of the tree's canopy). That's because a tree's roots don't just go straight down into the ground; they spread out and cover an area equal to or greater than the spread of the tree's branches. If you apply compost just around the base of the tree, it won't benefit much of the root system.

Plants native to beach and dune areas are adapted to dry, infertile sand and may not thrive in fertile soil rich in organic matter, so salt windbreaks and dune-stabilizing plantings may not require these yearly infusions of organic matter. But garden beds and borders will definitely benefit.

When applying compost or other soil amendments under a tree, spread the material over an area from a foot away from the trunk to the drip line, to ensure that the entire root system receives the benefit.

Roses and other flowering plants appreciate a fertilizer rich in phosphorus. Apply fertilizer around the base of each plant and work it gently into the soil.

HOW TO FERTILIZE

Fertilizing at the beach can be a tricky proposition. Garden beds and borders in very sandy soil will need fertilizing in order to thrive, especially if the soil is not being regularly amended with organic material. But well-adapted native plants will need less fertilizer than more conventional garden plants.

How and when you fertilize also depends upon the kind of fertilizer you are using. Synthetic fertilizers such as granular 5-10-5 and 8-8-8 products work quickly and can be very effective. But they are more concentrated than organic products, and they can cause problems in sandy soils if not handled correctly. For one thing, granular fertilizers mixed into soil that is mostly sand can become more concentrated if the sand dries out during spells of hot, dry summer weather. The concentrated salts can burn plant roots with which they come into direct contact. To avoid damaging plants, sprinkle granular fertilizers on top of the ground, in a circle around the base of each plant, and water them in, instead of placing them into planting holes.

Synthetic fertilizers also leach quickly through very porous, sandy soil. You need to be careful not to overfertilize your garden. Fertilizers that are not absorbed by plant roots travel through soil in rainwater and can eventually reach the water table.

From there the runoff can get into rivers, estuaries, and bays. Fertilizer runoff wreaks havoc with coastal waterways. (On eastern Long Island, for example, fertilizer runoff is believed by many environmentalists and other experts to be a possible contributor to the demise of the once abundant population of bay scallops and the subsequent ruin of the shellfishing industry.)

A better fertilizer option is to use a timed-release product or an organic formula, which will naturally release its nutrients gradually. Timed-release fertilizers are especially helpful for heavy feeders like annuals (either in the ground or in containers) and roses that repeat bloom. Read labels carefully: a timed-release fertilizer may not be effective until the soil temperature reaches 50°F. And fertilizers are used up more quickly in hot weather. Soaring temperatures may mean you will have to apply the fertilizer more frequently than the advertisements or the large print on the front of the package promises.

Use fertilizers rich in phosphorus, such as 5-10-10 and 5-10-5, for flowering and fruiting plants. Powdered rock phosphate is an organic source of phosphorus. For grasses, lawns, and other foliage plants, use a high-nitrogen fertilizer such as 20-10-10. Some plants need less fertilizer than others. Achillea and artemisia, for instance, need less fertilizing than lilies and roses.

Natives also will need little in the way of fertilization once they become established. See the plant profiles in chapter 5 for information on the nutritional needs of individual plants.

Liquid fertilizers are great for plants in pots, and you can also use them diluted to half or one-quarter strength as a foliar feed sprayed onto leaves to give plants a quick boost. Foliar feeding is a good way to provide plants with trace elements; use an organic liquid such as kelp or fish products or compost tea to supply them. There are numerous all-purpose liquid fertilizers available at garden centers and home improvement stores.

Intensively planted container combinations will need frequent water and fertilizer to keep them flowering through the summer.

WHEN TO FERTILIZE

You may or may not want to fertilize at planting time, depending on what you are planting and where you are planting it. As described below, many plants in beds and borders benefit from fertilization at planting time. But do not fertilize dune-stabilization plantings when you put them in unless you are using an organic product.

Trees and Shrubs. Fertilize new trees and shrubs with an organic fertilizer at planting time, working the material into the soil at the bottom of the planting hole. Fertilize young trees again in early summer with an organic or timed-release product, or monthly with a granular synthetic until six to eight weeks before the average date of the first fall frost in your area.

Fertilize established trees and shrubs once a year, when growth begins in spring, with an all-purpose organic or synthetic fertilizer. Follow package directions for rate of application. For shrubs and young trees, spread the fertilizer on top of the soil in a ring around the base of the plant and a couple of feet out from the trunk or main stems. Work it into the top inch of soil. For older trees, drill holes two feet apart and 12 to 18 inches deep over an area from two to three feet out from the trunk to the drip line (where most of the roots are concentrated). Put the fertilizer into the holes.

Perennials. Feed perennials at planting time with an all-purpose or high-phosphorus fertilizer. Thereafter fertilize every two or three weeks in sandy soil, once a month if you are using an organic fertilizer, or once in early summer if the soil is rich in organic matter. Stop feeding six weeks before the first expected fall frost — late July in the North, around the middle of August in the mid-Atlantic region, or September in the South. Cessation of fertilizing allows plants to slow their growth so they will not be producing a lot of tender new leaves right before the onset of cold weather (new growth can be seriously damaged by cold). Instead, plant tissues, especially in the crown, will be able to harden off in preparation for the winter dormant period.

Roses. Amend the soil for roses before planting with plenty of organic matter (this is less important for rugosas, which are very tough). Also work in an all-purpose or high-phosphorus organic or timed-release fertilizer, according to package directions. After planting, wait three to four weeks for plants to establish themselves in the soil, then begin to fertilize every two or three weeks in sandy soil, or once a month if you are using an organic fertilizer. In subsequent years, fertilize bush roses when plants begin to grow in spring, again after the first flush of bloom, and once a month until midsummer. Feed shrub roses and climbers in spring when growth begins and just once or twice more, in late spring and early summer. Stop fertilizing six to eight weeks before the first expected fall frost to allow plants enough time to harden their canes and buds before winter.

Annuals. Fertilize annuals at planting time with all-purpose or high-phosphorus products. As soon as the plants show new growth, begin to fertilize weekly in sandy soil, or monthly with organics throughout the growing season. If your soil is heavier, feed every two or three weeks. Follow package directions for rates of application. It's a good idea to water before fertilizing if the soil is dry.

Container Plants. Mix an organic or timed-release fertilizer into the potting mix when planting. Then feed every week or two with an all-purpose liquid fertilizer diluted according to package directions. Or fertilize at every watering with an all-purpose liquid fertilizer diluted to half or one-quarter strength.

If you want to use an organic liquid fertilizer, look for fish emulsion or a product that combines seaweed and fish. Use according to package directions. Liquid fertilizers may be applied to the soil or sprayed onto plant leaves as a foliar feed.

Mulching

Buckwheat hulls dress up the King garden in Cohasset, Massachusetts. Mulch helps slow evaporation of moisture from the soil and adds organic matter as it decomposes.

Mulching — covering the soil under plants — is a great help to seashore gardens. Mulches laid on the garden in summer slow the evaporation of moisture from the soil and reduce weed growth. Mulch will also help moderate soil temperatures, preventing them from rising to levels harmful to plants — the sun won't heat up the soil under a layer of mulch as much as it will bare soil that just bakes under the beating summer rays. Mulches of natural materials offer the additional benefit of contributing organic matter to the soil as they decompose, improving soil texture and overall quality. They'll add some nutrients, too.

Be aware that mulches of wood products, such as wood chips, bark nuggets, and uncomposted sawdust, use nitrogen from the soil as they decompose, so it's a good idea to apply a nitrogen-rich fertilizer before laying a wood mulch.

Covering the soil with mulch keeps soil from splashing up during rain or waterings onto plant leaves, where it could possibly encourage soilborne diseases in susceptible plants. At the seashore, mulch can also help protect the soil from salt deposits. In addition, a layer of mulch gives the garden a neat, finished look.

SEASONAL MULCHES

The best time to put down a summer mulch is in spring, after the soil warms but before temperatures really start to climb. Most mulches are best laid two to three inches deep; see below for more information on particular mulch materials.

Mulches can be extremely useful in winter, too, but at that time of year their purpose is different. Where the ground freezes in winter, mulch helps to keep the soil frozen during spells of warm winter weather. It prevents or at least minimizes the kind of freeze/thaw/refreeze cycle that can cause the ground to heave and push the roots of perennials out onto the surface. Exposed roots in winter are likely to die as they dry out and freeze. If you want to give your garden a protective winter mulch, apply a six-inch layer in late fall or early winter after the soil freezes. Note that mulches will be washed away or at least moved around by floodwaters. If your property is prone to flooding, you may want to forgo mulching.

APPLYING MULCH

When you spread mulch in your garden, don't just dump it on top of the plants. Tuck it in around the base of each plant, taking care to keep it away from direct contact with stems. Don't bury the crowns of plants that sit close to the ground — the mulch will hold moisture that can cause crowns to rot. If laid too deeply, the mulch could suffocate the plants.

There are some times when mulching

Mulching with natural materials gives the garden a neat, finished look. Pine needles and pine straw make good mulches for many seaside gardens.

may not be a good idea. Earwigs, slugs, and mice love to hide out in mulch. If they're a problem in your garden, it may be better not to mulch. Also, if you have some plants that you want to encourage to self-sow and spread, leave the soil under them bare so the seeds can reach the ground.

When applying mulch, tuck it around the base of each plant, but do not cover the crown; the plant could rot.

The most widely used mulches are shredded bark, wood chips, bark nuggets, cocoa bean hulls, and shredded leaves. Seashore gardeners can also look for saltmarsh hay, which works well, and in the South, pine straw, which is an attractive dark brown. You can also mulch with compost or pine needles. Be aware that organic mulches will lighten in color over the course of a season. To retain a good dark color, spread fresh mulch each year.

Some gardeners like to use plastic mulches, or a layer of gravel or pebbles, to cover the soil around plants. Both can work, but they do hold heat in the soil and are probably best for northern gardens.

Here are some of the characteristics of various mulches:

• **Bark chips or nuggets.** Long lasting. The larger the pieces, the longer they last, but smaller chips are finer textured and more attractive under perennials and smaller plants. Add nitrogen fertilizer to soil, and apply a two-inch layer.

• **Shredded bark.** Long lasting. Partially composted mulch is an attractive dark color. Add nitrogen fertilizer to soil, and apply a three-inch layer.

• **Cedar mulches.** Fine textured and available in natural and dyed colors. The orange-red type is popular but can clash with flower colors and call too much attention to itself; use with care. Apply a two- to three-inch layer.

• **Cocoa bean hulls.** Nice brown color, and they smell like chocolate when first applied. Expensive, but fine textured and nice in perennial beds and formal gardens. Lightweight and may blow around on windy sites. Apply a two-inch layer.

• **Compost.** Dark brown and crumbly, excellent soil conditioner, and invaluable for sandy soils. But it won't keep down weeds — they'll grow right up through it. Apply a one- to two-inch layer.

• **Shredded leaves.** Free or inexpensive if you shred your own or obtain them from municipal recycling operations. Excellent soil builder, but best in informal or naturalistic gardens. Apply a two- to three-inch layer in summer; six inches as a winter mulch. Leaf mold (composted leaves) is also good. Don't use unshredded leaves — they tend to mat down and look messy.

• **Pine needles, pine straw.** Attractive brown color, especially nice in naturalistic and native plant gardens. Will tend to make soil pH more acidic; add some lime if using around plants needing neutral to mildly alkaline soil. Apply a two- to three-inch layer.

• **Saltmarsh hay.** Effective where available, though expensive. It is finer textured than agricultural hay, and contains no weed seeds, the way agricultural hay can. Decomposes well and adds trace minerals to soil. Apply a two- to three-inch layer.

• **Seashells.** Crushed seashells, where they are available, can be used for mulching or for surfacing paths. They will tend to raise soil pH. Apply a two- to three-inch layer.

• **Seaweed.** Free when collected from beaches. Adds minerals and organic matter to soil, but can be smelly when it decomposes. Best used in compost.

• **Stone (pebbles, gravel, marble chips).** Won't suppress weeds unless you first lay down a weed-barrier fabric. Looks best in a rock garden or under trees and shrubs. Apply a two- to three-inch layer, depending on size of stones.

• **Wood chips.** Often available free from tree-care crews. Long lasting, but not terribly attractive when chips are large. Usually light colored. Add nitrogen fertilizer to soil and apply a two- to three-inch layer, depending on size of chips.

Shredded bark mulch suppresses weeds beneath a newly planted tree.

There is a standard procedure to follow in removing large branches without tearing the bark of the trunk. First, make a cut up into the underside of the branch one to two feet out from the branch collar (the raised ridge of bark where branch meets trunk), cutting about halfway through the branch. Second, a couple of inches out beyond the first cut, saw downward from the top of the branch all the way through it. Third, saw off the remaining stub by cutting right next to the collar (the cut will be slightly angled to follow the line of the collar). Do not cut into the collar or leave a stub beyond it — either could increase the possibility of disease.

Remove smaller branches with loppers, a pole pruner, or a pruning saw, cutting right alongside the collar.

If you need to prune a diseased branch, cut back to healthy wood, several inches away from the damaged site. Dip your tools into a solution of liquid chlorine bleach and water after each cut to sterilize them and avoid spreading the disease.

After pruning, make sure to water and fertilize according to the guidelines given earlier in this chapter, to keep the tree or shrub healthy and help it recover.

Shearing. Shearing is simply cutting off a certain amount from the ends of stems all over a plant to create a uniform surface or a precise, particular shape. The technique is

Keep hedges neat by shearing them at least once a year, in late spring or early summer. Where the growing season is long enough, you may shear again in mid- to late summer.

used to trim hedges and clip topiaries. In order to tolerate shearing, a plant must be able to sprout new growth from farther back on the stem than the tip. Many plants cannot tolerate shearing, so it's important to choose hedge and topiary plants carefully.

Shear hedges and evergreen topiaries in late spring or early summer every year, at least once. Do not shear late in summer in the North, or you will promote new growth late in the season that may not have time to harden properly by winter. Insufficiently hardened growth is susceptible to winterkill. Clip stray shoots from topiaries as needed throughout the growing season.

Controlling Pests and Diseases

This sea holly (*Eryngium* sp.) is one of the most deer-resistant plants you'll find.

Problems can crop up in even the most carefully tended gardens. Lots of seashore gardeners have to contend with deer, and diseases like mildew and black spot can be troublesome, too. In general, when dealing with pest and disease problems, the best approach is to try to prevent problems in the first place. As they say in the sports world, the best offense is a good defense. If you grow a lot of native plants in your garden, you're already a step ahead of the game. Natives are far less bothered by pests and diseases than are exotic plants, especially varieties bred to be bigger, brighter, and earlier than their less flamboyant ancestors.

But no matter what grows in your garden, keeping the garden clean will go a long way toward preventing disease and insect infestation. Practice good sanitation. Pick up and remove dead and fallen leaves and other debris. Deadhead to get rid of old flowers. Keep the weeds pulled — they offer good hiding places for bugs, and they compete with garden plants for water and nutrients. When you plant, allow enough space between plants for air to circulate freely. Mulch the garden to prevent mud that could contain pathogens from splashing up onto plant leaves. Clean up the garden promptly after a storm.

To prevent disease, don't use overhead sprinklers. Instead, install a drip-irrigation system or lay soaker hoses. If you do water from above, do it in the morning or late afternoon (early enough so foliage will dry before dark). Try not to work among the plants when they are wet, so you don't inadvertently transfer any lurking pathogens from one plant to another.

Be vigilant. Keep an eye on your garden. If you spend time among your plants, you will notice when things go wrong before little problems turn into big ones. And after all, isn't a big reason you have a garden to enjoy the plants in it? When you do spot a problem, take action right away. Don't wait until a few bugs turn into a full-scale infestation or a disease spreads from one plant to many.

With experience, you will learn which pests and diseases are likely to invade your garden and which plants they are most likely to attack. But you can be proactive and investigate for yourself. Learn to identify the insects in your landscape. Some will actually help combat pests by preying on them. You don't want to get rid of the beneficial wasps, flies, and other insects that prey on pests. Indeed, you should encourage them. Growing native plants is one good way to support beneficial insects. Also, if you have an herb garden, include dill, caraway, angelica, and other plants in the Umbelliferae family — they attract a variety of beneficial insects. Include some blue lace flower (*Trachymene coerulea*) in a flower garden; it's in the same family.

PEST CONTROL

Deer take a toll on many a seaside garden. As the march of development eats up natural habitat areas, deer find their way into more and more gardens looking for food. If deer are a problem in your region, you will want to build your landscape with plants they aren't likely to eat. You might use deer-resistant plants in outlying parts of the landscape and put plants you and the deer both love in hard-to-access areas close to the house — in an enclosed courtyard, perhaps, or up on an elevated deck. "Deer-Resistant Plants for Seashore Gardens" (right) contains a listing of plants that deer are unlikely to eat. But there are no guarantees. When deer are hungry enough, they will eat just about anything. I've known them to chew rugosa roses, which have very thorny stems, nearly to the ground. Deer are usually hungriest at the end of winter, when food is hard to find. You may find them coming onto your property then even if they don't bother you the rest of the year.

The only way to really keep deer out of your garden is to fence it in. And you need a high fence — 8 to 10 feet — or the deer will leap right over it. You may find the best solution is to install black plastic mesh deer fencing all around the perimeter of the property. This kind of fencing can be camouflaged behind tree and shrub plantings, and it really does work. But you'll

DEER-RESISTANT PLANTS FOR SEASHORE GARDENS

Trees and Shrubs

Amelanchier canadensis, shadblow
Aronia spp., chokeberry
Clethra alnifolia, sweet pepperbush
Cotoneaster horizontalis, rockspray cotoneaster
Crataegus spp., hawthorn
Cytisus scoparius, Scotch broom
Ilex spp., holly
Juniperus spp., junipers
Lavandula spp., lavender
Myrica cerifera, wax myrtle
Myrica pensylvanica, bayberry
Picea abies, Norway spruce
Picea pungens var. *glauca,* blue spruce
Pinus densiflora, Japanese red pine
Pinus mugo, mugo pine
Prunus maritima, beach plum
Quercus spp., oak
Spiraea spp., spirea
Thuja plicata, western arborvitae
Viburnum dentatum, arrowwood viburnum
Vitex agnus-castus, chastetree

Perennials

Achillea spp., yarrow
Artemisia spp., artemisia
Asclepias tuberosa, butterfly weed
Aster spp., aster
Astilbe spp., astilbe
Baptisia australis, false indigo
Cerastium tomentosum, snow-in-summer
Cimicifuga spp., snakeroot
Ferns
Gaillardia × *grandiflora,* blanketflower
Hibiscus moscheutos, rose mallow
Iberis sempervirens, perennial candytuft

Kniphofia spp., red-hot poker
Monarda didyma, bee balm
Nepeta × *faassenii,* catmint
Nipponanthemum nipponicum, Montauk daisy
Oenothera spp., evening primrose
Perovskia atriplicifolia, Russian sage
Rudbeckia spp., black-eyed Susan
Salvia spp., sage
Santolina chamaecyparissus, lavender cotton
Solidago spp., goldenrod
Stachys byzantina, lamb's ears
Thalictrum spp., meadow rue
Veronica spp., veronica
Yucca spp., yucca

Annuals

Arctotis venustum, African daisy
Lantana spp., lantana
Lobularia maritima, sweet alyssum
Mirabilis jalapa, four-o'clocks
Pelargonium spp., geranium
Petunia cvs., petunia
Salvia spp., sage
Tagetes spp., marigold
Tropaeolum majus, nasturtium

Ground covers and Vines

Ajuga spp., bugleweed
Arctostaphylos uva-ursi, bearberry
Ceratostigma plumbaginoides, false plumbago
Clematis spp., clematis
Euonymus fortunei, wintercreeper
Hedera helix, English ivy
Lonicera spp., honeysuckle
Thymus spp., thyme
Vinca minor, periwinkle

need tall gates to close the driveway, too, or the deer will stroll right on in.

Another option, if deer are really problematic, is to enclose plants you really prize in cages made of hardware cloth or plastic mesh. It's not an aesthetically pleasing solution, but it will save the plants. Wrap the trunks of young and newly planted trees with tree wrap for protection.

Scent-based repellents can be effective, but you have to reapply them after rain washes them away. Sooner or later the deer will get used to the smell, too, so you have to switch products often. Some people hang bars of deodorant soap in the bushes or suspend bags of hair clippings from tree branches. These methods seem to work well for some gardeners and not at all for others.

OTHER FOUR-LEGGED PESTS

Deer aren't the only four-legged pests you may encounter, although they are usually the most destructive, unless you have a vegetable garden. Rabbits may nibble herbaceous plants, and they also like to eat crocuses and tulips. Groundhogs and raccoons may bother vegetables, if you grow them. A three-foot fence will keep these smaller critters out of beds and borders, or you can sprinkle dried blood over the planting area or spray plants with a deer repellent.

Under the ground, moles and voles devour bulbs (except for narcissus, which they avoid), and sometimes they will eat the roots of perennials and annuals. Chipmunks, too, may get into the garden. If you notice that some plants in the garden die suddenly, and there is no sign of pests or disease, it's possible the roots were eaten by voles or other tunnelers. These creatures are hard to keep out of the garden. One control strategy is to surround entire garden beds with a barrier of hardware cloth sunk two feet into the ground. It might also help to try and eliminate hiding places for them by removing any piled-up brush and other debris that has accumulated in odd corners of the property.

SMALL INVADERS

It's not necessary to drench the garden with insecticide at the first sign of a bug. Indeed, spraying with broad-spectrum insecticides, whether they are of synthetic or organic origin, should be a last resort. Many of these products kill beneficial insects along with the pests, and even organic products are quite toxic when first applied (although they do break down more quickly in the environment than do synthetic insecticides).

This deer-resistant planting of sedum, globe thistle, nepeta, and hyssop also attracts many beneficial insects.

Even plant-based insecticides such as pyrethrum can kill butterflies and beneficial insects along with pests, so use them only when absolutely necessary.

Whatever type of pest-control products you use, always follow package directions explicitly for application, storage, and handling. Dress appropriately — wear long sleeves, long pants, shoes and socks, a respirator mask, and industrial (not kitchen-type) rubber gloves. Don't spray or dust on a windy day, and stand upwind when applying the material. If you need to dispose of leftover, unused insecticides, don't ever pour them down the drain or dump them on the ground. Instead, dispose of them when your town has special hazardous waste disposal times.

Learn to identify beneficial insects in your garden, and leave them alone when you see them. When pests do attack the garden, use the least invasive control measures first. For larger beetles or caterpillars that aren't present in great numbers, put on a pair of gloves and pick them off by hand. Drop them into a can of soapy water. If you spot small pests like aphids and whiteflies, try washing them off plants with a strong spray of water from a hose.

Here are some control measures to take to combat more serious infestations:

- **Insecticidal soap.** Effective on contact for a wide variety of small insects on many kinds of plants. Spray thoroughly so plants are wet. Be sure to spray both tops and bottoms of leaves, leaf axils, and new growth of affected plants. Keep an eye on plants after application; you may need two or more applications of insecticidal soap, several days apart, to control serious infestations.

- **Horticultural oils.** Oils kill pests by smothering them, and are effective for mealybugs, adelgids, scales, and mites. They are mixed with water and sprayed onto affected plants. Some oils (called dormant oils) are applied to trees and shrubs in winter when the plants are dormant. Lighter-weight summer oils are applied during the growing season. Both petroleum-based and vegetable-based oil sprays are available. Monitor plants after application and repeat if necessary.

- **Traps.** Various sorts of traps can catch stubborn pests that are hard to get by other methods. Sticky yellow cards placed among plants can catch whiteflies and other small flying insects. There are also traps available for Japanese beetles and yellow jackets. An old-fashioned way to trap slugs and snails is to sink small containers of beer into the ground so the tops are at ground level (you can also kill them with commercial baits). Rolled-up newspapers or boards laid on the ground can trap earwigs that hide under them.

- **Barriers.** Other kinds of barriers can be useful, too. Some gardeners keep slugs from the garden by edging with copper strips. Diatomaceous earth sprinkled around sensitive plants or the perimeter of beds and borders will keep out caterpillars, slugs, and other soft-bodied pests. Be sure to get diatomaceous earth meant for horticultural use, not the kind used in swimming pool filters.

- **Biological controls.** Biological control means using living organisms to kill pests. Many of these controls are predatory insects or their larvae (praying mantids, green lacewings, ladybird beetle larvae, various kinds of tiny flies and wasps) that are available by mail

Timely pruning can help prevent damage from insects and disease. The leader branch of this old apple tree has split off in a ragged way, leaving an entry point for infection.

and sometimes from local garden centers. A useful biological control for caterpillars is Bt or Btk (*Bacillus thuringiensis* subsp. *kurtaki*). Treating the lawn with milky spore disease (sold under various trade names) will kill Japanese beetle grubs that incubate under the ground and chew on grass roots. Biological controls are not very good as preventive measures, though. If the target pests are not present in your garden, the predators will move on in search of food.

- **Botanical insecticides.** Some very potent insect killers are derived from plants. The best known are rotenone, pyrethrum (look for ingredients listed on labels as pyrethrum or pyrethrins, not pyrethroids, which are synthetic imitations), sabadilla, and neem (which works as both an insecticide and a fungicide). Botanical insecticides break down much more quickly after application and do not linger in the environment like most synthetic (chemical) materials do. They are also less harmful to people, pets, and wildlife when the product dries after application. But they are quite toxic when applied and must be handled with appropriate caution. Follow package directions explicitly.

Some botanical insecticides kill beneficial insects along with pests — they may

Roses are often plagued by black spot. To avoid it, use the "Homemade Disease Prevention" recipe below.

wipe out butterflies and honeybees along with aphids and whiteflies, so use them only as a last resort.

DISEASE CONTROL

The air along the coast is generally humid, and high humidity can promote the development of fungal and bacterial diseases in plants: blights, rusts, rots, mildews, and other nasties. Powdery mildew can be a big troublemaker, attacking roses, lilacs, phlox, zinnias, and bee balm. Although powdery mildew does not usually kill plants, it does disfigure the leaves. Black spot is a notorious plague of rose gardens, and bush roses —hybrid teas, grandifloras, and floribundas — are especially susceptible to it. Shrub roses are less likely to suffer from black spot.

The best way to control plant diseases is to prevent them in the first place. One helpful measure is to allow space between plants so air can circulate freely around them. When plants are crowded together, disease pathogens can collect in the still, humid air.

When and how you water the garden also can influence the likelihood of disease. If possible, water at ground level, with soaker hoses or a drip irrigation system, rather than with overhead sprinklers. If you do use overhead watering, do it in the morning. If you have to water later in the day, do it early enough that the plants dry off before dark. Wet leaves in sticky,

still air at night offer an ideal breeding ground for disease pathogens.

Keep the garden clean. Don't let dead leaves and other debris lie on the ground. If you notice any leaves on plants showing signs of disease, pick them off and dispose of them. (Do not put them on the compost pile; even a hot pile is probably not hot enough to destroy all disease pathogens.) If you need to prune to remove diseased stems or branches, remember to dip your shears or loppers in a bleach solution after each cut so you don't spread the infection. Use a solution of one part liquid household chlorine bleach to nine parts water. Mulch the garden, so water droplets that pick up pathogens when they hit the ground won't splash back up onto foliage.

Take care of the plants to keep them healthy. Plants that are weakened or stressed from lack of water or insufficient nutrients are at greater risk of disease. Grow disease-resistant varieties if possible. (The phlox cultivar 'David', for example, is less prone to mildew than others.)

Finally, if you just can't live without some favorite plants, such as hybrid tea roses, even though you know they are susceptible to disease problems, try using the preventive baking soda spray described in "Homemade Disease Prevention" (right). This spray is effective on roses, and may work on other susceptible plants, too. Other preventive measures include dust-

ing plants with sulfur and spraying the foliage with neem oil.

If you do need to use fungicides in the garden, whether you use organic or synthetic products, follow the label directions for handling, application, and storage. Use only as much as the package directs — more is not better. Dress appropriately, as described in the section on pesticides. Dispose of unused fungicides when your town has hazardous waste collection days.

HOMEMADE DISEASE PREVENTION

Use this spray to prevent mildew and black spot on roses. Dissolve one tablespoon of baking soda in one gallon of water. Add a few drops of insecticidal soap, liquid Ivory soap, or horticultural oil to help the spray stick to plant leaves. Spray every four to seven days in summer.

Winterizing the Garden

The pillar-like yews (*Taxus* sp.) that anchor the arches in this Long Island garden are wrapped in burlap each winter to prevent windburn.

IT'S A GOOD IDEA TO PROVIDE SOME winter protection for plants, especially nonnatives, growing close to the water or in windbreaks or other exposed locations in northern gardens. Trees and shrubs that will be going through their first winter in your garden are also candidates for some extra TLC when the weather gets cold.

As the growing season winds down, make sure garden areas, and individual trees and shrubs, get plenty of water. If the weather has been dry, continue to water regularly until the ground begins to freeze and plants go into dormancy. When the soil freezes, apply a winter mulch as described in the "Mulching" section on page 68. Southern gardeners can lay down a fresh layer of mulch any time during autumn if the soil will not freeze solid over the winter.

CUTTING BACK PLANTS

Perennial gardeners can cut back most of their herbaceous perennials to a few inches from the ground in fall. Some later bloomers, such as perovskia, sedums, and asters, can be allowed to stand in the garden over the winter, then be cut back in early spring before new growth begins. Pull the summer annuals when they stop blooming, or when frost shuts them down. Southern gardeners can replant with winter annuals such as pansies, stocks, larkspur, and calendula.

Ornamental grasses also need to be cut back to within a few inches of the ground once a year. If your grasses are in a location that is sheltered from the wind, you can let them stand in the garden through the winter to bring structure and interest to the landscape. Cut them back in early spring before new growth begins. But in locations that are exposed to winds or winter snows, grasses will be tattered and broken long before spring and are best cut back in late fall. Depending on the size of your grasses, you may need to use hedge clippers, electric hedge shears, or even lopping shears to cut back the tough-stemmed plants.

WINTERBURN PROTECTION

Winter winds are very drying, and bright winter sun can be harmful, too. Broad-leaved evergreens such as hollies and rhododendrons can suffer damaging winterburn to their foliage. Junipers and other conifers also can be damaged. Spraying these plants with an antidesiccant will give them some protection. To shield new trees and shrubs, including hedges, and older woody plants close to the water, you can build little shelters for them. First wrap tree trunks with tree wrap to protect them from sunscald. Stake each tree to keep it upright during storms until it has grown enough roots to be securely anchored. Drive two tall stakes into the ground, one on either side of the trunk, angled into the prevailing wind. Tie the tree to the stakes with strips of sturdy fabric, old panty hose, or other soft but strong material. Don't use wire or rope, which could damage the branches when the tree strains against the ties in the wind. Do allow the trunk to have some flex, though. Allowing it to move somewhat in the wind will strengthen the tree.

After the tree is anchored, erect a burlap windscreen around it. Pound four tall stakes into the ground in a ring around the tree several feet out from the trunk. Wrap burlap around the stakes and secure it with twine to form an enclosure. If you are really worried about the tree's survival, fill the enclosure with shredded leaves.

To protect a row of new trees or shrubs, you can erect a windscreen by placing the stakes in a row on the side of the plants facing into the prevailing wind and attaching the burlap to them.

After the first winter, new trees and shrubs should be well enough established that you won't have to provide these shelters in subsequent years.

STORM AFTERCARE

Storms can be intense at the seashore, and they can damage plants in several ways. Strong winds can knock down stems, snap branches, and even topple whole trees. Salt can blow into gardens and settle onto plants, burning foliage. Saltwater may flood lawns and gardens. Taking prompt action after a storm can help to ameliorate the damage.

Any tree branches broken or damaged by storms need to be addressed at once. Prune to remove the damaged wood, or to completely remove broken branches. Trees that are left leaning or even toppled, if the root-ball is still mostly in the ground, may be able to be reset and supported by stakes and cables to hold them upright while they reestablish themselves in the soil. Consult an arborist for advice.

If flooding has occurred, wait until the water has drained away to take any remedial action. Most plants can usually survive an occasional saltwater flooding unless the soil is poorly drained and the salt remains in the garden for an extended time. When the floodwaters recede, get out the hose. Rinse off all your plants, and as high into the trees as you can, with a strong spray of water. Pay particular attention to evergreens, which keep their leaves all year and are thus at greater risk of suffering long-term damage than are deciduous trees and shrubs that lose their leaves each year, or herbaceous perennials that die back to the ground in winter. Deciduous trees and shrubs will sometimes lose their leaves after a severe storm; the salt will cause the leaves to turn brown and fall off. Most of the woodies will recover, however, and produce new leaves the following spring.

To create a protective winter windscreen for an evergreen shrub, surround it with four tall stakes and wrap a length of burlap around them.

These trees and shrubs can tolerate periodic saltwater flooding.

Acer pseudoplatanus, sycamore maple

Aronia arbutifolia, red chokeberry

Baccharis halimifolia, groundsel bush

Calluna vulgaris, heather

Campsis radicans, trumpet vine

Clematis terniflora, sweet autumn clematis

Clethra alnifolia, sweet pepperbush

Cryptomeria japonica, Japanese cedar

Hibiscus syriacus, rose of Sharon

Ilex glabra, inkberry

Juniperus chinensis 'Pfitzeriana', Pfitzer juniper

Juniperus virginiana, eastern red cedar

Ligustrum amurense, Amur privet

Ligustrum ovalifolium, California privet

Myrica pensylvanica, bayberry

Nyssa sylvatica, tupelo

Parthenocissus tricuspidata, Boston ivy

Picea pungens 'Kosteri', blue spruce

Pinus sylvestris, Scotch pine

Prunus maritima, beach plum

Prunus serotina, chokecherry

Quercus alba, white oak

Rhus spp., sumacs

Rosa cvs., rambler roses

Rosa rugosa, saltspray rose

Rosa virginiana, Virginia rose

Rosa wichuraiana, memorial rose

Vaccinium corymbosum, highbush blueberry

Viburnum dentatum, arrowwood viburnum

Vitis labrusca, fox grape

Wisteria sinensis, Chinese wisteria

Water the soil and lawns thoroughly to wash away excess salt and dilute the concentration of whatever salt is left. If your lawn was flooded with saltwater, flush with freshwater to get rid of as much of the salt as you can. Let the water run until the soil is saturated. Then you may want to spread ground limestone over the lawn, at a rate of 20 to 50 pounds per 1,000 square feet, and water again. Kentucky bluegrass and bent grasses are very susceptible to saltwater damage. But crabgrass, naturally, can easily survive being under saltwater for 24 hours. The lawn may look burned and dry, but if the roots of the grass have survived, new grass blades will emerge next spring. If no new growth appears in spring, the lawn will have to be dug up and replanted.

Trumpet vine, or trumpet creeper (*Campsis radicans*), tolerates saltwater flooding and salty winds, thrives even in poor soils, and attracts hummingbirds.

These hawthorns (*Crataegus* 'Winter King') are very hardy and salt tolerant. Hair grass (*Deschampsia caespitosa*) tumbles about at their feet.

CHAPTER 4

Garden
Profiles

GARDENS NEAR THE SEA ARE AS VARIED AS THE GARDENERS and homeowners who create them. Some seashore gardeners succeed in spite of the difficult conditions they face — the English-style perennial border in a seashore town, for example, is a triumph over nature. Other gardeners embrace the seaside's salt and wind to create native plant gardens of a wilder, more natural beauty that do not overcome the limitations of the environment but instead work within them.

The gardens profiled in this chapter represent a variety of styles and ways to solve the problems of coastal conditions. They exist in different settings and climate zones along the Atlantic coastline, from New England to South Carolina. Each garden is unique in its own way, with its own inspired solutions to the challenges of its site.

ABOVE: Along the coast of northern New England, rocky cliffs drop right into the sea.

RIGHT: Gardens tucked into the natural rock ledges on this Maine property anchor the house and unite it with its setting.

Preserving a Historic Garden

SOUTHERN MAINE

In the kitchen garden, hoops made from forsythia prunings support spring plantings of peas. Several kinds of lettuce also grow here, along with other vegetables and herbs.

BRAVE BOAT HARBOR FARM OVERLOOKS the ocean on the coast of Maine. A magical place of over 100 acres, the farm has a long history. The land was settled in 1638 as a king's grant, and for the next 300 years it was a subsistence farm. Then, in 1949, the property was purchased by the Hosmer family. Calvin and Cynthia Hosmer live there today, and are the stewards of this beautiful land by the sea.

The gardens are concentrated on approximately three acres immediately surrounding the house. The plantings were begun by Mr. Hosmer's parents. "When my parents-in-law came here in 1949," explains Mrs. Hosmer, "there was a circle of old lilacs here, and the burying ground. Otherwise, what's here they put in." Some of those old lilacs still exist, and have been joined over the years by apple trees, lush vegetable gardens, and magnificent perennial beds. "It's really quite wonderful to see what a mature garden is all about," says Mrs. Hosmer. "It really is the most incredible gift that anyone could be given."

The house is situated some distance above the ocean, with rolling hay fields stretching beyond the landscaped parts of the property toward the sea. Salt wind and spray are seldom a problem for the plants here except during stormy weather. Most of the storms come in from the northeast, and a large grove of hickory trees on that side of the property affords protection.

Deer are present in abundance, and the Hosmers deploy a variety of defensive measures to protect their gardens. Fencing is part of the strategy, as is the use of Milorganite (a fertilizer manufactured from treated sewage sludge) as a deer repellent. "I go around like a fairy godmother in the spring and drop it around," Mrs. Hosmer says with a laugh. Another important part of the deer-repellent program is Daisey May, a two-year-old golden retriever who is a dedicated chaser of the four-hoofed visitors.

The grounds around the house are extensively cultivated, and Mrs. Hosmer does much of the gardening herself, along with the caretaker of 28 years. "He is the

history" of the place, explains Mrs. Hosmer. "He knows everything that's been planted — he can remember planting it."

The lane coming into the yard is lined with crab apple trees. The Hosmers have cleared the brush from the woods and planted rhododendrons and laurels beneath the old beech trees, along with small kousa dogwoods. Preserving the beech trees is an ongoing battle; over the years they've been besieged by a number of imported pests and diseases. The beech woods are extensive, so the Hosmers fight on in the hope of saving as many of the trees as they can.

There are many apple trees on the property — 'McIntosh', 'Cortland', and 'Macoun'. The trees are quite old now, and are pruned to keep them about 15 to 20 feet high, with arced branches that curve downward. "It's very English in that respect," explains Mrs. Hosmer. It takes a week to ten days to prune the trees, and

RIGHT: Oriental and Asiatic lilies grace the perennial garden in summer. The walls are built of stone dug from the property.

LEFT: Stately old arborvitaes, with their lower limbs removed to admit more light, line the drive leading to the house.

pruning is done in August rather than in late winter, when many orchardists prune. By mid-August the trees have completed their new growth, and pruning then allows enough time for tissues to harden before winter sets in. The weather is far more forgiving in late summer than in February, when the nor'easters blow.

Part of what Mr. and Mrs. Hosmer have done since moving to the farm eight years ago is to open up vistas and limb up the trees. The old lilacs were limbed up, rather than cut back, to open up views of the sea.

The gun house (built by Mr. Hosmer's father) faces the sea, offering a relaxing spot for evening cocktails.

The venerable old arborvitaes along the drive also had their lower branches removed. Mrs. Hosmer had wanted to put in a pleached hornbeam hedge there but was advised that it would be too formal to suit the farm. So instead, the arborvitaes were limbed up and trimmed to even out their tops, "and they've become such a wonderful way in here, architecturally," Mrs. Hosmer says.

Near one corner of the house the Hosmers removed some old shadbushes that were tipping over and generally falling apart, and replaced them with a single columnar copper beech that will grow taller over time but remain narrow. "We wanted to have that exclamation point at that corner of the house," says Mrs. Hosmer. "It's a statement unto itself." Enhancing that elegant statement, the English ivy climbing the nearby walls of the house is kept neatly trimmed.

Not far from the copper beech, along the side of the house nearest the driveway, is a kitchen garden. The garden is divided into quadrants, with intersecting paths of stepping-stones. At one end of the main axis path is a white moon gate that frames a view of magnolias beyond. In the center of the garden sits an old millstone upon which rests a large glass ball—it's actually a solar-powered fountain, with the water reservoir in a five-gallon pickle jar buried below.

Plantings are done on the diagonal. In spring there are several kinds of lettuce, including 'Nevada', 'Merveille Quatre Saisons', 'Arctic King', and 'Red Sails', and peas supported on hoops Mrs. Hosmer fashions from forsythia prunings. Parsley grows along the edges of the path. There are broccoli, beans, peppers, and other favorites, too, along with lots of herbs — thymes, basils, and oregano among them. In summer there are luscious raspberries.

Part of the walkway near the moon gate is carpeted with chamomile, which Mrs. Hosmer trims by hand to keep it low and cushiony. Thyme grows in the path, also, both plants releasing their aromatic scents when trodden upon. They are important elements of the garden for Mrs. Hosmer "because sometimes," she says, "I think the sensory pleasure you get from walking through a garden comes from underfoot."

There are cutting flowers in the kitchen garden, too — Oriental poppies, calendulas, salvias, sea holly (*Eryngium*), rubrum lilies, and roses. There are several David Austin varieties, some old roses, and the shrub rose 'Bonica'. All the roses grow on their own roots except for one hybrid tea, 'Tropicana', which "seems to like it here," says Mrs. Hosmer.

In front of the house is a perennial garden enclosed by a stone wall and an old boxwood hedge. The wall — as well as the house, the walkways, and all the walls on the property — is built of stone dug from the ground here. This garden is mostly blues and yellows, with occasional touches of pink. There are golden 'Stella de Oro' daylilies, and lots of Oriental and Asiatic lilies. The fragrant lilies are particular favorites. On hot summer days their delicious scents drift into the house on breezes drawn by a fan placed in a nearby window.

Tall violet monkshood (*Aconitum*) stands in the back of the garden until the weight of its flowers pulls the stems over, then Mrs. Hosmer props them up on the wall and some nearby lilies. Blue delphiniums also supply vertical accents, and the blue spheres of *Allium caeruleum* add substance. A shrub clematis (*Clematis integrifolia*) dangles its blue bells of blossoms. In spring there are pots of tulips in the garden for early color; when the tulips finish, they are removed and replaced with dahlias.

At the end of the day, the Hosmers like to sit near the small stone gun house to enjoy a glass of wine and watch the passing ships. Such moments of leisure are well earned. For Calvin and Cynthia Hosmer, preserving and maintaining the property is a sacred trust, a way of carrying on the family tradition of serving as guardians of this beautiful land. "It is my stewardship and legacy for the rest of my life," says Mrs. Hosmer. The land and its glorious gardens are in good hands.

A moon gate at one end of the kitchen garden frames *Magnolia* 'Elizabeth', part of a collection of magnolias that includes 'Merrill', 'Leonard Messel', 'Butterflies', 'Yellow Bird', and 'Ballerina'.

Tapestry on a Ledge

SOUTHERN MAINE

ABOVE: A seashell planter suggests beach grass and ocean waves with upright *Juncus* 'Quartz Creek', donkeytail spurge (*Euphorbia myrsinites*), and flowering *Laurentia fluviatilis.*

BELOW: Passionflowers follow sweet peas in the formal kitchen garden.

ATOP A PROMONTORY ON THE MAINE ledge, bordered on three sides by the ocean, sits an elegant stone house that has weathered many storms. Salt spray and wind are constants in the gardens here, and winter winds pose the greatest seasonal challenge of the year. But the plants thrive in a landscape designed to blend the house seamlessly into its breathtaking setting.

The landscape gardener Tony Elliott designed this garden. An agronomist by training, and the proprietor of Snug Harbor Farm, Mr. Elliott has been designing gardens since he was 13. To integrate this house into the site, he created a series of garden rooms that are more formal close to the house and become progressively less formal as one moves outward from the house into the landscape. The informal parts of the garden create a graceful transition to the dramatic natural landscape beyond.

Mr. Elliott amended the soil on the site with dehydrated cow manure, peat moss, and lime to prepare it for planting. The gardens are fertilized with an all-purpose granular 5-10-5 product. Drought is not a problem here; the gardens are irrigated, but even if they were not, says Mr. Elliott, the frequent Maine fogs that roll in would provide adequate moisture for the plants. The moist conditions can encourage disease, however, and plants that develop ailments are removed and replaced with tougher substitutes.

Winter winds pose the biggest challenge to this garden, and the plants must be hardy enough to stand up to them. Mr. Elliott is not a believer in wrapping evergreens and other shrubs to coddle them through the winter. "I'm a do-or-die gardener," he declares. Instead, he chooses plants he believes will be tough enough to withstand the wintry blasts. So far, nothing has been lost. He does, however, make an exception in the case of lacecap hydrangeas, which he finds do better with a winter wrapping of burlap; the wrap goes on in December.

The most formal rooms in this garden are located immediately adjacent to the house. Near the front door is an elegant gathering of blue-flowered lacecap hydrangeas (*Hydrangea macrophylla* 'Mariesii'), one of Mr. Elliott's favorite varieties. Climbing hydrangea (*H. petiolaris*) scales the wall of the house behind them, clinging to the stone with no additional support. Its delicate white lacecap flowers bloom in summer against the glossy, deep green leaves. The hydrangea garden has a serene, elegant feeling that creates a graceful segue into the foyer, a welcome into the home.

Across the walkway from the hydrangea garden is a woodland garden anchored by some old existing junipers that have attained interesting, windswept shapes of the sort bonsai growers aim to re-create.

An opening from the hosta garden allows a view of the ocean and leads to the pool and the marvelous perennial borders. The perennial garden is about 100 feet long, and sweeps in graceful curves across the front of the property. The Kings brought in lots of compost to create the garden, then installed a drip irrigation system before beginning to plant. More compost is added each year, as needed. The basic structure of the garden comes from a series of low, rounded blue spruces (*Picea pungens* 'Montgomery') backed by red-leaved sand cherries (*Prunus × cistena*). "The dark reds and blues anchor the garden," explains Mrs. King. Hydrangeas also contribute year-round form to the border, and reinforce the blue theme. The rest of the garden is filled with blues, pinks, and some yellow. The protection of the hedge allows her to grow some plants that aren't often seen so close to the ocean. There are blue delphiniums and nepeta, pink carpet roses, soft yellow 'Moonbeam' coreopsis,

RIGHT: A privet hedge affords enough protection for classic perennials such as nepeta, 'Moonbeam' coreopsis, daylilies, delphiniums, and hydrangeas.

LEFT: A few steps lead down from the rose garden to a shady garden full of hostas, lady's mantle (*Alchemilla mollis*), astilbes, and other perennials.

Grass-covered steps lead from the pool to a more naturalistic garden. The rocky ledge alongside is planted with sea pinks (*Armeria maritima*), small junipers, rugosa roses, and other tough plants.

and lots of daylilies, which she plants for their adaptability. "I love those because they grow anywhere," Mrs. King says. "They bloom where nothing else blooms."

A couple of years ago, an especially severe winter killed the buds on all the hydrangeas — that summer they had plenty of foliage but no flowers. Thus the Kings pulled them all out and replaced them with the variety 'Endless Summer', which blooms on both old and new growth, all but guaranteeing at least some flowers even after the hardest winter. So far 'Endless Summer' has done just fine. The white-flowered *Hydrangea arborescens* 'Annabelle', which blooms on new growth, also thrives in this garden.

The perennial border receives a mulch of buckwheat hulls, which Mrs. King highly recommends. "I love it," she says. "It doesn't get slimy, doesn't have any odor. It's attractive, it works into the soil nicely every year, and nonacidic plants love it."

In a reclamation area near the pool, the couple planted natives (in a trade-off with the town to get permission to construct a pool house). Here there are eastern red cedar, highbush and lowbush blueberries, and native azaleas.

At the end of this garden room is a 12-foot-wide gate, and then a descent down some broad, half-round, terraced steps in the lawn. These lead to the lowest part of the garden, which is a very natural area.

"I try to keep my hands off it," says Mrs. King, laughing. "I'm generally a more-is-better person." She has planted the rocky ledge there with tough plants like sea pink, or thrift (*Armeria maritima*), in the cracks, and small junipers in larger crevices in the rock. There are also some small cedars and rugosa roses. This is rocky ground — the entire town is built on ledge. The Kings blasted out rock to create their gardens, and used the stone to build structures on the property.

To hold an embankment in this area, Mrs. King planted bayberries, which she thought would be sure to do well. Inexplicably, they didn't. But rugosa roses did, and now they hold the soil on the exposed slope.

Other plants that thrive in the more exposed parts of the property are rose of Sharon (*Hibiscus syriacus*) and lilacs. "I have really good luck with lilacs," says Mrs. King, "especially 'Miss Kim'."

A gardener through and through, Mrs. King devotes many hours to her plants. Once a week someone comes in to help her, and they work together all day. And Mrs. King works some part of every summer day in the garden. "It's my pleasure to get a cup of coffee in the morning and go outside and work for an hour or so," she says. Spoken like a true gardener. And her love of plants shows in the breathtaking gardens she has created here.

The wild, rocky transition from the Kings' garden to the sea.

A Seaside Retreat

A riot of colorful annuals surround the entrance to the house.

ALONG THE COAST OF RHODE ISLAND there exists a property like no other. It's the kind of place that needs a very special owner to appreciate the exceptional beauty of its rugged terrain. On this property an extraordinary garden took shape over a period of six years. Created by Oehme, van Sweden and Associates, the principals involved in the project were Sheila Brady, OVS partner in charge of design, and James van Sweden, founding partner.

The property is huge — 85 acres — and when the owner took possession, it was a tangled wilderness of briars and brush and poison ivy. But the owner, born and raised in the city, had long cherished a dream of having a farm by the sea where he could retreat from urban pressures and walk the land. This was the place where he believed his dream would come true.

The property had once been a farm, but the land had not been cultivated for 45 years. Oehme, van Sweden's first year on the job involved a slow process of discovering what was really there underneath all the vines and brambles. Half the property is framed by water, with a classic rugged, rocky New England shoreline. Craggy outcrops of shale drop sharply to the water. It is undoubtedly, says Sheila Brady, one of the most extraordinary pieces of land she has worked with in her 25 years as a landscape architect.

First the team set about removing the thickets of briars and scrub. They uncovered groves of tall, native eastern red cedars (*Juniperus virginiana*) whose trunks had not even been visible. They found big old highbush blueberries (*Vaccinium corymbosum*) that had been twisted by the wind into compelling, gnarled forms.

When they found the remains of the old stone walls surrounding former farm fields, they decided to use them as an organizing principle for the landscape. When the strangling brushy and weedy growth was cleared away, the incredible beauty of the site revealed itself, and the design team worked with it.

Key to Oehme, van Sweden's success with coastal gardens is their understanding of the soil in each location. They work with a skilled and extremely knowledgeable soil scientist, Dr. Frank Gouin, who studies the parent soil on each site, performing extensive testing to determine what sorts of amendments are needed to support a sustainable landscape that will not require the addition of fertilizers or other foreign materials. Before planting, they work with the soil, incorporating compost specially formulated with local materials for each site, such as a crab-based compost or a cranberry bog compost. The goal is to work with the parent soil rather than disturb it. Compaction is broken up, then compost is tilled in to create a balanced, self-sustaining growing medium for plants that are native or naturally suited to the site. The result is a sustainable landscape that requires no synthetic fertilizers or pesticides.

On the Rhode Island property, the team replaced the old broken stone walls with a series of low retaining walls built mostly of stone found on the property, to provide an organizing framework for the design. The walls divided the land into a series of precincts through which visitors pass as they enter the property and proceed toward the house. A long, winding entrance drive weaves through these precincts until it reaches the house, which is situated at a high point.

Following the drive feels suspenseful and mysterious — you don't know what's around the next bend. The first precinct you encounter is the inland meadow, which was probably the most recently farmed part of the property. No trees or shrubs grew here, and the design team cleared the old fields and allowed the meadow to come back naturally. From there, a series of low stone walls announce the transition into the evergreen woodland collection, the groves of cedars. The trees here were limbed up to admit more light and air, and the ground beneath them was planted with grasses mowed to a height of six to eight inches. This area is quiet and green, a textural and visual contrast to the sunny openness of the inland meadow. The next precinct is a deciduous seaside woodland

An ancient highbush blueberry, uncovered as the property was being cleared of overgrown vines and brambles.

The winding drive creates a sense of mystery as it passes through each precinct of the property. When visitors reach the seaside meadow, the bay is revealed.

with trees and shrubs, such as yellowwood, carefully chosen to enhance that theme. From there the drive enters the eight-acre seaside meadow, where at last the sea becomes visible. Finally, the drive arrives at the expansive three-acre garden surrounding the house.

Passing through the fluid, graceful transitions from one precinct to the next enables owner and visitor alike to shed the stresses and tensions of city life in anticipation of the rest and solitude of this remarkable seaside retreat.

The designers carved a series of walking trails through the property, including three that lead to ocean overlooks. Working with the shoreline was a challenge, because the Rhode Island Coastal Resource Council strictly regulates a 200-foot buffer zone along the waterfront. The buffer of natural vegetation had to remain intact except for the three overlooks where access to the shoreline was permitted. Oehme, van Sweden turned that potential liability into an asset by siting the house, drives, and walking trails on high ground to take advantage of the breathtaking view. "You actually have the feeling of being surrounded by water," says Ms. Brady. Had the house been set closer to the shoreline, the view would have been lost behind the buffer vegetation.

Close to the house the gardens are rich with color and texture, alive with the movement of plants in the wind and the interplay of light and shadow. The plantings here are a tapestry of texture, light, and color. It's a painterly approach to design that resonates with Ms. Brady's fine arts background. The ground plane is her canvas, the plants a composition of light and shadow, mass and space, form and texture, patterns of color. All the elements here and throughout the property combine to express the spirit of this most special place, a landscape and garden united with their setting.

STRATEGIES FOR SUSTAINABLE DESIGN

- Organize a large, open landscape around existing features, such as old stone walls, highbush blueberries, and red cedars.
- In areas where natural vegetation will be preserved, create a series of scenic overlooks instead of one sweeping vista.
- Improve and maintain existing soil using local materials, such as crab and cranberry waste.

RIGHT: A series of walking trails lead to ocean overlooks and allow an intimate experience of the beauty of the landscape.

BELOW: Long drifts of foxtailed *Pennisetum alopecuroides* and lavender-blue Russian sage (*Perovskia atriplicifolia*) sway in the passing breezes, forming dynamic patterns of color, texture, light, and shadow.

Making the Most of a Narrow Lot

MARTHA'S VINEYARD, MASSACHUSETTS

The heart of the garden is a small pool surrounded by cut bluestone, in perfect scale with the narrow property.

On one side of the property, a pink rose of Sharon (*Hibiscus syriacus*) screens a utility area from view.

FOR MANY LANDSCAPE DESIGNERS, THE most rewarding kinds of projects are those in which they help a homeowner realize his or her vision for the garden. This New England garden is the result of such a partnership. Landscape designer Robbie Hutchison, of Donaroma's Nursery and Landscape Services in Edgartown, Massachusetts, worked with the owner to create a garden that combines elegant structure with lots of multiseason color.

The house is located on Martha's Vineyard, in a historic district full of old whalers' houses. Space was the greatest challenge posed by the site. The houses here are close together on narrow lots, so privacy is a major consideration. Another issue is getting access for equipment onto the property; the design team had to plan construction carefully. They started work behind the main house and worked their way to the back edge of the property. The environment was less of a limiting factor here than it is in many seaside gardens.

This house is not directly on the water; the nearest water is a harbor located behind the houses across the street from this one. Although deer and direct salt winds do not trouble the garden, it is nonetheless a windy place, and that had to be taken into account. But there are sheltered nooks and crannies that are used to good advantage.

The landscape here began with the pool. The owner had found a picture of a small pool — really a large spa — that spoke to her. And she had made a sketch showing paths weaving through the property. That was the genesis of the design, with the pool as a focal point in a series of interlocking paths. The owner, explains Ms. Hutchison, "had this great bubble of an idea, and we just helped her organize it, to make it more real." The owner had a vision of what she wanted in the landscape, Ms. Hutchison goes on, "and I think we captured it for her."

In the backyard the homeowner wanted a similar small pool with space around it for chaise longues. It left plenty of room for gardens. "I commend her for that," declares Ms. Hutchison. Many people

A moon gate near one end of the garden frames a view of the pool and pool house with its vine-covered arbor, and the back of the main house. In the foreground is one of the brick circles edged with boxwood.

would tend to want to put in a big swimming pool, then cram some landscaping around it. But the pool here is on a scale that's very comfortable for the property.

An elegant bluestone patio surrounds the pool. An existing shed was transformed into the pool house. An arbor built onto the front of the pool house is planted with wisteria and trumpet vine (*Campsis radicans*), which climb up the framework to the roof, forming a leafy canopy in summer. The white columns supporting this structure are repeated in a freestanding arbor marking the junction of the patio with one of the paths.

The paths arc away from the patio in pairs — two heading toward the main house at the front of the property and two more toward the garage and guesthouse at the rear. The paths are made of unmortared brick set into the lawn, and they have a lovely antique charm. Together, all the paths form a series of ellipses that flow down the length of the property. Where the paths intersect, Ms. Hutchison created circular areas of brick pavement ringed by two varieties of dwarf boxwood on either side of a taller variety, all of them kept neatly clipped. On each brick circle is displayed an elegant antique urn full of flowers. The plants are changed seasonally and the urn overflows with color. In summer there are lush combinations of annuals; in winter there are cut evergreens. The urns

provide yet another opportunity for color, as well as focal points that help to break up the long, narrow stretch of the lot.

Another thing the homeowner wanted in her garden was color — and there is an abundance of it. When you walk through the gate into the yard, says Ms. Hutchison, you feel like you're in the original version of *The Wizard of Oz*, where suddenly everything is in color. Magnificent borders run along the sides of the property. These plantings were designed by Janice

A focal point of the garden is an antique urn of annuals including Persian shield (*Strobilanthes dyerianus*), coleus, scaevola, 'Margarita' and 'Blackie' sweet potato vines, and angelonia.

Donaroma, owner of the nursery. They are full of classic perennials — delphinium, Shasta daisy (*Leucanthemum × superbum*), foxglove (*Digitalis*), bee balm (*Monarda didyma*), catmint (*Nepeta × faassenii*), and black-eyed Susan (*Rudbeckia* spp.). In shadier areas there are astilbes and heucheras, along with annuals like coleus and impatiens. The borders gain structure from shrubs, including Tardiva hydrangea, chastetree (*Vitex agnus-castus*), and blue mist (*Caryopteris × clandonensis*).

Close to the house a row of pink and white rose of Sharon (*Hibiscus syriacus*) screens a small utility area. Nearby, under a cryptomeria limbed up to let in more light, the pink and white are echoed in mounds of impatiens edging a shady part of the border. The colorful borders and overflowing urns and window boxes soften the controlled, elegant structural elements of the landscape.

For Ms. Hutchison, designing this landscape was a most rewarding and satisfying collaboration with the homeowner. "What I really enjoyed," she says, "is that she had a vision and she wanted to participate. To me that's rewarding. Now I feel like I know her."

Indeed, the goal for any good garden is to express the spirit and sensibility of the gardener or homeowner. The ability to capture that essence is part of the landscape designer's art.

In the perennial border, late-summer flowers blooming in front of white Tardiva hydrangea include black-eyed Susans (*Rudbeckia hirta*), Shasta daisies (*Leucanthemum × superbum*), sunflowers, pink cosmos, red bee balm (*Monarda didyma*), and blue-mist shrub (*Caryopteris × clandonensis*).

One Garden, Many Styles

LONG ISLAND, NEW YORK

In the walled garden, Indian architectural elements are a focal point at the end of the brick path. A venerable agave that is overwintered in a greenhouse provides dramatic punctuation below.

ON THE EASTERN END OF LONG ISLAND, between the Atlantic Ocean and a saltwater pond, is a uniquely beautiful garden that's a blend of formal elements and a wilder kind of informality. Designed by Ryan Gainey, the garden evolves and changes each year, in an ongoing collaboration among the designer, the homeowners, and head gardener John Hill. Here's one example of the juxtaposition of formal and informal style in this garden: a row of large yews that are kept neatly clipped look very classical and English, but nasturtiums climb all over them, adding a wild look. The yews anchor a border of perennials and annuals that is lush and overflowing with rambunctious boltonia, dahlia, agastache, and other flowers. There are also some large old boxwoods (*Buxus sempervirens* 'Suffruticosa') on the property—another nod to traditional English garden style.

It's a very exposed site here, with sandy soil and lots of deer and rabbits. But despite

A comfortable seating area, surrounded by cosmos, in front of the guesthouse.

the challenges posed by the site, the entire garden is managed in a highly ecological way — the method is almost 100 percent organic. The organic approach here is not simply a matter of using organic products; it's a mind-set as well. There's a willingness to coexist with wildlife, using fences and repellents to keep them away from the plants. There are beehives on the property, and birdhouses to attract the purple martins that are part of the pest-control program.

The sandy soil is lean and low in nutrients, and Mr. Hill has put in place an ongoing amendment program. Before planting, he brought in soil that is a mix of equal parts topsoil, compost, and sand. Each year the gardens are top-dressed with compost in winter and during the growing season, and more compost is mixed into the soil. In addition, Mr. Hill uses chicken manure, which he gets from a local farm six months before he plans to use it. By the time the manure is applied to the garden, it is well rotted and ready to release its nutrients into the soil. Mr. Hill has also been experimenting with compost teas. And an organic plant care company comes in to do root feeding with microbial products intended to boost the population of beneficial microorganisms in the soil and foster their work. (Mr. Hill has been experimenting, too, with fish emulsion as a foliar feed, but he can't yet say for sure whether it has been effective.)

Salt wind is a great challenge in this garden. When the winds come off the ocean — from the south rather than the east, on the spit of land upon which this property lies — they strike the oceanfront side of the house, hitting the dunes and flowing up and over them, then slamming down hard onto the lower part of the property. In winter, the winds whip across the property from the pond. "They're relentless," says Mr. Hill.

The house itself, sitting on the crest of the dunes, protects the gardens behind it, especially in summer. From this high spot, the grade level drops about 20 feet as the property slopes down toward the pond on the opposite side. One part of the garden is enclosed by walls. A hedgerow of yews (*Taxus* species) also shelters the gardens. Heroic measures are taken to protect some of the plants. "We didn't go out of our way to choose salt-resistant plants," explains Mr. Hill, "but we do go to extraordinary lengths to get the plants to succeed" in the difficult environment.

A canal in the formal walled garden serves as an axis in the design. Lotus grow in the water, and carefully shaped yews edge the canal. Potted 'Meyer' lemon trees trained as standards mark the intersection of the canal and the main brick path.

The lush, informal perennial borders are given structure from a series of clipped columnar yews anchoring arches made of copper tubing.
In late summer there are masses of white boltonia, and the nasturtiums begin to show renewed vigor after a midsummer slump.

In winter they wrap all the yews and other sensitive plants with burlap. "It looks like [Dr. Seuss's] Whoville," Mr. Hill says. The wrappings go on right after Christmas and remain in place until the weather starts to moderate in spring, usually around the beginning of April. Antidesiccant sprays are applied to evergreens in fall, before the wrapping occurs. During the growing season, especially after storms in the autumn hurricane season, the garden staff wash down the evergreens with water to rinse salt from the foliage.

Other plants are wind sheared and never attain their full growth potential, but the owners are willing to put up with that for the particular visual contribution the plants make to the garden at a specific time. For example, there's a photinia whose perfect moment comes when its branches spill over a wall in an especially beguiling way. The rest of the season the wind takes its toll, but by then the photinia has already had its time to shine.

On the lower parts of the property, the blend of formal and informal elements is beautifully orchestrated in the garden. Leading to the guesthouse, a series of arches made of copper tubing mark a mown grass path that runs between a pair of colorful borders. A series of clipped, flat-topped, columnar yews march alongside the arches. This formal structure is engulfed by masses of perennials and annuals that spill onto the path. Annual nasturtiums (which are started from seed in three successions two weeks apart) clamber up the yews. 'American Pillar' and other roses climb the arches.

The walled garden is also formally structured, then softened with lush plantings. Brick walls enclose a classically laid-out space with a brick walkway forming the main axis of the garden, bisected by a canal that serves as the secondary axis. Lotus and papyrus grow in the canal, and there are fish. Cone-shaped yews (cleverly tied and clipped into that form) punctuate the garden with a series of vertical spires. Neatly pruned 'Meyer' lemon trees in large pots provide additional vertical accents. One year they tried planting Italian cypress in this garden; the trees looked great for a season, but perished in winter, despite their best efforts. One exotic plant that does last here is a 'Brown Turkey' fig, which has grown to eight feet tall. How do they get it through the winter? "We build a little house around it," says Mr. Hill.

Tender plants such as agave and rosemary lend exotic touches to the garden in summer, and they overwinter in a cool greenhouse. Asian and Indian architectural elements enhance the air of faraway places that infuses this garden.

Like most seaside gardens, this one continues to develop. It's an ongoing process of growth and change, and with each passing year the garden becomes more fully integrated with the special piece of land it occupies. It's a unique blend of sophisticated design and cutting-edge horticultural technique.

PROTECTING PLANTS FROM THE ELEMENTS

- Offer delicate plants more protection by siting them on the leeward side of a building or hedge. Spray salt-sensitive evergreens with an antidesiccant product, then wrap them with burlap for the winter.
- After storms, hose down evergreens that haven't been wrapped in burlap, to remove salt residue.
- Overwinter tender plants like agaves, rosemary, and fig trees indoors, or cover individual plants with a large cold frame.

Capturing a View

LONG ISLAND, NEW YORK

Looking back at the house from the meadow. In late summer, the mown grass path is bordered by native goldenrod and the airy panicles of an ornamental grass, *Miscanthus sinensis* 'Gracillimus'.

RIGHT: An intimate dining area overlooks the meadow full of goldenrod with a view of the pond. In the distance at the horizon is the ocean.

ON THIS EASTERN LONG ISLAND PROP-ERTY, the goal of the landscape design is to take maximum advantage of the expansive view in a very low-maintenance way. Land-scape designer Edwina von Gal used native plants and ornamental grasses to reveal and enhance the innate character of the land. The result is a casual, simple land-scape that requires very little in the way of maintenance, allowing the homeowners to relax and enjoy the magnificent natural surroundings.

From the property there is a view across a somewhat brackish pond to the ocean in the distance. The soil is classic "Bridge-hampton loam," as it is called in these parts — three to eight feet of clay loam over sand. It is some of the best farmland in the country, and it supports a varied commu-nity of plants. The mix of soils on the east-ern end of Long Island is one of the most interesting aspects of the landscape. Unlike many regions, not all the soil here is sandy. The area is, geologically speaking, a terminal moraine, where retreating gla-ciers left behind rock and soil carried here during the last ice age. Despite relentless development, there are still a few places where you can look across fields of pota-toes growing in rich loam to see rolling sand dunes and the ocean beyond. It is a place of breathtaking beauty, and this property exemplifies the unique grandeur of the place.

Ms. von Gal's mission was to leave the view undisturbed and to bring aspects of the ocean view back into the landscape nearer the house. "You can't plant in front of an incredible view," Ms. von Gal told the owners. There are massive clumps of bay-berry (*Myrica pensylvanica*) out on the dis-tant dunes, so she planted bayberry on the property to connect it to the view. The rep-etition of plants visually annexes the ocean to the property, making the entire view part of this landscape. The result is a sense of expansive openness that is both majestic and serene. It's a sight you feel you could take in forever.

On the farther, more exposed reaches of the property there were areas in need of screening, and autumn olive (*Elaeagnus umbellata*) was planted. This tree is contro-versial because it spreads so vigorously

Grass paths mown regularly along with the lawn bring definition to the landscape. This path leads to a bench placed for viewing the pond, a vista that connects this property to the natural landscape beyond.

that it has become invasive. But it is extremely tough, and many landscape designers feel it still has its uses in harsh seaside environments where little else will grow. It also provides food and good habitat for birds. In this landscape, the trees are prevented from spreading because self-sown seedlings are cut down when the adjacent meadow is mowed.

Although it does not front on the ocean, this property is close enough that salt-tolerant plants are an important component of the landscape. There are bayberries and native wild cherries. "Once you have bayberries," says Ms. von Gal, "you'll get more if you have the right conditions." London plane tree (*Platanus × hispanica*) was planted too. It is not a native, but it can take quite a bit of salt as long as it's not right on the beach. Butterfly bushes (*Buddleia*) also thrive here despite the salt winds that sweep across the property.

In one area the owners needed screening plants to replace Japanese black pines that had died. Ms. von Gal put in Hinoki cypresses (*Chamaecyparis obtusa*), which have flourished. "They're remarkably salt tolerant," she observes.

A portion of the property is devoted to an expansive meadow of goldenrod, through which paths are mowed for strolling and benches are placed for contemplating and observing the landscape. As with all else in this garden, the meadow

was achieved very simply — by mowing. "There was an old field, and we just mow it," Ms. von Gal explains. "If you time the mowing right, you can encourage what you want. In this case we got goldenrod, and that's fine."

Some wild cherries and bayberries were allowed to come up in the meadow. Although we generally think of bayberries as dune plants, they do quite well in the loamy soil here. The only regular maintenance the meadow receives is a twice-yearly mowing, to keep down unwanted woody plants. The bayberries and cherries are allowed to stay.

Paths through the meadow are kept mowed by the lawn service. The paths are an important structural component of the garden. "I think paths are one of the best and easiest ways to landscape," says Ms. von Gal. "The areas you don't mow are defined by the areas you do."

One thing that does trouble her about the meadow is the emergence of miscanthus seedlings coming up from seeds blown in from nearby plantings. The seedlings in the meadow are coarser and less attractive than the *Miscanthus* 'Gracillimus' planted in the garden, and mowing the meadow doesn't really slow them down (they are, after all, grass). "I'm worried that at the rate they're seeding in, they might be a new invasive," she says. When asked if she thought the miscanthus might

In an area of lawn near the house, wisteria frames a pair of swings. The soil here is excellent — several feet of clay-loam over sand.

outcompete and overwhelm the golden-rod, Ms. von Gal said she believes they may be evenly matched. Time will tell.

Bordering the meadow closer to the house are plantings of *Miscanthus* 'Gracillimus', pennisetum, and mugo pine. Mugo pine is another plant that does quite well here. Several were used to screen the pool from the house, as they are high enough to serve that purpose.

Elsewhere are a number of Kwanzan cherries that are lovely when they bloom in spring. There's also a grove of hawthorns with a carpet of fine-textured hair grass (*Deschampsia caespitosa*) underneath. Several existing hawthorns on the property were thriving, so Ms. von Gal decided to add more to create a grove. She was told the existing trees were 'Winter King' hawthorn, which is reputed to be highly salt tolerant, so 'Winter King' was planted. Alas, the old hawthorns are doing better than the new ones, and they were apparently not, after all, 'Winter King.' "I wish I could find out what they are," Ms. von Gal says. "But once you find out what they are, it doesn't mean you'll be able to find them." In any case, there's a mystery hawthorn growing in this garden that's remarkably salt tolerant.

That kind of adaptability is the key to this landscape. It's a paragon of subtle, low-maintenance design that lets the natural beauty of the site shine through.

SALT-TOLERANT LANDSCAPE PLANTS

Buddleia spp., butterfly bush
Chamaecyparis obtusa, Hinoki cypress
Crataegus 'Winter King', hawthorn
Deschampsia caespitosa, hair grass
Myrica pensylvanica, northern bayberry
Pinus mugo, mugo pine
Platanus × *hispanica,* London plane tree
Solidago spp., goldenrod

In late summer and early autumn, the low, slanting rays of the sun illuminate the bottlebrush inflorescences of fountain grass (*Pennisetum* sp.) in the foreground and the fanlike plumes of *Miscanthus sinensis* 'Gracillimus' farther back.

A Secret Garden by the Sea

REHOBOTH, DELAWARE

Assorted culinary herbs —golden oregano, red-veined dock (*Rumex sanguineus*), and French tarragon — thrive in pots on the sunny patio.

FROM THE BEACH, THIS REHOBOTH house looks like a quintessential beach house with a typical garden. There's a boardwalk heading toward the sea. Beach grass grows in the sand. Low pots of wind- and salt-tolerant annuals line the brick wall around the patio. But from other angles, surprises abound. The other side of the house, which faces a quiet lake, looks elegant and traditional, even English. Some of the brick walls enclose a hidden courtyard that is home to plenty of plants you'd never expect to see at the beach. The lady of the house, Meredith Marshall, is an accomplished gardener who has had a passion for gardening since her childhood.

Mrs. Marshall comes from a gardening family — both her mother and grandmother were gardeners, too. "My grandmother had a beautiful kitchen garden," she says, "with roses, larkspur, sweet William, and bachelor's buttons — plants that reseeded — and a huge vegetable garden." Carrying on the family tradition, Mrs. Marshall has created an amazingly lush and colorful courtyard garden near the beach. The garden is the summer home of Mrs. Marshall's prized plant collection, including award-winning myrtle topiaries. It's also a peaceful haven, offering respite from the busyness of the beach and the crash and boom of the nearby ocean waves.

The Marshalls' landscape was designed by landscape architect Mario Nievera, of Mario Nievera Designs, based in Palm Beach, Florida. Mr. Nievera used structural elements — walls, walkways and other hardscape elements, and large old trees — to anchor the design and organize the outdoor space. The courtyard is the quiet heart of the property. It is full of deliciously fragrant plants — sweet-smelling

An enclosed courtyard offers a protected environment for a host of plants not usually associated with seashore gardens, including topiaries trained by Mrs. Marshall.

the bay is clean. Indeed, says Mr. van Swe-den, "I see my garden, which has no lawn and uses no chemicals, as one huge filter for the water that runs across it going to the bay."

The meadow also attracts its share of wildlife; black snakes, rabbits, and, of course, deer are common, but they don't bother the plants. The ornamental grasses and most of the other plants in the garden are deer resistant. Plants that are suscepti-ble to deer browsing, such as oakleaf hydrangea and viburnum, get sprayed peri-odically with a garlic mixture that has proved sufficient to keep away the deer.

The only other regular maintenance required is some weeding. The garden is well established now, and the plants shade out a lot of the weeds. The poison ivy that grew on the property initially is gone now. The worst problem is Canada thistle, but it is removed as soon as it pops up. The yellow-flowered compass plant (*Silphium*

RIGHT: Hackberry trees (*Celtis occidentalis*) punctu-ate a tapestry of lower plants that includes blocks of *Aster oblongifolius* and *Eupatorium hyssopifolium* near the pond and wild rice (*Zinzania latifolia*) and *Thalia dealbata* in the water.

LEFT: A planting of *Schizachyrium scoparium* and *Coreopsis tripteris* connects the house to the bay.

Paths maintain the natural look of the rest of the property; they are surfaced with crushed oyster shells, a traditional paving material along the East Coast in times past when oysters were plentiful in the waters.

laciniatum), a prairie native, is a prolific self-sower that has become invasive, so unwanted seedlings have to be pulled every year. The silphium that remains is striking, however; in some places it is nine feet tall.

The three-acre property had once been a soybean field. When Mr. van Sweden took possession, he planted soybeans once more but did not fertilize them. After the soybeans were gone, he left the land alone, and horsetail came up. The horsetail was gone the next year. Then 50 pounds of panicum and schizachyrium seed were planted with a seed drill. Then there was a drought and none of the grass came up. Finally, though, the rains came and then the grasses grew.

Closer to the house, sturdy perennials such as giant black-eyed Susan (*Rudbeckia maxima*), asters, and grasses including broom sedge (*Andropogon virginicus*), wild oats (*Chasmanthium latifolium*), and little bluestem (*Schizachyrium scoparium*) were planted in bands and blocks and then allowed to go their own way. Paths through the garden are made of flagstones set in crushed oyster shells — a traditional paving material at the seashore that, these days, is difficult to come by.

Like all gardens, this one has evolved over time. Even a meadow requires a certain amount of experimentation and revision to arrive at the ideal mix of plants.

Switchgrass (*Panicum virgatum* 'Cloud Nine') planted right off the deck grew quickly to eight feet high and blocked the view of the bay from the expansive windows of the house. It was moved and replaced with *Pycnanthemum muticum*, a lower-growing perennial with aromatic, minty foliage.

In and around the pond, Mr. van Sweden planted Asian wild rice (*Zinzania latifolia*), butterbur (*Petasites japonicus*), rose mallow (*Hibiscus moscheutos*), and *Thalia dealbata*. Cattails (*Typha* sp.) have to be weeded out to prevent them from taking over and crowding out the other plants.

Hedgerows run along the property lines and they were overgrown with poison ivy, which was removed. Poison ivy is tenacious, but repeated pulling or mowing will eventually get rid of it without the need for herbicides. Native eastern red cedars populate the hedgerows (and don't burn from salt wind, as they often do near the ocean) and produce new seedlings. Mr. van Sweden has added desirable trees such as *Oxydendrum arboreum* and *Magnolia grandiflora* to the hedgerows, as well.

Another tree that grows in the garden is hackberry (*Celtis occidentalis*). The eminent tree authority Donald Wyman said the hackberry had no landscape value whatsoever, but Mr. van Sweden's business partner, Wolfgang Oehme, likes the tree, so several found their way into the land-

scape. As Mr. van Sweden describes them, hackberries are not pretty, they have no fall color, and they don't have nice flowers — that is, they fit his criterion of not having pretty plants in his garden. But the birds like them, he says. And they are very tough.

Mr. van Sweden's Chesapeake retreat demonstrates that a naturalistic landscape can have a positive effect on the environment that surrounds it and still be attractive (even when "pretty" flowers aren't employed).

RIGHT: Hackberry trees, while not conventionally beautiful, are tough and resilient, and they provide habitat for birds, so they have earned their place in this landscape.

BELOW: Because it uses no chemical inputs and relies largely on native plants, this garden helps in its own small way to preserve the incomparable beauty of the Chesapeake Bay.

TOUGH PLANTS FOR A NATURALISTIC LANDSCAPE

Andropogon virginicus, broom sedge
Baccharis halimifolia, groundsel bush
Celtis occidentalis, hackberry
Magnolia grandiflora, southern magnolia
Pycnanthemum muticum, mountain mint
Rudbeckia maxima, giant black-eyed Susan
Schizachyrium scoparium, little bluestem

Designing with Nature

KIAWAH ISLAND, SOUTH CAROLINA

A winding driveway paved with crushed slag ends in a parking area near the house. Here, the soaring branches of old live oaks create a cathedral effect. Sandanqua viburnum (*Viburnum suspensum*) and dwarf palmetto (*Sabal minor*) grow beneath the oaks.

ON A BARRIER ISLAND OFF THE SOUTH Carolina coast, there's a wonderful example of how native plants can be used to integrate a seaside house into a beautiful natural setting and create a landscape that is sophisticated yet low maintenance.

The house is built of wood and stone; it's natural and rustic, yet elegant and stylish. To take advantage of the unspoiled character of the maritime forest site, landscape architect Clyde Timmons, of Design-Works, LC, in Charleston, created a garden that relies heavily on native plants to fit the house comfortably into its surroundings.

To reach the house, you travel along a winding drive paved with crunchy, dark crushed slag through a woodland planted with ferns and dwarf palms. The natural environment here is so beautiful that the designer and the owners agreed they wanted a landscape that blended into its surroundings, with some added touches of color and texture.

As a starting point, they decided to preserve the magnificent huge old live oaks (*Quercus virginiana*) that graced the property. The architecture of the house already embraced the trees — the outstanding feature of the house is a circular glass block tower with a spiral staircase that is located right under one of the live oaks. Climbing the stairs feels like walking through the branches of the tree.

There were also native wax myrtles (*Myrica cerifera*), yaupon hollies (*Ilex vomitoria*), and palmettos (*Sabal palmetto*). The natural vegetation was enhanced with additional plantings on the grounds just beyond the house. Once established, these natives need little in the way of maintenance, tolerating drought, heat, and the salt winds off the river that flows behind the property. Another plus is that the plentiful deer population leaves the plants alone. Needle palm (*Rhapidophyllum hystrix*), a hardy and shade-tolerant native, was added here for greater textural contrast.

Close by the river at the rear of the property is a marsh dominated by a native cordgrass, *Spartina alternifolia*. Along the edge of the marsh, Mr. Timmons and his team planted another native marsh cordgrass, *Spartina patens*, which can tolerate periodic saltwater flooding.

Closer to the house, the plantings combine with striking architectural features to create a more controlled, elegant, but still natural look. The house itself is actually two separate buildings linked by a courtyard. Here there is a rectangular lap pool surrounded by a terrace of cut bluestone, which is bordered with rippling bands of rounded river stone alternating with dwarf mondo grass (*Ophiopogon japonicus*) that reinforce the linear feeling but create an interesting contrast of textures. In a bit of serendipity, the homeowners had chosen tiles with a wavy pattern to run down the

ABOVE: Saw palmetto (*Serenoa repens*) is hardy and resilient in this garden, tolerating salt, wind, and drought, and it's not tempting to deer.

RIGHT: The crisp lines of the courtyard and lap pool are softened with plantings of sago palm, and Confederate jasmine climbing the pillars. Dwarf mondo grass planted in undulating lines echoes the wavy tile pattern down the center of the pool.

center of the bottom of the pool, a perfect complement to the pattern of the mondo grass and river stone. Designer and owners were thinking on the same plane, which made for a very successful collaboration.

For the plantings in this area, the design team amended the naturally quite sandy soil with compost, peat moss, and fertilizer to support a wider range of plants. Along the sides of the pool, magnificent columns of Confederate jasmine (*Trachelospermum jasminoides*) scale the posts supporting the roof. When the fragrant jasmine flowers in the spring, the effect is intoxicating, but there's still plenty of interest when the jasmine is not in bloom. In the river stone below are several sago palms (*Cycas revoluta*), which can eventually become quite large but grow very, very slowly. Here at the northernmost limit of its hardiness range, the palm can burn in a very severe winter, but it has so far done just fine. Taller windmill palm (*Trachycarpus fortunei*) is not a native, but it is hardy.

Perennials and annuals in the courtyard bloom at different times of year. The garden includes agapanthus, plumbago (*Plumbago auriculata*), gaura, and crocosmia, along with pink lantana. All of them do well there.

Behind the house a series of terraced planters step down toward the marsh. The strong architectural lines of the planters are softened with native sweetgrass (*Muh-*

The fragrant white flowers of Confederate jasmine (*Trachelospermum jasminoides*) perfume the courtyard in spring. The sago palm (*Cycas revoluta*) below grows very slowly but can eventually reach an impressive size.

lenbergia filipes), which is used locally to make sweetgrass baskets. "It has a beautiful little pinkish purple bloom in late summer and fall," says Mr. Timmons. He also used saw palmetto (*Serenoa repens*) in the planters. This is about as far north as it can grow, but there are some natural stands of it on the island, and it is fairly low growing. He also used some creeping rosemary in the planters, a plant he likes because "it takes the salt, takes the dryness, takes the winds." Plants here are mulched with local pine straw to help retain moisture.

In front of the house, the driveway ends in a parking area that's an architecturally strong space, again blending house and garden. The main houses, the guesthouse, the garage, and some tall live oaks with their overhanging branches combine to form three sides of this cathedral-like space. One feels a sense of both enclosure and verticality. "The live oaks are absolutely beautiful," says Mr. Timmons. The plantings simply reinforced the structure that was already there. Beneath the live oaks are palmetto (*Sabal palmetto*), *Viburnum suspensum* (which, although not native, has a natura-

listic feel and tolerates the shady conditions under the trees), evergreen giant liriope (*Liriope muscari*), and a redbud tree (*Cercis canadensis* 'Forest Pansy').

The sensitive design and use of native plant materials unite this remarkable house with the unspoiled natural environment that surrounds it. The courtyard plantings reinforce the architectural lines of the house while adding color and texture. It's an ideal marriage of house and landscape.

NATIVE PLANTS FOR THE SOUTH

Cercis canadensis, redbud
Ilex vomitoria, yaupon holly
Muhlenbergia filipes, sweetgrass
Myrica cerifera, wax myrtle
Quercus virginiana, southern live oak
Rhapidophyllum hystrix, needle palm
Serenoa repens, saw palmetto
Spartina patens, marsh cordgrass

Behind the house, a series of terraced planters are filled with native sweetgrass (*Muhlenbergia filipes*), trailing rosemary, creeping fig (*Ficus pumila*) and saw palm (*Serenoa repens*).

Inspired by Frank Lloyd Wright

KIAWAH ISLAND, SOUTH CAROLINA

Planters near the house contain ornamental grasses, palms, and a creeping shore juniper (*Juniperus conferta* 'Blue Pacific') that drapes itself over the edges.

FRANK LLOYD WRIGHT BELIEVED THAT landscape and architecture should connect to each other; his houses were all designed to fit into their surroundings, with landscaping to enhance the connection. Many of his houses are low to the ground, to blend with their flat prairie sites. The owners of this property on a barrier island off South Carolina wanted a house and landscape in the spirit of Frank Lloyd Wright. But this house had to be tall — there were setback and flood requirements, and the owners wanted to have enough space and a good view. The verticality of the house made it more challenging for landscape architect Clyde Timmons, of DesignWorks, LC, in Charleston, South Carolina, to tie together the landscape and house. But he employed a number of creative design strategies to accomplish the goal.

There were also a number of landscape challenges presented by the site. The property is buffeted by strong salt winds coming off the ocean. There are plenty of hungry deer in residence. The house sits on a flag lot, and a driveway had to be constructed in a narrow corridor lined with live oaks (*Quercus virginiana*) that both designer and homeowners wanted to preserve. There is a range of soils, from sand to muck, each with different watering needs. In addition, the property lies in a swale between two dune fields, and water naturally collects there. The water table is only three feet down, even in dry weather. Local development has channeled ever more water into the swale — there's no place for it to run off. The water problem exists on the landward side of the property (the sandy beachfront side drains well). The design team solved the water problem by building up mounds of soil to improve drainage. They created a berm to accommodate plantings near the street, graded

Terraces and porches help to unite the house with the landscape, and their horizontal lines evoke the feeling of Frank Lloyd Wright's prairie style of architecture.

carefully, and made raised planting areas with drainage pipes installed underneath.

In the end, the owners wanted a low-maintenance landscape that was respectful of and appropriate to the environment — and they got it. First, they left intact as much of the indigenous vegetation as was practical, and added some new, primarily native, plants. On the seaward side of the house, they used dune and beach plants. They added some grasses and palms that are visually compatible although not necessarily native. They also added a few gingers to strike a tropical note. A few unhealthy loblolly pines were removed on the beach side, and they selectively pruned the remaining pines and oaks to frame views of the ocean that had been blocked. A boardwalk leading to the beach was carefully located to wind through the existing vegetation, making a stroll to the beach visually more interesting while still protecting the dunes and plants.

On the landward side of the house, Mr. Timmons relied on plants suited to the maritime forest. Along the driveway, most of the existing vegetation, including wax

The boardwalk leading to the beach is carefully designed to wind through the existing vegetation, protecting the dunes and the plants.

myrtle (*Myrica cerifera*), yaupon holly (*Ilex vomitoria*), redbay (*Persea borbonia*), and *Magnolia grandiflora*, remained in place, with just some cleanup and pruning, and some new plants were added to provide better screening and more textural interest.

A second design strategy was to bring some dune plants close to the house. Mr. Timmons installed palms and dune grasses in terraced planters off the first floor. Conditions were different from one planter to another — wind exposure and amount of sunlight varied — and the plants had to be suited to the particular environment. Another consideration was not to block the view with plants. To evoke the spirit of Frank Lloyd Wright, who liked to use trailing plants and vines in his own landscape designs, Mr. Timmons included trailing rosemary in the planters.

The planters hold a variety of ornamental grasses — sweetgrass (*Muhlenbergia filipes*), maidengrass (*Miscanthus sinensis* 'Gracillimus'), and pennisetum. Dwarf yaupon holly, which forms a large mound that can be clipped to keep it small or left to assume its natural form, also figures in the planters. (The holly is, says Mr. Timmons, tough and durable as well as attractive — an all-around good, versatile plant.)

More planters grace the broad porches that forge another link between house and landscape. Here the grasses are joined by yellow lantana, aspidistra, variegated ginger, and a creeping shore juniper (*Juniperus conferta* 'Blue Pacific').

Mr. Timmons connected the landscape to the house by pulling architectural materials into the landscape; he also made design recommendations for creating a covered walkway or breezeway leading to the front door. He designed angular retaining walls that reach out into the landscape in front of the house to create terraced planting areas right alongside the building. In these beds are holly fern (*Cyrtomium falcatum*), the finer-textured autumn fern (*Dryopteris erythrosora*), and yellow lantana for color. To introduce a vertical line close to the wall of the house there are cast-iron plants (*Aspidistra elatior*), which are very

The pool and spa offer a view down the boardwalk to the beach. Native loblolly pines were selectively pruned to frame the vista.

Angular planters are sided with wood to match the house, bringing an architectural element into the landscape. At the base, native sweetgrass is mulched with local pine straw, connecting planted areas to the surrounding natural landscape.

tough and can take a lot of shade. Close to the breezeway is a trident maple (*Acer buergerianum*), planted to lighten up the brick wall against which it is seen. Red maple was rejected for this space because it is too large, and Japanese maple was considered too fragile for the seaside environment.

A higher wall, sided with wood like the house, creates a second, elevated level for planting. Masses of Confederate jasmine (*Trachelospermum jasminoides*) spill over the edges of this higher wall, in another nod to the style of Frank Lloyd Wright.

Altogether, this landscape achieves its aim — that of uniting a well-conceived and beautifully detailed home with a wonderful seaside setting.

STRATEGIES FOR UNITING HOUSE AND LANDSCAPE

• Leave existing vegetation intact as much as possible; prune selectively and replace damaged specimens with healthy plants.

• Select native (or native-looking) plants to mix effectively into the existing landscape.

• Use plants close to the house that also occur in the distant landscape.

• Repeat architectural elements from the house in the landscape, in the form of paths, beds, breezeways, and retaining walls.

CHAPTER 5

Top Seaside Plants

THIS SECTION IS A CONCISE GUIDE TO MORE THAN 100 plants that do well in seaside gardens. There are many more plants suited to seashore conditions than can be described here, so don't be afraid to experiment. Some of the plants in this chapter will grow in beachfront gardens, and some will work near the beach if sheltered by a windbreak or the house itself. Others have less tolerance for salt or wind, and are best located away from the beach.

ABOVE: *Dahlia* 'Caboose'

RIGHT: Astilbes, hostas, and ferns thrive in a protected, shady spot on the rocky coast of Mane.

Understanding Environmental Conditions

Growing conditions vary widely near the beach. If you have shade, it is important to understand its density and duration.

WHEN CHOOSING PLANTS FOR YOUR seaside garden, it is essential that you have a very clear understanding of the environmental conditions they will face in your garden or in their particular spot in your garden. Seashore conditions vary significantly from one property to another. The closer you are to the beach, the greater the variation can be. At the beach, growing conditions just a thousand feet apart can be totally different from one another.

To select plants that will thrive in your garden, it is important to know the direction from which the prevailing winds blow in summer and in winter. Find out when the stormiest weather usually occurs.

Sun exposure is another critical factor. You will need to know how many hours of direct sun the garden will receive each day, and how the sun shifts in the sky over the course of the growing season, which will alter the patterns of light and shadow across the property. If you have shade, be realistic about the type and degree of shade it is. Sun-loving plants will just not thrive in the shade. But there are plenty of plants that will. See "Kinds of Shade" (below) for more information.

KINDS OF SHADE

The quality of shade varies greatly, and understanding what constitutes partial shade or full shade will help you make better plant choices for your garden.

Partial shade, semi-shade, or half shade. A partially shady location receives two to six hours of sun, either in the morning or in the afternoon. It can also refer to a full day of dappled sunlight. Partial shade is usually cast to the east or west of a relatively solid body, such as a wall, building, or thick hedge, or beneath an arbor or lattice.

Light or thin shade. This can be found under young trees, or mature trees with a light, lacy canopy. Light shade can also be cast by trees or buildings at some distance from the garden. While not sunny, this environment is still bright and airy.

A lightly shaded garden may receive only an hour or two of direct sun during the day, but it is bright enough the rest of the time to allow a variety of plants to thrive. The thin canopy creates shifting patterns of light and shadow, or intermittent shade, as some of the sun's rays pass through spaces between the leaves.

Full shade. This is found under mature trees that have dense, spreading foliage. Unpruned oaks and maples cast this kind of shade in summer. A fully shaded location is fine for woodland plants.

Heavy shade. Cast by tall buildings and mature evergreens, heavy shade is too dim, and often too dry, for all but a few plants.

The other key factors are soil and moisture. Don't automatically assume your soil is sandy — not all seashore gardens are. If you do have sandy soil, how sandy is it? How well does the soil drain and how long does it retain moisture? What is the pH? What are nutrient levels like? Have a good soil test done. In addition to providing test results, USDA county Cooperative Extension offices and good private testing labs will make recommendations on amending and improving your soil.

The answers to all these environmental questions will guide you both in your choice of plants and in how you manage the plants in the garden. If you work with nature and choose plants that are naturally suited to the growing conditions present on your property, your chances of success will be much greater. You'll also have to do less work to coddle and nurse them along. Use this chapter as a guide to help you find plants that will work in your garden.

THE ROLE OF NATIVE PLANTS

Many, but certainly not all, of the plants covered in this chapter are native to the United States or eastern North America. Native plants have a special role to play in seashore gardens. Especially at or very near the beach, it is frequently native plants that are best able to hold up under the very difficult conditions. Often they will grow where little else will.

Natives are sometimes less showy than more traditional garden plants, but you can come to appreciate them as part of the special environment that is the seashore. You may have to adjust your idea of the garden and learn to enjoy a wilder, more natural kind of beauty. When you do, you will find that native plants truly express the spirit of what it means to live near the sea, and you will also find them incredibly easy to care for. If your heart is set on roses and peonies and irises, you can certainly still have them — you will just have to learn how to create a protected environment in which to grow them, as explained in chapter 3.

As more and more gardeners are including native plants in their gardens and more landscape professionals are designing with them, these plants are becoming more widely available in nurseries. It is important when gardening with natives that you obtain them from a reputable source. Don't collect plants yourself from the wild; some are endangered and it's illegal to take them. Seek out nursery-propagated stock.

Beach grass and bayberry, like other native plants, are adapted to seashore conditions and will do well with little help.

Making Good Choices

Beach peas are among the few plants that thrive in the harsh dune environment.

Hᴏᴍᴇᴏᴡɴᴇʀꜱ ʟɪᴠɪɴɢ ɴᴇᴀʀ ᴀ ʙᴀʏ often have more leeway in terms of plant choices than do oceanfront dwellers, especially if the property is elevated on a bluff. Farther away from the water, the choices become even broader.

Still, seaside gardening is always a process of trial and error, and you have to resign yourself to losing plants. Over time, you'll find out which ones work in your garden and which ones don't. But unusually severe winters and hard storms can wipe out plants that have done well in your garden for years. It's part of life at the shore, and you don't have much choice but to accept it. Still, for those of us who live near the sea, the trials and tribulations of seashore gardening are worth it.

For each of the plants in this chapter you will find a quick capsule of information on its hardiness, sun and shade requirements, and approximate degree of salt tolerance. You will also find out whether the plant tolerates drought, and if deer are likely to eat it. There is a description of the plant, suggestions on how to use it in the garden, and, where applicable, recommended varieties.

There is also basic information on how to grow and care for the plant. Just bear in mind that plants do not perform the same way in all gardens, especially at the shore. So many different environmental factors come into play that it is really difficult to make generalizations about how plants will perform. Use the information in this chapter as a basic guide, but observe your plants carefully and get to know the growing environment that exists on your property. And remember: Never, never stop experimenting!

Trees and Shrubs

Amelanchier species
Shadbush, serviceberry

Zones: 4–8

Exposure: Full sun to partial shade

Salt Tolerance: Good

Drought Tolerance: Poor

Deer Resistance: Good

There are actually two woody plants called shadbush — *Amelanchier canadensis* and *Amelanchier arborea* (also known as downy serviceberry). The two are often confused, and are used in similar ways. Both are natives, and both may take the form of a large, dense, clump-forming shrub. Downy serviceberry may also grow as a small tree with an oval to rounded crown, and is a bit taller, growing to 25 feet high. *Amelanchier canadensis* reaches about 20 feet with a 10-foot spread.

Serviceberries, also known as shadbush, have oval, toothed leaves and clusters of white flowers in spring. In early summer they produce juicy, purple-black berries that can be used for pies and jellies, if the birds don't get to them first. Fall color is mostly yellow in *Amelanchier canadensis* and ranges from yellow to orange and sometimes red in downy serviceberry. Their light grayish bark is attractive in winter.

Shadbush prefers moist but well-drained soil with an acid pH. It grows wild in boggy areas up and down the coast from Maine to South Carolina, but it adapts to a range of soils. These trees can tolerate dry soil, but need watering during prolonged spells of dry weather. They look best in a naturalistic or informal garden. Plant at the edge of a woodland or alongside a pond, or in a shrub border. Shadbush is sometimes affected by scale, fire blight, or black spot.

Amelanchier species

Aronia species
Chokeberry

Zones: 5–9

Exposure: Full sun to light shade

Salt Tolerance: Good

Drought Tolerance: Moderate

Deer Resistance: Good

Red chokeberry (*Aronia arbutifolia*) is a leggy, upright shrub with arching stems that spreads by suckers to form a clump. It grows 8 to 10 feet high and may be 5 feet or more across. Leaves are oval, finely toothed, and dark green. They turn rich red in fall. Large clusters of small, fragrant white flowers bloom in spring, then from fall into winter the plants are covered with bright red berrylike fruits. The cultivar 'Brilliantissima' has spectacular autumn foliage and larger, shinier fruits than the species.

Red chokeberry grows well in full sun to light shade. It adapts to a range of soils from wet to dry. Moderate fertility suits it well, but it will grow in poor soils, too.

Black chokeberry (*Aronia melanocarpa*) is similar to the red species but bears dark purple-black fruits; the cultivar 'Autumn Magic' has especially large, glossy fruits. It is a bit smaller than red chokeberry (growing to six feet high), and its fall foliage is usually a deep purplish red. Like red chokeberry, this species adapts to a range of soils.

Both chokeberries are best grown in a shrub border or massed together.

Aronia arbutifolia 'Brilliantissima'

Baccharis halimifolia

Baccharis halimifolia
Groundsel bush, saltbush, salt myrtle

Zones: 3–8
Exposure: Full sun
Salt Tolerance: Excellent
Drought Tolerance: Good
Deer Resistance: Fair

This bushy deciduous shrub is rather weedy looking, but it's extremely tough. Saltbush stands up to salt spray, strong winds, and dry, sandy soil with no problem, and it's not bothered by saltwater flooding. It grows wild along the East Coast in a variety of habitats from sandy to marshy.

Groundsel bush grows to about 5 feet high at the beach, but will reach 10 or 11 feet in less exposed locations, with a spread of about 12 feet. The leaves are leathery and grayish green, oblong and coarsely toothed, and poisonous. Large clusters of white to yellowish white flowers appear on female plants in late summer and fall, and are followed by ornamental, foamy-looking, thistle-like seed heads. The plant self-sows and spreads; its vigor can be problematic in good soils.

Give saltbush a location in full sun, with very well-drained soil. It is useful in windbreaks at the beach, for screening in exposed locations, and to hold soil and control erosion on dunes and slopes. Away from the beach, it can fill space in poor soil where few other plants would thrive. Space plants two to three feet apart in a windbreak or other screen planting, or set them three feet apart in a double row. Cut back plants occasionally to promote bushier growth.

Buddleia species
Butterfly bush

Zones: 5–9
Exposure: Full sun to partial shade
Salt Tolerance: Fair
Drought Tolerance: Fair
Deer Resistance: Good

Butterfly bushes are lovely additions to gardens. They are adaptable and easy to grow, and their wands of little flowers bloom for a long time and are magnets for butterflies. Butterfly bushes prefer full sun, although cultivars with variegated leaves will do better with some afternoon shade in southern gardens. *Buddleia davidii* has some salt tolerance, but all species need protection from salt spray and strong winds.

Butterfly bushes thrive in soil that is well drained and reasonably fertile, but they can tolerate poorer soils, too, although they won't bloom as well. Deadhead plants to prolong flowering. Prune once a year if you want to limit their size.

Common butterfly bush (*Buddleia davidii*) grows to 20 feet if left unpruned, and can be cut back to the ground in early spring to rejuvenate old bushes or keep plants shorter. It has lance-shaped, grayish green leaves. Its fat, conical spikes of lightly fragrant flowers bloom in late summer and fall in shades of purple, violet, pink, burgundy, and white. This butterfly bush holds up well in dry conditions but needs some water during periods of prolonged drought.

Fountain buddleia (*B. alternifolia*) is a more graceful plant, with arching stems lined with narrow, dark green leaves. In late spring its branches are lined with dense clusters of light purple flowers that from a distance look like long wands of bloom. Fountain buddleia grows 10 to 15 feet high when unpruned, but can be pruned right after it finishes blooming to control its size.

Buddleia davidii

Calluna vulgaris
Scotch heather

Zones: 4–7
Exposure: Full sun
Salt Tolerance: Fair
Drought Tolerance: Fair
Deer Resistance: Good

This small evergreen shrub grows just two feet high with an equal spread, and forms a low mat. The thin, needlelike leaves are a rich medium green in summer and may take on a bronze cast in winter. From midsummer into fall plants produce long clusters of tiny bell-shaped flowers of deep purple-red, rosy pink, or white, which bees love.

Shear back plants after blooming to remove the old flowers, or prune occasionally to keep plants looking neat.

Heather needs plenty of sun and moist but

Calluna vulgaris

very well-drained soil with a mildly acid pH. It grows well in poor, infertile soil, but it can dry out in an exposed, windy location. Water well during periods of dry weather.

Heather can be used in a number of ways — in a rock garden, on a slope, or as a ground cover in an area that does not get foot traffic.

Caragana arborescens
Siberian peashrub

Zones: 2–7
Exposure: Full sun
Salt Tolerance: Good
Drought Tolerance: Good
Deer Resistance: Good

Siberian peashrub is an upright deciduous shrub to 20 feet high, with a spread of about 15 feet. Its compound leaves are composed of pairs of bright green oval leaflets with spiny tips. Clusters of bright yellow flowers bloom in spring, and pealike brown seedpods follow in mid- to late summer. Like legumes, Siberian peashrub fixes nitrogen in the soil.

Although not a terribly ornamental plant, Siberian peashrub is deep rooted, very cold

Caragana arborescens

hardy, and easy to grow. It tolerates salt, stands up well in strong winds, and can take poor soils and alkaline pH. Use it in a windbreak or screen near a bay beach or in other difficult sites. If you start with young plants, they will likely adapt to conditions near the ocean, too.

Clethra alnifolia
Sweet pepperbush

Zones: 4–9
Exposure: Partial to light shade
Salt Tolerance: Fair
Drought Tolerance: Poor
Deer Resistance: Poor

Sweet pepperbush offers its wands of fragrant white flowers in late summer to early fall, when they are especially welcome. Native to the eastern United States, this deciduous shrub forms a clump of stems about eight feet high and spreads by means of suckers but is not invasive. Leaves are oval and medium green in color, turning bright yellow in autumn. Dwarf and pink-flowered cultivars are also available.

Grow sweet pepperbush in a sheltered, partly shaded spot. Reliable and easy to grow, it does best in moist but well-drained, humusy soil that is reasonably fertile and has an acid pH, but it can adapt to a range of soils. Although it is not considered deer resistant, deer have not touched it in my garden.

Sweet pepperbush works well in informal shady borders away from the water.

Clethra alnifolia

Cryptomeria japonica
Japanese cedar

Zones: 6–9
Exposure: Full sun to partial shade
Salt Tolerance: Fair
Drought Tolerance: Fair
Deer Resistance: Poor

This stately evergreen is a tough, attractive plant for seashore gardens. It can grow 60 to 80 feet high, but many cultivars are available, in a range of heights. Some varieties are conical in form, others narrow and columnar, still others rounded and dense. Sprays of soft, medium to deep green needles turn bronze or brownish in winter in cooler climates. The bark is an attractive reddish brown and peels in strips.

Japanese cedar thrives in moist but well-drained soil that is fertile and rich in organic matter, but it will tolerate a range of soils as long as they are well drained. It is reasonably salt tolerant, but the foliage will burn right at the beach. Though generally a tough plant, the tree is sometimes attacked by leaf spot and blight.

Use Japanese cedar for screening or as a specimen tree in a lawn, where its attributes can be fully appreciated. It is best used away from the ocean, but will do reasonably well near a bay.

Cryptomeria japonica 'Sekkan-sugi'

× Cupressocyparis leylandii
Leyland cypress

Zones: 6–10
Exposure: Full sun to partial shade
Salt Tolerance: Good
Drought Tolerance: Moderate
Deer Resistance: Poor

This tough, fast-growing, pyramidal evergreen is widely used for hedges and screening. Leyland cypress can grow to 60 or 70 feet in home landscapes, with a spread of 10 to 15 feet, but it can be kept smaller with pruning. A graceful, handsome plant, Leyland cypress has feathery, scalelike, dark green foliage and reddish brown bark.

Leyland cypress is most often used in screens and informal hedges, but it can be sheared for a more formal look. It can also be planted in pairs flanking an entry or at the end of a driveway, or as a single specimen.

Leyland cypress needs well-drained soil, and it will tolerate poor, infertile soil. The tree can withstand salt spray and wind, and survives in difficult locations. It works well near a bay.

The best spot for Leyland cypress is a location in full sun. It will also grow in partial shade, but it won't be as dense. A quick grower even in poor soil, this plant will grow even faster in moist but well-drained, fertile soil. Pests and diseases seldom trouble it. If you prune or shear the tree for a hedge, do not cut back so far that you slice into old wood. Some gardeners find that touching the foliage irritates their skin, so wear gloves to work around the plant if you are sensitive.

RECOMMENDED CULTIVARS
- 'Gold Nugget' — golden foliage
- 'Naylor's Blue' — blue-green foliage
- 'Silver Dust' — white splotches on the foliage

× Cupressocyparis leylandii

Cytisus scoparius
Scotch broom

Zones: 5–8
Exposure: Full sun
Salt Tolerance: Good
Drought Resistance: Good
Deer Resistance: Good

In California, Scotch broom is an invasive nuisance, but along the East Coast it's a useful plant for sandy seaside gardens. Not a candidate for formal gardens, Scotch broom is a deciduous shrub to five or six feet high, with a mass of slender, upright, light green stems that arch over at the ends. The leaves are small and oblong, and masses of small, bright yellow flowers bloom along the stems in spring. A more compact variety with light yellow flowers is 'Moonlight'. There are also varieties with garnet red or red-violet flowers available in the nursery trade.

Grow this plant in full sun. It is not fussy about soil, so long as it has good drainage. In fact, broom does best in light, sandy soils of low fertility. Rich, wet soil will kill it. It also tolerates a range of pH levels. Scotch broom is susceptible to blight and leaf spot, which can kill the plant. It is reputedly difficult to transplant, but starting with young plants will reduce the risk of transplant shock. If you need to prune the plant, do it soon after it finishes blooming.

A word of caution: Scotch broom often self-sows. Be sure to pull up any unwanted seedlings.

Cytisus scoparius

Erica carnea

Erica carnea
Spring heath

Zones: (5) 6–8
Exposure: Full sun to partial shade
Salt Tolerance: Good
Drought Tolerance: Fair
Deer Resistance: Poor

A familiar plant to rock gardeners, spring heath has a place at the seashore, too. Low and spreading, it's a good addition to a sunny bed or border, or perhaps massed on a bank. Or you can use it as a ground cover in low-traffic areas.

Spring heath has dark green, needlelike, evergreen leaves. In late winter to early spring, depending on your location, it bears masses of tiny, tubular, rosy purple flowers. There are many cultivars in various shades of pink and purple, plus white. Some varieties also have golden foliage, which adds another season of color.

This heath grows just 8 to 12 inches high, forming a low mat or mound, and needs well-drained soil. Like other ericaceous plants, spring heath thrives in acid soil, but unlike many of its relatives, it will also tolerate alkaline soils. It is seldom bothered by salt or wind—they just blow right over it.

RECOMMENDED CULTIVARS
- 'December Red' — deep rose-pink flowers
- 'King George' — dark pink flowers, early blooming
- 'Myretown Ruby' — flowers open pink and darken to ruby red as they age
- 'Springwood Pink' — profuse, clear pink flowers; plant has a trailing habit
- 'Springwood White' — masses of white flowers on trailing plants

Euonymus species

Zones: *E. fortunei,* 5–9; *E. japonicus,* 7–9
Exposure: Full sun to full shade
Salt Tolerance: Fair to good
Drought Tolerance: Poor
Deer Resistance: Poor

These two members of a large and varied genus are both evergreen and able to stand up to salt winds to varying degrees. They grow in sun or shade, and tolerate a range of soils. If your soil is mostly sand, though, amend it with compost and topsoil before planting euonymus, to provide nutrients and help hold moisture for the plants. Fertilize annually with a balanced organic fertilizer, or with an all-purpose synthetic according to package directions.

Evergreen euonymus is more salt tolerant but less hardy than wintercreeper, which generally does best behind a windbreak near the beach. Evergreen euonymus can stand direct hits from salty wind. Its stems will swell from water buildup in very salty conditions, but the plant will generally keep on growing anyway.

Most kinds of euonymus are, unfortunately, subject to scale, and may also be bothered by mildew, galls, leaf spots, or aphids. Deer will eat them, too.

Euonymus fortunei 'Emerald Gaiety'

Euonymus fortunei
Wintercreeper

This woody vine has small, oval, leathery, dark green leaves with serrated edges. Plants form roots at nodes along the stem and sprawl across the ground or climb, clinging to walls and tree trunks. When left unsupported, the plants become rather shrubby. In fall, they sport small reddish fruits that open to reveal orange seeds.

You can use wintercreeper as a ground cover under shrubs or trees, in a mixed border, or to prevent erosion on a slope. Clip the plants as needed. Space plants 1½ to 2 feet apart.

RECOMMENDED CULTIVARS
- *E. f.* var. *coloratus* — glossy deep green leaves that turn reddish or purplish in winter
- 'Emerald Gaiety' — grows three to four feet high, with white-edged leaves
- 'Emerald 'n' Gold' — a low-growing, shrubby form to two feet high and three feet across, with yellow-edged green leaves
- 'Green Lane' — with glossy, thick leaves said to resist windburn
- 'Harlequin' — green leaves splashed with pink and white
- 'Kewensis' — a low-growing ground hugger just a few inches high, with small, dense leaves

Euonymus japonicus
Evergreen euonymus

An upright shrub growing 8 to 10 feet high and 4 to 6 feet wide, evergreen euonymus has leathery, glossy, oval leaves with slightly toothed edges. Clusters of tiny white flowers bloom in late spring and are followed in autumn by orange-red fruits. Less hardy than wintercreeper, this species is rated to Zone 6, but it doesn't do well where I live on the south shore of Long Island (Zone 7). It is a better choice for southern gardens.

Use evergreen euonymus in a windbreak, as a hedge or screen (spacing plants three feet apart), or in a mixed border. It takes shearing well.

RECOMMENDED CULTIVARS
- 'Aureo-variegata' — a compact variety 5 to 10 feet high, with yellow-splotched leaves
- 'Grandifolia' — a dense variety to eight feet high that has larger leaves
- 'Microphyllus Albovariegatus' — tiny leaves resemble those of boxwood and are edged in white
- 'Silver King' — upright grower to about six feet high, with leaves edged in white

Euonymus japonicus

Fatsia japonica
Japanese fatsia

Zones: 8–10
Exposure: Partial to full shade
Salt Tolerance: Fair
Drought Resistance: Fair
Deer Resistance: Fair

Northerners know fatsia as a houseplant, but homeowners in warm climates can grow it outdoors as a bold accent plant or to bring a tropical note to shady beds and borders. It also creates a striking effect when massed in front of a wall or next to the house.

This large-leaved shrub grows about three to six feet high near the water. Its leathery evergreen leaves are dark green and divided into seven to nine pointed segments with wavy edges splayed around a central point. The leaves can be more than a foot across. In fall, spherical clusters of tiny white flowers bloom on thin, branched stems and are followed by blue-black berries.

Fatsia has moderate resistance to salt spray, but it does best behind a windbreak at the beach. Its large leaves will turn brownish in sunny, windy locations and can become damaged and tattered in extremely windy spots. Cold, drying winds will also take their toll. The plant is fairly vigorous and prefers humusy, moist, well-drained soils, but will tolerate sandy soils. Give it a shady location where it will receive a couple of hours of sun a day. Fertilize plants with an all-purpose organic fertilizer at the beginning of the season, or once a month with a soluble fertilizer while the plant is growing actively. Cut back on watering during the winter to let the plant rest.

Northern gardeners who want to use fatsia for a tropical effect in the garden can grow it in a large container and move it indoors to a bright location to spend the winter.

Fatsia japonica

Gleditsia triacanthos var. *inermis*
Thornless honey locust

Zones: 4–9
Exposure: Full sun
Salt Tolerance: Good
Drought Tolerance: Good
Deer Resistance: Poor

The species *Gleditsia triacanthos* is native to the eastern and central United States. It has sharp thorns along the trunk, so most homeowners prefer the thornless variety, *inermis*. This medium-size tree has been widely planted around the country, and it can be useful in seashore gardens, too, planted in an open space or close to garden beds and borders.

Honey locust varies in size with the particular variety and the growing conditions, ranging from 30 to 60 or more feet high, with a spreading crown. The graceful leaves are bright green and lacy looking, made up of pairs of small, oblong leaflets. They cast a dappled shade, which is hospitable to shade-tolerant perennials and annuals or lawn grasses that are planted near the tree. Small yellow-green flowers in late spring are extremely fragrant but not very showy, and are followed by brown seedpods.

Honey locust is shallow rooted but will stand up well in wind once it becomes established. Stake it during its first year or two in the garden. Tough and adaptable, honey locust will grow in a range of soils. Fertile, moist but well-drained soil with a neutral to mildly alkaline pH will promote maximum growth, but the tree will also grow in poor, sandy soil. It is quite salt tolerant.

Unfortunately, honey locust sometimes can be troubled by webworms, borers, and spider mites, as well as a variety of diseases including leaf spot, rust, powdery mildew, and cankers. All of these conditions are less likely to occur, however, if only a few trees are present.

RECOMMENDED CULTIVARS
- 'Elegantissima' — shrubby and dense, grows 15 feet high and equally wide
- 'Aurea' — grows 30 to 40 feet high, with leaves that emerge bright yellow-green in spring and deepen to dark green in summer
- 'Rubylace' — leaves start out burgundy in spring and turn deep green by late summer

Gleditsia triacanthos var. *inermis* 'Sunburst'

Hibiscus syriacus
Rose of Sharon

Zones: 5–9

Exposure: Full sun

Salt Tolerance: Fair

Drought Tolerance: Fair

Deer Resistance: Poor

Easy to grow and adaptable, rose of Sharon is an upright shrub with prominent-stamened, single or double flowers of pink, lavender-blue, white, or red in midsummer to early fall. You can treat rose of Sharon like a small tree and prune to keep it neat and limited in size. Or grow it in a row along a driveway, as an informal screen, or in a mixed border.

Rose of Sharon grows 6 to 12 feet high and half as wide, but can be kept smaller with an annual pruning. Give it a sunny location and it will thrive in a range of well-drained soils, even poor ones. Plants need regular watering until they are established, but can tolerate some drought after that. They have some tolerance to salt but generally do best behind a windbreak near the beach or in a spot farther away from the water. Rose of Sharon is seldom troubled by pests or diseases, although deer may nibble on it. Its biggest drawback is that it self-sows and produces a lot of seedlings that you'll have to pull up.

RECOMMENDED CULTIVARS

- 'Aphrodite' — rich rose-pink flowers with a red central eye; does not self-sow
- 'Blue Bird' — lavender-blue flowers with a red eye
- 'Diana' — large, pure white flowers
- 'Lucy' — deep red, double flowers
- 'Minerva' — lavender-pink flowers with a dark red eye

Hibiscus syriacus

Hippophäe rhamnoides

Hippophäe rhamnoides
Sea buckthorn

Zones: 3–8

Exposure: Full sun

Salt Tolerance: Good to excellent

Drought Tolerance: Good

Deer Resistance: Good

This bushy, spiny-stemmed shrub handles salt spray, wind, and sand with aplomb. Use it in a windbreak near the beach, to hold soil on the back of the dunes, as an informal hedge or screen, or as a barrier along property boundaries. It would also be at home in a very informal or naturalistic bed or border near the water.

Sea buckthorn grows as a clump of upright, thorny stems to 20 feet high and wide, lined with narrow, silvery green leaves somewhat similar to willow leaves. If both males and females are planted, females will follow their tiny yellow-green spring flowers with orange berrylike fruits in autumn, which persist and brighten winter landscapes (they are very acidic, and birds will pass them by). The plants take shearing and pruning well, and they spread by means of suckers to form colonies.

Plant sea buckthorn in a sunny location in light, well-drained, preferably sandy soil with a neutral to alkaline pH. High fertility will probably kill the plant, so fertilize only lightly, if at all. If you need to prune or clip the plant to improve its shape or limit its size, fall is the best time.

RECOMMENDED CULTIVAR

- 'Sprite' — a dwarf, grows just three to four feet high

Hydrangea macrophylla

Hydrangea macrophylla
Bigleaf hydrangea

Zones: 6–9
Exposure: Full sun to light shade
Salt Tolerance: Fair
Drought Tolerance: Poor
Deer Resistance: Poor

The big round or flat-topped flower heads of hydrangea are synonymous with summer in most East Coast seashore towns. Although they have only a modest tolerance for salt spray, when planted behind a windbreak or away from the water hydrangeas are lovely additions to mixed beds, foundation plantings, screens and space dividers, and borders along drives and walkways. You can also use them as specimen plants or in groupings in a lawn.

Bigleaf hydrangea grows three to four feet high near the beach and to six feet or taller farther inland. Size varies somewhat with cultivar, however. The large leaves are glossy green and broadly oval with toothed edges. The summer flowers may be full, round "snowball," "mophead," or "hortensia" types, or flattened, more delicate "lacecap" flowers with tiny fertile flowers in the center surrounded by a ring of larger, petal-like sterile flowers.

Blue-flowered varieties will be blue in acid soil but will turn pink in alkaline soil. White-flowered varieties do not change their color with soil pH. Grow hydrangeas in full sun to partial or light shade; afternoon shade is particularly helpful in southern gardens. The ideal soil for hydrangeas is moist but well drained and rich in organic matter. Amend very sandy soils with lots of compost before planting. To encourage blue flowers in neutral or perhaps mildly alkaline soil, add sulfur to the soil. For pink flowers in neutral to very slightly acid soil, work in lime or phosphate.

The plants bloom on old wood, setting their buds for next year's flowers after they finish blooming. If you need to prune your hydrangeas for reasons other than removing damaged or diseased growth, prune right after the plants finish blooming or you will remove some of next year's flower buds. But it's better not to prune hydrangeas if you don't have to. Leave them alone and they'll be happy.

Hydrangeas are cold sensitive — or at least their buds are. Cold winters or late frosts that strike when plants have broken dormancy in spring can kill the developing flower buds and eliminate this year's crop of flowers.

Hydrangeas don't usually suffer a lot of pest and disease problems, although the leaves may develop small burned spots where droplets of water sat on them in the sunlight.

RECOMMENDED CULTIVARS

- 'All Summer Beauty' — long blooming and compact, three to four feet high, with blue mophead flowers that form on the current season's growth
- 'Ayesha' — unusual pale lilac-pink mophead
- 'Blue Wave' — lacecap type with big heads of tiny blue or pinkish fertile flowers surrounded by lilac to white sterile florets
- 'Endless Summer' — blooms all summer on both new and old wood, so there's less chance of losing the flowers by pruning at the wrong time or from a late frost that nips the buds; deadhead to encourage continued production of blue (or pink) flowers
- 'Forever Pink' — pink flowers that deepen to rose in cool weather, on three-foot plants; early blooming
- 'Lanarth White' — compact, three to four feet high with lacecap fertile flowers of blue or pink surrounded by white sterile flowers
- 'Mariesii' — to four feet high, with blue to pink lacecap flowers
- 'Nikko Blue' — considered the most salt-tolerant variety by many gardeners and widely grown; big flower heads of rich, true blue (in acid soil)
- 'Pia' — dwarf variety just one to two feet high, with rosy pink flowers in any soil pH

Ilex species

Zones: Vary with species

Exposure: Full sun to light shade, varies with species

Salt Tolerance: Varies with species

Drought Tolerance: Varies

Deer Resistance: Good

Many of us associate holly with Christmas wreaths, but the genus includes trees and shrubs of varying sizes, forms, and leaf types, and not all of them are evergreen. One characteristic shared by all hollies is that only female plants bear the berrylike fruits that are so brightly colorful in many *Ilex* species, and they need a male nearby to pollinate them. Birds love the berries, too. Hollies come in a host of sizes and growth habits, from dense and globelike, to pyramidal, to narrowly upright.

The hollies discussed here are all good choices for seaside gardens. They each have some degree of salt tolerance; how much varies from one species to another. Some make good hedges or screens, others are useful in windbreaks, and some are striking as specimen plants displayed on a lawn or used as accents in mixed borders.

Moist but well-drained soil of average fertility will suit many hollies, but some will grow in dry, very sandy ground and others will tolerate wet, almost boggy, conditions. A location in full sun to partial or light shade is best, although light needs do vary somewhat among the species.

Ilex crenata
Japanese holly

This is a dense, slow-growing shrub with small, oval, leathery, glossy dark green leaves. It looks rather like boxwood and is used in much the same way: for sheared formal hedges or informal plant screens; in mixed borders or foundation plantings; or massed along a driveway or walk.

Japanese holly grows in sun or shade, as much as 15 feet high (although many cultivars are much smaller) and does best in light, moist but well-drained soil with a mildly acid pH. It has slight resistance to salt spray but is best planted behind a windbreak or in another protected spot at the beach. Female plants produce small, glossy black berrylike fruits. Although considered hardy in Zones 5 to 8, Japanese holly generally does best in Zones 5 to 7. Plants take clipping and shearing well, and older plants can be pruned severely to rejuvenate them. Spider mites and black knot disease are sometimes a problem.

RECOMMENDED CULTIVARS
- 'Beehive' — male pollinator, dense and mounded, to four feet high
- 'Compacta' — densely branched dwarf, four to six feet high and equally wide; good choice for an informal, unclipped screen
- 'Glory' — another male, grows four to six feet high and has small leaves
- 'Golden Gem' — has golden leaves and grows five feet tall
- 'Lemon Gem' — has golden leaves in spring that deepen to chartreuse by summer
- 'Helleri' — a dwarf, just one and a half feet high by three feet wide, with very small leaves
- 'Hetzii' — a pyramidal form growing four to five feet high and equally wide
- 'Sky Pencil' — very narrow and upright; it grows fast, takes shearing, and works well in a hedge

Ilex crenata 'Sky Pencil'

Ligustrum species

Zones: Vary with species
Exposure: Full sun to light shade
Salt Tolerance: Good to moderate
Drought Tolerance: Good
Deer Resistance: Good

Privet is ubiquitous up and down the East Coast, and with good reason. It makes a dense, high hedge that can be sheared into neat green walls (angled slightly outward for best plant growth). There are both evergreen and deciduous species, and even a deciduous hedge is effective in winter because of its dense growth. At the seashore, privet hedges protect gardens from salt and wind, although they're not usually tough enough to serve as a first line of defense. The garden profiled on page 96, however, relies on a privet hedge for its protection. Behind the dunes, or as a second line of defense, privet is very effective.

Privet isn't limited to hedging, although that's how most people use it. For a different look, consider planting privet as a billowy, informal, unclipped screen.

The plants are sturdy and adaptable with good tolerance for salt. They grow well in full sun to light shade. They will adapt to a range of soils, except for very wet, soggy ones, and are easy to grow. Both deciduous and evergreen species have dark green oval leaves and, in summer, sprays of highly scented white flowers that are pleasantly fragrant or headache inducing, depending upon your point of view. Privets are occasionally plagued by leaf diseases or attacked by aphids, scale, or other pests, but for the most part you can expect them to be healthy and trouble-free.

Set plants about two feet apart when planting a formal hedge, or three to four feet apart for an unclipped screen planting. Older hedges periodically need to be severely pruned to rejuvenate them. Clipping the hedge so the sides slope slightly outward will allow all the leaves to receive good light and will prolong the time a hedge can grow before needing rejuvenation.

Ligustrum japonicum
Japanese privet

An evergreen shrub, Japanese privet grows vigorously to 12 feet high and about 6 feet wide. The oval leaves are glossy and very deep green, and flowers bloom in spring. Small, shiny black berries appear in late fall and remain into winter. Hardy in Zones 7 to 10, Japanese privet is moderately salt tolerant, but needs some protection from salt wind, especially in the North.

RECOMMENDED CULTIVARS
- 'Texanum'—a compact six to eight feet high and four to six feet wide
- 'Texanum Silver Star'—a slower grower with white-edged leaves
- 'Variegatum'—with leaves edged and splotched with white

Ligustrum japonicum hedge

Ligustrum ovalifolium
California privet

This is shrub that may be deciduous, semievergreen, or evergreen, depending on the climate. It is considered hardy in Zones 6 to 8 and tends to be deciduous in the northern part of its range and evergreen in the south. Vigorous and dense, California privet makes a good salt barrier, although southern gardeners have reported it as being less salt tolerant for them than Japanese privet. On Long Island, it affords good protection, and holds on to its leaves until the end of December in most winters. The glossy, dark green leaves turn purplish in winter in locations where the plant is evergreen. The sprays of tiny, white, late-spring flowers are followed by small black fruits in fall.

RECOMMENDED CULTIVARS
- 'Argenteum'—white-edged leaves
- 'Aureum'—leaves have a broad golden border surrounding a green center
- *L. o.* var. *regelianum*—regal privet; a low and dense, rounded form growing five to six feet high and equally wide

Zones: *M. pensylvanica*, 3–6; *M. cerifera*, 6–9
Exposure: Full sun to partial shade
Salt Tolerance: Good to excellent
Drought Tolerance: Good
Deer Resistance: Good

Both these plants can be used for informal screening and to help control erosion on dunes after beach grass or sea oats have become established. Bayberry is an excellent addition to beachfront windbreaks, and it can also be useful for screening farther from the water. Wax myrtle tends to do best in the lee of the dunes, and it also makes a good specimen or accent plant when pruned as a small tree. Both species tolerate a range of soils and have good tolerance for both salt and drought. Bayberry is arguably the tougher of the two, adapting to soils from dry sand dunes to moist and almost marshy or clayey situations.

Myrica pensylvanica
Northern bayberry

Though considered semievergreen, bayberry can lose all its leaves in a hard winter. Plants grow to 10 feet high and spread by suckers to form colonies. The leaves are oblong, two to four inches long, and deep green. They are wonderfully aromatic when crushed.

In fall female plants bear clusters of grayish white berries, which can be used to make candles. They also attract birds — in fall along the beaches of southern New Jersey, great flocks of tree swallows descend on the dunes to eat the bayberries.

Like wax myrtle, bayberry can fix nitrogen in the soil. It will grow in practically any soil from sand dune to wetland. It's a tough, adaptable plant, a good choice for a windbreak at the beach, to stabilize dunes once beach grass is established, and for low-maintenance beds and borders. It combines well with broad-leaved evergreens. Bayberry can take salt and drought, and isn't bothered by strong winds. In a screen or windbreak, space plants two to three feet apart. Otherwise, set them four to five feet apart.

Myrica cerifera
Wax myrtle

This broad-leaved evergreen shrub or small tree grows from 10 to 15 feet high or taller. The variety *pumila* is just three feet tall. Its leathery, narrowly oblong leaves are yellowish green, and aromatic when crushed. Its light gray bark is attractive. In fall, female plants produce clusters of small, waxy white berries (if a male plant grows nearby) that can be used in making candles. Birds like them, too.

The roots of wax myrtle fix nitrogen in the soil like legumes do, enabling the plant to grow in poor soils. It tolerates drought and salt wind, although it does best behind the dunes where it receives a little protection. It is sensitive to cold, and the leaves will turn brown or fall when the mercury hits zero. In the wild, wax myrtle inhabits the swales between dunes, where the soil is a bit moister than higher up on the dunes. Leaf diseases are sometimes a problem.

Use wax myrtle as a hedge or screen, spacing plants three to four feet apart. Otherwise, space plants five or six feet apart. Or prune its lower limbs to turn it into a small tree and use it as a specimen or accent plant. Wax myrtle combines well in the landscape with junipers and other evergreens. It is also useful for controlling erosion on the lee side of dunes.

Myrica pensylvanica

Myrica cerifera

Nerium oleander
Oleander

Zones: 8–10	
Exposure: Full sun to partial shade	
Salt Tolerance: Good	
Drought Tolerance: Good	
Deer Resistance: Good	

This warm-climate evergreen is an upright shrub that generally grows quickly to 6 to 10 feet high near the beach and to 15 feet away from the water in protected locations. It has a spread of up to 10 feet. The lance-shaped leaves are dark green. In summer, plants bear clusters of single or double flowers in shades of pink, red, and yellow, as well as white, at the tips of the stems. Red-flowered varieties are said to be hardiest. All parts of the plant are poisonous if eaten, or if burned and the smoke is inhaled. Handle it with care.

Oleander has good tolerance to salt wind, and is reasonably drought tolerant. Give it well-drained, moderately fertile soil. Fertilize monthly with an all-purpose fertilizer when plants are growing actively, or two or three times during the growing season with an all-purpose organic fertilizer. The most common pests are scale, aphids, and mealybugs.

Oleander makes a lovely clipped hedge or informal screen; space plants three to four feet apart. It is a nice addition to mixed borders and back-of-the-garden plantings, and makes a handsome specimen or accent plant. You can also grow it in a tub or other large container.

RECOMMENDED CULTIVARS
- 'Algiers' — dark red, single flowers
- 'Casablanca' — single white flowers
- 'Hardy Pink' — single, salmon pink blossoms
- 'Isle of Capri' — single, soft yellow flowers
- 'Ruby Lace' — large, ruby red flowers with wavy edges

Nerium oleander

Nyssa sylvatica
Black tupelo

Zones: 4 to 9	
Exposure: Full sun to partial shade	
Salt Tolerance: Fair	
Drought Tolerance: Poor	
Deer Resistance: Poor	

A native of eastern North America, the black tupelo can be found growing in the wild in woodlands and swamps. It's a handsome tree, growing as tall as 50 feet or so, with a spread of 20 to 30 feet. It is pyramid shaped when young, but becomes more spreading with age. At the seashore it may take the form of a multistemmed tree without a central leader. The lower branches tend to droop. Black tupelo's greatest asset, ornamentally speaking, is its brilliant autumn color. The three- to five-inch-long oval leaves, which are leathery and glossy dark green in summer, turn rich shades of yellow, orange, red, and even purple in fall. Female trees produce small blue fruits in fall.

Black tupelo grows well in full sun to partial shade. The ideal soil is rich and moist but well drained, with an acidic pH, but the tree is somewhat adaptable. It has a fair degree of salt tolerance, but does best with the protection of a windbreak near the beach.

Trees adapt best if planted when still small; larger trees are difficult to transplant because of the large taproot. Black tupelo sometimes suffers dieback of branch tips, scale, or leaf miners, but these are not usually major problems. Fall is the best time to do any necessary pruning.

Nyssa sylvatica

Picea species

Zones: *P. abies,* 2–7; *P. pungens* var. *glauca,* 3–8
Exposure: Full sun to partial shade
Salt Tolerance: Fair
Drought Tolerance: Poor
Deer Resistance: Good

The stately spruces are mostly big trees and belong to the cooler regions of the Northern Hemisphere. Some of them are good choices for seashore gardens in Zone 7 and north, with some protection from a windbreak or dune or away from the water. The root system is spreading and fairly shallow, so give new trees good support until they become well established in the garden. Spruces tolerate a range of soils, although they thrive in moist but well-drained, sandy soil with an acid pH. They need water during dry weather, especially during their first few years in the garden. Spruces sometimes suffer from spider mites, spruce gall aphids (which cause branch tips to die), and spruce budworm.

Spruces, especially blue spruce, make interesting specimen trees. Dwarf varieties can add year-round interest to beds and borders or rock gardens, or you can plant them behind a retaining wall or in a foundation planting.

Picea abies

Picea abies
Norway spruce

Pyramidal in form, Norway spruce grows 40 to 60 feet high and 25 or so feet wide. Its needles are rich green, and the cones are slender and brown, up to six inches long.

RECOMMENDED CULTIVARS
- 'Argenteospicata' — has white-tipped branches
- 'Aurea' — new needles are golden, then deepen to yellow-green
- 'Flat Top' — just one foot tall and three feet across; forms a dense, flat-topped mound
- 'Inversa' or 'Pendula' — weeping Norway spruce, forms a large, low mound that will tumble over a wall or rocks, or can be staked and trained to grow upright with weeping branches
- 'Nidiformis' — bird's nest spruce, forms a dense, spreading mound with branches in horizontal layers and a hollow central "nest," two feet high and three feet across
- 'Pumila' — globe-shaped dwarf variety three to four feet high with an equal spread

Picea pungens var. glauca
Blue spruce

Known for its blue-green color, blue spruce is quite tough and durable at the seashore. The tree grows 30 to 40 feet high, with a spread of 10 to 15 feet, and numerous cultivars have been bred from it. Blue spruce is pyramidal in form and has oblong brown cones two to four inches long. It does best in full sun and can tolerate drought better than does Norway spruce.

RECOMMENDED CULTIVARS
- 'Fat Albert' — broadly pyramidal, 10 to 12 feet high and 7 to 8 feet wide, with good blue-green color
- 'Globosa' — round and shrublike with a flat top, to three feet high and four to five feet wide
- 'Hoopsii' — silvery blue, especially new needles, pyramidal form, to 30 or more feet tall and 5 feet wide
- 'Montgomery' — broadly pyramidal; dwarf to five feet high and four to six feet wide
- 'R. H. Montgomery' — popular older variety with very blue needles, grows to six feet tall and five feet wide

Picea pungens var. *glauca*

Quercus species

Zones: Vary with species
Exposure: Full sun
Salt Tolerance: Varies
Drought Tolerance: Fair
Deer Resistance: Good

Oaks are valued for their hard wood, the shade they cast, and the acorns that feed wildlife. Many of them would have a hard time at the seashore, but the ones discussed here can handle the conditions. Near the beach they are best planted behind a wind-break or in another sheltered location. Live oak can take more salt than the others. Away from the water you have more leeway. In seashore landscapes, oaks can serve as shade trees or specimens in a lawn or other large space.

Quercus virginiana

Quercus alba
White oak

This big, sturdy tree grows slowly to 60 feet or higher (taller inland), with a rounded, spreading crown. It has the lobed leaves typical of many oaks, and these turn deep burgundy in fall. Native to the eastern United States, white oak is hardy in Zones 4 to 9. It prefers seashore conditions when the sandy soil is amended with compost. Oaks in general are subject to a host of pest and disease problems, but white oaks seem to be seldom bothered by them.

Quercus marilandica
Blackjack oak

A southeastern native, blackjack oak is a shrubby tree with a low, spreading habit. It has glossy, leathery, dark green leaves and rough dark bark. Blackjack oak can grow as high as 40 feet, but it is usually smaller and shrubbier at the shore. It is hardy in Zones 6 to 9.

Blackjack oak has good tolerance for salt and wind. It also grows naturally in poor, often sandy, acidic soils. Blackjack oaks aren't widely sold in nurseries, although they are available. If you have them on your property, think twice before getting rid of them in favor of showier species.

Quercus alba

Quercus virginiana
Live oak

This is another native that has become a southern classic. Hardy in Zones 8 to 10, live oak is tall and stately inland with wide-spreading branches that come almost to the ground. At the seashore, though, it is often more shrubby, kept lower by the fierce salt winds. But older specimens can be magnificent even near the beach. They can be anywhere from 6 to 40 feet high, depending on conditions.

Live oak grows very slowly and sends a large taproot deep into the ground in search of moisture and nutrients. As the taproot develops, live oak is slow to become established in the garden — it can take three or four years for it to settle in. Live oak needs good drainage and will grow in poor, sandy soil. Fertilize each year in spring with an all-purpose fertilizer. Trees have moderate to good tolerance for salt spray and wind, but generally they do best behind the dunes or at a modest distance back from the water. Live oak can also be planted on the lee side of a dune to help control erosion.

Rhus species

Zones: Vary with species
Exposure: Full sun
Salt Tolerance: Good
Drought Tolerance: Good
Deer Resistance: Good

Sumacs are wild-looking shrubs most at home in naturalistic or informal gardens.

Their brilliant autumn color is arguably their most ornamental feature. They are very tough, and able to tolerate salt wind and spray. They adapt to a range of soils, although their preference is for moist but well-drained soil of reasonable fertility. Sumacs are spreaders and not for small gardens. Use them in windbreaks, to hold soil on a bank or slope, or in dry, stony soil. One note of caution: Make sure you do not bring into your garden poison sumac (*Rhus vernix*), which has whitish fruits. It causes a nasty skin rash in susceptible people. The following sumacs are all natives and are good choices for seaside gardens.

Rhus copallina
Flameleaf sumac

The aptly named flameleaf sumac has glorious autumn foliage of bright scarlet and red. Hardy in Zones 4 to 9, it grows in the wild as a shrub or small tree in acidic, poor soils in the Southeast. It grows to 10 feet high at the seashore, with an interesting spreading form. The compound leaves are divided into up to 21 oblong leaflets that are shiny and dark green in summer and brilliant in fall. Clusters of red fruits are produced on female plants in fall and attract birds.

Flameleaf sumac spreads by suckers to form vigorous colonies and can be a pest in the South. It prefers some moisture but will get by in poor, dry soil. This sumac is less salt tolerant than the others described here and needs some protection from salt wind or the foliage may burn. That said, it can be used to control erosion on the lee side of dunes. Set plants six to eight feet apart.

Rhus typhina

Rhus glabra
Smooth sumac

Hardy in Zones 4 to 9, smooth sumac grows as an upright shrub or small tree to 12 feet high and wide. Its compound green leaves, composed of oblong, toothed leaflets, turn bright orange, red, and purple in fall. Scarlet fruits hang on female plants into winter if the local wildlife doesn't get to them first. This species is good for planting in groups or even masses in poor, dry soil.

RECOMMENDED CULTIVAR
- 'Laciniata' — finely dissected leaflets

Rhus glabra

Rhus typhina
Staghorn sumac

This sumac was named for the resemblance its branches bear to deer antlers. Hardy in Zones 3 to 8, it grows to about 15 feet high and wide. It grows as an open, spreading shrub, or sometimes a small tree. The compound leaves are made up of oblong leaflets with toothed edges. The velvety stems are covered with soft hairs.

Staghorn sumac adapts to many kinds of soil as long as it is well drained; it can't stand soggy ground. It tolerates a good amount of drought. Like other sumacs, this one is not seriously bothered by pests or disease. You can rejuvenate old, overgrown plants by cutting them back to the ground in late winter. Plant staghorn sumac in groups or masses; it is especially useful where little else will grow.

Rosa species

Zones:	Vary with type
Exposure:	Full sun
Salt Resistance:	Varies
Drought Tolerance:	Poor, except *R. rugosa*
Deer Resistance:	Poor

Roses are part of many seashore gardens. With good protection from salt spray and wind, and in soil well amended with compost, many kinds of roses will thrive. Which kinds are right for your garden depends upon your location and the amount of time and effort you want to devote to them.

TYPES OF ROSES

Shrub roses take up the most space but require the least amount of effort from the gardener. Just deadhead them to remove faded flowers and prune as needed to remove dead or damaged growth. Look for stems that are pale and dry and snap when bent, or canes that are shriveled, not firm. Shrub roses make lovely additions to mixed beds and borders.

Hybrid teas are harder to mix with other plants, so many gardeners like to grow them in beds of their own. Low, sprawling perennials such as nepeta, perennial candytuft, dianthus, and lamb's ears and annuals like sweet alyssum and Wave petunias make good companions for hybrid teas and other bush roses. Just don't let them get too close to the base of a rose-bush. Clematis is lovely trained with climbing roses or clambering over shrub roses.

Train climbing roses on trellises, arches, and arbors for beautiful architectural accents in the garden. Rambler roses are lovely trained on a fence or allowed to scramble over the ground.

Hybrid tea roses (hardy in Zones 5 to 10) and climbers (hardy in Zones 4 to 10) need special protection close to the ocean in winter. They also need pruning, and climbers need training, too. Prune hybrid teas in spring, when the weather has settled and they begin to break their buds. For the greatest vigor, remove all but the strongest four or five canes, and cut those back to about eight inches. On climbing roses, cut back to the ground old, woody canes on older plants that have developed bark. Lightly prune other canes, cutting them back by just a few inches.

WINTER PROTECTION

In northern areas, gardeners near the beach may want to protect hybrid teas over the winter by covering them with a loose mulch of salt hay or shredded leaves and sur-rounding the bed with a burlap windscreen. Climbers can be wrapped in burlap and left on their supports where winter temperatures do not drop below –5°F. In colder areas, carefully remove canes of climbers from their support and lay them on the ground. Cover with a loose mulch at least six inches deep, and cover with burlap.

PESTS AND DISEASE

One thing all kinds of roses need by the seaside is good air circulation. Roses are prone to disease, especially black spot and mildew. The heavy, humid summer air and frequent fogs along the coast can provide the perfect environment for disease pathogens to develop. Although some gardeners believe the salty air actually discourages disease, it is wise to allow plenty of room between plants so air can circulate freely. Space hybrid teas, climbers, and ramblers two to three feet apart, and shrub roses four to five feet apart. Use the larger spacing in warm parts of Zone 7 and south.

If Japanese beetles are a problem in your area, be on the lookout for them and take appropriate measures if they appear. Treating lawns with milky spore helps prevent future infestations by killing the larvae that develop under the lawn.

Rosa banksiae

Rosa banksiae
Lady Banks' rose

Southern gardeners in Zones 8 and 9 can grow Lady Banks' rose. This vigorous semievergreen rambler can grow to 15 feet with proper support. Left to its own devices, the thornless stems will ascend to four or five feet, then arch over to trail on the ground. In late spring, plants produce clusters of fragrant, single or double yellow or white flowers.

Lady Banks' rose has some resistance to salt spray, but needs the protection of a windbreak at the beach. It will grow in full sun or partial shade. Some gardeners train it on a trellis or let it climb a tree; others let it spill over a wall. The only pruning it needs is the removal of old stems. Provide mulch or other protection in winter.

Rosa rugosa
Saltspray rose

One of the absolute best roses for the seaside is the saltspray or beach rose, *Rosa rugosa*. Rugosas, hardy in Zones 3 to 10, bloom through much of the summer with gloriously fragrant magenta, pink, white, or yellow flowers. Pink and magenta varieties are generally the most vigorous, yellows the least. The plants are robust, very thorny shrubs to six feet high that tolerate salt and will grow in very sandy soil. They spread by means of suckers and can become a bit of a pest. In fall, large, orange-red hips decorate the plants. Rugosas make a good barrier or screen, and can be planted on the lee side of dunes or on slopes and banks to help control erosion.

RECOMMENDED CULTIVAR
- 'Thérèse Bugnet' — double pink blossoms

Rosa rugosa

Memorial rose

Rosa wichuraiana
Memorial rose

Hardy in Zones 5 to 9, memorial rose is a semi-evergreen shrub with long, vinelike stems that can reach 20 feet. It can be trained on a trellis or fence, or allowed to ramble over the ground as a low, mounded ground cover. The stems will root where they touch the ground if you cover them with soil. In summer, plants bear fragrant, single white flowers with golden stamens. In fall there are red hips. Memorial rose needs some protection from salt winds, but it can take sandy, infertile soil and a fair amount of drought. Try it on a bank or slope.

Ramblers

Rambler roses, with their clusters of small, full flowers, also have good tolerance for wind and salt. Plants produce slender stems 15 or more feet long and are hardy in Zones 5 to 10. You can train ramblers on a fence or use them to cover swales and banks — the stems will root where they touch the ground. They are not fussy about soil. Ramblers bloom on stems produced the previous year. Prune them in spring to remove thin canes that crowd together in the center of the plant. After blooming, cut off at least some of the canes that produced flowers to make room for the stems that will bloom next year. Fasten those new stems into place.

RECOMMENDED CULTIVARS
- 'American Pillar' — deep pink with a white eye
- 'Goldfinch' — yellow
- 'May Queen' — pink
- 'Seagull' — white, fragrant
- 'Veilchenblau' — purple and white

Ramblers

Sabal palmetto
Cabbage palmetto

Zones: 8–11
Exposure: Full sun to partial shade
Salt Tolerance: Good to excellent
Drought Tolerance: Good
Deer Resistance: Good

The state tree of North Carolina, cabbage palmetto grows as far north as about Wilmington, North Carolina, although it is sometimes damaged by cold temperatures in the northernmost parts of its range. This native palm grows slowly to 10 to 20 feet high near the beach and can reach 30 or more feet inland. Its large, fan-shaped, evergreen leaves, each a cluster of narrow, five- to six-foot-long blades, are gathered into a rounded clump atop a straight, narrow trunk. The bases of old leaf stems remain on the trunk as the tree grows, giving the trunk a classic palm tree look. In summer, palmetto bears clusters of creamy white flowers that are followed by small black fruits.

A tough, adaptable plant, cabbage palmetto brings a tropical look to warm-climate landscapes. It can tolerate salt spray, high winds, drought, and sand. It will grow in sand dunes, but does best there if given some fertilizer. Plant the tree as a specimen or accent, or in a row along a driveway or property boundary. Space trees 8 to 10 feet apart.

Cabbage palmetto may need to be staked at planting time, especially in exposed, windy locations, until the roots become well established. Fertilize with a balanced, all-purpose fertilizer at planting time. Water regularly until you see signs of new growth, indicating that the tree has sent new roots into the soil.

Sabal palmetto

Spiraea species

Zones: 4–8
Exposure: Full sun to partial shade
Salt Resistance: Fair
Drought Tolerance: Good
Deer Resistance: Good

Spireas are adaptable, easy-to-grow deciduous shrubs that bloom beautifully in summer.

They thrive in moist but well-drained soil that is reasonably fertile, but will tolerate poorer, drier soils, too. Give them a location in full sun to partial shade and provide some water during extended periods of drought. Spireas have some tolerance for salt, but need the protection of a windbreak near the beach. Use spireas in beds and borders, massed alongside a driveway, or as an informal screen or space divider. Dwarf varieties are nice in rock gardens. Like other plants in the rose family, spireas are sometimes subject to diseases such as mildew and leaf spots and pests including aphids and scales. In my experience, however, both species described here are mostly trouble-free.

Spiraea japonica 'Anthony Watereri'

Spiraea japonica
Japanese spirea

This is a highly variable species, encompassing a range of sizes from two or three to five or six feet high and wide. Plants sometimes listed as a separate species, *S. × bumalda*, are now classified by taxonomists as belonging to this one. You may find them for sale under either name. The plants have oblong leaves with toothed edges and in mid- to late summer, flat-topped clusters of small pink or white flowers appear at the ends of the stems.

RECOMMENDED CULTIVARS

- 'Anthony Watereri' — three to four feet high; has raspberry pink flowers and leaves sometimes edged with cream
- 'Fire Light' — three to four feet high; has pink flowers in summer and red fall foliage
- 'Goldflame' — dwarf, to two and a half feet high; has young leaves that start out reddish, turn golden, then yellowish green, and, finally, orange, red, and yellow in autumn; pink flowers
- 'Little Princess' — dwarf, two to three feet high and four to five feet wide, with pink flowers and red fall foliage

Spiraea × vanhouttei
Bridalwreath spirea

Hardy in Zones 3 to 8, bridalwreath spirea is a tougher plant than Japanese spirea, and just as easy to grow. It forms a tall mound five to six feet high, with graceful, fountainlike stems that arch over toward the ground. In midspring the plants are covered with clusters of tiny white flowers. This species is especially lovely as an informal hedge or screen.

RECOMMENDED CULTIVAR

- 'Pink Ice' — leaves that are pink at first and then change to green and white

Spiraea × vanhouttei

Tamarix ramosissima
Tamarisk

Zones: 3–8
Exposure: Full sun
Salt Tolerance: Excellent
Drought Tolerance: Good
Deer Resistance: Good

Tamarisk is among the most rugged of seashore plants, with excellent tolerance for salt spray, drought, wind, and sand. It prefers poor, infertile soil and will even grow in sand. Reaching to about 15 feet high and 8 to 10 feet wide at the shore, tamarisk has tiny, feathery, aromatic, light green leaves on graceful arching stems. The leaves have glands that secrete salt absorbed by the plant. In early to late summer, depending upon your location, tamarisk produces long, feathery plumes of soft, rosy pink flowers. Tamarisk is fast growing and can take very strong sun. The only quality that argues against it is that in winter, when the leaves are gone, the plant can look awfully weedy.

Tamarisk works well in windbreaks at the beach or as an informal hedge. Space plants three feet apart. Give tamarisk a spot in full sun, in practically any well-drained soil, ideally with an acid pH. Tamarisk blooms on new growth, so do any necessary pruning in early spring.

RECOMMENDED CULTIVARS
- 'Cheyenne Red' — darker pink flowers
- 'Pink Cascade' — vigorous grower with flowers of rich, rosy pink
- 'Rosea' — very hardy, later blooming, rose-pink flowers
- 'Rubra' — rich pink blossoms

Tamarix ramosissima

Taxus cuspidata
Japanese yew

Zones: 4–7
Exposure: Sun or shade
Salt Tolerance: Fair
Drought Tolerance: Moderate
Deer Resistance: Good

Yews are generally somewhat sensitive to salt and wind close to the beach, but this species does better than the rest of them at the seashore. I have seen a row of them growing just feet from the back of the dunes (in improved soil, of course). Nevertheless, Japanese yew is best planted behind a windbreak. Without protection, it will sometimes burn under fierce salt winds, on the side facing into the wind, close to the beach. In time, plants usually recover. Farther from the beach burning is much less of a problem. Japanese yew can take all the pruning and shearing you care to give it, which is why it's traditionally used in formal gardens. Use Japanese yew as a hedge or informal screen, as a specimen plant, in groups, or in a foundation planting or mixed border.

An upright evergreen shrub with soft, needle-like, evergreen leaves, the form varies with cultivar, from columnar to pyramidal, to broad and flattened. Size varies, too. Japanese yew grows slowly. Female plants produce a hard brown seed inside a fleshy red aril.

Japanese yew will grow in sun or shade. It prefers moist but well-drained, sandy loam soil but adapts to a range of soils as long as there is excellent drainage. In cool climates it is moderately drought tolerant; in hot climates it needs summer moisture. One thing this plant will not tolerate is wet feet. It has no serious pest or disease problems. If you grow it as a hedge, trim it in summer and again in early fall.

Taxus cuspidata, trained as pillars

RECOMMENDED CULTIVARS
- 'Bright Gold' — to three feet high, mounding; young needles turn from golden to green
- 'Nana' — to three feet high and six feet wide, dark green needles
- 'North Coast' — round form three to four feet high, six to eight feet wide; drought resistant, olive green needles
- 'Silver Queen' — spreading semidwarf, white-edged new needles appear silvery

Thuja occidentalis
American arborvitae

Zones: 2–7
Exposure: Full sun
Salt Tolerance: Fair
Drought Tolerance: Good
Deer Resistance: Good

Native to eastern North America, arborvitaes are among the most widely planted of evergreens. At the seashore, they hold up well if given some protection from salt spray and wind near the beach. Use arborvitae as a specimen plant or as a hedge or screen. Size and form vary with cultivar. It grows at a slow to moderate rate.

Plants grow best in full sun, in moist but well-drained soil. Once it is established, arborvitae can tolerate drought and heat. If you grow it as a hedge, clip it in spring and again in late summer. Bagworms and spider mites can cause problems.

RECOMMENDED CULTIVARS
- 'Aurea' — small globe or broad cone to three feet high and wide, golden yellow leaves; hardy to Zone 4
- 'Wintergreen' — pyramidal to 30 feet high and 10 feet wide; holds its color well in winter

Thuja occidentalis 'Degroot's Spire'

Zones: *V. angustifolium,* 2–6; *V. corymbosum,* 3–7
Exposure: Full sun to partial shade
Salt Tolerance: Fair
Drought Tolerance: Poor
Deer Resistance: Poor

The two species of blueberries described here can be found in the wild in eastern North America, and offer the rewards of edible fruit and fiery fall color. Both must have acid soil or they will not thrive.

Vaccinium angustifolium

Vaccinium angustifolium
Lowbush blueberry

A low, spreading shrub to two feet high and wide, lowbush blueberry bears clusters of small white flowers in spring and petite sweet berries in summer — the famous Maine blueberries. Hardy in Zones 2 to 5 or possibly 6, lowbush blueberry does well in poor, dry soil as long as the pH is acid. If you can find plants for sale, use them for massing or ground cover in an open space, or include them in informal mixed beds and borders.

Vaccinium corymbosum

Vaccinium corymbosum
Highbush blueberry

This is the blueberry that's widely grown commercially, with different varieties suited to northern or southern gardens. Check with your county Cooperative Extension office to see which varieties are recommended for your area. Plants are dense, compact, and rounded, growing slowly to 6 to 12 feet high and 8 to 12 feet wide. The dark green oval leaves turn yellow, orange, and red in fall. There are clusters of small white flowers in spring, and the berries follow in summer. The ideal soil is humusy, moist but well drained, and acidic. In the wild, highbush blueberry is found in wet, swampy places, but it does well in sandy soil as long as the pH is quite acid. Mulch to conserve moisture. Prune, if needed, after the fruit is picked.

Viburnum species

These two viburnums are good choices for seashore gardens. Both have good to excellent salt tolerance and are attractive landscape plants. Use them in groups or masses, in mixed beds and borders, or for an informal hedge or screen planting.

Vitex agnus-castus

Viburnum dentatum
Arrowwood viburnum

Hardy in Zones 2 to 8, arrowwood viburnum is a big, rounded shrub growing to 8 feet or so high and up to 15 feet wide. A native of eastern North America, it has glossy, dark green, toothed oval leaves that turn yellow, red, or red-purple in fall and flat-topped clusters of tiny white flowers in late spring. In fall, plants produce lots of little blue-black fruits that birds love. Give it a location in full sun to partial or light shade. It adapts to a range of well-drained soils. At the beach, grow arrowwood viburnum behind a windbreak.

RECOMMENDED CULTIVARS

- 'Blue Muffin' — compact, five to seven feet high, rounded form; fruits are rich blue
- 'Chicago Lustre' — rounded, to 10 feet high, glossy leaves turn red-purple in autumn
- 'Northern Burgundy' — upright, 10 to 12 feet high, burgundy leaves

Viburnum dentatum

Vitex agnus-castus
Chastetree

This lovely shrub deserves to be better known. In the northern part of its range, it dies back to the ground in winter like herbaceous perennials do. In the South, it may take the form of a small tree. It grows 6 to 10 feet high and as wide, with aromatic (when crushed), dark grayish green compound leaves composed of five to seven oblong leaflets splayed around a central point. In mid- to late summer the plant bears many long, slender wands of fragrant lavender-blue flowers. White and pink varieties are available, but they are less robust than the species.

Give chastetree a location in full sun, protected by a windbreak near the beach, with moist but well-drained soil of reasonable fertility. Amend very sandy soil with compost before planting. Fertilize with an all-purpose fertilizer after planting, and annually in spring thereafter.

Chastetree makes an elegant specimen plant, or you can incorporate it into a mixed border.

Viburnum tinus
Laurustinus

Hardy in Zones 7 to 10, laurustinus is an evergreen growing about 10 feet high and wide, with glossy, deep green, oval leaves. Small white flowers open from pink buds in winter and are followed by small blue fruits that turn black when they ripen; birds love them. Laurustinus tolerates sun to light or medium shade, and grows best in well-drained, humusy soil, although it is drought tolerant once established.

Viburnum tinus

Perennials

Achillea cultivars
Yarrow

Zones:	3–9
Exposure:	Full sun
Salt Tolerance:	Fair
Drought Tolerance:	Fair
Deer Resistance:	Good

Yarrow is grown for its flat-topped clusters of small flowers in warm shades of yellow, orange, red, and pink, as well as white. Flowers bloom in early to midsummer, and regular deadheading extends flowering of some varieties. The gray-green leaves are ferny and finely divided. Heights range from one and a half to four feet. Good companions are salvia, nepeta, artemisia, daylilies, coreopsis, echinacea, and perovskia.

Yarrow prefers a well-drained, loamy soil of average fertility, but it adapts to a range of soils including dry, sandy ones, as long as drainage is good. Plants need full sun. They hold up well in the wind, but are best behind a windbreak at the beach. Achillea needs little fertilizing; once a year in spring with an all-purpose product should be fine. Yarrow can tolerate heat and a fair degree of drought once it is established, but it appreciates some water during extended spells of dry weather. Cut back plants to the basal mound of foliage after they finish blooming.

RECOMMENDED CULTIVARS
- 'Coronation Gold' — bright gold flowers on two- to three-foot plants
- *A. filipendula* 'Gold Plate' — bright gold flowers on taller plants, to four or five feet
- 'Moonshine' — soft yellow flowers on one-and-a-half- to two-foot plants; does better in northern than in southern gardens; needs some protection from salt winds
- *A. millefolium* 'Cerise Queen' — deep rosy pink flowers; plants spread to form clumps
- *A. millefolium* 'Paprika' — bright orange-red flowers

Achillea cultivar

Armeria maritima
Sea pink, thrift

Zones:	3–9
Exposure:	Full sun
Salt Tolerance:	Fair
Drought Tolerance:	Good
Deer Resistance:	Poor

Sea pink is a small, clump-forming perennial about eight inches high, with a basal mound of narrow, grassy, dark green leaves. In late spring and early summer, plants send out many spherical heads of rose-pink, pink, or white flowers on stiff, slender stems (regular deadheading will keep them blooming longer). Sea pink grows well in a rock garden or at the front of a bed or border. It's a good companion for small sedums, rock cresses (*Arabis* and *Aubrieta*), perennial candytuft (*Iberis sempervirens*), and basket-of-gold (*Aurinia saxatilis*).

This diminutive plant needs well-drained soil of average to poor fertility and does fine in sandy soils. Sea pink will not thrive in heavy, wet soil — it will suffer crown rot. Wind doesn't bother the plant, and while it can tolerate some salt, it is best behind a windbreak near the beach. Otherwise, it's a good choice for coastal gardens.

Armeria maritima

Artemisia species

Zones:	4–9, varies with species
Exposure:	Full sun
Salt Tolerance:	Fair to excellent, depending on species
Drought Tolerance:	Good
Deer Resistance:	Good

The silvery leaves of artemisias are an asset to flower gardens, where the foliage serves as a foil or a softener for the colors of annuals and other perennials. Planting artemisias with pink and blue flowers gives the garden a soft, misty look, especially in northern climes where the sun is less glaring than it is in the South. Surrounding hot red, orange, and yellow flowers with artemisias produces a cooling effect, toning down some of the flowers' intensity. In a garden of many colors, artemisias can soften strong contrasts and make the garden look more unified. The leaves of many artemisias are lacy or feathery, finely cut or dissected, and contribute textural interest as well. Artemisias produce small white or yellow flowers in summer, but many gardeners feel the flowers detract from the plants' appearance and cut them off.

Artemisias range in size from one to three or more feet high, and their leaves are strongly aromatic. They need full sun and well-drained soil of average fertility. Sandy soil suits them just fine. Very good drainage is critical to their success in southern gardens. What they don't like is heavy, soggy soil and continual high humidity. Plants may become floppy or straggly looking in hot, humid weather; if this happens in your garden, cut them back by half to clean them up and to encourage fresh growth. Large artemisias, if you have a lot of them, can be pruned and shaped with hedge shears if they become weedy, but do not cut into the woody base of a plant or you could injure or even kill it.

Most artemisias are moderately salt tolerant, but one species, *A. stelleriana*, is native to sand dunes along the East Coast and has excellent salt tolerance.

Artemisia 'Powis Castle'

This hybrid is very fine textured, forming a two-foot-high clump of feathery, finely dissected silver leaves. It's a beauty, but a vigorous grower; trim it if needed to keep it neat. It does best in Zones 5 to 8.

Artemisia abrotanum

Artemisia abrotanum
Southernwood

Hardy in Zones 5 to 9, southernwood is a four-foot-tall, back-of-the-garden plant. Its divided, ferny leaves are greener than those of many other artemisias but are still grayish.

Artemisia 'Powis Castle'

Artemisia stelleriana
Beach wormwood

This artemisia can be seen growing on the dunes at the beach. It is hardy and adaptable, flourishing in Zones 4 to 9, and is an excellent choice for oceanfront gardens. Plants vary in size from 1 to 2½ feet high, and spread by means of rhizomes to form a mat. The leaves are deeply cut and very silver. This tough customer can handle poor soil, sand, salt, and drought. 'Boughton Silver' and 'Silver Lace' are two attractive cultivars.

Artemisia stelleriana

Artemisia ludoviciana
White sage

White sage, a tall species, can grow four feet high, with narrow, lance-shaped silver leaves. Its salt tolerance is moderate to good. Allow some space for it to spread in the garden.

RECOMMENDED CULTIVARS

- *A. l.* var. *albula* has a fuzzy silver-white leaves
- 'Silver King' — grows two to three feet high, with lance-shaped, silvery leaves; it's a good choice for southern gardens
- 'Silver Queen' — is similar, growing about two and a half feet high and with slightly larger leaves
- 'Valerie Finnis' — also does well in the South, is two feet tall, and its silver-gray leaves have deeply cut edges

Artemisia ludoviciana 'Silver King'

Asclepias tuberosa
Butterfly weed

Zones: 4–9	
Exposure: Full sun	
Salt Tolerance: Fair	
Drought Tolerance: Good	
Deer Resistance: Good	

Butterfly weed (*Asclepias tuberosa*), a relative to milkweed, really does attract butterflies. It's a nectar source for monarchs, among others. It can be a bit weedy looking and is best for an informal garden, but the plant is easy to grow and its brightly colored flowers enliven summer beds and borders or meadow gardens. Possible garden companions for butterfly weed are black-eyed Susan (*Rudbeckia* species), goldenrod (*Solidago* species), asters, purple coneflower (*Echinacea purpurea*), and smaller ornamental grasses.

Butterfly weed grows two to three feet high, with lance-shaped leaves and clusters of yellow-orange to reddish orange flowers in midsummer. Deadhead spent flowers to encourage another round of bloom in late summer.

Give butterfly weed a location in full sun; it can take a bit of shade in southern gardens. As you would expect of a plant native to the midwestern prairies, butterfly weed needs well-drained soil and can withstand a fair degree of drought. It has some salt tolerance and will grow near the beach if given a little protection.

Plants often self-sow, so deadhead them before the fruits mature and drop their seeds to prevent lots of volunteer seedlings. Butterfly weed is late to come up in spring; you might want to mark its location so you remember where it is. Once the plant is established, it does not take kindly to transplanting, so try not to move it.

Two good cultivars to look for are 'Gay Butterflies', with a mix of red, orange, and yellow flowers, and 'Hello Yellow', with bright yellow blossoms.

Asclepias tuberosa

Aster species

Zones: (4) 5–8
Exposure: Full sun
Salt Tolerance: Fair
Drought Tolerance: Fair
Deer Resistance: Good

Asters are a terrific source of late-season color for seashore gardens. Easier to grow and more reliably perennial than the ubiquitous chrysanthemum, asters have a casual look that's well suited to an informal bed or border. The daisylike flowers come in a range of pinks, blues, and purples, along with white. Plants have narrow, linear leaves. Asters look fine with ornamental grasses, goldenrod (*Solidago* species), boltonia, black-eyed Susan (*Rudbeckia* species), 'Autumn Joy' sedum, and *Eupatorium*.

Give asters a sunny location with well-drained soil. To encourage bushier, more compact plants, you can cut or pinch back taller varieties in early summer. Be sure to allow for plenty of air circulation around your asters — crowded plants are prone to mildew and other leaf diseases. Cutting back the plants once — or, in southern gardens, twice — as they grow can also help them avoid mildew problems. But don't cut back after mid- to late July unless you want the plants to bloom later than usual.

Aster carolinianus
Climbing aster

As its common name implies, this southeastern native has vining stems that can grow 10 to 15 feet long. Plants bear yellow-centered lavender flowers in late fall, and may continue blooming into winter in mild southern locations. Hardy in Zones 7 to 10, climbing aster is best suited to mild climates. Cut back the plants in early spring to make way for the new season's growth.

Aster carolinianus

Aster laevis
Smooth aster

This aster is vase shaped and forms clumps of nonbranching stems 3½ to 4 feet high, with grayish green oblong leaves up to 5 inches long. In late summer and into fall, plants bear clusters of lavender-blue flowers with yellow centers. Hardy in Zones 4 to 9, it is native to the eastern and central United States.

Like other members of the clan, smooth aster brings color to the garden when most other perennials have finished blooming.

Aster laevis

Aster novae-angliae 'Fanny'

Aster novae-angliae
New England aster

Another native species, New England aster was long overlooked here, but English plant breeders took to it and developed lots of cultivars, calling them Michaelmas daisies. Now there are New England asters in shades of pink-rose, red, purple, and violet, along with white. Plants grow one to five feet high, depending on the cultivar. They can take partial shade in the South. Hardy in Zones 4 to 8.

Baptisia species
False indigo

Zones: 4–9

Exposure: Full sun

Salt Tolerance: Fair to good

Drought Tolerance: Good

Deer Resistance: Good

False indigos provide the look of shrubs in the garden, but they are really herbaceous perennials that die back to the ground in winter. The plants grow as a bushy clump of upright stems to four feet high, and bear loose spikes of pealike flowers in spring or early summer, depending on the climate. The plants have oblong leaves of bluish green. They are attractive additions to beds and borders of ample size, where they will not look crowded into the space. False indigo can be at home in a garden with yarrow (*Achillea* species), coreopsis, Shasta daisy (*Leucanthemum super-bum*), bearded or Siberian iris, and Russian sage (*Perovskia atriplicifolia*).

Both species discussed here are natives, and grow well in loose, well-drained, sandy soil. To grow them near the beach, though, add some compost to soil that is very sandy before planting. False indigo has decent salt tolerance and can withstand salt wind as long as it is set back from the beach. False indigos tolerate partial shade in warmer climates. To keep the plants from becoming loose and floppy, you can cut back the stems by a foot or so after they finish blooming.

White false indigo (*Baptisia alba*) bears white flowers. Blue false indigo (*B. australis*) has deep blue flowers that are followed by dark, rattling seedpods. This species may take several years to really settle in, but once it does, it's impressive.

Baptisia species

Cerastium tomentosum
Snow-in-summer

Zones: 3–7

Exposure: Full sun

Salt Tolerance: Fair

Drought Tolerance: Good

Deer Resistance: Good

Snow-in-summer is a low-growing spreader that can be a real pest in decent soil, but it's useful in poor, dry soils and windy, exposed locations. The plant forms a low mat of leaves only a few inches high. The leaves are small, narrow, and grayish green, and there are lots of small white flowers in late spring and early summer.

You can use snow-in-summer in the front of beds and borders, to spill over a retaining wall, or in a rock garden. It will cover a bank or slope, too. In the garden it can keep company with small sedums, perennial candytuft (*Iberis sempervirens*), sea pinks (*Armeria maritima*), and plumbago (*Ceratostigma plumbaginoides*).

Give snow-in-summer plenty of sun and well-drained soil. Wet soil and high humidity can cause it to rot. At the beach it does best behind a windbreak or other protection. Shear back plants when they finish blooming to keep them looking neat and to keep the centers of the plants dense and full. Wait until spring, before new growth really gets started, to cut back the plants close to the ground.

Cerastium tomentosum

Zones: (4) 5–9
Exposure: Full sun
Salt Tolerance: Slight to moderate
Drought Tolerant: Fair
Deer Resistant: Good

Perennial garden favorites and for good reason, coreopsis are easy to grow, adaptable, and long blooming; many will flower right through the summer and into autumn if you deadhead them regularly. Most coreopsis are yellow, although there are now also pink- and red-flowered forms, which in my experience are less resilient and not as long lived as the ones described here. All coreopsis tend to be longer lived in northern gardens than in southern ones.

Depending on the depth of your bed or border and the sizes of the other plants in it, coreopsis can go in the middle or near the front of the garden. Good companions are salvia, veronica, nepeta, bee balm (*Monarda*), daylilies (*Hemerocallis*), Siberian irises (*Iris sibirica*), perovskia, and many other perennials and annuals.

Plant coreopsis in full sun, or perhaps partial shade in the South. They need well-drained soil that is not too rich. Coreopsis thrives in hot sun and tolerates a fair degree of drought, although it will need water during prolonged periods of dry weather.

Coreopsis grandiflora

Hardy in Zones 4 to 9, this coreopsis forms a clump of oblong leaves above which rise daisy-like flowers of rich golden yellow, 1½ to 3 feet high. 'Early Sunrise', also grown as an annual, is 1½ feet high, with semidouble flowers; 'Goldfink' is a dwarf, just 8 to 10 inches high; 'Sunburst' has full, double flowers.

Coreopsis grandiflora 'Early Sunrise'

Coreopsis verticillata

Coreopsis verticillata
Threadleaf coreopsis

This is an airy, delicate-looking plant with thin, threadlike leaves on slender, branching stems and daisylike flowers about two inches across. Threadleaf coreopsis keeps on blooming well into autumn.

RECOMMENDED CULTIVARS
- 'Crème Brûlée' — has large, pale yellow flowers on bushy, mounded plants
- 'Golden Shower' — has rich yellow flowers
- 'Moonbeam' — has lovely, soft yellow flowers that mix beautifully with many other flowers in the garden
- 'Zagreb' — has bright golden flowers

Eryngium amethystinum
Amethyst sea holly

Zones: 3–8
Exposure: Full sun
Salt Tolerance: Good
Drought Tolerance: Good
Deer Resistance: Good

Sea hollies are unusual-looking plants. They are not very colorful, but they have an arresting textural presence in the garden. Amethyst sea holly has spiny, pointed leaves and, in late summer, tight, cone-shaped clusters of tiny amethyst or steely blue flowers atop branched stems. It's not the flowers that get your attention, though; it's the spiny, metallic steely blue to silver-green bracts surrounding the stem immediately beneath them that stand out. The bracts look soft and feathery, but they're sharp.

Amethyst sea holly makes an interesting addition to a bed or border. It grows two to two and a half feet high. The bluish color is not as pronounced in southern gardens, perhaps due to the warmer nighttime temperatures.

Despite their name, not all sea hollies do well at the seashore, but this one does. Amethyst sea holly adapts to a range of soils, from ordinary garden soil to poor, sandy beach soils. With a long taproot that stretches deep underground in search of water, it is drought tolerant. It needs plenty of sun. Amethyst sea holly is evergreen in warm climates.

A wild species, sea holly eryngo (*Eryngium maritimum*), grows on sand dunes and beaches, and is sometimes available for gardens.

For an unusual, modernistic planting, you might combine sea holly with silver lavender cotton (*Santolina chamaecyparissus*) and artemisia, and bolder, more sculptural plants like yucca, agave, and phormium.

Eryngium amethystinum

Gaillardia × *grandiflora*
Blanketflower

Zones: 3–8
Exposure: Full sun
Salt Tolerance: Good
Drought Tolerance: Good
Deer Resistance: Good

This blanketflower is a hybrid species that can be short lived in the garden, but it's worth replanting every few years, if necessary, for its long blooming time and ease of care. Plants grow two to three feet high, with daisylike yellow flowers with a maroon central disk and a red band on the base of each petal-like ray. The lance-shaped leaves may be lobed, and are grayish green with toothed edges. Although the plants may not survive for many years, they do self-sow. And they bloom all summer into fall. Use blanketflower in beds and borders, along with perovskia, salvia, achillea (pictured), coreopsis, rudbeckia, and ornamental grasses.

Blanketflower needs lots of sun, and it can tolerate poor, sandy soils. Good drainage, in both summer and winter, is critical to its success. Blanketflower has good salt tolerance and will grow near the beach.

Another species, Indian blanket (*Gaillardia pulchella*), is an annual native to the prairie, growing one to two feet high. Its flowers may be yellow, red, or bicolor, single or double. Indian blanket also does well near the beach, withstanding fierce sun, salt, and very sandy soil.

RECOMMENDED CULTIVARS
- 'Baby Cole' — a dwarf just eight inches high; flowers are mostly deep red, with yellow tips
- 'Burgundy' — deep wine red flowers on plants to two feet high
- 'Goblin' (a.k.a. 'Kobold') — a dwarf 9 to 12 inches high, with yellow-tipped red flowers

Gaillardia 'Goblin' with *Achillea* 'Fanal'

Hemerocallis cultivars
Daylily

Zones: 3–9	
Exposure: Full sun to partial shade	
Salt Tolerance: Fair	
Drought Tolerance: Fair	
Deer Resistant: Poor	

Daylilies are beautiful and versatile, among the most popular of all perennials. They are terrific in beds and borders, or planted in masses along a driveway, in front of a fence or wall, or on a slope. There are thousands of cultivars available, in practically every color except true blue. You can have daylilies in shades of yellow, peach, orange, red, pink, purple, white, even chartreuse and reddish brown. Some have a contrasting central eye, some have ruffled petals, others have narrow, spidery petals. Some daylilies repeat-bloom, and some, such as 'Stella de Oro', bloom all summer. There are early-, mid-, and late-season varieties that range in size from 10 inches to 6 feet high (although many are around 3 feet). Some daylilies are evergreen; these less-hardy varieties are good for southern gardens.

Hemerocallis 'Midnight Magic'

Each daylily flower lasts just a single day, but the plants produce many of them and they open in succession, so every plant flowers for several weeks. The best daylilies for seashore gardens, especially gardens near the beach, are those with shorter scapes (flower stems); the taller varieties are more likely to be damaged by strong winds. Daylilies can handle some salt, but do better behind a windbreak right near the beach. Good partners for daylilies include coreopsis, Siberian iris, phlox, aster, kniphofia, salvia, and many other perennials.

Daylilies will bloom in full sun to partial shade. They appreciate moist but well-drained soil, but they can tolerate some drought. Top-dress your daylilies with compost once a year, and give them a handful of balanced, all-purpose fertilizer in spring. If you have a really tough spot, with poor, dry soil, try growing tawny daylily (*Hemerocallis fulva*), the orange-flowered species that has naturalized along roadsides all over the eastern United States.

Daylilies do require some maintenance to keep them looking fresh and neat. Remove old flowers by twisting them off the plant with your thumb and forefinger. Be careful not to snap off nearby buds at the same time. After the plants have finished blooming, the foliage starts to look ratty. Reach into the mound of leaves to pull out withered and drying leaves. If you have lots of plants, you can use hedge shears to cut back all the leaves. New foliage will grow in by fall, so you won't be left with holes in the garden for a long time.

There are far too many daylily cultivars to even begin to recommend any here. Consult with gardening friends, your county Cooperative Extension office, and knowledgeable nursery personnel for suggestions regarding good varieties for your area.

Hibiscus moscheutos
Rose mallow

Zones: 5–10	
Exposure: Full sun	
Salt Tolerance: Fair	
Drought Tolerance: Poor	
Deer Resistance: Good	

With its huge flowers, rose mallow looks like it belongs in the tropics. But it's a perfectly hardy perennial that grows with gusto and brings bold, late-season color to the garden.

Rose mallow forms an open, loose clump of thick stems five to eight feet tall with green, pointed-lobed leaves. In mid- to late summer there are huge, saucer-shaped flowers to eight inches across in shades of red, pink, and white.

Grow rose mallow in full sun, in moist soil of average fertility. It can tolerate some salt and does fine up on a bluff overlooking a bay, but it's not a good bet for an oceanfront garden unless it has wind protection and soil amended with compost. Plants will need water during dry weather.

Japanese beetles sometimes trouble rose mallow, but deer avoid it. Cut back the stout stems to a few inches above the ground in fall or spring. Plants are slow to get growing in spring, so be patient.

Hibiscus moscheutos

Hosta species and cultivars
Plantain lily

Zones: 3–9	
Exposure: Partial to full shade	
Salt Tolerance: Fair	
Drought Tolerance: Poor	
Deer Resistance: Poor	

Hostas are practically indispensable in shady gardens, even at the seashore. Although they're not good beachfront plants, they can manage if protected from salt spray and wind, and are fine in woodland or shade gardens away from the water.

Numerous species and hundreds of different cultivars are available, ranging from six-inch sprites to four-foot giants with huge, wide leaves. Those leaves can be narrow and lance shaped to broad and round; they may be smooth or puckered and quilted; in shades of green from golden to chartreuse to smoky blue-green; solid colored or streaked, edged, or striped in assorted combinations of green, gold, chartreuse, and creamy white.

In summer to fall, depending on variety, hostas send up stalks of trumpet-shaped white or lavender flowers that are fragrant in some species. Hostas mix beautifully with astilbes, foamflowers (*Tiarella cordifolia*), bleeding hearts (*Dicentra* species), ferns, snakeroots (*Cimicifuga* species), and other shade lovers.

If you have deer on your property, don't plant hostas; it's like setting a salad bar for them. But where deer are not a problem, hostas have myriad uses: large ones can anchor a bed or border, medium varieties can populate the middle ground, and small growers can work as edgers. You can plant hostas under trees or shrubs or mass them as ground covers. Large ones make impressive specimen plants.

Hostas grow best in soil that is moist but well drained and fertile, but they adapt to a range of conditions. When the clumps get too large, you can dig and divide them. Slugs love hostas as much as deer do, and voles can be pests, too, if you have them on your property.

There are hundreds, maybe thousands, of hosta varieties — too many to make recommen-

Hosta 'Blue Angel'

dations here. You'll be sure to find one you like if you visit local nurseries and peruse mail-order nursery catalogs.

Iberis sempervirens
Perennial candytuft

Zones: 3–8	
Exposure: Full sun	
Salt Tolerance: Fair	
Drought Tolerance: Poor	
Deer Resistance: Good	

Perennial candytuft is a low, sprawling, mat-forming plant that is often seen in rock gardens, and can be used at the front of beds and borders. It grows up to a foot high, with small, narrow, dark green, evergreen leaves and, in early spring, dome-shaped clusters of tiny white flowers. It is

Iberis sempervirens

lovely spilling over a wall or tucked into a soil pocket in a dry stone wall. Try it with tulips and daffodils, pansies, basket-of-gold (*Aurinia saxitilis*), and other early bloomers.

This is a plant that likes to bake in the sun in well-drained soil. But it also needs to be watered when the soil dries out. It has some tolerance for salt, but needs the protection of a windbreak near the beach. Amend very sandy soil with compost before planting, to improve fertility and boost humus content. To keep the plants looking neat, cut them back by about one third to a half when they finish blooming. Clubroot can be a problem. Perennial candytuft tends not to do as well in southern gardens as in northern ones.

Kniphofia cvs.
Red-hot poker, torch lily

Zones: 5–9
Exposure: Full sun
Salt Tolerance: Fair
Drought Tolerance: Good
Deer Resistance: Good

Red-hot poker grows as a clump of grassy, arching leaves 1½ to 5 feet high, with spikes of tiny, tubular flowers in shades of red, orange, yellow, pink, or cream on straight, slender stems in early summer. Flowers bloom from the bottom up, and some change color as they mature. Deadheading will keep the plants blooming longer, and some varieties rebloom in late summer or fall. The plants spread by rhizomes to form clumps.

Red-hot poker is a good choice for adding some vertical line to a bed or border. Good companions for it include coreopsis, salvia, gaillardia, nepeta, and Shasta daisy.

Give red-hot poker a place in full sun, with very well-drained soil that is moist in summer but dry in winter. Wet winter soil will surely kill it. Choose the location carefully; kniphofia does not like to be moved once it is established. As the flowers fade, cut back each flower stem to the ground.

RECOMMENDED CULTIVARS

- 'Alcazar' — three and a half feet high, salmon flowers, reblooms, very hardy
- 'Bressingham Comet' — one and a half feet high; orange flowers have red tips, yellow at the base
- 'Earliest of All' — two feet high, rosy coral flowers, reblooms, very hardy
- 'Gold Mine' — three feet high, golden flowers
- 'Green Jade' — five feet high, pale green flowers turn to cream, then white
- 'Primrose Beauty' — three feet high, soft yellow flowers, reblooms
- 'Royal Standard' — three feet high, scarlet buds open to bright yellow flowers, very hardy

Kniphofia 'Royal Standard'

Lavandula angustifolia
English lavender

Zones: 5–9
Exposure: Full sun
Salt Tolerance: Fair
Drought Tolerance: Good
Deer Resistance: Good

Lavender is loved by flower and herb gardeners alike for its beguiling fragrance. Actually a subshrub, not a true herbaceous perennial, lavender is part of many perennial and herb gardens. It can be used for edging or planted along a wall, or, since it takes shearing well, it can be a low hedge. Possible garden companions include coreopsis, dianthus, nepeta, evergreen candytuft (*Iberis sempervirens*, which blooms earlier but likes similar conditions), lavender cotton (*Santolina*), and thyme.

Plants grow one to two feet high and about two feet wide, with narrow, fragrant, gray-green leaves and wands of tiny, fragrant purple flowers in midsummer. Lavender loves the sun, and it must have well-drained soil, preferably with an alkaline pH, to thrive. It cannot tolerate heavy, wet soil in summer or winter. In fact, the two most common causes of lavender demise are wet soil and pruning in fall. Average to poor fertility suits it; wet soil does not. Lavender has some ability to tolerate salt, but it needs to be behind a windbreak when growing near the beach.

If you deadhead lavender, it may reward you with a second, less lavish, round of bloom in late summer. To deadhead, cut off individual flower stems or use hedge clippers. Any other pruning is best done in spring, when new growth has begun and you can see which plants are still viable. Don't prune in fall or plants will not have enough time to harden off before winter.

Every few years, cut back the plants to six to eight inches above the ground to keep them more compact and shapely. But take care not to cut back into very old, woody growth or the plant can be harmed.

Lavandula angustifolia

Limonium latifolium
Sea lavender

Zones: 4–9
Exposure: Full sun
Salt Tolerance: Good
Drought Tolerance: Good
Deer Resistance: Good

Sea lavender looks a bit as though the ocean mist has descended into the garden. The plants take the form of a low basal rosette of leathery, dark green leaves. During mid- and late summer, branched clusters of tiny, papery, lavender-blue flowers bloom on thin stems two feet or more high. The effect in the garden is soft and misty. Grow sea lavender near the front of a bed or border. Because of its airy, delicate texture, you can also plant it as a scrim in front of the garden through which other plants are seen. It is also a good companion for lavender, germander, lavender cotton (*Santolina* species), and thyme. Sea lavender attains a spread of about two feet.

Sea lavender is a sun lover, and it thrives in very well-drained, sandy soil. It can handle salt and wind and generally does well near the beach, as well as farther inland. You can leave old flowers on the plants—they will dry in place. Instead of cutting back the plants in fall like most perennials, wait until the following spring.

RECOMMENDED CULTIVARS
- 'Blue Cloud'—mauve flowers
- 'Violetta'—deep violet blossoms

Limonium latifolium

Monarda didyma
Bee balm

Zones: 3–8
Exposure: Full sun to partial shade
Salt Tolerance: Fair
Drought Tolerance: Poor
Deer Resistance: Good

Bee balm, or bergamot, native to the meadows of the eastern United States, is often found in herb gardens and is a traditional tea plant. These days it is often found in perennial gardens, too, where its shaggy flowers attract bees, butterflies, and hummingbirds. Plants grow two to four feet high, with oval, toothed leaves that have a fresh scent of citrus and mint. From mid- to late summer, the stems are crowned with whorls of tubular flowers surrounded by colorful bracts, in shades of red, pink, purple, and white. They can be three to four inches across. Possible companions include goldenrod and meadow rue (*Thalictrum*).

Monarda didyma

Bee balm grows in full sun to light shade, and needs moist, humusy soil of average fertility. It can't be allowed to dry out in summer. That wouldn't seem to describe a seashore plant, but bee balm does quite well away from the water. Over time, the plants spread to form clumps. Deadheading the plants keeps them blooming over many weeks. One problem that does trouble bee balm is mildew, and that susceptibility makes bee balm a gamble for many southern gardens. Allowing for good air circulation among plants helps minimize it, as does thinning out crowded stems. Mildew usually strikes when the plants are well along in their blooming, and if it becomes too severe, just cut back the plants close to the ground. New leaves will grow but bloom will be over for the season. There are some mildew-resistant cultivars, which are noted below.

RECOMMENDED CULTIVARS
- 'Cambridge Scarlet'—bright red
- 'Croftway Pink'—rosy pink
- 'Jacob Kline'—dark red, mildew resistant
- 'Marshall's Delight'—clear pink, mildew resistant
- 'Violet Queen'—red-violet, mildew resistant
- Another species, wild bergamot (*Monarda fistulosa*), is less showy, bearing pale lavender flowers with purple bracts, but it is more heat tolerant and mildew resistant than bee balm.

Nepeta × faassenii
Catmint

Zones: 4–8
Exposure: Full sun to partial shade; partial to light shade in southernmost gardens
Salt Tolerance: Fair
Drought Tolerance: Fair
Deer Resistance: Good

Catmint is among the easiest and most accommodating of perennials. Not a plant for formal gardens, it is floppy and lax, but its flowers are a soft shade of lavender-blue that goes beautifully with pinks or yellows, and they bloom for quite a few weeks in early to midsummer. Catmint can be charming in the front of a bed or border where it can spill over the edges of a path. It's a good underplanting for roses and a congenial companion for many summer perennials, such as coreopsis, daylilies, achillea, Shasta daisies, peonies, and artemisia.

Catmints are loose, spreading plants ranging from 10 inches to 3 feet high, with aromatic, oval, grayish green leaves with toothed edges. In early to midsummer, they produce loose spikes of lavender-blue flowers. When blooming slows, shear back the plants to promote a new, though spottier, round of flowers. In this case, shearing back the whole plant works better than deadheading individual flowers to promote more bloom. It also helps keep the plants from flopping all over the place.

Give nepeta well-drained soil of average fertility; it can tolerate a range of soils but doesn't like soggy conditions. In northern gardens, catmint likes sun and will tolerate partial shade as well. In the South, a little shade is good for it. Catmint has some tolerance for salt, doing best behind a windbreak near the beach and thriving in many locations away from the water.

RECOMMENDED CULTIVARS
- 'Blue Wonder' — 12 inches high, greener

Nepeta × faassenii

leaves than most nepetas; flowers are larger than other types and bloom longer
- 'Dropmore Hybrid' — to 18 inches high, more upright and less floppy than other nepetas
- 'Six Hills Giant' — to three feet high and as wide, popular and widely planted, a better choice for moist conditions than other catmint varieties
- 'Souvenir d'Andre Chaudron' — 18 inches high, said to do well in southern coastal gardens

Nipponanthemum nipponicum
Montauk daisy, Nippon chrysanthemum

Zones: 5–9
Exposure: Full sun
Salt Tolerance: Good
Drought Tolerance: Good
Deer Resistance: Good

Gardeners in either the North or the South in search of a durable, easy-to-grow plant that offers an alternative to autumn chrysanthemums should consider Montauk daisies. They don't always fit comfortably into beds and borders, although they can work with sedums, asters, and ornamental grasses. But in their brief few weeks

of autumn glory, they make an impression when massed on a bank or slope.

Montauk daisy forms a clump of stems about three feet high (or taller, when not cut back), with fleshy, oblong leaves with scalloped edges. For a few weeks in fall, the plants bear classic yellow-centered white daisies.

This tough-as-nails plant needs sun but can grow in practically any well-drained soil, including poor, sandy ones. It tolerates drought and salt spray and can withstand a lot of neglect. One thing Montauk daisy does need is pruning, or the stems flop over, especially in a wet summer. Cut back the plants to a few inches from the ground every year in fall when plants finish blooming, or early the following spring. If plants are not cut back, they will become progressively woodier,

and eventually you will end up with almost shrublike, unkempt bases with flowers blooming on new growth at the top of the gnarled woody parts. To keep the plants more compact and the stems less floppy, cut back the plants in late spring. Buds usually are not set until fall, so the pruning should not delay bloom.

Nipponanthemum nipponicum

Oenothera species

Zones: Vary with species
Exposure: Full sun
Salt Tolerance: Moderate to good
Drought Tolerance: Good
Deer Resistance: Good

This group of native wildflowers adds color to informal flower beds and borders. Their cup-shaped flowers bloom in early to mid-summer on sprawling plants. Although they tend to spread, they are valuable for their ability to grow in poor soils and tolerate drought. They do not thrive in wet, soggy conditions. Good companions in the garden are blue salvias, daylilies, nepeta, artemisia, and pennisetum.

Oenothera speciosa 'Siskiyou'

Oenothera drummondii

Oenothera drummondii
Beach evening primrose

If you can find it for sale, beach evening primrose is meant for seaside conditions. Hardy only in Zone 8 and south, it thrives in poor, sandy soil and has good tolerance for salt spray and wind. Plants have hairy, gray-green leaves and a sprawling, spreading form. The flowers are pale yellow.

Oenothera fruticosa
Sundrops

Hardy in Zones 4 to 8, sundrops grow from one to three feet high, with lance-shaped green leaves that turn reddish in cool fall weather. The summer flowers are bright, clear yellow. When the plants die back in fall, a low clump of evergreen leaves remains through the winter. Sundrops do best in soil of average fertility — it's a bit more demanding than the other types discussed here. The yellow flowers of the cultivar 'Fireworks' open from red buds. 'Summer Solstice' blooms practically all summer, and its leaves turn red in summer, deepening to burgundy in fall.

Oenothera fruticosa

Oenothera speciosa 'Rosea'
Showy evening primrose

Suited to Zones 5 to 8, showy evening primrose grows about a foot high, with narrow, toothed leaves on arching stems. The pretty flowers are light pink with deeper pink veining, and bloom for a long time in summer. The cultivar 'Siskiyou' has flowers of a richer pink. The plants spread by runners and can become a pest in small gardens. They have naturalized in parts of the South. Showy evening primrose does tolerate poor soil.

Perovskia atriplicifolia
Russian sage

Zones: 5–9	
Exposure: Full sun	
Salt Tolerance: Fair to good	
Drought Tolerance: Good	
Deer Resistance: Good	

This lovely late-season perennial brings a soft haze of misty, lavender-blue flowers to the garden starting in midsummer and continuing into fall. It's a good addition to beds and borders and looks fine with black-eyed Susans (*Rudbeckia* species), salvia, coreopsis, sedum, heliopsis, and ornamental grasses.

Russian sage can grow as high as four feet, though it is often closer to two or three feet. The stems near the base of the plant are woody; it is actually a subshrub, like lavender, rather than a true herbaceous perennial. The aromatic leaves are silvery gray-green in color, finely divided and fernlike. In mid- to late summer, many tall, branched clusters of tiny purple-blue flowers grace the plants, and last for many weeks.

Give Russian sage a sunny spot and well-drained soil of average fertility. It is easy to grow and undemanding. Plants bloom for a long time. Some southern gardeners find that pruning back some of the spent flower stems promotes new growth and fresh bloom. It is generally best to let the plants stand through the winter and cut them back in spring, though you may want to trim them a bit when they finish blooming to give them a neater look. Plants can be slow to start growing in spring, so be patient with them.

RECOMMENDED CULTIVARS

- 'Blue Spire' — to four feet high, with deeper violet flowers
- 'Filigran' — has more finely cut, feathery, silvery leaves
- 'Longin' — more compact and narrow in habit

Perovskia atriplicifolia with *Hibiscus moscheutos*

Phlox paniculata
Garden phlox

Zones: 4 to 8	
Exposure: Full sun to partial shade	
Salt Tolerance: Fair	
Drought Tolerance: Poor	
Deer Resistance: Poor	

Garden phlox is actually a native of the eastern United States, found in the wild from New York to as far south as Georgia. Wild phlox is purple-pink or magenta in color, but garden varieties come in shades of pink, cherry red, salmon, and lilac to purple, as well as white. Plants grow from one and a half to about four feet tall, and if you deadhead them regularly to remove old flower heads, they'll bloom through much of the summer and into fall. The five-petaled flowers, which are fragrant in many varieties, are gathered into rounded or dome-shaped clusters atop tall, straight stems lined with oblong to lance-shaped leaves.

Although garden phlox has only a modest degree of salt tolerance, it flourishes in many seashore gardens. Grow it away from the water, or provide a good windbreak near the beach. The worst problem for garden phlox is a susceptibility to mildew. Seek out mildew-resistant varieties such as 'David', 'Laura', and 'Shortwood'. It is also a good idea to thin crowded clumps, removing some stems to promote better air circulation that can in turn help prevent disease.

Grow garden phlox in full sun to partial shade. Bluer varieties are said to do best with some shade because they tend to bleach out in strong sunlight. Moist, fertile soil is best, so enrich sandy soil with lots of compost, and water plants during dry weather. Tall varieties will need staking to stand up in windy seashore weather. Cut back the plants to the ground in late fall.

Phlox paniculata 'Laura'

Rudbeckia species

Zones: Vary with species
Exposure: Full sun
Salt Tolerance: Fair to good
Drought Tolerance: Good
Deer Resistance: Fair

The familiar black-eyed Susan is ubiquitous in seashore gardens in late summer. The golden, slightly orangey yellow daisy flowers have a dark center and bloom for many weeks, continuing into fall. Black-eyed Susan works best in an informal garden and can keep company with asters, sedums, boltonia, perovskia, and ornamental grasses.

The plants tolerate heat and drought, and grow in average soil. They are generally deer resistant, too, although I have seen them eaten in some gardens. In short, black-eyed Susan is about as foolproof as a perennial can be. It does, however, spread itself around. If you plant it, you will have more and more as years go by. Pull up unwanted seedlings, and dig up the plants when they spread beyond their boundaries. Plants are also sometimes susceptible to mildew. Make sure they get plenty of sun and good air circulation to minimize the risk of trouble. Deadhead the flowers after bloom, or leave the seed heads in the garden for winter interest or for birds to eat. Or cut back flowering stems near the ground after the plants finish blooming.

Rudbeckia fulgida

Rudbeckia fulgida

The parent of many varieties is *Rudbeckia fulgida*, hardy in Zones 3 to 9. It grows two to three feet high and about one and a half feet wide, with lance-shaped, hairy, rather coarse leaves and many flowers from late summer into autumn. The best-known variety is 'Goldsturm', which grows about two feet high.

Rudbeckia 'Herbstonne'

An imposing hybrid often categorized as a cultivar of shining coneflower, *Rudbeckia nitida*, is 'Herbstonne' or 'Autumn Sun'. This impressive plant grows to six feet high, with oblong leaves and many branched clusters of green-centered yellow flowers with down-curved rays atop the tall stems. 'Herbstonne' makes a dramatic statement in the back of the garden, but it will need staking in windy locations.

Rudbeckia hirta

The other most widely grown black-eyed Susan is *Rudbeckia hirta*, which is a short-lived perennial hardy in Zones 3 to 10 that is often grown as an annual. Plants are hairy, even bristly, with oblong to oval green leaves; they grow from one to three feet high. The Gloriosa Daisy group of cultivars comes from this species, with deep red, bronze, or red-brown coloration on their golden rays. Other cultivars are 'Goldilocks', two feet high, double or semidouble flowers; 'Irish Eyes', two to two and a half feet high, with bright yellow rays and a green center; and 'Rustic Dwarfs', to two feet high, with flowers of gold and mahogany.

Rudbeckia hirta

Rudbeckia 'Herbstonne'

Stachys byzantina
Lamb's ears

Zones: 4–8
Exposure: Full sun
Salt Tolerance: Fair
Drought Tolerance: Fair to good
Deer Resistance: Good

The fuzzy, silvery leaves of lamb's ears serve as a softener or blender for strong flower color in beds and borders, and they bring some shimmer to a garden of soft pink, blue, and purple flowers. Lamb's ears have some tolerance for salt, but they need the protection of a windbreak close to the beach. The plant grows as a clump of thick, oblong, green leaves that are covered with soft white hairs. In midsummer a thick stem lined with small purple flowers arises from the middle of the clump. The flowers aren't very attractive; in fact, their appearance actually detracts from the overall look of the plant. In addition, the foliage starts to decline when the flower spike appears. Most gardeners cut off the flowering stems to preserve a better look for the plant.

The two most important environmental considerations for success with lamb's ears are well-drained soil and plenty of sun. Excellent drainage is absolutely critical — the plant will rot in wet or heavy soil. Lamb's ears don't like high humidity, and do not take well to life under overhead sprinklers, either. This would argue against its inclusion in southern gardens, but the cultivar 'Countess Helene von Stein' holds up better than other lamb's ears in heat and humidity.

Given the right growing conditions, lamb's ears don't need a lot of maintenance in the garden. You will want to cut off flower stems as they form, unless you grow the variety 'Silver Carpet', which does not bloom. Remove any leaves that rot or just start to look bad. It is better to wait until the following spring to clean up the plants for the season and remove all the old foliage, rather than doing it in fall.

RECOMMENDED CULTIVARS

- 'Countess Helene von Stein' — sometimes known as 'Big Ears', grows to 10 inches high, with larger leaves than those of the species
- 'Primrose Heron' — has yellow-gray leaves that are really interesting or sickly looking, depending on your point of view
- 'Silver Carpet' — does not bloom, and its leaves are very silver-white

Stachys byzantina

Teucrium chamaedrys
Germander

Zones: 4–9
Exposure: Full sun
Salt Tolerance: Fair
Drought Tolerance: Good
Deer Resistance: Good

Germander is familiar to herb gardeners as one of the plants used in the low hedges that create the patterns in knot gardens. It can also figure into rock gardens and beds and borders. Germander is quite drought tolerant, but it's not a plant for the beach — winter winds would burn the foliage. Away from the water, however, it can be a good choice.

Germander is a low, woody subshrub growing about a foot high and one to two feet wide, with small, glossy, dark green leaves. In summer it bears tiny pink or purple flowers. The plant must have very well-drained soil in order to thrive; it cannot abide soggy conditions. A neutral to mildly alkaline pH is ideal. Germander doesn't take well to very high humidity. Southern gardeners may prefer to grow a different species, the silver-leaved *Teucrium fruticans*, which is suited to Zones 8 to 10. This germander grows two to three feet high and spreads as wide, with light blue flowers in summer. Good companions for germander include santolina, lavender, sea lavender, African daisy (*Arctotis*), and thymes.

Germander takes clipping and shearing well. Shear back the plants to shape them, if you like, after they bloom, but do it by the end of summer so they have time to harden off before the onset of cold winter weather. In spring, cut back the plants to a few inches from the ground if you want to keep them compact, such as for a small hedge. Otherwise, just shear the plants lightly at this time to shape them and remove any stem tips that were damaged over the winter.

Teucrium chamaedrys

Yucca filamentosa
Adam's needle

Zones: 5–10
Exposure: Full sun
Salt Tolerance: Good to excellent
Drought Tolerance: Good
Deer Resistance: Good

The stiff, sword-shaped leaves of Adam's needle make a bold, architectural statement in seashore gardens, both at the beach and farther inland. The leaves point to the sky and provide a strong vertical line that offers a good counterpoint to the softer, rounder forms of perennials or the lower cylindrical shapes of cacti. Yucca has excellent tolerance for salty wind, making it a candidate for inclusion in a windbreak or helping to control erosion on the dunes. In the garden it mixes well with other architectural plants such as palmetto, crested celosias, and New Zealand flax (*Phormium tenax*), along with sedums, sea holly (*Eryngium*), blue lyme grass (*Elymus*), and other ornamental grasses.

Adam's needle forms a clump of pointed evergreen leaves two to two and a half feet high, with curly threads along their edges. In summer a tall, thick stalk of bell-shaped white flowers shoots up from the center of the plant. If plants are not deadheaded, the flowers are followed in fall by nonornamental oblong fruits.

Yucca needs full sun and very well-drained soil. It will rot in wet conditions. The plants demand little in the way of care. They do look best if old flower stalks are cut down when blooming is finished (use lopping shears for the task).

RECOMMENDED CULTIVARS
- 'Bright Edge' — yellow-edged leaves
- 'Variegata' — blue-green leaves edged with white
- 'Color Guard' — leaves have a gold center and edges that turn pink in winter

Yucca filamentosa 'Garland Gold'

Annuals and Tender Perennials

Arctotis × hybrida
African daisy

Exposure: Full sun	
Salt Tolerance: Moderate to good	
Drought Tolerance: Good	
Deer Resistance: Good	

African daisies are native to dry, rocky soils in South Africa. They thrive in hot sun and handle drought with aplomb, which makes them prime candidates for adding color to seaside gardens. They are perennials that usually are grown as annuals in East Coast gardens, and they bloom heartily all summer and well into fall, often continuing beyond the first frost.

The rather sprawly plants grow from 8 to 12 inches high and about a foot wide, with a basal rosette of lobed, silvery green leaves covered with soft hairs, and daisy flowers 2 to 3 inches across, usually with dark-colored or blue centers, on long stems. Flowers come in a range of colors, including clear pink, rose-pink, burnt orange, bright pumpkin orange, soft apricot, gold, yellow, cream, white, burgundy, and purple. The blossoms of older varieties would close in the afternoon and during cloudy weather, but newer cultivars stay open longer.

Grow African daisies in garden beds or borders or in containers. They are good partners for blue lyme grass, blue oat grass, yarrow, catharanthus, lantana, nepeta, snow-in-summer, lavender, and portulaca. Give them a location in full sun with very well-drained soil. The plants will fail in soggy soil. Although they love heat, African daisies do not handle continual high humidity well, making them a better bet for northern gardens than southern ones.

Deadhead the plants regularly in summer to keep the plants producing lots of new flowers. Water only when the soil is dry an inch or two below the surface.

Arctotis × hybrida

Catharanthus roseus
Madagascar periwinkle

Exposure: Full sun to partial shade	
Salt Tolerance: Some	
Drought Tolerance: Good	
Deer Resistance: Good	

Madagascar periwinkle is a colorful little plant that doesn't look nearly as heat and drought tolerant as it is. It's pretty as an edging for a bed or border, and is an excellent source of summer-long color in pots and planters, where it works beautifully with lantana, Victoria salvia, geraniums, petunias, verbena, sweet potato vine, and vinca, among others.

Plants grow 6 to 12 inches high, with dark green oval leaves and flat-petaled flowers, resembling those of phlox, in tropical shades of magenta, pink, lilac, purple, salmon, and white, some with a contrasting eye.

Madagascar periwinkle loves sun, heat, and sandy soil, and it can tolerate drought. Do not plant it outdoors until all danger of frost is past in spring. Although it is a sun lover, it will bloom in partial shade, too. With some deadheading, the plants will bloom all summer.

RECOMMENDED CULTIVARS
- Cooler series — large flowers in a range of colors including pink, lavender, and white, some with a contrasting eye
- Pacifica series — includes a red, as well as several shades of pink, rose, lavender, and white
- 'Parasol' — grows eight inches high, with white flowers with a deep red eye
- 'Santa Fe Deep Salmon' — has salmon-pink flowers

Catharanthus roseus

Celosia argentea var. cristata

Exposure: Full sun
Salt Tolerance: Fair
Drought Tolerance: Poor
Deer Resistance: Poor

Celosias count among their number some of the weirdest-looking flowers in the plant world. They can be real conversation pieces, and make your garden look like a science project. For the less flamboyant souls among us, there are also celosias with plumelike flowers that work very well with other garden flowers. Try them with yuccas, phormium, and other spiky-leaved plants. Or combine them with round or daisylike flowers. They can also work in a garden with ornamental grasses in the background.

Celosias grow from eight inches to four feet high, depending on the variety, with oval to lance-shaped leaves. The flowers come in many warm colors — shades of red, rose, pink, orange, gold, yellow, and white.

They need full sun and warm temperatures; so do not plant them out until all danger of frost is past in spring and the soil has warmed. Celosias need well-drained soil but they don't like to get too dry; water during spells of dry weather. They stand up nicely to heat and humidity.

This is a confusing group of plants, taxonomically speaking. You may see variations in nomenclature in different places, but here are the main groupings.

Cristata Group

These are really oddball flowers — they can look like alien life-forms beamed in from across the galaxy. The flower heads resemble the combs of roosters, fans with ruffled edges, brains, or coral, or just impossible-to-describe curled and twisted things. The colors include lurid magentas and brilliant reds. Childsii Group is similar and sometimes included with this one.

RECOMMENDED CULTIVARS
- 'Big Chief Mix' — three feet high, twisted, rounded flower heads in red, pink, and yellow

Cristata Group

- Olympia series — dwarf, eight inches high, with fan-shaped flowers in shades of red and yellow

Plumosa Group

Plumosa Group has the most appealing (to my eye) varieties, with feathery, plumelike flowers.

RECOMMENDED CULTIVARS
- 'Apricot Brandy' — two feet high
- Castle series — 12 inches high, 8-inch-long, feathery plumes in several colors: pink, yellow, orange, and scarlet
- 'New Look' — to one and a half feet high, with reddish bronze leaves and deep scarlet flowers

Plumosa Group

Spicata Group

Spicata Group, also called wheat celosias, have narrow, plumy flower spikes on branched stems atop the plants.

RECOMMENDED CULTIVARS
- 'Flamingo Feather' — two to three feet high, pink flowers that fade to cream as they age
- 'Flamingo Purple' — three to four feet high, rosy purple flowers and purple leaves
- 'Pink Candle' — two to three feet high, rosy pink flowers

Spicata Group

Cosmos species

Cosmos are charming additions to summer flower gardens and cottage gardens. The slender stems and finely cut leaves give the plants a rather willowy grace until late in the season, when they start to look weedy. The bowl-shaped flowers come in shades of pink, crimson, white, yellow, orange, and maroon. Sometimes they self-sow. In the garden, cosmos work well with annuals like celosia, lantana, and four-o'clocks, and with such perennials as heliopsis, daylilies, sea lavender, perovskia, salvia, and black-eyed Susan. They also do well in containers.

Give cosmos a location in full sun, with well-drained soil of average fertility. They grow well in sandy soils and can tolerate a fair amount of drought. Cosmos need some protection near the beach but are reasonably salt tolerant. Regular deadheading keeps the plants blooming, but they do begin to look straggly by fall.

Cosmos atrosanguineus

Cosmos atrosanguineus
Chocolate cosmos

Perennial in Zones 7 to 10, chocolate cosmos grows as an annual elsewhere. It gets to be about 2½ feet high, with divided, fernlike leaves and velvety maroon flowers with reddish brown centers. The flowers really do smell like chocolate.

Cosmos sulphureus

Cosmos bipinnatus

The most familiar type of cosmos, *C. bipinnatus* grows three to four or more feet high. The leaves are thin and threadlike, and flowers may be pink, rose, white, or crimson.

RECOMMENDED CULTIVARS
- 'Seashells' — petals are rolled into tubes
- 'Sensation' — grows three feet high, with large pink or white flowers
- 'Sonata' — shorter, one to two feet high, in red, pink, or white

Cosmos bipinnatus 'Sensation'

Cosmos sulphureus
Golden cosmos

This cosmos produces semidouble yellow or orange flowers on two- to three-foot plants.

RECOMMENDED CULTIVARS
- 'Bright Lights' — gold, red, and yellow
- Cosmic series — double flowers in orange, yellow, and gold
- Klondike series — one to one and a half feet high
- 'Lemon Twist' — soft yellow flowers, a different color for cosmos

Dahlia cultivars
Dahlia

Exposure: Full sun
Salt Tolerance: Good
Drought Tolerance: Poor
Deer Resistance: Poor

Dahlias are excellent additions to seashore flower gardens and containers. Use tall varieties near the back of the garden and shorter ones closer to the front. The plants bloom nonstop all summer until frost shuts them down; they reach their peak in many gardens in August and September. There's a range of warm colors avail-

Dahlia 'Jitterbug'

able: shades of red, rose, pink, yellow, orange, and white, and a variety of flower forms — from small, round pompoms to single and daisylike to slender petaled and spidery. The flowers come in many sizes, too, although the big dinner-plate types are hard to mix with other plants in the garden. Plants range in size from foot-high dwarfs to three- and four-footers. Use dwarf dahlias in the front of garden beds and borders or in pots. Taller varieties can go into the middle ground of a sunny bed or border, or you can combine them with other annuals in large containers. Dahlias combine well with daisylike flowers such as coreopsis, spiky blossoms like salvia and veronica, small-flowered baby's breath and *Verbena bonariensis*, and many other flowers.

Dahlias are not true annuals; they grow from tuberous roots that are tender — they must be dug and stored indoors over winter except in very warm climates where the ground does not freeze. Plants grow best in soil that is fertile and moist but well drained. Amend soil with compost in fall for planting the following spring. Good drainage is important; dahlias will rot in soggy soil.

If you are starting with tubers, plant them in the garden in spring, when the danger of heavy

frost is over (a few weeks before the average last frost date in your area). Place the tubers deep enough that the "eyes," or growth buds, are two to four inches below the soil surface. Set in dahlia plants from the nursery outdoors when all danger of frost is past. Set plants in the garden at the same depth they were growing in their nursery pot.

As the plants grow, pinch off the stem tips when there are four sets of leaves on the stems; pinch back to the next set of leaves. Pinching will result in bushier plants with more flowers.

Like many annuals, dahlias are heavy feeders. Feed them every couple of weeks with a balanced, all-purpose fertilizer. Water plants during dry weather. Plants growing in containers may need daily watering during hot weather, depending on the size of the pot. Tall varieties may need staking.

To store dahlia tubers for replanting next year, dig them in fall after the first couple of light frosts. Cut back the stems to five or six inches, and when the soil is dry, brush it off the tubers. Store in a cool place indoors over winter, in peat moss.

There are far too many dahlia varieties to make recommendations here. Visiting local nurseries and investigating mail-order catalogs will give you numerous choices.

Euphorbia marginata
Snow-on-the-mountain

Exposure: Full sun to partial shade
Salt Tolerance: Moderate
Drought Tolerance: Good
Deer Resistance: Good

Snow-on-the-mountain, a relative of the poinsettia, is primarily a foliage plant. Its white-edged leaves, some of which are mostly white, can inject sparkle into a garden that contains lots of deep-colored flowers and dark green foliage.

The branched plants grow two to three feet high; pinching back the stem tips when plants are young promotes bushier growth. Tiny white flowers cluster in the leaf axils in late summer, but they are not particularly decorative. Plants may need staking in warm climates.

Give plants full sun and well-drained soil of average to poor fertility. Do not plant outdoors until frost danger is past. Plants don't need much except for some water during prolonged dry spells. The white sap in the leaves and stem is toxic when ingested and is a skin irritant for many people; wear gloves if needed.

Euphorbia marginata

Lantana cultivars
Lantana

Exposure: Full sun
Salt Tolerance: Good
Drought Tolerance: Good
Deer Resistance: Good

Lantana is a woody-stemmed perennial that is hardy in the warmest climates but is grown as an annual in most East Coast gardens. Plants grow one to three feet high and have dark green, rather coarse-textured, toothed, oblong leaves. Throughout the summer they bear many dome-shaped clusters of little flowers in warm shades of red, orange, gold, yellow, pink, lavender, and white. There are solid colors and bicolors. Some varieties change color as the flowers mature, so individual flower heads may be two or three different colors at once. The flowers attract butterflies.

Lantana cultivar

Use lantana in the front of an informal bed or border, or grow it in containers or window boxes where it can cascade over the edge. Good companions for lantana are verbena, salvia, coreopsis, achillea, geraniums, petunias, butterfly weed (*Asclepias tuberosa*), and nepeta.

Lantana needs full sun and adapts to a range of soils. It does best in well-drained soil but will tolerate moister conditions, too, as long as the soil is not continuously soggy. The best bloom usually occurs in sandy or gravelly soils that are low in nutrients. Plants will also tolerate partial shade. Lantana generally does well near the beach, and holds up well in summer heat. If lantana is hardy where you live, don't cut it back in fall; instead, wait until early the following spring. Aphids and whiteflies sometimes cause trouble for lantana.

RECOMMENDED CULTIVARS
- 'Alba' — white flowers on trailing stems to three feet
- 'Feston Rose' — pink and yellow flowers
- 'Gold Mound' — variegated yellow leaves, golden yellow flowers
- 'Patriot Rainbow' — multicolored flowers of red, orange, yellow, and purple; 'Confetti' is very similar
- 'Tangerine' — orange and yellow-orange flowers

Lobularia maritima
Sweet alyssum

Exposure: Full sun to partial shade
Salt Tolerance: Fair
Drought Tolerance: Poor
Deer Resistance: Good

These sweet little plants have many uses in the garden. They are classic edging plants, and are widely grown in pots, window boxes, and hanging baskets, where they can spill over the edges. Less common but quite delightful ways to use sweet alyssum are as a carpet under spring bulbs, taller perennials and annuals, or roses; between paving stones in a patio or path; and as an annual ground cover in an area that does not get foot traffic.

Sweet alyssum grows just 3 to 6 inches high and 8 to 12 inches wide, forming a low mat of small, oblong green leaves. The plants bear many clusters of small, white, honey-scented flowers. There are also pink- and purple-flowered varieties.

Sweet alyssum grows best in cool weather. It will bloom through the summer, too, although it does not like heat. If bloom slows and plants begin to look ragged in midsummer, shear then back to promote fresh growth and renewed bloom. In southern gardens, sweet alyssum is fine in winter and spring gardens, but doesn't do well in summer heat.

Give sweet alyssum well-drained soil of average fertility, in full sun or partial shade. Water during spells of dry weather. Sweet alyssum will self-sow if its location suits it.

RECOMMENDED CULTIVARS
- Easter Bonnet series — flowers in purple, lavender, violet, rose, and dark pink
- 'Rosie O'Day' — six inches high, with rose-pink flowers
- 'Snow Crystal' — six to nine inches high; white flowers are larger than those of most other varieties
- 'Violet Queen' — deep violet flowers

Lobularia maritima

Pelargonium × *hortorum*
Geranium

Exposure:	Full sun
Salt Tolerance:	Fair to good
Drought Tolerance:	Poor
Deer Resistance:	Good

Geraniums are the most widely grown annuals in American gardens, and they perform well in a variety of situations. At the seashore they grow happily even near the beach. A location behind the dunes or a windbreak is ideal if you are on the ocean, but I have seen them flourishing on the exposed upstairs deck of a house right behind the dunes. Away from the water, they just need a sunny spot.

Geraniums are most often grown in containers, where they are excellent for adding volume to pots. In a large container you can combine them with spiky Victoria salvia, dracaena or a small fountain grass (*Pennisetum*) for height; some smaller fillers such as calibrachoa or million bells, narrow-leaved zinnia, lobelia, and sweet alyssum; with trailing vinca, Wave petunias, or sweet potato vine to spill over the edges. Geraniums can work as bedding plants, too, in formal or informal gardens.

Geraniums have rounded to kidney-shaped, lobed leaves that may or may not have the dark purplish, orange, or yellow bands, or zones, that gave rise to the name "zonal geranium." The round flower heads come in a range of warm shades — red, scarlet, rose, pink, salmon, and white. The plants grow one to two feet tall, with an equal spread.

Geraniums need lots of sun to do their best. Give them moist but well-drained, fertile soil that is rich in organic matter. Deadhead regularly to keep the plants blooming—they will continue until frost shuts them down.

Geraniums are usually trouble-free, although virus diseases can afflict them, as can aphids and whiteflies. Mildew and rot can occur when soil is poorly drained or plants are overwatered.

RECOMMENDED GROUPS

- Americana series — vigorous, with medium green leaves and flowers in a range of colors; Eclipse series is similar, but the plants are smaller and the leaves more bronzy
- Candy series — dark green leaves and plants with names like 'Bubblegum' (single flowers combining magenta and deep pink), 'Cotton Candy' (semidouble salmon pink flowers), and 'Lollipop' (semidouble coral-red flowers)
- Orbit series — widely available and comes in 17 colors
- Tango series — has zoned leaves and flowers in deep red, red, orange, salmon, and violet

Orbit series pelargoniums

Petunia × hybrida
Petunia

Exposure: Full sun to partial shade
Salt Tolerance: Fair
Drought Tolerance: Poor
Deer Resistance: Good

Petunias are colorful and easy to grow, and they come in a broad range of colors and several different sizes and flower types. Colors include many shades of purple, rose, pink, salmon, red, and white, plus some yellows. True blue is hard to find; although numerous cultivars are called "blue," most of them, to my eye, are more violet.

Petunias are terrific in pots, planters, window boxes, and hanging baskets, and they are useful in the front of beds and borders, too. Trailing kinds can even serve as ground covers in areas that get no foot traffic. Probably the greatest drawback to petunias is that they take a pounding during heavy rain and can look bedraggled for days afterward.

The most familiar and widely grown petunias are cultivars of the hybrid species *Petunia × hybrida*. At the seashore, the smaller, single, multiflora types generally hold up better than the big, ruffly grandiflora varieties, which can look tattered and disheveled after doing battle with strong winds and heavy rains. The trailing Wave varieties are vigorous and free blooming, but they tend to peter out and look bad toward the end of summer. An old-fashioned trailing species, *Petunia integrifolia*, stays attractive and vigorous longer than the Wave varieties, at least in my experience. Its dark-eyed, purple-pink flowers continue blooming nicely into fall. Calibrachoa, or million bells, which is like a miniature petunia with a cascading habit, also does well at the seashore and is terrific in hanging baskets and pots.

Good companions for petunias are salvia, celosia, marigolds, marguerites (*Argyranthemum frutescens*), catharanthus, New Guinea impatiens, lantana, and tradescantia.

Plant petunias in full sun to partial shade, in well-drained soil. They will tolerate poor, sandy soils as long as you fertilize them regularly. Frequent deadheading will keep the plants blooming. In late summer, when the stems get long and floppy, especially on Wave petunias, start cutting them back by half, a few stems at a time, to promote fresh growth and renewed flowering.

Petunias may be attacked by botrytis or tobacco mosaic virus, aphids, and whiteflies.

RECOMMENDED GROUPS
- Carpet series — these multiflora types are especially heat tolerant and good for southern gardens
- Celebrity series — comes in more than 20 colors, including bicolors, flowers with contrasting veining, and some with a central star
- Supermagic series — larger than average plants, in a good range of flower colors
- Surprise series — low and mound forming, and good bloomers
- Wave petunias (which are actually multifloras) — bloom on long, vining stems in purple, magenta, pink, white, rose, or lilac

Wave petunias with purple tradescantia

Phormium tenax
New Zealand flax

Exposure: Full sun to partial shade
Salt Tolerance: Fair
Drought Tolerance: Poor
Deer Resistance: Good

New Zealand flax makes a great foliage accent where you want a vertical line and bold, spiky, sword-shaped leaves. It is hardy in Zones 8 and south, but everywhere else we grow it as an annual. The leaves of different cultivars come in various colors and combinations of colors. The leaves of some varieties are longitudinally striped or infused with pink, red, orange, yellow, or white. The most common sizes available seem to be two to three feet high, although there are varieties ranging from one to six feet. You can use phormium in beds and borders or large contain-ers. They lend a contemporary or tropical touch to the garden. Try them with hibiscus, cannas, castor bean (*Ricinus communis*), yucca, dahlias, celosia, or salvia.

Give New Zealand flax full sun to partial shade and moist but well-drained, humusy soil of average to good fertility. Shade is especially good for them in southern gardens where the strong sun can tend to fade the colors. The plants are easy to care for — they need no deadheading or staking. At the end of the season, you can bring them indoors in pots to a bright room to use as houseplants.

RECOMMENDED CULTIVARS
- 'Apricot Queen' — two to three feet high; leaves are infused with apricot-orange and striped in yellow and green
- 'Atropurpurea' — to six feet, with bronzy purple leaves
- 'Aureum' — green leaves striped with yellow
- 'Bronze Baby' — two to two and a half feet high, with bronze leaves
- 'Dazzler' — three feet high, arching leaves striped in orange, pink, and red
- 'Flamingo' — pink, green, and yellow leaves

Phormium tenax

Portulaca grandiflora

Portulaca grandiflora
Rose moss

Exposure: Full sun
Salt Tolerance: Good
Drought Tolerance: Good
Deer Resistance: Good

These tough little plants, with their warm-colored flowers, are at their best in the front of dry, sunny beds and borders. Good companions include lantana, smaller artemisias, dusty miller, coreopsis, yarrow, nepeta, perovskia, and African daisy. Rose moss is a low, sprawling plant to six or eight inches high, with succulent, fleshy, needle-like leaves and ruffly, cup-shaped flowers in many shades of red, rose, pink, orange, yellow, and white. The flowers close up at night and on rainy days.

Portulaca loves the sun, and withstands heat and drought with no problem. What it doesn't like is humidity, so it's not a great performer in southern gardens. Give it well-drained, sandy soil of average to poor fertility. It has good salt tolerance and will grow near the beach. In humid conditions, rose moss is prone to rot or disease, but otherwise it is generally trouble-free. Plants often self-sow in conditions to their liking.

RECOMMENDED CULTIVARS
- 'Calypso Mixed' — with double flowers in bright, hot colors
- Sundance hybrids — large, double flowers in many bright colors on semi-trailing plants; the flowers remain open into the evening
- Sundial series — varieties that perform better in cooler, cloudier conditions, with double flowers in a good range of colors

Salvia species

Exposure: Full sun to partial shade
Salt Tolerance: Fair
Drought Tolerance: Poor
Deer Resistance: Good

The two tender sages described here are both good choices for coastal gardens. Red-flowered varieties look best when planted by themselves as a group or combined with white flowers, foliage plants such as dusty miller and snow-on-the-mountain, or lots of green foliage to tone down their bright colors. Or you can use them sparingly as accents in beds and borders of softer-hued flowers. White-flowered sages can mix with many other annuals and perennials.

Salvia splendens

Salvia coccinea
Texas sage

A perennial in Zones 9 and south, Texas sage is an annual for the rest of us. The bushy plants grow one to two feet high, with oval green leaves and loose spikes of cherry red, coral or white flowers all summer. It looks similar to the very familiar scarlet sage, but the plants are bushier and more compact. A good plant for informal beds and borders, Texas sage attracts butterflies and sometimes hummingbirds.

Texas sage is easy to grow in full sun to partial shade in the North, with afternoon shade in the South, in almost any well-drained soil.

RECOMMENDED CULTIVARS
- 'Cherry Blossom' — bicolored flowers of salmon and white
- 'Coral Nymph' — red and white flowers
- 'Lady in Red' — flowers of brilliant scarlet
- 'Snow Nymph' — with white flowers

Salvia coccinea

Salvia splendens
Scarlet sage

This often-used sage figures into many municipal park and roadside plantings. The flaming scarlet flowers can be hard to mix comfortably with other colors in the garden, but surrounding it with lots of green and white helps tone it down. There are also varieties with pink, purple, and creamy white blossoms that are easier to work with. Plants grow six inches to two feet high, depending on variety, with dark green oval leaves.

Scarlet sage can fade in intense sun; planting in partial shade can help the flowers hold their color better. Give them moist but well-drained soil of good fertility. Pinch the stem tips of young plants to promote bushier growth.

RECOMMENDED CULTIVARS
- 'Blaze of Fire' — lighter green leaves, red flowers
- 'Bonfire' — two to three feet high, scarlet flowers
- Empire series — comes in purple, red, rose-pink, burgundy, salmon, and white
- 'Flare' — grows to one and a half feet and has tall scarlet-red spikes
- Sizzler series — flowers of red, burgundy, lavender, purple, salmon, white, and a salmon-and-white bicolor

Senecio cineraria
Dusty miller

Exposure: Full sun to partial shade	
Salt Tolerance: Good	
Drought Tolerance: Good	
Deer Resistance: Good	

What artemisias do for perennial gardens dusty miller does for annual beds and container plantings. The silvery white leaves soften color contrasts in the garden, tone down bright, hot colors, and blend mixtures of colors. Dusty miller is especially pretty with pink and blue flowers. Plants grow from about 10 inches to 2 feet high, with silver-white leaves whose edges are cut and filigreed.

Dusty miller thrives in full, baking sun, but it can also handle partial or even light shade. Too much shade, however, will cause the leaves to lose their whiteness and turn green. The plants have no trouble with heat and are quite drought tolerant. They don't hold up well in high humidity. They can withstand wind and salt spray and grow well near the beach. You can grow them in practically any soil, as long as it is not soggy. Pinch the stem tips when plants are young to encourage bushier growth. If the plants bloom, remove the yellow flowers to preserve the best foliage quality (the flowers aren't very ornamental). Plants sometimes winter over in southern gardens.

RECOMMENDED CULTIVARS
- 'Cirrus' — eight inches high, very white leaves
- 'New Look' — 8 to 10 inches high; very white, somewhat broader leaves
- 'Silver Dust' — 10 to 12 inches high, an old variety with silvery, deeply cut leaves
- 'Silver Lace' — to 15 inches high; leaves are finely cut and lacier than those of 'Silver Dust'

Senecio cineraria

Strobilanthes dyerianus

Strobilanthes dyerianus
Persian shield

Exposure: Full sun to partial shade	
Salt Tolerance: Moderate	
Drought Tolerance: Poor	
Deer Resistance: Poor	

Persian shield deserves to be better known. A shrubby plant in its native Burma, it is an annual or greenhouse plant for American gardeners. Grow this plant for its stunningly beautiful leaves. They are oval to lance shaped with toothed edges, and up to six inches long. The upper surface is a bronzy green but is covered in magenta-purple and overlaid with a silvery sheen — the effect is one of shimmering iridescence. On the underside, the leaves are a darker purple.

Over the course of a growing season the plants will grow tall — to three feet or even more. Pinching them while they are young will promote more branching, but the plants will still be upright rather than full and bushy. Use them as vertical accents in containers or in the middle ground of a bed or border. Persian shield produces tubular blue flowers in autumn when grown in a greenhouse, but you probably won't see them in a summer garden.

Persian shield does best away from the water or behind a windbreak, although it does have a reasonable degree of salt tolerance. It likes sun but appreciates some afternoon shade, especially in southern gardens. Give the plant moist but well-drained soil of reasonable fertility; feed it once a month if you grow it in a container. Persian shield does poorly in cool weather, so wait until the weather warms in spring before planting it outdoors.

Exposure: Full sun	
Salt Tolerance: Fair	
Drought Tolerance: Good	
Deer Resistance: Good	

Cheerful marigolds are garden stalwarts, with a role to play in beds and borders and containers. Marigolds look good with other red, orange, and yellow flowers such as coreopsis and gaillardia, and also with blue flowers like salvia and bachelor's buttons (*Centaurea cyanus*) or purples including verbena and petunias. They love the sun, although signet marigolds will also grow in partial shade. All three tolerate poor, well-drained soil, but signet marigold prefers even moisture while the other two like it drier. Rich, fertile soil is not recommended for any marigolds — it makes them floppy and weak, and they won't bloom as well. Deadhead often to keep the plants blooming and looking neat. There are three main types of marigolds, and many cultivars within those types.

Tagetes erecta
African marigold

This largest of the marigolds grows one to four feet high and has yellow, orange, or creamy white flowers two to four inches across. The leaves are dark green and deeply divided, with a strong aroma. The plants tend to grow as one or two straight stems unless you pinch them when they are young to encourage bushiness. Use the tallest ones in the back of the garden; smaller ones can go into the front of a bed or border, or in pots, tubs, or window boxes.

RECOMMENDED CULTIVARS
- Crush series — 10 to 15 inches high, large, double yellow or orange flowers
- Discovery series — 8 to 10 inches high, compact and heat tolerant, orange or golden yellow flowers need no deadheading
- Inca series — 14 inches high, orange, yellow, or gold double flowers, heat tolerant, hold up well in rain
- 'Snowball' and 'French Vanilla' — both are creamy white

Tagetes patula
French marigold

These are the smallest marigolds, growing 6 to 12 inches high. They sport 1- or 2-inch flowers in golden yellow, orange, or bicolors including brownish red. The plants are naturally bushy and need less pinching than African marigolds.

RECOMMENDED CULTIVARS
- Bonanza series — 10 to 12 inches high, double flowers, early blooming
- 'Bolero' — 12 inches high, gold-edged maroon petals
- Bounty series — 10 inches high, good for hot, humid climates; gold, orange, yellow, and bicolor flowers
- Disco series— 12 inches high, single flowers in various bicolor combinations

Tagetes tenuifolia
Signet marigold

Intermediate between the previous two is the signet marigold, which grows from 8 to 18 inches high but has the smallest flowers. The finely cut, feathery foliage has a pleasant, citrusy scent, and the yellow or orange flowers, if you grow them organically, are edible. The plants are looser and less rigidly upright in form than the other two types.

RECOMMENDED CULTIVARS
- 'Lemon Gem' — 6 to 12 inches high, single yellow flowers
- 'Tangerine Gem' — 6 to 12 inches high, single orange flowers
- 'Starfire Mix' — single, bicolor flowers in orange, red, and yellow

Tagetes 'Tangerine Gem'

Tropaeolum majus
Nasturtium

Exposure: Full sun	
Salt Tolerance: Fair	
Drought Tolerance: Poor	
Deer Resistance: Good	

Nasturtiums grow on long, sometimes trailing stems that can sprawl over the ground, spill over the side of a container, or scramble up a shrub (see photo at right). The bright, warm-colored flowers are delightful in informal flower beds and borders, in a cottage garden, or in a kitchen garden. They're edible, too, as are the round, blue-green leaves, which have a peppery tang similar to watercress, to which nasturtium is related. Flowers bloom in shades of red, rose, pink, orange, gold, creamy white, and mahogany.

Give nasturtiums a place in full sun in the North; in the South they do better with some afternoon shade. They need well-drained soil of average to poor fertility; in rich soil there will be few flowers. Nasturtiums may slow down and sulk in summer, but if you can keep them going, they will come roaring back in fall. The plants don't like to be disturbed, so sow seeds where you want the plants to grow, or transplant them with care.

RECOMMENDED CULTIVARS

- 'Alaska' — to 15 inches high, leaves splashed with white, flowers in various colors
- Climbing Hybrids Improved — to five feet, many colors
- 'Empress of India' — 12 inches high, with non-trailing, orangey red flowers
- Gleam series — trailing plants with double red or yellow flowers
- 'Jewel Mix' — 12 inches high and non-trailing, semidouble flowers in mixed colors
- 'Jewel of Africa' — similar to 'Alaska', but with trailing stems

Tropaeolum majus

Zinnia angustifolia
Narrow-leaved zinnia

Zinnia angustifolia

Exposure: Full sun	
Salt Tolerance: Fair	
Drought Tolerance: Good	
Deer Resistance: Poor	

Narrow-leaved zinnia is a smaller, less flashy plant than the more familiar common zinnia (*Zinnia elegans*). That makes it better able to withstand the heat, humidity, and drought it will encounter near the sea. It is less prone to the mildew and foliar diseases that disfigure its larger, showier relatives. Narrow-leaved zinnia grows 12 to 15 inches high, with slender leaves and small, single flowers of yellow, orange, or white. It's charming in the front of a bed or border and grows beautifully in pots and window boxes.

Give narrow-leaved zinnia full sun and well-drained, fertile soil. The small flowers need no deadheading; in general, the plants are easy to grow, and take to all kinds of climates.

Varieties include 'White Star' and 'Crystal White' (white flowers), 'Gold Star' (golden yellow), and 'Orange Star' (orange flowers).

Ornamental Grasses

Ammophila breviligulata
American beach grass

Zones: 3–9	
Exposure: Full sun	
Salt Tolerance: Excellent	
Drought Tolerance: Good	
Deer Resistance: Good	

This perennial native grass is the first line of defense in stabilizing dunes, and, in fact, that is how it is best used, although you can also plant it in very well-drained, sandy soil on a slope or a bank. Beach grass traps and holds sand on both the ocean side and the lee side of dunes. The plants spread widely from rhizomes. Interestingly, when the stands of grass have grown dense enough to hold the sand in place, the grass begins to lose its vigor. At that point, if the dunes are on your property and you are permitted to plant on them, you can begin to replace the beach grass with more permanent grasses or shrubs (or with new plugs of beach grass).

American beach grass grows one to three feet high, with narrow leaves that are green in spring and fade to brownish beige in winter in the North; in the Carolinas, the leaves often remain partially green in winter. In summer or fall, plants produce tall seed stalks, each bearing a slender seed spike 6 to 10 inches long.

Plant beach grass during cool weather. In the North, that means spring (March and April on Long Island, where I live). In the Carolinas, the best planting time is in winter, from November to March. If you're in doubt about when to plant, check with your local nursery — they'll usually have plugs of beach grass available at the proper time for planting in your area. Set the plugs upright in the sand about eight inches deep. It's all right to bury part of the leaf. Pack the sand firmly around each plug when you plant it.

Space the plugs 12 to 18 inches apart on center, in staggered rows 2 to 2½ feet apart. (If you have a large space to fill and use 1-foot spacing, plan on using about 1,000 grass plugs per 2,000 square feet.) Fertilize with a balanced or high-nitrogen fertilizer three times during the first year after planting (in early spring, late spring, and early fall). The second year fertilize twice, in spring and in fall. Thereafter, fertilize just once a year, in spring.

Ammophila breviligulata

Elymus arenarius 'Glauca'
Blue lyme grass

Zones: 4–10

Exposure: Full sun to light shade

Salt Tolerance: Good

Drought Tolerance: Good

Deer Resistance: Good

Blue lyme grass has been grown in gardens for a hundred years, and it's a rugged, reliable plant in seascape gardens today. The plant forms a clump of blue-green leaves to ½ inch wide that grow to three feet long but arch over, so the visual height is closer to two feet. Spiky gray-green seed heads appear in summer, but they are not very ornamental — the leaves are the reason to grow this plant. Blue lyme grass is a spreader, but is less problematic in poor, sandy soils.

Given its vigorous nature, blue lyme grass is probably best used in poor soil, but it will grow practically anywhere. It can be planted to stabilize dunes or control erosion on slopes, and it

Elymus arenarius

will tolerate salt spray and salt-laden winds off the ocean. The gray-blue leaves look especially good with deep purple foliage, pink, rose, and lavender flowers, and silver foliage in beds and borders. Or you might just plant it by itself in a mass where you want to strike a cool note.

Cut back the plants in early spring, to a few inches above the ground. If they start to look ragged during the growing season, mow or trim them back to encourage fresh new growth. Pests and diseases don't attack this plant, and, like most ornamental grasses, it is deer resistant.

Helictotrichon sempervirens
Blue oat grass

Zones: 4–9

Exposure: Full sun

Salt Tolerance: Fair

Drought Tolerance: Good

Deer Resistance: Good

Blue oat grass grows as a clump of thin, metallic-blue leaves to two feet high and wide that are evergreen in warmer climates and semievergreen in cooler climates. In late summer, plants produce on stiff, upright, four-foot stems graceful clusters of flat seed heads resembling oats. They

begin white and age to light beige as they dry. Plants do not always bloom in warm climates.

In seashore landscapes, blue oat grass makes an interesting accent in beds and borders or massed together.

Blue oat grass likes full sun for the most part, though it appreciates some shade in the southernmost gardens. It needs very well-drained soil with some fertility, but will adapt to a range of soil types. It does not tolerate heavy, soggy soils. Allow adequate air circulation between plants; otherwise they may suffer in very humid conditions.

Helictotrichon sempervirens

Miscanthus sinensis
Maiden grass, eulalia grass

Zones: 5–9
Exposure: Full sun to partial shade
Salt Tolerance: Fair to good
Drought Tolerance: Fair
Deer Resistance: Good

Miscanthus is among the most widely bred and planted of all ornamental grasses. A visit to a good nursery will show you cultivars ranging from two to seven feet high, with leaf blades varying from about an inch wide to thin and almost needlelike. The clump of arching, grassy leaves may be plain green, edged or striped in creamy white, or banded in gold. In late summer and fall, plants bear glistening, airy, fan-shaped seed heads that may be pinkish, coppery, or silvery. Seed heads turn beige or white as they age, as do the leaves. Where winter winds are not too fierce and snow and ice not too heavy, the seed plumes may stay on the plants through winter.

One problem with miscanthus is that it is vigorous and can become invasive in good growing conditions. To be safe, you might do best to plant it where its spread can be contained, such as in a built-in planter bed, in a large tub, or in an area bounded by pavement. And watch for unwanted seedlings that may come up where you don't want them; pull them when they are young.

Miscanthus will grow in full sun to partial shade. It thrives in moist but well-drained, reasonably fertile soil but will tolerate drier conditions, too, and even a fair degree of drought.

RECOMMENDED CULTIVARS
- 'Adagio' — two to four feet high, gray-green leaves; pink flower plumes age to white
- 'Gracillimus' — five to six feet high, has narrow leaves with a white midrib and bronze seed heads in fall
- 'Morning Light' — four to five feet high; has thin, white-edged leaves that appear luminous from a distance and coppery seed plumes that age to tan or beige
- 'Purpurascens' (flamegrass) — three to four feet high and less hardy than most varieties, turns purplish in the cool weather of fall except in very warm southern gardens; has silvery seed plumes in late summer
- 'Silver Feather' or 'Silberfeder' — to six feet high; has gracefully arching leaves and silvery to pinkish brown plumes
- 'Zebrinus' — five to seven feet high; has green leaves horizontally banded with yellow, and coppery seed heads in late summer

Miscanthus sinensis 'Zebrinus'

Panicum virgatum
Switchgrass

Zones: 5–9
Exposure: Full sun to partial shade
Salt Tolerance: Fair to good
Drought Tolerance: Good
Deer Resistance: Good

Switchgrass is native to the tallgrass prairies of the Midwest, and makes a fine addition to seashore gardens, too. It forms a clump of narrow, bluish green leaves. In late summer, plants produce delicate, airy, reddish brown seed clusters. The leaves turn golden or reddish in fall, fading gradually to beige.

Switchgrass is lovely in mixed beds and borders. You can use it as a background plant behind an informal flower garden, mix it with other grasses in a low-maintenance border, or plant it in groups or masses. Or plant tall varieties in a row on a berm or alongside a deck or patio for a summer privacy screen.

Not fussy about soil, switchgrass will grow in a range of soils from wet to dry and sandy. It does best in full sun but tolerates partial shade. Plants can withstand a fair degree of drought (they curl in their leaf edges when it's very dry), but they appreciate water during prolonged periods of hot, dry weather. Cut back plants to a few inches above the ground in early spring to remove old foliage and encourage new growth.

RECOMMENDED CULTIVARS
- 'Cloud Nine' — six feet high, bluish green
- 'Haense Herms' — three to four feet high; turns red in fall with silvery seed heads
- 'Heavy Metal' — narrow, upright clump of metallic-blue leaves to four feet high

Panicum virgatum

Pennisetum species

Zones: Vary with species
Exposure: Full sun to partial shade
Salt Tolerance: Fair to good
Drought Tolerance: Good
Deer Resistance: Good

Fountain grasses are valued for their handsome bottlebrush flowers in late summer and their gracefully arching leaves. They vary in their hardiness and cultural requirements, so be sure to read the descriptions below for more information.

Fountain grasses are lovely in beds and borders, massed or grouped with other ornamental grasses, and even in pots. They can handle salt and are attractive near the beach or alongside a garden pool. They will grow in full sun to partial shade, and prefer well-drained soil with varying degrees of moisture. Like other ornamental grasses, fountain grass is not troubled by pests or diseases, and deer don't eat it.

Pennisetum alopecuroides 'Moudry'

Pennisetum alopecuroides

This is the hardiest species familiar to gardeners, growing well in Zones 6 to 9. It grows actively in warm weather and forms a clump of bright green leaves two to three feet high. In midsummer, stiff bottlebrush flowers begin to bloom, starting out creamy white or beige and maturing to coppery-red. They remain in good shape until fall, when the flower heads shatter and drop their seeds. These may take root and grow into new plants, so pull up any unwanted seedlings. This species prefers moist but well-drained soil, but once established it is generally drought tolerant in cooler climates.

RECOMMENDED CULTIVARS

- 'Hameln'—one and a half to two feet high, with narrower, deeper green leaves than the species form and earlier blooming flowers; grows best where winters are cold, and can struggle in Zones 8 and 9
- 'Little Bunny'—a dwarf just eight inches high, for the front of the garden, a rock garden, or containers
- 'Moudry'—black-flowered pennisetum, grows about two and a half feet high with reddish–purple-tinged leaves and dark brown-black flower heads; foliage turns yellow to orange in fall; a prolific self-sower, so be warned

Pennisetum villosum Feathertop

This is another warm-climate fountain grass grown as an annual north of Zone 9. It grows one and a half to two feet high, with narrow, bright green leaves. In midsummer, plants bear fuzzy-looking, arching seed plumes of creamy white. Feathertop is extremely drought tolerant, and will grow in almost pure sand. It's a good bet near the beach. The plants are striking in a mass and as individuals in pots or at the front of a garden bed.

Pennisetum setaceum 'Rubrum' Purple fountain grass

Mostly grown as an annual north of Zone 9, purple fountain grass grows to three feet high. Its narrow leaves are a striking deep purplish red. The bottlebrush flowers are red-purple and beige. It prefers moist but well-drained soil and generally does well in sandy coastal soils. Once established, it is somewhat drought tolerant. One thing it won't tolerate, though is heavy, wet soil.

Pennisetum setaceum 'Rubrum'

Pennisetum villosum

Spartina pectinata
Cordgrass

Zones: 4–9	
Exposure: Full sun	
Salt Tolerance: Good	
Drought Tolerance: Good	
Deer Resistance: Good	

Spartina pectinata

Cordgrass is native to the eastern half of the United States and is found both in marshes and on prairies. It grows as a clump of arching leaves about ½ inch wide and three to six feet high. In midsummer, plants produce narrow flower spikes that start out green and mature to a brownish color. The leaves turn yellow in fall. The plants spread by means of rhizomes (underground stems).

Cordgrass is very drought tolerant once it is established, and it grows well in sand. Plants spread aggressively in moist soils but are better behaved in dry conditions. Dig up rhizomes around the edges of a clump of plants to help contain their spread if you find them getting out of bounds. They can handle plenty of wind and a range of soils but will get floppy if planted in the shade.

Use cordgrass on the back of dunes, to cover ground in difficult locations, or massed alongside a pond or pool. It also grows well in containers.

The cultivar 'Aureomarginata' has a thin yellow edge along its leaves.

Uniola paniculata
Sea oats

Zones: 7–10	
Exposure: Full sun	
Salt Tolerance: Excellent	
Drought Tolerance: Good	
Deer Resistance: Good	

Sea oats is native to coastal areas from Virginia to Florida and along the Gulf Coast. It is the predominant dune grass in the Southeast. But it is an endangered species now and is protected by law in many places. The plants grow three or more feet high, with tough, narrow, light green leaves; in late summer to early fall, brownish seed heads top long, arching stems. The plants spread by means of long rhizomes and root to form colonies in the sand. Sea oats is excellent for holding sand dunes, and unlike American beach grass, it continues to thrive after the sand

is stabilized. It is illegal to dig plants from the wild, but you may be able to find plants available commercially. Contact the county Cooperative Extension office in your area to see what the regulations are locally, and if plants are available from approved sources.

If you have existing plants on your property, you may be able to divide them to get more. Make sure each division has a piece of the rhizome attached. Replant the divisions at least one foot deep — it's all right to partially bury the leaves. Water well after planting and fertilize with a high-nitrogen or balanced fertilizer three times during the first year after planting (early spring, late spring, and early fall). The second year, fertilize in spring and fall. Thereafter fertilize once a year, in spring.

Uniola paniculata

Vines and Ground Covers

Ajuga reptans
Bugleweed

Zones: 3–10
Exposure: Partial to full shade
Salt Tolerance: Fair
Drought Tolerance: Poor
Deer Resistance: Good

Bugleweed is a familiar, easy-to-grow ground cover that adapts to a variety of situations. The oblong evergreen leaves sit close to the ground and may be deep green, bronze, purple-red, or multicolored, depending on the variety. In late spring or early summer, the plants bear small, upright spikes of deep lavender-blue flowers. Bugleweed spreads well but is not generally invasive, although if planted next to a lawn, it will spread into the grass.

Bugleweed does well in partial to light shade in northern gardens, but in the South it is best in light to full shade. The leaves will scorch under full, blazing sun. The plants adapt to a range of soils, tolerating most types except for very wet and very dry soils. Bugleweed grows even in poor, sandy soil, although it can die if allowed to dry out too much. Water it during spells of dry weather.

RECOMMENDED CULTIVARS
- 'Braunherz' — deep burgundy leaves and lavender flowers
- 'Burgundy Glow' — flushed leaves with burgundy, violet-blue flowers
- 'Catlin's Giant' — large, bronze-purple leaves and eight-inch violet flower spikes
- 'Jungle Beauty' — gold- and purple-splotched leaves, violet-blue flowers
- 'Multicolor' or 'Rainbow' — deep bronzy green leaves splashed with cream and purple and suffused with pink
- 'Pink Surprise' — bronze leaves and pink flowers

Ajuga reptans

Arctostaphylos uva-ursi
Bearberry

Zones: 2–6
Exposure: Full sun to partial shade
Salt Tolerance: Excellent
Drought Tolerance: Good
Deer Resistance: Good

Bearberry is a low, mat-forming evergreen shrub with small, rounded, leathery, glossy dark green leaves that may take on a bronze tone in winter. In spring it bears clusters of small, pinkish white flowers, and in late summer or fall there are bright scarlet-red berrylike fruits. Bearberry grows just four to six inches tall and spreads to form a wide mat several feet across.

Extremely tough and durable, bearberry makes a superb ground cover for seaside gardens. It thrives in well-drained, sandy soil with an acidic pH, but it will adapt to beach sand — you can grow it practically down to the dunes.

Space plants one to two feet apart. Once established, they need little or no fertilizer. Plants are sometimes prone to leaf diseases, but resistant varieties are available, including 'Massachusetts' and 'Vancouver Jade'.

Arctostaphylos uva-ursi

Campsis radicans
Trumpet creeper

Zones: 5–9
Exposure: Full sun to light shade
Salt Tolerance: Fair
Drought Tolerance: Fair
Deer Resistance: Good

Trumpet creeper is a familiar late-summer sight in seashore towns along the East Coast. The bright red-orange trumpet flowers can be seen on fences and sturdy trellises, and trained over arbors. You can let trumpet vine climb a tall, sturdy tree trunk or use it as a ground cover to hold soil on a slope or a bank. In many places the vines grow wild, along roadsides and clambering over trees and shrubs. A tough, vigorous vine, trumpet creeper has become rampant in parts of the South.

Trumpet creeper is a woody, clinging vine that can grow to 40 feet long climbing by sticky aerial rootlets. Its pinnate leaves are divided into pairs of oblong, deep green leaflets. In late summer the clusters of tubular, trumpet-shaped blossoms burst forth. They are red-orange in the species, and there are orange- and yellow-flowered forms, too. Hummingbirds are drawn to the flowers, especially the redder ones.

Trumpet vine has a long taproot that goes deep into the ground, giving the plant good tolerance for drought. The vine blooms best in full sun, but it will also grow in partial to light shade, and afternoon shade is helpful in southern gardens. The ideal soil is fertile, moist, and well drained, but given its vigor, it is probably best to plant it in leaner, less-fertile ground. Trumpet creeper has a fair degree of tolerance for salt and wind. At the beach it generally does best behind the dunes. It may take a few years for young vines to bloom after they are planted, so be patient.

Prune the plants severely in spring to keep them from getting out of hand. A hybrid, *Campsis* × *tagliabuana* 'Mme. Galen', is less rampant, with clusters of apricot-orange flowers.

Campsis radicans

Ceratostigma plumbaginoides
Plumbago

Zones: 6–9
Exposure: Full sun to partial shade
Salt Tolerance: Fair
Drought Tolerance: Fair
Deer Resistance: Good

Plumbago's greatest assets are the clusters of electric blue flowers that bloom in abundance from late summer into fall. When the weather turns cool in fall, the oblong, dark green leaves develop a reddish tinge, further accentuating the flowers.

The plants stay close to the ground, growing no taller than 1½ feet (and usually considerably less than that, in my experience). They spread by means of rhizomes and make a handsome ground cover in low-traffic areas. You can also use them in the front of beds and borders. Ceratostigma can be paired in the garden with daylilies (*Hemerocallis*), asters, black-eyed Susan (*Rudbeckia*), salvia, nepeta, and sedum, among other plants. It is also a good companion for crocuses, small narcissus, grape hyacinth (*Muscari*), crested iris (*Iris cristata*), and other small spring bulbs — it will grow in around them and camouflage their maturing leaves.

Plumbago is a familiar sight in southern gardens, where it is semievergreen. It prefers full sun in the North, but is better with some afternoon shade in the South. Moist but well-drained soil of average fertility suits plumbago well. Near the beach, plant it behind a windbreak or in a sheltered location. It can tolerate some drought but will need watering during prolonged dry spells. The plants are slow to send out new leaves in spring, so don't give up on them.

Ceratostigma plumbaginoides

Clematis species and cultivars

Zones: Vary with species
Exposure: Full sun to light shade
Salt Tolerance: Fair
Drought Tolerance: Poor, except sweet
   autumn clematis
Deer Resistance: Good

Clematis are among the most beloved of woody vines, and for good reason. They offer an array of flower sizes, forms, and colors, and blooming times from spring to fall. Most gardeners are familiar with the large-flowered hybrids that bloom in late spring or summer, but there are also lovely species clematis that flower at other times of the year. One that does quite well in seaside gardens is sweet autumn clematis (*Clematis terniflora*). Clematis comes in a spectrum of colors that is weighted toward the purple to pink range. There are no real oranges and only a few yellows, but there are a host of other colors to choose from: purples ranging from palest lavender to rich, deep violet, and also several shades of blue; pinks from soft blush to bright magenta, vibrant crimson, and wine red; and white, rounding out the palette.

All vining clematis are tendriled and climb by twisting their leafstalks around a support. The vines can grow to 5 to 20 feet long, depending on the species or variety. Many are quite hardy, growing as far north as Zone 3 and south to Zone 8 or 9. They have some tolerance for salt, but need the protection of a good windbreak near the beach. They can be challenging in southern seaside gardens.

Clematis are lovely on a lamppost, trellis, or lattice panel, or clambering over a shrub. They weave their stems among the branches of the host shrub, and decorate it with their blossoms like ornaments on a Christmas tree. A clematis can make an evergreen tree appear to bloom. They are classic companions for roses, too. They can be planted in the ground or in a large tub to decorate a patio or deck. Vigorous sweet autumn clematis is excellent for camouflage; this species will envelop fences and walls in a blanket of greenery that in late August to early September is spangled with fragrant white stars.

Large-flowered clematis hybrids are often divided into three groups, according to their flowering habit. Mature clematis can benefit from pruning, but the time and manner of pruning depends upon the flowering habit. The Patens Group bloom in spring on old wood. Prune them lightly after they bloom, and only if necessary to keep them under control or to remove damaged growth. Cultivars in this group include 'Barbara Jackman', 'Bees Jubilee', 'Guiding Star', 'Lasurstern', 'Miss Bateman', 'Mrs. Spencer Castle', and 'President'.

The Florida Group hybrids bloom in summer on old wood. They need only light pruning, if any. Prune after flowering. 'Belle of Woking', 'Dr. Ruppel', 'Duchess of Edinburgh', 'Enchantress', and 'Nelly Moser' belong to this group.

The Jackmanii Group bloom in summer and autumn on new wood. You can prune them all the way back to the ground when they are dormant. These hybrids are more cold tolerant than the other two groups. Jackmanii hybrids include 'Ascotiensis', 'Comtesse de Bouchard', 'Crimson King', 'Duchess of Albany', 'Elsa Späth', 'Ernest Markham', 'Etoile Violette', 'Hagley', 'Lady Betty Balfour', 'Minuet', 'Prins Hendrik', 'Ramona', 'Ville de Lyon', and 'W. E. Gladstone'.

Clematis appreciate a fertile, loamy soil that is light and well drained. Amend sandy soil with compost and topsoil before planting. The ideal pH is neutral to mildly alkaline; if your soil is acidic, add lime or crushed seashells to raise the pH.

Keep the soil evenly moist for the first few weeks after planting clematis to let the plants settle in. Thereafter, water when the soil dries out an inch below the surface. To encourage bushier growth, cut back the long stems by half their length during their first year in the garden. It takes two or three years for clematis to begin producing its full complement of mature growth; if your plants look a little spindly their first year or two, be patient.

Install the supports when you plant clematis, and begin guiding or attaching the vines to them as soon as they are long enough; the stems are slender and stiff, and likely to break in strong wind if not secured. Clematis benefits from a good layer of mulch to help conserve moisture and keep the roots cool. An old gardening saying is to plant clematis with its head in the sun and its feet in the shade.

Clematis 'Elsa Späth'

Gelsemium sempervirens
Carolina jessamine

Zones: 7–9
Exposure: Full sun to light shade
Salt Resistance: Fair
Drought Tolerance: Poor
Deer Resistance: Good

This classic southern vine, the state flower of South Carolina, has a multiplicity of uses in the garden. It is lovely trained on a fence or trellis, allowed to climb small trees, trailing from containers, or spilling over the ground. You can use it to prevent erosion on slopes or banks.

Jessamine will twine and climb to 15 to 20 feet, or, used as a sprawling ground cover, the stems will form roots where they touch the ground. The small, waxy, dark green leaves are evergreen, pointed, and narrowly oblong, taking on a purplish tone in winter. Masses of small, fragrant, bright yellow flowers bloom in spring, and may appear again in smaller numbers in fall. The cultivar 'Pride of Augusta' has double flowers. The flowers, leaves, and roots are poisonous, so avoid planting Carolina jessamine where young children or nibbling pets are present.

Native from Virginia to Florida and westward, jessamine will grow in sun or shade, but blooms best in a sunny location. At the seashore, it needs a location protected from salt winds. It grows quickest in moist but well-drained soil of good fertility, but it will tolerate dry, sandy conditions. Prune plants, if needed, within a month after they finish blooming in spring.

Gelsemium sempervirens

Liriope muscari
Lilyturf

Zones: 6–10
Exposure: Partial to full shade
Salt Tolerance: Fair
Drought Tolerance: Good
Deer Resistance: Poor

Lilyturf is a tough but graceful plant with a clump of narrow, grasslike, evergreen leaves about a foot high that remain in good shape through much of the winter. In autumn, plants send up slender spikes of tiny, round violet flowers that are followed by small black berries. Another species, *Liriope spicata*, is quite similar, and hardier, but it is a very vigorous spreader that can turn into an invasive nuisance. *L. muscari* spreads, but not aggressively, and is easily divided to fill new space.

The plants grow well in partial to medium shade. In the North they can take full sun, but not in the South or the foliage will burn. But they can handle full shade in southern gardens. Plants are adaptable and will grow in practically any soil. They don't have problems with pests or diseases, though deer may eat them. By late winter the leaves start to look ragged, so cut back the plants in early spring to make room for new growth.

RECOMMENDED CULTIVARS

- 'Big Blue' — 8 to 10 inches high, violet-blue flowers
- 'Majestic' — tall spikes of rich violet flowers
- 'Monroe White' — white flowers
- 'PeeDee Ingot' — yellow-green leaves that make a striking combination with red- or purple-leaved plants
- 'Variegata' — leaves edged in ivory, violet flowers

Liriope muscari

Lonicera species
Honeysuckle

Zones: Vary with species
Exposure: Full sun to partial shade
Salt Tolerance: Fair
Drought Tolerance: Fair
Deer Resistance: Good

Honeysuckles are a group of vines with trumpet-shaped or two-lipped flowers in white, yellow, orange, pink, or red. They can be lovely covering a fence or rambling about a hillside, and some offer the bonus of sweet fragrance in their flowers. As a group, honeysuckles are easy to grow and need little in the way of maintenance. Where space is limited, prune them to control growth. Some honeysuckles, however, grow too well and can easily become invasive pests. Chief among these is Japanese or Hall's honeysuckle (*Lonicera japonica* 'Halliana'), which is still widely sold and planted along the East Coast for its ability to survive in tough seaside locations. It is best to avoid planting this honeysuckle on your property. The species described here are better behaved and very beautiful, although they will need the protection of a windbreak near the beach.

Everblooming honeysuckle (*Lonicera* × *heckrottii* 'Goldflame') has lovely flowers that begin as carmine-red buds and then open into fragrant blossoms that are yellow inside and rose-red on the outside. The flowers gradually fade to pink as they age. Everblooming honeysuckle flowers profusely in early summer and continues sporadically into fall. The vines twine and climb, reaching about 15 feet in height. It is hardy in Zones 6 to 9.

Trumpet honeysuckle (*Lonicera sempervirens*), native to the eastern United States, is hardy in Zones 4 to 9 and good for screening. Its stems are typically about 12 to 15 feet long, and are dressed in oval to oblong leaves that are evergreen in southern gardens. From late spring to late summer, the plant sends forth clusters of trumpet-shaped orange, scarlet, or yellow flowers. The flowers are not fragrant, but they do attract hummingbirds. A number of cultivars are

Lonicera sempervirens

available, including 'Cedar Lane', with dark red flowers; 'Magnifica' and 'Superba', with scarlet flowers; and 'Sulphurea', with yellow blossoms.

Honeysuckles take to a range of soils, as long as they are well drained. The plants do not need pruning, but over time they tend to grow into tangled thickets of stems that bloom only at the ends. Pruning after they finish blooming keeps the plants neater. Cut away all the dead old growth from underneath the younger stems with hedge clippers.

Ophiopogon japonicus
Mondo grass

Zones: 6–10
Exposure: Partial to full shade
Salt Tolerance: Fair
Drought Tolerance: Good
Deer Resistance: Poor

Mondo grass is very similar to lilyturf (*Liriope* species), and is grown in many southern gardens. The two groups of plants are often confused, but liriope has violet flowers while those of mondo grass are white. Both plants are ideal for edging a sidewalk, path, or driveway. Or you can use them as ground covers, or for a leafy accent in a mixed container planting. Mondo grass is hardy in Zones 7 to 10, grows 8 to 12 inches high, and has white flowers.

Gardeners in Zones 6 to 10 can plant *Ophiopogon planiscapus* 'Nigrescens' or 'Ebony Knight'. This is a showstopper, about eight inches high, with very dark, nearly black leaves.

RECOMMENDED CULTIVARS
- 'Kyoto Dwarf' — grows just four inches high, with purple-black leaves.
- 'Silver Dragon' — grows to 12 inches, with white-variegated leaves

Ophiopogon planiscapus 'Nigrescens'

Parthenocissus species
Virginia creeper, Boston ivy

Zones: Virginia creeper, 3–9; Boston ivy, 4–8
Exposure: Sun or shade
Salt Tolerance: Fair to good
Drought Tolerance: Good
Deer Resistance: Good

Virginia creeper and Boston ivy are two tough, adaptable vines that are salt resistant and wind tolerant. Both are clingers that will hold on to a wall or tree trunk with no help from the gardener. They will also climb an arbor, trellis, or fence. You can use these vines for screening or camouflage, or as ground covers on a slope or a bank. Virginia creeper will also grow on the back side of a dune and can be useful for erosion control. Both vines are at their best in fall, when the foliage turns rich red, although the color may not be as bright in southern gardens.

Virginia creeper is native to eastern North America and can be found growing wild in woodlands and along roadsides up and down the coast. Its compound leaves are composed of five toothed, oblong leaflets radiating from a central point. The leaves turn fiery scarlet or red in fall. In late summer the plants bear dark blue-black berries that birds enjoy. The vines can grow to 30 feet or more.

Boston ivy is the plant from which the Ivy League universities got that name. It can grow to 50 feet, with lobed leaves somewhat resembling maple leaves that turn dark red in autumn. In late summer the plants produce blue-black berries attractive to birds. Numerous cultivars are available, including 'Lowii' and 'Veitchii', whose small leaves are purplish when young; 'Minutifolia', which also has small leaves; 'Purpurea', with dark purple leaves; and 'Robusta', which is exceptionally vigorous.

Both plants grow well in either sun or shade, although they need sun to produce fruit. They tolerate just about any kind of soil, including dry, sandy, and alkaline soils. They don't really need maintenance, except to trim them to keep the vines away from windows and rain gutters if you let them climb the walls of a building. To use the vines as ground cover, space plants about four feet apart. Set them closer together to grow vertically up a wall.

Parthenocissus tricuspidata

Thymus species
Woolly thyme, creeping thyme

Zones: 5–9
Exposure: Full sun
Salt Tolerance: Good
Drought Tolerance: Good
Deer Resistance: Good

Thymes are well known to cooks and herb gardeners, of course, but they make good ground covers too, especially the creeping kinds. These small-leaved plants spread slowly to form low mats. On hot, sunny days, and when stepped upon, the foliage is wonderfully aromatic. Thymes are delightful growing in spaces left between paving stones in a path or patio,

tumbling out of pockets in a dry stone wall, or hugging the ground in a dry, sunny spot. They are also fine in rock gardens and in containers.

Woolly thyme grows just a couple of inches high, with tiny, fuzzy, silver-gray leaves and clusters of little rose-pink flowers in summer.

Creeping thyme, or mother of thyme, grows to 10 inches high and forms a mat 1½ feet across. It has tiny, hairy leaves and clusters of minute purple flowers in summer.

All thymes need full sun and light, porous, very well-drained soil. In wet conditions they will rot. A near neutral to mildly alkaline pH is ideal. Average to poor fertility is fine; they don't take well to rich soil. Thyme doesn't always do well in southern gardens due to the high humidity.

RECOMMENDED CULTIVARS
- 'Annie Hall' — light purplish pink flowers
- 'Carol Ann' — yellow-variegated leaves, lavender flowers
- 'Minimus' and 'Minor' — both very compact, just a few inches high
- 'Snowdrift' — white flowers

Thymus serpyllum 'Snowdrift'

Vinca species
Greater periwinkle, common periwinkle

Vinca minor

Zones: Greater periwinkle, 7–11; common periwinkle, 4–9

Exposure: Sun or shade

Salt Tolerance: Fair

Drought Tolerance: Poor

Deer Resistance: Good

Periwinkles are easy-to-grow vines that are popular ground covers and container plants. Greater periwinkle (*V. major*) has rounded leaves, edged in cream in the variety 'Variegata', and in spring bears funnel-shaped lilac-purple flowers. Gardeners in the South can use it as a ground cover, but in the North it is strictly a container annual, spilling over the sides of window boxes everywhere. Greater periwinkle does best with at least some sun in the North.

Common periwinkle (*V. minor*) has smaller, oval leaves of deep, glossy green, and purple flowers in early spring. It is seemingly everywhere as a ground cover, and in fact has escaped from cultivation and can be seen weaving its way through woodlands in many parts of the Northeast. In the seaside garden it is tough and dependable, and has much better salt tolerance than does large periwinkle.

Both plants will grow in partial to light shade. Greater periwinkle needs some sun in the North but can take full shade in the South. Common periwinkle can also take full shade. Greater periwinkle is best in moist, fertile soil, while common periwinkle is less fussy and can tolerate drier conditions. Both are best with the protection of a windbreak near the beach.

Trachelospermum jasminoides
Confederate jasmine

Zones: 8–10

Exposure: Full sun to partial shade

Salt Tolerance: Good

Drought Tolerance: Poor

Deer Resistance: Poor

An evergreen vine from China, Confederate jasmine got its common name from its long history in southeastern gardens. Confederate jasmine is a vigorous twiner that grows quickly to 15 feet or more. It has small, oblong to elliptical evergreen leaves that are dark green and glossy. In spring and early summer, the plant bears clusters of intensely fragrant, star-shaped, tubular-throated flowers of creamy white. The cultivar 'Variegatum' has green-and-white variegated leaves, and 'Japonicum' has leaves veined in white and turning bronze in autumn.

Confederate jasmine is excellent for screening or covering a trellis. Locate it where you can enjoy the fragrance when the plants are blooming. You can also plant it as a ground cover and let it sprawl over a slope.

The ideal location for Confederate jasmine is sunny or partially shaded, with moist but well-drained soil. Plants may take two or three years to become established, so give them time. Prune as needed to keep Confederate jasmine under control.

Trachelospermum jasminoides

Wisteria species
Wisteria

Zones: Japanese wisteria, 4–9; Chinese wisteria, 5–10

Exposure: Full sun to partial shade

Salt Tolerance: Fair

Drought Tolerance: Poor

Deer Resistance: Good

The fragrant flowers of wisteria are pure delight in mid- to late spring. It's too bad the vines that produce them can get so out of control. If you intend to grow wisteria, plan on pruning every year to keep it under control. Southern gardeners, especially, should beware the rampant habit of wisteria, and prune regularly. For those of us who love the sweet-scented flowers, the extra work is well worth it.

Wisteria is lovely trained on an arbor or pergola, on a fence, or on a sturdy trellis. It is dense enough to use for screening. It will also climb a tree trunk and even the wall of a building. For a formal treatment, you can, over a period of years, train wisteria to take the form of a tree. Allow one main stem to develop, and support it with stakes until it is sturdy enough to stand by itself. Careful pruning and training of lateral stems will allow you to develop a canopy of foliage and flowers atop the main trunk. Over time, the stems of wisteria become thick, woody, and interestingly gnarled and twisted.

There are numerous native wisteria species, but the two most often grown for ornamental purposes are both from Asia. They are twining vines whose deciduous leaves consist of pairs of oval leaflets. The leaves turn an attractive yellow in autumn before they drop. The vines bear long, drooping flower clusters in spring.

Japanese wisteria (*W. floribunda*) grows to 25 feet, twining its stems in a clockwise direction, and is the hardier of the two. It also has the longer and more fragrant flower clusters. The species has pealike flowers of a light violet color, but there are cultivars with white, pink, red, or deeper violet flowers. The flowers of both wisterias are followed by flat, velvety seedpods in summer.

Chinese wisteria (*W. sinensis*) grows to 30 feet long, twines in a counterclockwise direction, and blooms a week or two ahead of the Japanese species. Its lightly fragrant, blue-violet flowers come in clusters 8 to 12 inches long. There are cultivars with white, and deeper violet-purple, flowers.

Wisteria flowers best in full sun but can also take partial to light shade. It enjoys fertile soil, but will tolerate poor, dry soils once established. Even moisture is important during the plant's first year in the garden. Transplant wisteria with care; like all legumes, its roots resent being disturbed. Fasten the young stems to their support until the vines are able to twine on their own.

Amend very sandy soil with compost before planting, and top-dress with fresh compost every fall. Young plants may take up to 10 years to bloom, so be patient when planting them.

The vines need regular pruning to keep them in bounds and looking their best. In summer, prune the long, straggly stems that develop, except for the ones the vine needs to climb. Also one third to half their length, to produce the best flowers. In late winter, while plants are still dormant, you can prune again, cutting back the previously pruned shoots to two or three buds. Cut back to six inches any long shoots that developed after last summer's pruning.

Wisteria floribunda

WHEN WISTERIA WON'T BLOOM

If your wisteria doesn't flower, ask yourself:

Is the plant old enough? Wisteria often takes six or seven, or more, years to produce its first flowers.

Is the soil too rich? Very fertile soil, especially soil rich in nitrogen, causes lavish foliage growth but no flowers. As a remedy, try digging a trench around the base of the plant and working in superphosphate or another phosphorus fertilizer to balance the excess of nitrogen. A more labor-intensive way to stimulate bloom is to prune the roots. Push a sharp spade into the soil in a circle around the base of the plant, 1½ feet out from the trunk, to cut the roots. Severely pruning long stems (back to two or three buds) may also help.

Is there enough light? Wisteria needs a sunny location.

Was last winter too cold? Low temperatures may kill flower buds. If you are in a very exposed location or northern Zone 4 or 5, try removing the vines from their support and laying them out on the ground in late fall. Cover with a foot-deep layer of leaves, hay, or evergreen boughs over winter.

Acknowledgments

Wᴵᵀʜᴼᵁᵀ ᵀʜᴱ ʜᴱᴸᴾ ᴼᶠ ᴬ ᴺᵁᴹᴮᴱᴿ ᴼᶠ people, this book could not have come together. Special thanks to the homeowners, gardeners, garden designers, and landscape architects who so generously shared their time to talk with me about the gardens profiled in chapter 4. They are:

Cynthia Hosmer, in Maine; Tony Elliott, landscape gardener and owner of Snug Harbor Farm, in Kennebunk, Maine; Geraldine King, in Massachusetts; James van Sweden, founding partner, and Sheila Brady, partner, Oehme, van Sweden & Associates, Inc., in Washington, D.C.; Robbie Hutchison, designer, Donaroma's Nursery & Landscape Services, in Edgartown, Massachusetts; John Hill, head gardener, in East Hampton, New York; Edwina von Gal, Edwina von Gal and Company, East Hampton, New York; Mario Nievera, Mario Nievera Design, in Palm Beach, Florida; Meredith Marshall, in Delaware; and Clyde Timmons, senior designer, DesignWorks, in Charleston, South Carolina.

Many thanks also to Kevin Coffey, of Marders, in Bridgehampton, New York, for sharing his knowledge of coastal trees and shrubs; to Tom Stubelek, of Southampton, New York, for sharing his insights and experience gained in more than 20 years of gardening on oceanfront property; and to geologist Thomas Moyer, PhD (also my brother), for reviewing the coastline information in chapter 1.

Finally, thanks to my editor, Carleen Perkins, and to everyone else at Storey Publishing for their support of this book.

— *Anne Halpin*

Tʜᴵˢ ᴮᴼᴼᴷ Wᴼᵁᴸᴰ ᴺᴼᵀ ʜᴬᵛᴱ ᴮᴱᴱᴺ possible without the generosity of people who love gardens. Whether it's digging in the dirt, designing a landscape on a bluff above the Atlantic, or sitting beside a marsh under a lichen-speckled olive tree, garden folks want to share their beautiful world with others. Photographing this book, I was the lucky beneficiary of this phenomenon. People shared their homes and gardens, hours of their day, years of their accumulated knowledge, and, of course, plants for my fledgling garden back home. It was my privilege and pleasure to spend time with each of these contributors in their beautiful gardens.

In Maine, Tony Elliott, at Snug Harbor Farm in Kennebunk, spent a day zipping me around to a collection of rock-strewn seascapes, and created a bold sunny border against the sea when Mother Nature wasn't accommodating our timetable. After the sun set on Cynthia and Calvin Hosmer's garden, they wouldn't let me go home without supper. Thanks also to Ed Lowrie, the Molsons, the Sahins, and Frank and Brook Todd.

On the Massachusetts coast, Deborah and Hart Peterson were indispensable. This project wouldn't exist without their vision and their introduction to the gardens around them. Thanks also to the Flannerys, the Goldensons, the Kings, the MacLeods, the McBratneys, and the Michauds.

On a rugged spit of land on Narragansett Bay in Rhode Island, Oehme, van Sweden & Associates shared a landscape that resembles a lucky accident until you spy a plant tag hiding in a thicket.

My friend and frequent garden collaborator, Jane Berger, hosted me and introduced me to the talent of Robbie Hutchison on Martha's Vineyard. Robbie lined up exquisite gardens designed by her and Mike Donaroma's staff at Donaroma's Nursery & Landscape Service. Many thanks also to the Eberstadts, John Glendon, Claudia Miller, the Point Way, and the Shanes.

Once again, I'm indebted to Mac Griswold, who pointed me toward gardens in the Hamptons, New York, that ranged from a series of wistful garden rooms, created by Ryan Gainey, to a spare contemporary meadow, designed by Edwina von Gal. At short notice, David Seeler, at The Bayberry in Amagansett, offered up an array of seaside garden retreats tucked among the dunes and beside the marshes. Thanks also to Susan Calhoun, John Hill, Mark Perlbinder, Steve Perlbinder, the Raphaels, the Rayners, the Rosenbergs, and Barbara Slifka.

At the Delaware beaches, thanks to Meredith and James Marshall, whose beachfront garden, designed by Mario Nievera, unwinds from the dunes into a formal garden.

In Maryland, Jim van Sweden invited me to his retreat on the Eastern Shore — a bold meadow that floats above the Chesapeake Bay. He cooked meals, discussed the landscape value of hackberry trees, and offered me the guestroom next to the pond, where the frogs serenaded me to sleep at night. Thanks also to the Brillembourgs.

In South Carolina, Clyde Timmons at DesignWorks made sure I had plenty of beautiful and inventive gardens to choose from, including a Japanese garden and another that rose out of the pink-tinged marshes. Thanks to the Ackermans, Peter Bartlett, Howell Beach at Robert Marvin/Howell Beach & Associates, the Dursts, Roger Good at Cloverleaf, Kiawah Development Partners, the Luries, and the Pennells.

Many thanks to Anne Halpin for bringing her vast experience in gardening and garden-book writing to this project, and to all those at Storey Publishing: Gwen Steege, for believing I was the "right" person to capture the drama of gardens shaped by wind and sea; Kent Lew and Vicky Vaughn in the art department, for their crisp, elegant design style; my editor, Carleen Perkins, whose calm professionalism guided the project; and the president, Pam Art, who said the words any garden photographer loves to hear: "We take every step to make sure the photographs look as beautiful on the page as they did when you took them."

— *Roger Foley*

ADDITIONAL PHOTO CREDITS

© Henry W. Art: 160 left, 164 right, 205 right; © Joseph DeSciose:140 left, 155 left, 178 right; © Global Book Publishing Photo Library/James Young: 139 top and bottom left, 141 left, 142 left, 146, 148 bottom right, 149, 150 top, 154 left, 156, 157, 161, 163, 168 left, 176 left, 177 bottom, 182 center, 184 left, 189, 193 bottom, 196 left, 197, 210 bottom, 211 bottom, 212 left; © Saxon Holt: 204 bottom right, 205 left; © Macore, Inc.: 143 bottom, 152 right, 153 bottom, 155 right, 158 left, 162 left, 167 left and bottom, 169 right, 170 bottom left, 173 right, 180 center and right, 181 bottom, 183 left, 184 right, 187 bottom, 190, 191 left and center, 194, 198 left, 199, 206; © Adam Mastoon: 70; New England Wild Flower Society, Garden in the Woods, Framingham, Massachusetts (508-877-7630, www.newenglandwildflower.org). © New England Wild Flower Society/Catherine Heffron: 147 top, © New England Wild Flower Society/William Cullina: 166 top, 171 left, 186 center, © New England Wild Flower Society/ John Lynch: 186 right; © Raintree Nursery: 144 bottom

GARDEN DESIGN CREDITS

Anthony Elliot, Snug Harbor Farm: 5, 55 (top), 92–95; Calvin and Cynthia Hosmer: 88–91; Clyde Timmons, DesignWorks: 35, 124–131; Edwina von Gal: 85, 112–115; Frank Todd & Associates: 87, 133; Geraldine King: 68, 96–98; James van Sweden, Oehme, van Sweden & Associates: 120–123; Mario Nievera Designs: 2, 24, 25, 66, 69, 116–119; Robbie Hutchison, Donaroma's Nursery: 104–107; Ryan Gainey: 26, 30, 40 (right), 82, 108–110; Sheila Brady, Oehme, van Sweden & Associates: 6, 40 (left), 52, 100–103

USDA Plant Hardiness Zone Map

THE UNITED STATES DEPARTMENT OF Agriculture (USDA) created this map to give gardeners a helpful tool for selecting and cultivating plants. The map divides North America into 11 zones based on each area's average minimum winter temperature. Zone 1 is the coldest and Zone 11 the warmest. Once you determine your zone, you can use that information to select plants that are most likely to thrive in your climate.

Range of Average Annual Minimum Temperatures for Each Zone

Zone 2	-50° to -40°F
Zone 3	-40° to -30°F
Zone 4	-30° to -20°F
Zone 5	-20° to -10°F
Zone 6	-10° to 0°F
Zone 7	0° to 10°F
Zone 8	10° to 20°F
Zone 9	20° to 30°F
Zone 10	30° to 40°F

Other Storey Titles You Will Enjoy

Grasses
by Nancy J. Ondra. Here is a complete
introduction to using ornamental grasses
in combination with perennials, annuals,
shrubs, and other garden plants. Beautiful
full-color photos illuminate complete
plans for 24 gardens featuring grasses.
144 pages. Paperback with French flaps.
ISBN 1-58017-423-X.

The Weather-Resilient Garden
by Charles W.G. Smith. Plant a garden
that is beautiful but tough enough to
withstand almost anything nature deliv-
ers. Smith's encyclopedia of 100 hardy
plants helps you garden defensively and
includes detailed advice on what to do
when a weather disaster strikes your garden. 416 pages. Paperback.
ISBN 1-58017-516-3.

The Perennial Gardener's Design Primer
by Stephanie Cohen and Nancy J. Ondra.
Learn how to create stunning perennial
gardens using basic design principles for
putting plants together in pleasing and
practical ways. 320 pages. Paperback.
ISBN 1-58017-543-0.

Shell Chic
by Marlene Hurley Marshall. Capturing
the romance of the beach and a lush
eccentricity, *Shell Chic* features creative
works from today's shell artisans and tells
you how to bring their decorative flair
into your home. Gorgeous photography,
design ideas, and practical instructions for
shell art make this book a beautiful
memento from a beach vacation and an
inspiring book of craft projects. 160 pages.
Hardcover; jacketed. ISBN 1-58017-440-X.

Garden Stone
by Barbara Pleasant. Practical information
and more than 250 inspiring photographs
explain how to use stone and plants
together to create contrasting textures
and colors in the garden. 240 pages.
Paperback. ISBN 1-58017-544-9.

*The Complete Houseplant
Survival Manual*
by Barbara Pleasant. This friendly
approach to selecting and caring for
indoor plants — with personality profiles,
growing needs, and troubleshooting tips
for 160 blooming and foliage varieties —
helps guarantee that you'll never kill
another houseplant. Whether you're looking for a hip flamingo flower, a delicate
orchid, or a sturdy Swedish ivy, you'll find
it here. 384 pages. Flexibind.
ISBN 1-58017-569-4.

The Flower Gardener's Bible
by Lewis and Nancy Hill. All the inspira-
tion and advice you need on flower gardening is gathered here in a single volume
with basic plant information, design ideas
and theme gardens, and a photographic
encyclopedia of more than 400 plants.
384 pages. Paperback. ISBN 1-58017-462-0.

*The Gardener's A–Z Guide to Growing
Flowers from Seed to Bloom*
by Eileen Powell. This encyclopedia of 576
annuals, perennials, and bulbs includes
information on sowing, regional suitabil-
ity, transplanting, flowering schedule,
propagation, and general care for each
plant listed. 528 pages. Paperback.
ISBN 1-58017-517-1.

PREP FOR SUCCESS

was made possible through the selfless efforts of those who worked tirelessly to see this project to fruition. In particular, the members of the Cooking & Tasting Committee, whose names are listed on page 239, have given countless hours of their time to ensure that all of our recipes have been tried and tested. All proceeds from the sale of this cookbook will be used for the continued development of Cayman Prep and High School.

COOKBOOK COMMITTEE

Production Manager	*Mrs. Terri Merren*
Book Title/Editor	*Mrs. Jennifer Hunter*
Cover Design/Art Consultant	*Mrs. Shelley Leonard*
Advisor	*Mrs. Jean Bahadur*
Production Assistant	*Miss Brenda Bryce*
Photography	*Mrs. Jennifer Hunter* *Mrs. Shelley Leonard* *Mrs. Terri Merren*
Promotions/Marketing	*Mrs. Jennifer Hunter* *Mrs. Terri Merren* *Ms. Caren Wight*

MAJOR SPONSORS

The Brasserie Restaurant ■ *Café Med/Casanova by the Sea/Coconut Joe's*
Copper Falls Steakhouse ■ *Edoardo's Restaurant*
Guy Harvey's Island Grill/Guy Harvey Gallery and Shoppe

MONETARY DONATIONS

Affordable Insurance ■ *Clyde & Helen Allen and family* ■ *Aon Insurance Managers (Cayman) Ltd.*
Calypso Grill ■ *Sydney & Claire Coleman and family* ■ *Colin & Kathryn Daniel and Nicholas*
Jon & Pamela Fowler and family ■ *Richard & Sandy Hew and family* ■ *Island Builders Co. Ltd.*
J E C Property Consultants Ltd. ■ *Bud & Sheila Johnson and family* ■ *Greg & Joan Link and Danny & Emily*
Kevin & Lyne Lloyd and family ■ *Steve & Pam McFadin and family*
Q & H Corporate Services Ltd. ■ *Billy & Lolli Reid* ■ *William & Sharon Walmsley and family*

CAYMAN PREP AND HIGH SCHOOL

Founded in 1949 by the United Church of Jamaica and the Cayman Islands (formerly the Presbyterian Church), Cayman Prep and High School provides a stimulating learning environment, firmly rooted in Christian principles, in which our students become critical, creative thinkers, responsible citizens and lifelong learners in an ever changing world.

With over 700 boys and girls of all demographics and academic abilities the school, one of the leading providers of quality education on the island, is located on two sites: Smith Road houses the Primary School and the High School is located on Walkers Road. Although weighted towards the British education system, Cayman Prep and High School satisfies U.K., U.S., Canadian and Caribbean entrance requirements. It is, in fact, one of only two schools in Cayman able to offer full Advanced Level examinations and has had an excellent results record in these examinations as well as in the International General Certificate of Secondary Education (IGCSE), and Scholastic Achievement Tests (SATs).

Highly qualified staff from Cayman and around the world teach at the school, which is headed by Principal, Jean Bahadur. To ensure that every child receives the best possible education, classes are kept to a manageable number and work is carefully differentiated to allow each child to operate at his/her level. Learning support is available throughout both the Primary and High Schools from specialist teachers.

Students strike a healthy balance by combining their study of subjects such as English, Maths, Business Studies, Art, French, Spanish, Coordinated Science, Biology, Chemistry, Physics, Music, Drama, Information Technology, History, Geography, Religion, and P.E. with diverse extracurricular activities including Key Club, Spanish Club, Dancing Club, Rugby, Soccer, Netball, to name just a few. There are opportunities to learn a variety of musical instruments and to play in the school's orchestras and also to sing in the many choirs in both the Primary and High Schools.

The excellent external examination results coupled with the good all around education prove that there is no longer a need to consider high school education elsewhere and has resulted in tremendous demand for places in our school.

LET US JOIN HANDS AS TOGETHER WE "KEEP BUILDING EDUCATION"

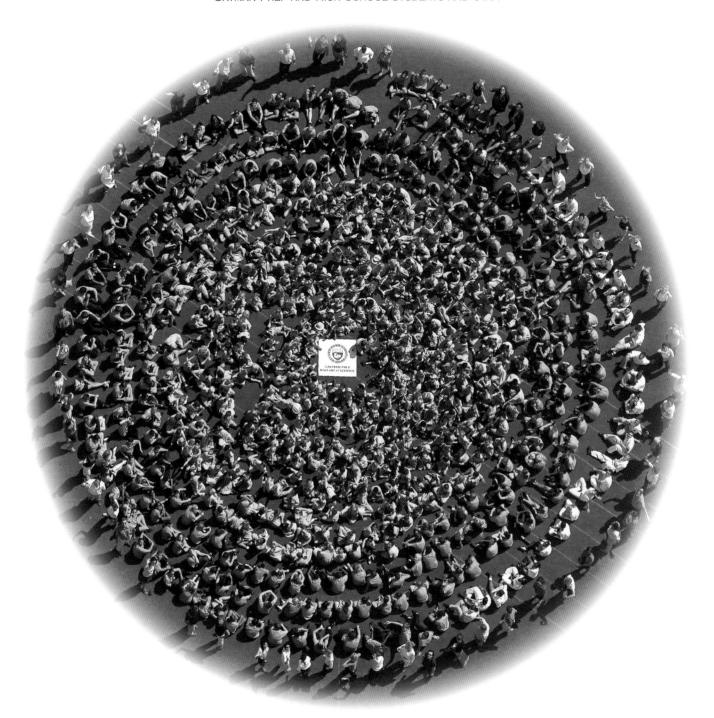

Cayman Prep and High School, Smith Road campus playfield

THE UNITED CHURCH IN JAMAICA AND THE CAYMAN ISLANDS

The United Church, which owns and operates Cayman Prep and High School, began its ministry in the Cayman Islands in 1846, when it was decided by the Church in Scotland and Jamaica to extend its mission to Cayman after it was discovered by Rev. Hope Waddell that there was no organised church in the Islands. Rev. William Niven, a Presbyterian missionary, lost his life at sea in a hurricane after bringing the Rev. James Elmslie to Grand Cayman, who volunteered to go when no one else was available for the mission. Once in Grand Cayman, Rev. Elmslie travelled all over the Island on horseback, by boat and on foot, setting up churches in each district of the Island. The Church then began to champion education, working tirelessly to improve primary schooling and spread its availability, before taking steps to provide secondary education in Grand Cayman in 1946. Thus began the Cayman High School as it was then called, with its Preparatory Department, and also a Commercial Department, which opened its doors in 1949. This was later to become what is now the Cayman Prep and High School. The role of the Church in education is no doubt reflected by the fact that two of the Government high schools are named in memory of two of the Church's ministers and educators in the aforesaid school, Rev. George Hicks and Rev. John Gray.

Elmslie Memorial Church (pictured on the opposite page) is the flagship of the United Churches located in the Cayman Islands. This Church has a lot of historical significance and has unofficially served as Cayman's "cathedral" for many years. Remembrance Day is observed each November, with persons placing wreaths around the Memorial Cross in the Churchyard and it also serves as a hallowed burial site. On 1st July 1920, the foundation for the Church was laid and at the same time it was decided to name the Church "Elmslie Memorial" in memory of Rev. Elmslie, who had ministered here from 1846 to 1863. Due to the fact that three churches on the same site had previously been destroyed by hurricanes, it was decided that the new Church should be built with cement blocks. At that time, structures here were made of wattle and daub or wood, and no one in Cayman had ever worked with cement blocks before. It was decided to send Capt. Rayal Bodden to the Portland Cement Works in Jamaica to learn how to work with cement and how to make the moulds to pour cement blocks. At the time Capt. Rayal Bodden was renowned as one of our best shipbuilders and it was suggested that he should build the Church. The architect who was based in Jamaica commented that "anyone who can build a ship can build a church, but not everyone who can build a church can build a ship." Each block was made by hand and this was a long and tedious job. Elmslie Memorial was the first structure in the Cayman Islands to be built with cement blocks. The wood and timber used for the roof and window frames were reportedly salvaged from a shipwreck. In his capacity as foreman for the building of the Church, Capt. Rayal Bodden employed many local and gifted finish carpenters, one of whom was his brother, Roland Bodden II, who was also a shipbuilder. Roland Bodden was responsible for the much admired ceiling in the Church which resembles the upturned hull of schooners that the two brothers had designed and built previously. The present pews in the Church were built by Elroy Arch, another of Cayman's finest shipbuilders. The Church therefore serves as a testament to the fine workmanship produced by some of our most gifted shipbuilders of that bygone era.

by Mrs. Joan Wilson (nee-Watler)
Former student, Cayman High School, Class of 1952

- CONTRIBUTORS -

A special thank you to the numerous families, staff and students (past and present) of the school who so generously contributed their favourite recipes and pieces of their lives to this book. We also wish to thank those families who sent in monetary donations in respect of the recipes they submitted which were chosen for inclusion herein.

Carlene Alexander-Kay, and
   Liam Kay & Cristin Alexander

Nan Alexander

Clyde & Helen Allen, and James & Charles

Tony & Karen Attenborough, and Claire,
   Hamish & Matthew

Joey & Jean Bahadur

Adrian & Kathy Barnett, and
   Ryan & Matthew

David & Michelle Bodden, and Jade, Wyatt & Jaxon

Queenie Bodden

Orlando Bonar

Bryan & Andrea Bothwell

Jeff & Michelle Boucher, and
   Michael & Jenna

Graham & Catharine Boyd-Moss, and
   Emma & Rachel

Brenda Bryce

Russell & Sheena Bunton, and Madison & Quincey

Tony & Christine Cleaver, and Alex,
   Jordyn & Bethany

Chris & Chrissy Cooke, and Matty & Amy

Wayne & Patricia DaCosta, and Aaron & Ashley

Darrin & Michelle Daykin, and Joshua & Emmi

Beatrice Dilbert

Leonard & Carol Ann Ebanks

Leslie & Michele Ebanks, and Jessica & Kaleb

Lina Dell Ebanks

Margaret Ebanks, and Megan

Petronella Ebanks

Robert & Paula Ebanks, and Ashleigh

Cy & Cheryl Elliott, and Jada

Scott & Kathryn Elphinstone, and
   Kaitlyn, Laura & Matthew

Rosa & Chantelle Esau

Andrew & Mary Falconer, and Luka & Evan

Ray & Jacqui Farrington, and Kyle

Vanda Fernandez

Jim & Janice Gillies, and Stephanie, James & Amy

Michael & Jennifer Godfrey

Mary Gray

Garry & Dinah Green, and Keelan

Kent & Stacey Green, and Megan

Roger & Rachael Hanson, and Thomas & Matthew

Sean & Liz Harrington, and Daniel & Caitlyn

Quatro & Penny Hatch, and Jason, Caitlin & Tanner

Richard & Sandy Hew, and Thompson,
   Lauren & Harrison

Violet Horner

Bryan & Jennifer Hunter, and Cory & Daniel

Arthur & Karen Hunter

Robin & Lana Jarvis, and Andrew & Aaron

Chris & Cheryl Kellett, and Brittney & Braydon

David & Melanie Khouri, and Jessica

David & Christina Kirkaldy, and Ryan & Taylor

Larry & Shelley Leonard, and Alex & Nicholas

Gary & Rose Lindsay, and Tia & Tamika

Kevin & Lyne Lloyd, and Jessica, Morgan & Ryan

Mark & Aoife Matthews, and Michael & Lara

Rod & Penny McDowall, and Jamie & Jessica

Mike & Anne McGrath

Rick & Kim McTaggart, and
   Jonathan, Katelee & Nicholas

Stephen & Debra McTaggart, and
   Sarah, Amelia & Matthew

Tony & Mary Mellin, and A.J. McKenzie

Edlin & Helen Merren

Gregory & Terri Merren, and Josh & Zachary

Lisa Merren

Suzan Merren

Leslie Metcalf

Andrew & Amanda Miller, and Romilly & James

Rex & Kim Miller, and Kayla, Corey & Halle

Hugh & Ann Murphy, and Daniel, Sean & Laura

Pearse & Alison Murphy, and Grace, Aoife & Sarah

David R. Myers, and Gabrielle

Celicea Myles & Kai-Leigh Haughton,
   and Trevor & Nicolo Tummings

Mike & Lauren Nelson, and Marc & Cari

Dwight & Shannon Panton, and Dylan & Frasier

Naomi Panton

Graham & Jane Peck, and Rebecca & Michael

Carlos & Fiona Pimentel, and
   Edward, Anna, Amelia & Jamie

Paul Peene & Toni Pinkerton, and
   Samantha, Derek & Andrew

Tony & Bridget Pitcairn, and Sophie

Don & Tracey Potkins, and Meghan & Sarah

Billy & Lolli Reid

Linda Dalton-Riley & Darren Riley, and
   Brittany & Sydney

Jim & Joan Ross, and Travis

Gordon & Lana Rowell, and Madeleine & Matthew

James & Kate Sauber, and Anne

Geoff & Liz Scholefield

Dan & Lisa Scott, and Juliette & Dani

Dean & Jennifer Scott, and
   Lauren, Hannah & Jonathan

Dervyn & Hio Scott

Charles Smatt & Lynn Bodden, and Kaylyn Bodden

Shelly Miller-Smith, and Chelsea & Amy Smith

Don & Jennie Stewart

John & Jillian Stone

Troy & Jewel Studenhofft, and Callhan & Gunnar

Antoinette Sturdivant

Bill & Donna Sullivan, and Michael

Chris & Olivia Sutton, and Laurence & Toby

Phil & Lindsey Turnbull, and Beth & Emma

Frans Vandendries & Suzanne Scheuneman,
   and Emma & Liora Vandendries

Richard & Meelin Vernon, and Elliot,
   Lauren and Yasmin

William & Sharon Walmsley, and Kirsten, Emma,
   Jonathan & Katherine

Terry & Susan Watling, and Tom, Lydia,
   Julia & Holly

Caren Wight, and Justin & Eric

Brian & Dorothy Wilson, and
   Jerrod & Brianna

Colin & Joan Wilson

TABLE OF CONTENTS

TIPS

ENTERTAINING WITH STYLE

Entertaining should be a fun and enjoyable experience. It gives you a chance to express your personality. Whatever the occasion, a beautifully arranged table always sets the mood. This charming dining table is ready for an elegant family Christmas lunch.

Table settings at the home of Dr. and Mrs. Edlin Merren, Grand Cayman
(previous page and above)

SETTING THE TABLE

Setting the table gives you an opportunity to show your creative side through your choice of colours and decorative accessories. Not only should the table be aesthetically pleasing but, more importantly, it should be set so that everything is placed conveniently and within easy reach. Functional place settings will enhance your guests' dining experience.

The first step in setting the table is to lay the tablecloth, runner, place mats and napkins. If using a tablecloth, it should have an overhang of about 12 inches. It is a good idea to iron all the linens before laying them on the table so that they will lay flat and the appearance of wrinkles will be reduced. On a round or oval table, lay rectangular place mats so that the corners are flush with the edge of the table. The napkins can be laid next or after the cutlery has been arranged for each place setting. Napkins will usually be placed to the left of the forks; however, for a formal dinner, the napkin should be folded very simply and placed on the plate. It is a nice touch to place the napkin in a decorative napkin ring or use a decorative folding technique. Napkins vary in size – a 12-inch napkin is used for breakfast and lunch whilst an 18-inch or larger napkin is used for dinner.

Individual place settings consist of dinnerware, glassware, cutlery and linens. Once you have figured out your menu you can then determine what items you will need for each place setting, if you are planning a sit down dinner. The order of courses will dictate the placement of the glassware and cutlery and the old saying, "start from the outside and work your way in," is always a handy reminder of how to arrange each place setting. This simply means that the cutlery for the first course (such as, salad or soup) goes on the outside, farthest away from the plate. As the plates and cutlery are used, they are cleared away for the next course, and the next cutlery in the line is used. The illustration on the following page is a useful example of how an individual place setting should be arranged.

The cutlery should be kept to a minimum by only using what is necessary for the menu that is planned. Generally, there should be no more than three pieces of cutlery on each side of the plate. Knives and spoons go to the right of the plate, with the cutting edge of the knife facing the plate. Soup spoons go to the extreme right. However, if seafood or cocktail forks are to be used, they are placed to the right of the soup spoon. All other forks go to the left of the plate and should be arranged from the outside in, so that the first fork to be used (usually the salad fork), is to the extreme left of the plate, followed by the fish fork, and meat/dinner fork which will be closest to the plate. If the menu does not include a salad, and a fork is needed for the dessert, the dessert fork can be laid to the right of the dinner fork. When the menu does include a salad, lay the dessert fork above the dinner plate so that the tines point to the right. If the table is to

Glassware is positioned above the knife in order of use.

are to be used, the salad plate should be placed to the left of the place setting and below the bread and butter plate which is placed near the tip of the fork.

Various accessories may be placed on the table to accompany the meal, such as salt and pepper shakers, butter dishes and condiment serving dishes. On a formal table, silver or crystal salt and pepper shakers are placed directly above the plates with at least one set for two guests.

Place cards can come in very handy whenever there are six or more guests to be seated and they always add a nice touch. Use your best handwriting and a nice black marker (such as a calligraphy one) when making each place card. Place cards are positioned at the top of each place setting after the table is set. The smart hostess will think carefully about her seating plan to ensure that her guests feel comfortable where they are seated and will enjoy themselves. The host and hostess are usually seated at opposite ends of the table, with the hostess being seated closest to the kitchen area. The seating should be arranged by following the old rule "boy, girl, boy, girl," and spouses should not be seated next to each other.

be completely cleared before dessert, the dessert fork or spoon can be laid to the right of the place setting just before dessert is served or it can simply be placed on the dessert plate along with the food. Similarly, if coffee is served, the beverage spoon can be placed directly on the coffee saucer. Like the cutlery, beverage glasses are also positioned in the order of use. The water glass should be placed closest to the tip of the knife. A pitcher of water should be on hand at the table so that guests can replenish their water throughout the meal. Wines are usually not poured until guests are seated and the appropriate course is presented. The wine glass is placed to the right of the water glass and a dessert wine glass may be placed to the right of the wine glass.

Bread and butter plates should be placed to the left of the place setting near the tip of the fork. If no bread and butter plate is to be used then the salad plate should be placed at the tip of the fork. In the event both plates

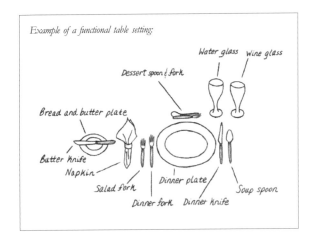

FLORAL ARRANGEMENTS

Anything worth doing is worth doing well! There is nothing quite like a beautiful floral arrangement to dress up your table and set the mood for the occasion, whatever it may be. Flowers are always appealing and serve as an expression of your personality. It is best to purchase and arrange them on the day of the event so that they will look fresh and bright. A simple arrangement of lilies (shown here) can be just as eye-catching and effective as a mixture of cut flowers.

Many hostesses enjoy creating their own unique floral arrangements, sometimes quite simple and at other times very dramatic. Flowers always add that special touch to any occasion.

Poolside table setting at the home of Arthur and Karen Hunter, Spotts, Grand Cayman

CREATING THE MOOD

Your personal taste and style is reflected in the way you entertain your guests. The decisions you make concerning the menu, decorations, flowers, candles etc. will create the mood that you wish to achieve. The location of your event is also another key ingredient to setting the mood. Eating at a dining room table can be both fun and intimate but a refreshing poolside party or beach barbecue can also be a terrific way to get people together. If opting for a poolside venue, the pool can be "dressed up" with balloons and floating floral arrangements. A large buffet table can be set up near the pool, while appetizers and beverages can be served on the patio or deck. It is also fun to invite guests over at easier times of the day. For example, instead of a Saturday night dinner you could host a Sunday breakfast and brunch – which can be simple but delicious with large pitchers of tropical smoothies, muffins (mixed the night before), fresh fruit platters, scrambled eggs and pots of coffee. Lunch can include easy comfort foods like bowls of soup, cold cuts and a crisp salad, followed by an easy key lime pie for dessert.

There are lots of ways to entertain besides the traditional Saturday night dinner. Be creative and imaginative – have a walk around your house and garden and consider all the possibilities. Keep in mind that plants and flowers, balloons, special garden lighting, tiki torches, lanterns and beautifully set tables can do wonders. Great music also adds to the occasion whether it be soft background jazz classics or something more contemporary.

The type of lighting you select will have a big impact on the mood and ambience. Candles are as popular as ever and come in a wide variety of shapes and sizes. A simple crystal bowl with floating candles at the dinner table can be a perfect centre-piece. Small votive candles are also wonderful, especially when they are grouped together on top of mirrors, around floral arrangements or along the table runner on the dining table. Of course tall candles in decorative silver or crystal candle holders are perfect on a fancy table. It is always wise to stock up on candles so that they will be on hand when needed.

If you entertain outdoors, keep in mind that strings of tiny white lights can be used in the trees and shrubs and create a special festive type of mood. At Christmas time, green and red lights can be added to the mix. Another great idea for casual outdoor parties is to use luminaries to outline walkways, the driveway or garden beds. These are easy to make – just anchor small white paper bags with sand and nestle a small votive candle in the centre. You can even cut a scalloped edge around the top of the bags using decorative scissors. Of course, these should not be used in windy conditions or if the grass is dry.

In addition to finding the perfect location to entertain your guests, try to plan a menu with food that is fun to eat. Aim to keep the stress of preparing the food to a minimum. For instance, avoid spending two days in the kitchen preparing a complicated dessert when a simple brownie sundae (using a store-bought brownie mix) or easy hot chocolate lava cakes will be equally enjoyed by your guests. In fact, your guests will have more fun this way since you will be relaxed and having fun too. Try not to be the hostess who gets stuck working in the kitchen and is unable to enjoy her guests. Plan a menu that is more about assembling the food than cooking it or where the food can be prepared well in advance and simply re-heated before serving.

Dessert, poolside by the beautiful Caribbean sea.

GREAT-GRANDPARENTS OF CHILDREN OF CAYMAN PREP AND HIGH SCHOOL

Some of the children attending Cayman Prep and High School are very fortunate to be able to enjoy the company of a great-grandparent. The Cookbook Committee felt it was appropriate to insert this section in the cookbook to honour the many great-grandparents of these children. The Committee also felt it appropriate to include a write-up about the late Rev. John R. Gray, who not only had a major impact on education in the Cayman Islands and was the first Principal of Cayman Prep and High School, but was also the great-grandfather of two of the school's current students.

These interesting people hail from many different countries and each has a story to tell. They have influenced many people along the way right down to their great-grandchildren who in turn have brought them much joy. Our school is pleased to have their great-grandchildren enrolled with us and through this book, we wish to share a bit of their lives with others.

Petronella Ebanks, "Mama Pet", as she is affectionately called by her grandchildren and great-grandchildren, was born in West Bay, Grand Cayman, on 9th June 1914. She is the grandmother of Alexandria Ebanks and great-grandmother of Kiaran Solomon, both students at Cayman Prep and High School. Ms. Pet lives with her daughter in Mount Pleasant, West Bay, where she is a member of the Wesleyan Holiness Church.

In her early years, she lived in Cuba and it was prior to the Revolution that she returned home to Cayman with her family. Her favourite Caymanian dish is Salt Beef and Beans, but she also enjoyed cooking Cuban food. In fact, her home was a haven for many of the refugees who passed through, and many were fed from her table. She was married to Leo Norman Ebanks and is the proud mother of 4 sons, Leonard, Richard, Alfred and Lewey Ebanks, and 1 daughter, Martha Bush.

Ms. Pet was employed for many years as Postmistress of the West Bay Post Office, and was awarded the British Empire Medal by Her Majesty the Queen for outstanding service. Following retirement, she enjoyed spending time with her family and traveling, until illness prevented her from doing so.

92 year old, Petronella Ebanks

The late **Rev. John Gray, MBE, B.Sc**, was born on 6th April 1910 in Scotland where he grew up. In his early adult years, he was a Church of Scotland missionary and then a minister in Kingston, Jamaica. In 1945, he married Mary, who was born in Glasgow, Scotland, on 15th April 1927. When Tommy and Elizabeth, their first two children, were still quite young, Rev. and Mrs. Gray moved to the Cayman Islands where Rev. Gray became Headmaster of the Cayman High School (now Cayman Prep and High School) and minister for the West Bay Presbyterian Church (now the John Gray Memorial United Church). After their arrival to Cayman, three more children were born; Sandy, Johnny and Mary.

Reverend and Mrs. John Gray

Despite being very busy raising five children and setting up house, in her early days in Cayman, **Mary Gray** found time to work at the Cayman High School in the Prep Department as a substitute teacher for the infants. She also worked as manager of Cayman Drug when it was first opened in the early '60s. After a short stint with Kirk Freeport, Mary retired. She was a leader in the Girls Guildry, which later became the Girls Brigade, as well as a Cub Scout leader. She also started the West Bay branch of the Women's Guild, now the Women's Fellowship.

Not many people know that among Rev. John's many accomplishments, he was also an excellent cook. Growing up in Scotland in a family of 8 children in the early 1900s one can only imagine what mealtimes were like, especially with none of the modern conveniences that we have today. Even in the Cayman that Mary and Rev. Gray came to in the late '40s, the availability of produce and provisions was not what it is today. There is one thing though that was abundant and that was fish and seafood, all of which they loved.

Rev. Gray loved cooking fish of any kind and his sauces to accompany were sublime. He made traditional white sauces but was a great improviser with ingredients, rarely using a cookbook but keeping certain strict rules of measurement. In Scotland, a favourite "High Tea" dish was a fish soufflé and he made the most amazing savory soufflés, be they cheese or salmon. He was very fond of a dish called Kedgeree and he made an excellent version, again improvising with what ingredients were to hand. Traditional Scottish scones and pancakes were whipped up in no time at all and cooked on the old fashioned griddle. Mary was (and still is – although she will tell you she has "hung up her apron") also an excellent cook and the family home was always filled with the welcoming smells of cooking and baking. People often speak of the old days in West Bay, when a storm would be approaching Cayman and the men would go around checking that everyone was okay and prepared for the storm. They would always stop by to see what Mary was cooking because she always had plenty of food to offer.

Rev. and Mrs. Gray have twelve grandchildren, two of whom have children who attend Cayman Prep and High School, Christopher Bodden and A.J. McKenzie. They refer to their great-grandmother as G.G.

86 year old, Violet Horner

Violet Horner, who was born in Stoke Newington, London, on 14th February 1920, is grandmother to Lindsey Turnbull and her sister, Beverley Hasler, and their cousins, Gary and Daniel Saxby. She is the mother of Carol Saxby and Marion Hasler, and mother-in-law to their respective husbands, Walter and Terry. Marion and Terry are Lindsey's parents. In addition to being a wonderful mother and grandmother, Violet is great-grandmother to Beth and Emma Turnbull, students at Cayman Prep and High School. She is better known to them as **"Nana."**

Violet lives with Carol and Walter in the heart of rural England, in a village called Heckington, Lincolnshire. She was married to James Horner for 59 and a half years, until he passed away in 2000. He was a much-loved great-granddad, as well.

Violet, who was 86 on St Valentine's Day, is famous for her pie making; in particular, her lemon meringue pie is legendary among the family and is still often requested today!

Laurie Gertrude Bodden (nee Panton), better known to most people as **"Miss Queenie,"** was born in George Town, Grand Cayman, on 16th September 1914. By the time of her birth, her parents, Albert and Effie Panton, already had five boys, so her brothers appropriately nicknamed her "Queenie" at an early age, since she was the only girl.

Miss Queenie married William Bodden, and to this union was born Zoe Bodden, Kay Coe (nee Bodden), Churchill Bodden, Bessie Arch (nee Bodden) and Ernie Bodden. At the age of 91, she has outlived all of her siblings.

Miss Queenie lives with her daughter, Zoe, on South Church Street in George Town, and her favourite activity is going on regular night drives, which she calls her "night cap."

Miss Queenie's family is very fortunate to have her with them to this day, still going strong and enjoying her nine great-grandchildren who affectionately call her "Nanee," two of whom, first cousins Andrew Jarvis and Stephanie Bodden, attend Cayman Prep and High School. Their younger siblings, Aaron and Natalie respectively, will soon follow.

91 year old, Queenie Bodden

Lina Dell Ebanks was born on 7th March 1915 in West Bay, Grand Cayman. **"Mama Dell"**, as she is affectionately known to her grandson, James Flatley, and great-grandson, Kiaran Solomon, both students at Cayman Prep and High School, lives on Elizabeth Street in West Bay. She attends worship and is a member of the John Gray Memorial Church.

Ms. Dell was married to Richard Ebanks who died at the age of 47, leaving her to raise 1 son, Richard Ebanks, and 4 daughters, Lina Dell Jackson, Ina Claire Orr, Carol Ann Ebanks and Nyda Mae Flatley.

Having operated a small shop on Elizabeth Street for several years prepared her with sufficient skills to rise to the position of Manager of Cayman Drug Ltd. Following her retirement, she busied herself with her sand yard and the many fruit trees in her garden. Today, she enjoys sitting in her swing on the front porch surrounded by her plants, waiting for passersby to drop in and visit. Ms. Dell's favourite dish is Fish Stew, but she has always enjoyed cooking Turtle Stew and Conch Stew.

91 year old, Lina Dell Ebanks

Orlando Bonar or "Bob", was born in Orlando, Florida, on 25th March 1924. He was called "Bob" because his mother wanted to name him Robert, and his dad wanted him to be a Jr., named for him. When he was 8 years old, he traveled to South Carolina to live with his aunt, and was educated there, then moved to Crownsville, Maryland, to be with his parents in 1941. In 1942, he met Emma Roebuck Dew, and they married in 1943. After over 53 years of wedded bliss, the love of his life, Emma, died. She is sadly missed by Orlando and the entire family.

In his early years, Orlando was a milkman, delivering milk door to door. He then served in the Infantry in the U.S. Army in WWII, and was honorably discharged with the rank of Staff Sergeant in 1946. After that, he was a law enforcement officer for 31 years, retiring in 1986.

Today, Orlando is a volunteer on the Transportation Committee for the Caring Network. He takes people to the doctor, dentist, hospital, and wherever they need to go for their health. He loves to cook, and has planned and presented several cook-outs in the area where he lives. He says, "We are all like a bunch of kids having fun!" Orlando Bonar is great-grandfather to Prep students, Jonathan, Katelee and Nicholas McTaggart.

83 year old, Orlando Bonar

86 year old, Beatrice Dilbert

Beatrice Vernett Dilbert, or **"Gramma Bea,"** as she is affectionately known to her great-grandchildren, Jade and Wyatt Bodden, students at Cayman Prep and High School, was born in West Bay on 10th February 1920. She also has 8 grandchildren and 10 other great-grandchildren. She was a single mother who raised 4 daughters, Annie Multon, (nee Dilbert), Annice Duffell (nee Dilbert), Beatrice Fazio (nee Dilbert) and Dawn Dilbert. To this day, she lives in the same "yard" where she was born. Gramma Bea worked for Caribbean Club for over 23 years and was well-known within the tourism industry. Her favourite meal to prepare was Turtle Stew with all the trimmings. One of her grandchildren's favourite desserts was her custard-topped cornbread. Not only was she famous for her cooking, but she enjoyed thatchwork and working in her white sand yard. After retirement she made every effort to ensure that her love of thatchwork was passed on to future generations by holding training sessions with Reina Jefferson at various private homes and schools. While the onset of Alzheimer's has changed their beloved Gramma Bea, her family still feels fortunate to have her with them today.

Antoinette Marie Simpson Sturdivant was born in Tampa, Florida, on 6th May 1914. She has 6 children, 15 grandchildren, 20 great-grandchildren and 4 great-great-grandchildren.

She was a seamstress for many years, then started quilting when she was in her early sixties. She made a lot of custom quilts for many people. Each of her grandchildren, great-grandchildren and great-great-grandchildren has at least four or more of them. She is 91 years old and now lives in Brandon, Florida. Except for a few years living in Louisiana and Georgia when she was younger, she has always lived in and around Tampa, Florida. She has always been there for all of her family whenever they needed her, or just needed someone to talk to. Also, she makes the best breakfast biscuits in the world!

Ann Sturdivant is the great-grandmother of Cayman Prep and High School student, Travis Ross.

91 year old, Antoinette Sturdivant

81 year old, Naomi Panton

Naomi Panton was born in George Town, Grand Cayman, on 17th September 1924 to the late Vibert Bodden and his wife, Annie Laurie. Naomi, like her mother, was an excellent cook in her younger years and was renowned in the Island for her cooking skills. In the 1950s, Naomi owned and operated a grocery store and snack bar on Cardinal Avenue in George Town, which sold many items including malted milks, sandwiches, hot dogs and burgers in homemade buns, patties, ice cream and frozen custards. In those days, ice cream was a novelty and she had many loyal customers.

In later years, Naomi would be the first to open a flower shop in Cayman. She is the great-grandmother of Cayman Prep and High School students, Cory and Daniel Hunter. She currently resides on Crewe Road where she has been living for over 30 years and she delights in spending time with her children, grandchildren and great-grandchildren.

Nan Alexander lives in a cottage in the town of Battle, Sussex in South East England. She is a wonderful lady and an exceptional cook who loves to entertain her friends and family.

Nan and her late husband, Gordon, lived in the Cayman Islands in the early 1970s when Gordon worked with PWD and subsequently Arch & Godfrey. Nan taught kindergarten at the Catholic School. They also lived in Africa, Iran and Saudi Arabia. Nan's cooking has been influenced by all these various cultures. Once, while in Cayman, she and Gordon roasted a suckling pig for Christmas using the old-fashioned method of building an in-ground "oven." It was an amazing Christmas.

81 year old, Nan Alexander

She is constantly experimenting with new recipes, using fresh ingredients. Being close to the South Coast, she has access to the bounty of the sea from the fish market in Hastings, and frequents the farm shop for all fresh vegetables and herbs. However, the one secret ingredient in all her dishes was taught to her at an early age by a nun at the Sacred Heart Convent where she was a student. No matter what you cook she was told, however simple or complicated the dish, as long as it is made with love, it will be a masterpiece. Nan is great-grandmother to Cayman Prep and High School student, A.J. McKenzie.

Conch Fritters, a local favourite (page 31), and Homemade Tartar Sauce (page 196)

APPETIZERS

SPINACH ARTICHOKE DIP

Nutrition Facts per serving: Calories 219.2, Protein 15.55 Gm, Carbs 11.65 Gm, Fat 12.04 Gm, Cholesterol 31.56 mg, Dietary Fiber 1.362 Gm, Sugar 0.698 Gm, Sodium 1429 mg, Calcium 500.6 mg, Potassium 102.3 mg, Iron 0.638 mg

SERVES 10

1 (8 oz.) pkg. cream cheese, softened
1 cup reduced fat mayonnaise
1 (10 oz.) pack frozen chopped spinach, thawed and well-drained
2 tsp. crushed garlic
2 cups fresh grated Parmesan cheese
2 (6 oz.) jars marinated artichoke hearts, drained
2 Tbsp. roasted red peppers (bottled)
1 scotch bonnet pepper, finely diced (remove seeds) or 1 tsp. Tabasco sauce

1. Preheat oven to 350°F.

2. Blend all the ingredients together in a food processor or electric blender until smooth.

3. Pour into an oven-proof serving dish.

4. Bake in preheated oven for 30 minutes, or until lightly browned.

5. Serve with tortilla chips.

[BRYAN & JENNIFER HUNTER, AND CORY & DANIEL]

BEV DACOSTA'S BLACK BEAN AND MANGO SALSA

Nutrition Facts per serving: Calories 288.9, Protein 15.36 Gm, Carbs 53.89 Gm, Fat 2.155 Gm, Cholesterol 0 mg, Dietary Fiber 6.06 Gm, Sugar 6.308 Gm, Sodium 651.7 mg, Calcium 101 mg, Potassium 977.2 mg, Iron 3.805 mg

SERVES 8 TO 10

1 (15.5 oz.) can Black Beans
1 (16 oz.) can Pinto Beans
1 (15.5 oz.) can Red Kidney Beans
1 (14.5 oz.) can chopped or diced tomatoes
1 lg. mango (not too ripe), cut into small squares
1 lg. red onion, chopped or finely sliced
¼ cup lime juice
½ cup olive oil
1 Tbsp. Adobo seasoning (preferably with pepper)
1 lg. bell pepper, finely or coarsely chopped (depending on preference)
Fresh cilantro (or dried, if fresh is not available), chopped
1 tsp. salt (optional)
1 Tbsp. sugar (optional)
1 (8 oz.) pkg. frozen corn or niblets

1. Drain all the cans of beans; rinse.

2. In a large mixing bowl, combine all ingredients.

3. Cover and refrigerate overnight.

4. Serve chilled, with tortilla chips.

This tasty recipe is often shared by Caymanian resident, Bev DaCosta, and is always the hit of the party. It is great when entertaining a large crowd, as it makes a very large bowlful!

[STEPHEN & DEBRA MCTAGGART, AND SARAH, AMELIA & MATTHEW]

PLANTAIN CHIPS WITH WARM CILANTRO DIPPING SAUCE

Nutrition Facts per serving: Calories 1088, Protein 4.501 Gm, Carbs 33.11 Gm, Fat 109.7 Gm, Cholesterol 0 mg, Dietary Fiber 2.087 Gm, Sugar 0.03 Gm, Sodium 682.2 mg, Calcium 89.82 mg, Potassium 704.5, Iron 4.515 mg

1. Trim off ends of plantains, and cut 4 vertical slits in skin of each (do not cut into fruit).
2. Microwave for 1 minute at 50% power, then pull off peel; cut diagonally into $^1/_8$" slices.
3. Pour both oils into a 3" to 4" deep frying pan; bring to Medium-High heat.
4. Working in batches, add plantain to the pan, and cook until golden brown, turning occasionally, for about 4 minutes.
5. Using a slotted spoon, transfer to paper towels; sprinkle with salt and pepper.
6. Cool slightly. Serve with Warm Cilantro Dipping Sauce.

Plantain Chips with Warm Cilantro Dipping Sauce

Warm Cilantro Dipping Sauce:
1. Blend first 4 ingredients in food processor until cilantro is finely chopped, about 15 seconds; transfer mixture to medium heat-proof bowl.
2. Heat oil in a skillet over Medium heat until hot; slowly whisk into cilantro mixture.
3. Mix in hot sauce; season to taste with salt and pepper, and transfer to a small bowl.

[LARRY & SHELLEY LEONARD, AND ALEX & NICHOLAS]

SERVES 6

Chips:
3 lg. unripe (green) plantains
1 cup Canola oil
1 cup extra virgin olive oil
Salt and black pepper,
   to taste

Warm Cilantro Dipping Sauce:
1 cup chopped fresh
   cilantro leaves
4 garlic cloves, minced
2 Tbsp. apple cider vinegar
1 Tbsp. fresh lime juice
¾ cup extra virgin olive oil
½ tsp. hot pepper sauce
Salt and black pepper,
   to taste

CRAB CAKES WITH ROASTED RED PEPPER COULIS SAUCE

Nutrition Facts per serving: Calories 259.3, Protein 18.07 Gm, Carbs 17.21 Gm, Fat 12.9 Gm, Cholesterol 139.5 mg, Dietary Fiber 0.446 Gm, Sugar 0.964 Gm, Sodium 1174 mg, Calcium 132.2 mg, Potassium 213.9 mg, Iron 1.502 mg

MAKES 16
SERVES 8

2 (16 oz.) cans of lump crabmeat
1/3 cup red onions, diced
1/3 cup green bell pepper, diced
1/3 cup red bell pepper, diced
1/2 small bunch fresh cilantro, minced (about 1/4 cup)
2 eggs
3/4 cup mayonnaise
6 dashes Worcestershire sauce
3 dashes Tabasco sauce
1.5 Tbsp. Old Bay seasoning
1/2 tsp. black pepper
2 cups fresh bread crumbs
Salt, to taste
Japanese style Panko bread crumbs, ground fine in a blender

Roasted Red Pepper Coulis Sauce:
1 red bell pepper
1 Tbsp. olive oil (for roasting pepper)
1 bottle of roasted red peppers (optional)
2 cloves garlic
3/4 cup red wine vinegar
Pinch of salt
Pinch of cayenne pepper
3 Tbsp. salad oil
1 cup mayonnaise

1. Mix all ingredients well (except the Panko crumbs) and let rest overnight in the refrigerator.

2. Form into crab cakes, coat in Panko bread crumbs and, just before serving, deep fry until golden brown or fry in a pan of hot vegetable oil until browned on both sides.

Roasted Red Pepper Coulis Sauce:

1. Fire roast the red pepper by placing it on a baking sheet lined with foil; drizzle with 1 tablespoon olive oil. Broil 5 inches from heat for about 10 minutes or until the pepper looks blistered. Place pepper in a Ziploc bag; seal and let stand for 10 minutes to loosen the skin. Peel off the skin and remove seeds. Alternatively, purchased bottled roasted red peppers can be substituted.

2. In a blender, add the roasted red pepper, garlic cloves, red wine vinegar, salt and cayenne pepper; puree well and then slowly add the salad oil to the blender while it is still running.

3. To make the sauce, mix three-quarters of the pepper coulis mixture with the mayonnaise. Use the remaining one-quarter of the mixture for decoration.

[GUY HARVEY'S ISLAND GRILL]
- SEE ADVERTISEMENT ON PAGE 252 -

CRABMEAT & ARTICHOKE DIP

Nutrition Facts per serving: Calories 131.7, Protein 6.48 Gm, Carbs 2.735 Gm, Fat 11.16 Gm, Cholesterol 19.56 mg, Dietary Fiber 0.006 Gm, Sugar 0.003 Gm, Sodium 299.3 mg, Calcium 74.57 mg, Potassium 7.24 mg, Iron 0.658 mg

SERVES 10 TO 12

1 (13.75 oz.) can artichoke hearts, drained
1 (6 oz.) can crabmeat, drained
1/2 cup mayonnaise
1/2 cup shredded Parmesan cheese
1 clove garlic (or to taste)
Paprika, to taste

1. Mix together in a blender artichoke, crabmeat, mayonnaise, garlic and 1/4 cup of Parmesan cheese, until well-blended, but still chunky.

2. Pour into an oven-proof baking dish. Top with the remaining Parmesan cheese and paprika. Bake at 350°F until bubbly. Serve hot with crackers.

[DAVID & CHRISTINA KIRKALDY, AND RYAN & TAYLOR]

SWEDISH MEATBALLS

Nutrition Facts per serving: Calories 212.8, Protein 10.3 Gm, Carbs 22.63 Gm, Fat 9.3,
Dietary Fiber 0.711 Gm, Sugar 1.451 Gm, Sodium 441.1 mg, Calcium 140.3 mg, Pota

Meatballs:

1. Mix all the ingredients together and form

2. Fry in vegetable oil, turning frequently, until

Sauce:

1. In a large saucepan, mix all the ingredie

2. Add cooked meatballs; simmer covered for

3. Serve with toothpicks.

[JEFF & MICHELLE BOUCHER, AND MICHAEL & JENNA]

ked onion
bs

per

stard
Approx. ¾ cup grated
Parmesan cheese (or enough
to bind)

Sauce:
1 cup brown sugar
1 cup white vinegar
1 can tomato soup
1 Tbsp. chili powder
1 Tbsp. celery seed

"This recipe was my
Grandma Braddock's,
and she made it for every
special family gathering
we had at her home
in Canada."
- Michelle Boucher

Swedish Meatballs

Swedish
MeatBalls

pd 29

VEGETABLE DIP

Nutrition Facts per serving: Calories 96.42, Protein 0.828 Gm, Carbs 6.566 Gm, Fat 7.907 Gm, Cholesterol 0 mg, Dietary Fiber 0.737 Gm, Sugar 0.9 Gm, Sodium 436.5 mg, Calcium 9.675 mg, Potassium 173.8 mg, Iron 0.486 mg

MAKES ABOUT 2 CUPS

¼ cup chili sauce
1 Tbsp. lemon juice
½ cup salad oil
1 clove garlic
½ tsp. salt
½ tsp. paprika
1 (8 oz.) can tomato sauce
¼ to ⅓ lb. blue cheese, crumbled
Celery sticks, carrots, or any fresh vegetables, or crackers

1. Place first 7 ingredients into a blender; blend until smooth.

2. Add blue cheese by simply folding it in.

3. Serve in a small bowl surrounded by favourite vegetables and/or crackers.

[STEPHEN & DEBRA MCTAGGART, AND SARAH, AMELIA & MATTHEW]

Vegetable Dip

SHRIMP CEVICHE

Nutrition Facts per serving: Calories 138.3, Protein 20.72 Gm, Carbs 11.65 Gm, Fat 1.528 Gm, Cholesterol 173.3 mg, Dietary Fiber 2.48 Gm, Sugar 3.164 Gm, Sodium 347.1 mg, Calcium 80.29 mg, Potassium 618.7 mg, Iron 3.893 mg

SERVES 4

1 lb. Black Tiger shrimp
¼ tsp. salt
Salt and freshly ground pepper, to taste
½ cup finely chopped red onion
¼ cup chopped cilantro
1 med. cucumber, peeled and chopped
Juice of 2 limes
3 Roma tomatoes, chopped
Tortilla chips
Hot salsa
Tabasco sauce (optional)

1. Boil shrimp with ¼ teaspoon salt for 3 to 4 minutes, or until pink in colour.

2. Peel and chop shrimp into bite-size pieces.

3. Mix all ingredients together.

4. Season with salt and ground pepper.

5. Serve with tortilla chips, salsa and Tabasco (if desired).

"Shrimp Ceviche, a very traditional Mexican seafood recipe, originates in the Pacific Coast area of Mazatlan in Mexico where I grew up in a family of seafarers, who were used to eating all varieties of seafood."
- Rosa Esau

[ROSA AND CHANTELLE ESAU]

CONCH FRITTERS

Nutrition Facts per serving: Calories 201.5, Protein 19.04 Gm, Carbs 20.57 Gm, Fat 4.215 Gm, Cholesterol 70.18 mg,
Dietary Fiber 1.246 Gm, Sugar 1.253 Gm, Sodium 218.8 mg, Calcium 19.93 mg, Potassium 477.8 mg, Iron 4.537 mg

1. Rinse the conch either with water or lime juice; run through a food processor.

2. Mix everything together, and form into about 1" balls.

3. Deep fry for about 5 minutes, or until brown.

4. Serve with tartar sauce (see page 196 for Homemade Tartar Sauce).

[TONY & CHRISTINE CLEAVER, AND ALEX, JORDYN & BETHANY]

SERVES 12 TO 14

2-½ lbs. conch
2 to 3 green bell
   peppers, diced
2 lg. onions, diced
1 lg. seasoning pepper
   or scotch bonnet pepper,
   seeded and finely
   chopped (optional)
1 Tbsp. cayenne pepper
1 egg, lightly beaten
2-½ cups self-rising flour
Salt and pepper, to taste
Vegetable oil, for frying

CALAMARI & GAMBERI ALL'AGLIO

Nutrition Facts per serving: Calories 377.8, Protein 15.3 Gm, Carbs 12.33 Gm, Fat 29.82 Gm, Cholesterol 186.7 mg,
Dietary Fiber 0.974 Gm, Sugar 1.625 Gm, Sodium 445.1 mg, Calcium 92.33 mg, Potassium 361.3 mg, Iron 1.95 mg

1. Heat olive oil in a frying pan over High heat.

2. Add shrimp, squid and garlic to hot oil; cook for about 1 to 2 minutes, or until garlic is almost pale yellow. Add white wine, lemon juice and parsley.

3. Season with salt and pepper; toss quickly. Do not over-cook.

4. Serve immediately.

[EDOARDO'S RESTAURANT]
- SEE ADVERTISEMENT ON PAGE 248 -

SERVES 1

2 jumbo shrimp
2.5 ozs. clean squid, sliced
1 oz. olive oil
1 oz. white wine
½ of a lemon, squeezed
1 pinch chopped parsley
1 pinch salt and black pepper
1 pinch chopped garlic

SHRIMP COCKTAIL

Nutrition Facts per serving: Calories 80.91, Protein 9.24 Gm, Carbs 9.376 Gm, Fat 0.742 Gm, Cholesterol 64.8 mg,
Dietary Fiber 0.154 Gm, Sugar 2.18 Gm, Sodium 205.7 mg, Calcium 39.73 mg, Potassium 268.3 mg, Iron 1.437 mg

1. Peel and de-vein fresh shrimp, leaving tails intact.

2. Cook in boiling water for 3 minutes, until shrimp turn pink; drain and chill.

3. In a bowl, mix together all the ingredients for the Cocktail Sauce.

4. Divide the Cocktail Sauce evenly between 8 shallow crystal bowls or cocktail glasses, and serve with about 6 jumbo shrimp to each bowl.

TIP:
To save on time, fully cooked shrimp may be purchased.

[BRYAN & JENNIFER HUNTER, AND CORY & DANIEL]

SERVES 8

48 jumbo shrimp uncooked

Cocktail Sauce:
½ cup chili sauce
½ cup ketchup
¼ cup horseradish
2 Tbsp. Worcestershire sauce
1 Tbsp. lemon juice
Tabasco sauce, to taste
Snipped fresh parsley (optional)

STUFFED MUSHROOMS IN GARLICKY WINE SAUCE

Nutrition Facts per serving: Calories 85.64, Protein 3.69 Gm, Carbs 2.168 Gm, Fat 6.163 Gm, Cholesterol 18.21 mg, Dietary Fiber 0.021 Gm, Sugar 0.413 Gm, Sodium 139.7 mg, Calcium 105.5 mg, Potassium 84.29 mg, Iron 0.541 mg

SERVES 8 TO 12

2 Tbsp. butter
2 shallots, finely chopped
4 cloves garlic, minced
⅔ cup dry white wine
⅔ cup chicken broth
1 (5.0 to 5.2 oz.) container semi-soft cheese with garlic and herbs, such as Boursin
2 doz. lg. mushrooms
2 Tbsp. snipped fresh herbs, such as basil, oregano or parsley

1. In a saucepan, heat butter over Medium heat.
2. Cook shallots and garlic in butter, until slightly browned.
3. Add wine and broth; bring just to a boil, then reduce heat.
4. Simmer uncovered for 15 minutes. Transfer to a 3-quart au gratin dish.
5. Preheat oven to 425°F.
6. Remove mushroom stems. Spoon a rounded teaspoon of cheese into each cap.
7. Arrange filled mushrooms, cheese side up, in the dish.
8. Bake uncovered for 10 to 12 minutes, or until heated through.
9. Top with herbs before serving hot.

[TONY & CHRISTINE CLEAVER, AND ALEX, JORDYN & BETHANY]

CODFISH FRITTERS

Nutrition Facts per serving: Calories 125.8, Protein 18.1 Gm, Carbs 8.036 Gm, Fat 1.903 Gm, Cholesterol 41.07 mg, Dietary Fiber 0.438 Gm, Sugar 0.479 Gm, Sodium 1901 mg, Calcium 64.34 mg, Potassium 472.8 mg, Iron 1.152 mg

MAKES 24

½ lb. salted codfish
½ lb. all purpose flour
2 onions, finely chopped
2 plum tomatoes, finely chopped
2 cloves garlic, minced
½ scotch bonnet pepper, seeded and finely chopped
2 stalks scallion, finely chopped
2 Tbsp. vegetable oil
2 tsp. baking powder
Vegetable oil, for frying

1. Soak codfish, preferably overnight. Drain, rinse under cold water, and flake the fish, making sure to remove fish bones.
2. Sauté tomatoes, onion, garlic, scallion and pepper in 2 tablespoons oil; drain off oil and let cool.
3. Add seasoning to raw codfish, and mix well; set aside.
4. Add baking powder to flour; stir in the codfish.
5. Add enough water to make a medium batter.
6. Scoop 1 tablespoon of mixture at a time into ½" of oil. Fry until golden brown; drain on paper towel.
7. Serve hot, with tartar sauce (see page 196 for Homemade Tartar Sauce) or cocktail sauce.

[CELICEA MYLES & KAI-LEIGH HAUGHTON
AND TREVOR & NICOLO TUMMINGS]

LOBSTER SALAD

Nutrition Facts per serving: Calories 86.2, Protein 11.27 Gm, Carbs 9.287 Gm, Fat 0.646 Gm, Cholesterol 53.71 mg, Dietary Fiber 0.557 Gm, Sugar 1.006 Gm, Sodium 448.8 mg, Calcium 38.08 mg, Potassium 290.9 mg, Iron 0.501 mg

1. Bring a medium or large pot of water to boil. Add lobster meat; simmer for about 10 minutes, or until fully cooked.

2. Drain meat, and chop into bite-size pieces.

3. In a bowl, mix together mayonnaise, ketchup and chili sauce, until smooth and well-blended.

4. Stir in the remaining ingredients.

5. Taste the sauce for seasonings. If more spice is desired, add an extra diced scotch bonnet pepper, or ½ teaspoon Tabasco.

6. Fold in the lobster; refrigerate, until chilled.

7. Serve over a bed of lettuce, or with crackers.

[BRYAN & JENNIFER HUNTER, AND CORY & DANIEL]

SERVES 4 AS A MAIN DISH AND 8 AS AN APPETIZER

1 lb. lobster meat
  (about 3 small lobster tails)
½ cup reduced fat mayonnaise
¼ cup ketchup
¼ cup chili sauce or
  cocktail sauce
1 tsp. Old Bay seasoning
1 scallion, finely chopped
1 scotch bonnet, seeded and
  finely diced (or more to taste)
1 stalk celery, finely chopped
12 grape tomatoes, chopped
  in half
1 Tbsp. small capers
1 Tbsp. sweet relish
Juice of 2 limes or 1 lemon
Black pepper, to taste
Tabasco sauce (optional, for
  added spice)

Lobster Salad and Shrimp Cocktail (page 31)

RED PEPPER WALNUT DIP

Nutrition Facts per serving: Calories 75.02, Protein 2.897 Gm, Carbs 7.37 Gm, Fat 4.501 Gm, Cholesterol 0.167 mg, Dietary Fiber 1.018 Gm, Sugar 5.253 Gm, Sodium 52.92 mg, Calcium 28.98 mg, Potassium 162 mg, Iron 0.475 mg

SERVES 10 TO 12

¾ cup walnuts, toasted
½ cup raisins
½ cup plain, low-fat yogurt
¼ tsp. salt
⅛ tsp. ground red pepper
1 (12 oz.) bottle roasted red
    bell peppers, drained

1. Place all ingredients in a food processor; process until smooth.

2. Serve with toasted pita wedges or sourdough baguette slices.

[TONY & CHRISTINE CLEAVER, AND ALEX, JORDYN & BETHANY]

Red Pepper Walnut Dip

GARDEN GREEN DIP

Nutrition Facts per cup: Calories 160.1, Protein 10.35 Gm, Carbs 27.14 Gm, Fat 1.792 Gm, Cholesterol 0.55 mg, Dietary Fiber 6.781 Gm, Sugar 2.438 Gm, Sodium 142.9 mg, Calcium 107.9 mg, Potassium 629 mg, Iron 4.324 mg

MAKES ABOUT 2 CUPS

1 (19 oz.) can Cannellini
    White Kidney Beans,
    rinsed and drained
1 cup finely chopped
    fresh parsley
2 Tbsp. fresh lemon juice
1 to 2 cloves garlic, minced
⅔ cup mayonnaise
½ cup snipped fresh chives
½ tsp. pepper
¼ tsp. salt

1. Process beans, parsley, lemon juice and garlic in a food processor using a metal blade until the consistency of paste (about 30 seconds).

2. Transfer white bean mixture to a mixing bowl; fold in mayonnaise, chives, salt and pepper.

3. Serve with vegetables or pita wedges.

[FRANS VANDENDRIES & SUZANNE SCHEUNEMAN,
AND EMMA & LIORA VANDENDRIES]

BLUE CHEESE TOASTS

Nutrition Facts per serving: Calories 202, Protein 4.52 Gm, Carbs 16.62 Gm, Fat 13.45 Gm, Cholesterol 33.24 mg,
Dietary Fiber 0.765 Gm, Sugar 0.112 Gm, Sodium 374.1 mg, Calcium 67.23 mg, Potassium 66.15 mg, Iron 0.879 mg

SERVES 8 TO 10

1 loaf of French bread, cut into 1" rounds
1 (4 oz.) pkg. crumbled blue cheese, or more to taste
1 stick (8 Tbsp.) butter, softened at room temp.
Sugar

1. Preheat oven to 375°F.

2. In a large bowl, mix together the blue cheese and butter until combined.

3. Spread the mixture onto the slices of French bread.

4. On each slice of bread, put a heaped teaspoon (or more) of sugar on top of the cheese mixture; pat it down with the back of a spoon.

5. Place slices in a single layer on a large cookie sheet.

6. Bake in preheated oven until the cheese has melted (about 10 minutes).

[DWIGHT & SHANNON PANTON, AND DYLAN & FRASIER]

VIDALIA ONION DIP

Nutrition Facts per serving: Calories 281.5, Protein 5.683 Gm, Carbs 2.985 Gm, Fat 29.22 Gm, Cholesterol 27.3 mg,
Dietary Fiber 0.453 Gm, Sugar 0.77 Gm, Sodium 367.8 mg, Calcium 188 mg, Potassium 63.19 mg, Iron 0.109 mg

SERVES 8 TO 12

2 cups Vidalia onion, chopped
2 cups grated Swiss cheese
1-½ cups mayonnaise
1 tsp. celery salt
¼ tsp. dill weed
¼ tsp. white pepper

1. Preheat oven to 350°F.

2. Mix ingredients all together.

3. Bake in an oven-proof (approximately 7" x 8") casserole for 30 minutes, or until browned and bubbly.

4. Serve with crackers.

[TONY & CHRISTINE CLEAVER, AND ALEX, JORDYN & BETHANY]

CURRIED ACKEE DIP

Nutrition Facts per serving: Calories 160.4, Protein 4.448 Gm, Carbs 11.56 Gm, Fat 10.9 Gm, Cholesterol 4.264 mg,
Dietary Fiber 1.647 Gm, Sugar 5.994 Gm, Sodium 488.7 mg, Calcium 73.05 mg, Potassium 199.6 mg, Iron 1.08 mg

SERVES 10

8 slices bacon, chopped
1 med. onion, chopped
2-½ Tbsp. curry powder
1 (14.5 oz.) can stewed tomatoes (or diced), drained
1 (19 oz.) can ackees, drained and rinsed
½ tsp. dried basil
½ tsp. Mrs. Dash

1. In a large saucepan, fry bacon until crisp. Drain off half the fat. Add onion and curry powder; cook for 3 to 5 minutes over Medium heat.

2. Add tomato, ackee and seasonings.

3. Gently stir to blend for 3 to 5 minutes.

4. Serve with Wheat Thin crackers.

[JOHN & JILLIAN STONE]

CRISPY WONTONS

Nutrition Facts per serving: Calories 48.14, Protein 3.082 Gm, Carbs 1.051 Gm, Fat 3.452 Gm, Cholesterol 11.83 mg,
Dietary Fiber 0.33 Gm, Sugar 0.104 Gm, Sodium 125.6 mg, Calcium 2.226 mg, Potassium 50.24 mg, Iron 0.169 mg

MAKES ABOUT 3 DOZEN

Approx. 1 lb. ground pork
   (or ground chicken)
1 can water chestnuts, chopped
4 scallions, chopped
2 Tbsp. low sodium soy sauce
1 tsp. salt
1 tsp. cornstarch mixed with
   equal water
2 tsp. fresh gingerroot, grated
Wonton skins (round ones
   from the Asian section
   of the supermarket
   or use square ones)

1. Combine pork, water chestnuts, scallions, soy sauce, salt, cornstarch and ginger in a medium bowl; mix well.

2. Place ½ teaspoon of the pork (or chicken) mixture in centre of each wonton skin; moisten the edge with water.

3. Fold wonton skin over filling to form a triangle.

4. Bring up other two sides to meet triangle at top.

5. Press firmly to seal.

6. Heat oil in wok or large saucepan over Medium-High heat to 375°F.

7. Deep fry wontons, a few at a time, 2 to 3 minutes, or until golden brown and crispy.

8. Drain on paper towels.

9. Serve warm with Asian Dipping Sauce (page 199).

[LARRY & SHELLEY LEONARD, AND ALEX & NICHOLAS]

Preparing the Wontons

Crispy Wontons with Asian Dipping Sauce

PEPPER JELLY DIP

Nutrition Facts per serving: Calories 263.7, Protein 4.912 Gm, Carbs 19.59 Gm, Fat 19.5 Gm, Cholesterol 20.21 mg, Dietary Fiber 0.793 Gm, Sugar 17.44 Gm, Sodium 323.9 mg, Calcium 112.8 mg, Potassium 104.5 mg, Iron 0.507 mg

1. Mix all ingredients together, and spread in a quiche plate.
2. Top with ¼" of pepper jelly, which can be bought or made.
3. Serve with crackers.

[TONY & CHRISTINE CLEAVER, AND ALEX, JORDYN & BETHANY]

SERVES 12

1 (10 oz.) jar pepper jelly
  (or see page 197 for homemade
  Red Pepper Jelly)
1 cup chopped pecans
1 cup grated sharp cheddar
  cheese
1 cup scallion, finely
  chopped
½ cup mayonnaise

Pepper Jelly Dip

SALMON PARTY LOG

Nutrition Facts per serving: Calories 434.25, Protein 11.77 Gm, Carbs 2.28 Gm, Fat 42.81 Gm, Cholesterol 106.54 mg, Dietary Fiber 0.47 Gm, Sugar 0.799 Gm, Sodium 810.5 mg, Calcium 1.092 mg, Potassium 262.62 mg, Iron 1.092 mg

1. Drain and flake salmon; remove skin and bones.
2. In a bowl, combine thoroughly the salmon, cream cheese, lemon juice, onion, horseradish, salt and butter.
3. Chill covered for several hours.
4. Shape into a log approximately 8" x 2", or use a fish-shaped mold sprayed lightly with no-stick cooking spray.
5. Combine pecans and parsley, and roll log or cover fish shape in mixture.
6. Chill thoroughly. Serve with crackers.

[DARRIN & MICHELLE DAYKIN, AND JOSHUA & EMMI]

TIP:
To eliminate having to take out the bones and skin from the canned salmon, which can be time-consuming, two (7.1 oz.) **salmon pouches** *(Chicken of the Sea brand) can be used instead.*

SERVES 8

1 (14.75 oz.) can red salmon
1 (8 oz.) pkg. cream cheese
1 tsp. lemon juice
2 tsp. grated onion
1 tsp. horseradish
1-½ tsp. salt
1 stick butter, softened
½ cup chopped pecans
3 Tbsp. chopped parsley

Slightly Sourdough Pancakes (page 45), left, and Mr. Cleaver's Crepes (page 41)

BRUNCH

EGGS

Bacon or Ham Strata....................................48
Breakfast Casserole.....................................42
Brunch Baked Eggs.....................................47
Choose-a-Flavour Quiche............................44
Easy Quiche...41
Egg Casserole..43
Eggs Fiesta..40
Ham and Cheese Omelette..........................46
Salmon Quiche...43
Scrambled Egg & Cheese............................48

COFFEE CAKES

Sausage Coffee Cake...................................45
Yum-Yum Sour Cream Coffee Cake.............52

BEVERAGES

Cayman Limeade...53
Mango & Raspberry Smoothie.....................44

BREADS

Apple Bran Muffins....................................49
Cinnamon Rolls..47
Macadamia Nut Muffins..............................50
Monkey Bread..40
Overnight Caramel French Toast................49

PANCAKES, ETC.

Buttermilk Banana Pancakes........................51
Mr. Cleaver's Crepes..................................41
Slightly Sourdough Pancakes.......................45

MISCELLANEOUS

Brown Sugar Bacon....................................51
Honey Nut Granola....................................53

EGGS FIESTA

Nutrition Facts per serving: Calories 258.4, Protein 20.17 Gm, Carbs 6.084 Gm, Fat 16.62 Gm, Cholesterol 214.9 mg,
Dietary Fiber 0.185 Gm, Sugar 1.34 Gm, Sodium 482.6 mg, Calcium 347.9 mg, Potassium 123.3 mg, Iron 1.182 mg

SERVES 12

10 eggs, beaten
1 lb. Monterey Jack
   cheese, shredded
½ cup self-rising flour
1 pint cottage cheese
1 (4 oz.) can green chiles, diced
¼ Tbsp. butter

1. Preheat oven to 400°F.
2. Combine all ingredients (except for butter), and mix with the eggs.
3. Grease the bottom of a casserole dish (approximately 9" x 7") with the butter.
4. Pour the egg mixture into the casserole.
5. Bake at 400°F for 15 minutes.
6. Turn the oven temperature down to 350°F, and bake for a further 30 minutes.

NOTE:
This dish is great alone, or served with salsa and/or sour cream.
Nice for large groups.

[STEPHEN & DEBRA MCTAGGART, AND SARAH ,
AMELIA & MATTHEW]

MONKEY BREAD

Nutrition Facts per serving: Calories 296.3, Protein 1.271 Gm, Carbs 22.92 Gm, Fat 23.27 Gm, Cholesterol 46.55 mg,
Dietary Fiber 0.439 Gm, Sugar 8.292 Gm, Sodium 271.6 mg, Calcium 24.72 mg, Potassium 85.12 mg, Iron 0.808 mg

SERVES 6 TO 8

2 cans refrigerated biscuits
⅓ cup white sugar
½ tsp. cinnamon
½ cup chopped nuts
   (preferably pecans)
¾ stick of butter
⅓ cup brown sugar
1 tsp. cinnamon

1. Preheat oven to 350°F.
2. Cut each biscuit into fourths.
3. In a large Ziplock bag, combine white sugar and ½ teaspoon cinnamon; add biscuits, and shake well.
4. Grease a Bundt or large cake pan. Sprinkle chopped nuts on the bottom of the pan.
5. Add sugar-coated biscuits.
6. In a microwave-safe bowl, or in a saucepan over Low heat, melt butter, brown sugar and 1 teaspoon cinnamon.
7. Pour over biscuits, and bake 20 to 30 minutes, until they pull apart done.

NOTE:
Monkey bread is nice for breakfast, but makes a great treat for
kids any time of the day or night!

[ROD & PENNY MCDOWALL, AND JAMIE & JESSICA]

EASY QUICHE

Nutrition Facts per serving: Calories 377.9, Protein 16.9 Gm, Carbs 20.58 Gm, Fat 24.24 Gm, Cholesterol 159 mg,
Dietary Fiber 0.718 Gm, Sugar 4.064 Gm, Sodium 1018 mg, Calcium 297 mg, Potassium 287.2 mg, Iron 0.976 mg

1. Preheat oven to 400°F.

2. In a large mixing bowl, combine all the ingredients.

3. Season with salt, black pepper and herbs, such as chopped basil, oregano, parsley or thyme, to taste.

4. Pour mixture into a greased 9" pie pan.

5. Sprinkle the top with cheese.

6. Bake for 35 to 40 minutes, until a toothpick inserted in the centre comes out clean.

[JEFF & MICHELLE BOUCHER, AND MICHAEL & JENNA]

SERVES 8

⅓ cup chopped onion plus a combination of other desired vegetables, such as chopped sweet bell pepper, chopped asparagus and chopped broccoli
¾ cup chopped meat, such as ham, cooked bacon, cooked breakfast sausage (or a combination thereof)
2 cups milk
1 cup Bisquick
4 eggs
1 cup shredded cheddar, Swiss or Brie cheese

MR. CLEAVER'S CREPES

Nutrition Facts per serving: Calories 89.2, Protein 3.221 Gm, Carbs 12.21 Gm, Fat 2.922 Gm, Cholesterol 30.8 mg,
Dietary Fiber 0.362 Gm, Sugar 1.705 Gm, Sodium 168.1 mg, Calcium 54.25 mg, Potassium 92.38 mg, Iron 0.639 mg

1. Mix flour, sugar, baking powder and salt together in a mixing bowl.

2. Stir in remaining ingredients; beat until smooth.

3. If necessary, spray frying pan with a little no-stick cooking spray.

4. Over Medium heat, pour small portions of the batter to desired size (as though making very thin pancakes) into the frying pan.

5. After about 1 to 2 minutes, when bubbles start to form on top or until lightly brown, flip the crepes. Cook a further 1 to 2 minutes.

6. Spread the crepes with butter and sugar; roll them up to eat.

"Growing up, we filled these with cottage cheese and jam, and some people in England like to sprinkle lemon juice over them. Whenever my oldest daughter has sleepovers, I prepare my crepes for her friends, and they are always a big hit."
- Tony Cleaver

[TONY & CHRISTINE CLEAVER, AND ALEX, JORDYN & BETHANY]

MAKES ABOUT 15

1-½ cups all purpose flour
1 Tbsp. sugar
½ tsp. baking powder
½ tsp. salt
2 cups milk
2 Tbsp. melted margarine
½ tsp. vanilla
2 eggs

BREAKFAST CASSEROLE

Nutrition Facts per serving: Calories 304.5, Protein 19.28 Gm, Carbs 20.82 Gm, Fat 16.14 Gm, Cholesterol 208.1 mg, Dietary Fiber 0.958 Gm, Sugar 4.389 Gm, Sodium 667.4 mg, Calcium 308.7 mg, Potassium 262.8 mg, Iron 1.819 mg

SERVES 8

16 slices of bread (crust removed)
20 slices of back bacon (Canadian bacon) or ham
8 ozs. grated sharp cheddar cheese
10 eggs
½ tsp. salt
½ tsp. pepper
½ tsp. dry mustard
¼ cup minced onion
¼ cup chopped green (or red) sweet bell pepper
1 tsp. Worcestershire sauce
3 cups whole milk
Dash of Tabasco sauce

1. Preheat oven to 350°F.

2. Sauté sweet pepper and onions, until soft.

3. Line a 9"x13" glass casserole dish with 8 slices of bread.

4. Cover the bread with bacon (or ham).

5. Cover the bacon (or ham) with grated cheese.

6. Cover the cheese with sautéed peppers and onions.

7. Top with 8 slices of bread.

8. In a mixing bowl, mix together eggs, salt, pepper, Worcestershire, dry mustard, milk and Tabasco; pour over top of casserole.

9. Cover and let stand in the refrigerator overnight.

10. Bake uncovered in preheated oven for 45 to 60 minutes.

[JEFF & MICHELLE BOUCHER, AND MICHAEL & JENNA]

This recipe belonging to Lynda Braddock, which is put together right before entertaining, is a favourite for weekend brunches.

Breakfast Casserole

EGG CASSEROLE

Nutrition Facts per serving: Calories 243.3, Protein 15.24 Gm, Carbs 4.09 Gm, Fat 18.33 Gm, Cholesterol 406.6 mg, Dietary Fiber 0.411 Gm, Sugar 1.305 Gm, Sodium 544.4 mg, Calcium 148.2 mg, Potassium 236.6 mg, Iron 1.686 mg

1. Preheat oven to 350°F.

2. In a medium mixing bowl, combine milk, salt and eggs.

3. In a frying pan, scramble the egg mixture until soft and fluffy.

4. In a small bowl, combine soup and mushrooms; mix thoroughly.

5. Spray a 9" x 13" casserole dish with cooking spray.

6. Spread the eggs in the casserole dish; pour the soup mixture over the eggs.

7. Sprinkle grated cheese on top.

8. Bake in preheated oven for 30 minutes.

[KENT & STACEY GREEN, AND MEGAN]

SERVES 10

18 eggs, beaten
¼ cup milk or cream
1 tsp. salt
1 (10 oz.) can Cream of
    Mushroom soup
1 (6 oz.) can sliced mushrooms,
    drained or 1 (8 oz. pkg.)
    fresh mushrooms, sliced
¼ lb. cheddar cheese
No-stick cooking spray

SALMON QUICHE

Nutrition Facts per serving: Calories 519, Protein 21.25 Gm, Carbs 34.97 Gm, Fat 32.95 Gm, Cholesterol 143.45 mg, Dietary Fiber 1.18 Gm, Sugar 8.16 Gm, Sodium 1212.3 mg, Calcium 412.5 mg, Potassium 389.16 mg, Iron 1.92 mg

Pastry:

1. If making the pastry from scratch, in a large bowl, combine flour, 1 teaspoon salt, mayonnaise and, using a fork, mix in enough water so that the mixture binds together. Roll out the pastry and press it into an 8-½" pie pan.

2. Alternatively, use a purchased frozen deep dish pie shell and follow the directions on the package.

Filling:

1. Drain salmon, remove skin and bones, flake and spread over the base of the flan; cover with mushrooms.

2. Stir eggs into the sour cream; add milk, and season with salt and pepper, to taste.

3. Stir in the cheese, and pour into flan.

4. Bake for 20 minutes at 425°F; reduce heat to 350°F, and bake for another 30 to 40 minutes.

[PEARSE & ALISON MURPHY, AND GRACE, AOIFE & SARAH]

SERVES 6

Pastry:
6 ozs. all purpose flour
1 level tsp. salt
3 ozs. mayonnaise
Cold water, to mix
    (or 1 frozen deep dish
    pie shell)

Filling:
1 (7.5 oz.) can red salmon
1 (3 oz.) can sliced
    mushrooms, drained
2 eggs, beaten
¼ pint sour cream,
    or plain yogurt
¼ pint milk
Salt and pepper, to taste
3 oz. grated cheddar or
    Swiss cheese
Parsley

MANGO & RASPBERRY SMOOTHIE

Nutrition Facts per serving: Calories 114.3, Protein 2.597 Gm, Carbs 25.43 Gm, Fat 1.302 Gm, Cholesterol 3.75 mg, Dietary Fiber 2.085 Gm, Sugar 17.09 Gm, Sodium 30.04 mg, Calcium 73.36 mg, Potassium 304.2 mg, Iron 0.329 mg

SERVES 2 TO 3

4 ice cubes
5 fl. ozs. milk
1 ripe mango (cut pulp from
   seed, and discard seed)
1 banana, chopped
3 ozs. frozen raspberries
Juice ½ lemon

1. Place all ingredients in a blender/liquidiser, and blend until smooth.
2. Serve immediately.

This delicious smoothie recipe is from Madelaine Lester, Matty & Amy Cooke's "Granny," who lives in the U.K.

[CHRIS & CHRISSY COOKE, AND MATTY & AMY]

CHOOSE-A-FLAVOUR QUICHE

Nutrition Facts per serving: Calories 413.6, Protein 20.74 Gm, Carbs 17.97 Gm, Fat 28.64 Gm, Cholesterol 70.95 mg, Dietary Fiber 0.962 Gm, Sugar 1.649 Gm, Sodium 482.9 mg, Calcium 628.3 mg, Potassium 194.6 mg, Iron 0.934 mg

SERVES 6

1 deep dish frozen piecrust
3 eggs, beaten
1 cup half & half (or
   whipping cream)
½ cup milk
¼ cup sliced scallion
¼ tsp. salt
⅛ tsp. pepper
⅛ tsp. cayenne pepper
Dash of ground nutmeg
¾ cup chopped cooked chicken,
   crabmeat or ham
1-½ cups shredded Swiss,
   cheddar, Monterey Jack
   or Havarti cheese
1 Tbsp. all purpose flour

1. Preheat oven to 425°F.
2. Bake piecrust for 10 minutes; remove from oven, and reduce oven temperature to 325°F.
3. Meanwhile, in a bowl, stir together eggs, half & half, milk, scallion, salt, pepper, cayenne pepper and nutmeg; stir in chicken, crabmeat or ham.
4. In a separate bowl, toss together shredded cheese and flour. Add to egg mixture; mix well.
5. Pour egg mixture into hot pastry shell.
6. Bake at 325°F for 35 to 40 minutes, or until a knife inserted in the centre comes out clean. Let stand for 10 minutes before serving.

Variations:

Salmon Quiche: Prepare as above, except omit chicken, crabmeat or ham, and substitute with 1 (7 oz.) can of red salmon. Drain the salmon and flake. Be careful to remove all bones and the skin. Swiss cheese is a good choice for this quiche.

Quiche Lorraine: Prepare as above, except omit chicken, crabmeat or ham. Cook 6 slices of bacon until crisp (can be cooked in the microwave, if desired). Crumble bacon and add to the egg mixture. Use Swiss cheese.

[BILLY & LOLLI REID]

SAUSAGE COFFEE CAKE

Nutrition Facts per serving: Calories 252.6, Protein 17.98 Gm, Carbs 20.26 Gm, Fat 33.46 Gm, Cholesterol 88.16 mg,
Dietary Fiber 0.478 Gm, Sugar 2.225 Gm, Sodium 575.6 mg, Calcium 214.7 mg, Potassium 127.7 mg, Iron 2.606 mg

1. Preheat oven to 400°F.

2. In a frying pan, cook sausage and onion until sausage is browned; drain well.

3. Add egg to the hot sausage first by mixing in a tablespoon at a time of the sausage to the egg, so as not to scramble the egg.

4. Add cheeses, Tabasco, salt and parsley; set aside.

5. Combine Bisquick, milk and mayonnaise to make a batter.

6. Spread half the batter into a greased 9" square baking pan.

7. Spread sausage mixture over batter.

8. Pour remaining batter over top.

9. Combine egg yolk and water; brush over batter.

10. Bake in preheated oven for 25 to 30 minutes.

11. Serve warm.

SERVES 6

1 lb. ground pork sausage
½ cup finely chopped onion
¼ cup grated Parmesan cheese
½ cup grated Swiss cheese
1 egg, beaten
½ tsp. Tabasco sauce
½ tsp. salt
2 Tbsp. chopped fresh parsley
1 cup Bisquick
¾ cup milk
¼ cup mayonnaise
1 egg yolk
1 Tbsp. water

SLIGHTLY SOURDOUGH PANCAKES

Nutrition Facts per serving: Calories 256.9, Protein 11.86 Gm, Carbs 37.34 Gm, Fat 6.361 Gm, Cholesterol 168.1 mg,
Dietary Fiber 0.905 Gm, Sugar 11.46 Gm, Sodium 638.2 mg, Calcium 274.7 mg, Potassium 517.3 mg, Iron 2.039 mg

1. Combine eggs, flour, yogurt and milk; beat until smooth.

2. Add remaining ingredients; stir until all ingredients are incorporated.

3. Let stand for 10 minutes.

4. Heat a non-stick skillet over Medium-Low, and drop the batter in tablespoonfuls into the hot skillet.

5. When bubbles form, flip the pancakes and cook until lightly browned.

SERVES 4

3 eggs, beaten
1 cup all purpose flour
⅔ cup plain yogurt
1 cup milk
2 Tbsp. granulated sugar
1 tsp. salt
2 tsp. baking powder
4 Tbsp. melted butter

The eggs and yogurt give these pancakes a really light and fluffy texture with a wonderful 'European' taste!

[JEFF & MICHELLE BOUCHER, AND MICHAEL & JENNA]

HAM AND CHEESE OMELETTE

Nutrition Facts per serving: Calories 577.9, Protein 30.56 Gm, Carbs 15.84 Gm, Fat 41.11 Gm, Cholesterol 517.9 mg,
Dietary Fiber 0.17 Gm, Sugar 0.767 Gm, Sodium 2017 mg, Calcium 465.7 mg, Potassium 379.4 mg, Iron 2.409 mg

SERVES 1

2 eggs
Salt and black pepper, to taste
2 tsp. vegetable oil
¼ cup chopped ham
1 Tbsp. chopped onion
   and/or bell pepper (optional)
¼ cup grated cheddar cheese

Variations:
Bacon Omelette:
¼ cup crisp,
crumbled bacon
Mushroom Omelette:
½ cup raw sliced or
chopped mushrooms,
sautéed in 2 Tbsp. butter
Herb Omelette:
2 tsp. finely chopped
parsley w/1 tsp. fresh sage,
tarragon, thyme or savory
Mexican Omelette:
¼ cup combination of
chopped black olives,
tomatoes, onions,
bell peppers and
Jalapaeno peppers
(optional)

1. Break the eggs into a small bowl; add salt and pepper, and whisk vigorously for about 10 seconds, just enough to thoroughly blend yolks and whites.

2. In an 8" to 9" non-stick skillet over High heat, cook the ham (and, if desired, the onions and sweet pepper) in the hot oil.

3. Add eggs, and let them set for about 5 seconds.

4. Using a spatula, pull the cooked egg from the edges of the pan toward the centre, allowing the liquid egg to run under onto the hot pan; continue this step until the egg is nearly cooked through and is still a little moist and creamy.

5. Sprinkle the cheese over half of the omelette.

6. Using a spatula, carefully fold the other half of the omelette over the side which is topped with cheese.

7. Allow the omelette to cook for several seconds more to lightly brown the bottom, and then quickly tilt the pan upside down over a plate so the omelette falls out bottom side up.

Ham and Cheese Omelette

BRUNCH BAKED EGGS

Nutrition Facts per serving: Calories 355.3, Protein 23.85 Gm, Carbs 8.417 Gm, Fat 25.06 Gm, Cholesterol 211.7 mg,
Dietary Fiber 0.581 Gm, Sugar 2.237 Gm, Sodium 559.8 mg, Calcium 489.2 mg, Potassium 266.4 mg, Iron 1.681 mg

1. Sprinkle 3 cups cheese in the bottom of a 13" x 9" x 2" baking dish.

2. In a saucepan, cook the mushrooms, onion, red pepper and ham (if desired) in the butter until vegetables are tender, but not brown; drain well.

3. Place vegetables atop cheese.

4. Arrange ham strips atop vegetables.

5. Sprinkle remaining 3 cups cheese atop ham.

6. Cover, and chill in the refrigerator overnight.

7. Next day, preheat oven to 350°F.

8. Combine eggs, milk, flour, herb of choice and parsley.

9. Pour over cheese layer.

10. Bake in preheated oven for approximately 45 minutes.

11. Let stand 10 minutes before serving.

[D W I G H T & S H A N N O N P A N T O N , A N D D Y L A N & F R A S I E R]

SERVES 12

3 cups (or 12 ozs.) shredded
  Monterey Jack cheese
12 ozs. fresh mushrooms,
  sliced
½ med. onion, chopped
¼ cup sweet red pepper,
  thinly sliced
¼ cup butter, melted
8 ozs. cooked ham, cut
  into julienne strips (optional)
3 cups (or 12 ozs.) shredded
  Monterey Jack cheese,
  for topping
8 eggs, beaten
1-¾ cups milk
½ cup all purpose flour
2 Tbsp. snipped fresh chives,
  basil, tarragon, thyme
  or oregano
1 Tbsp. snipped parsley

CINNAMON ROLLS

Nutrition Facts per serving: Calories 297.8, Protein 4.399 Gm, Carbs 54.72 Gm, Fat 7.226 Gm, Cholesterol 14.48 mg,
Dietary Fiber 0.906 Gm, Sugar 4.725 Gm, Sodium 333.1 mg, Calcium 72.12 mg, Potassium 126.1 mg, Iron 3.063 mg

1. Preheat oven to 350°F.

2. On a floured surface, roll the dough out into a 12" x 8" rectangle.

3. Combine the butter, sugar and cinnamon; spread evenly over the dough.

4. Starting from a short side, roll up the dough (jelly roll style) into a log; cut into 1" slices.

5. Prepare the sauce by combining all the sauce ingredients in a small saucepan; heat over Medium-Low heat, until sugar is melted, stirring constantly.

6. Place the sliced dough pieces side-by-side, 2" apart, flat on a baking sheet, and cover with warm sauce. Let stand and rise.

7. Bake in preheated oven for 20 to 25 minutes. Serve warm.

[L E S L I E & M I C H E L E E B A N K S , A N D J E S S I C A & K A L E B]

SERVES 8

1 loaf frozen "Ready Dough",
  thawed
3 Tbsp. each of butter,
  softened, sugar and
  cinnamon

Sauce:
½ cup brown sugar
¼ cup corn syrup
3 Tbsp. water

BACON OR HAM STRATA

Nutrition Facts per serving: Calories 680.4, Protein 36.7 Gm, Carbs 24.17 Gm, Fat 47.62 Gm, Cholesterol 227.4 mg, Dietary Fiber 1.013 Gm, Sugar 5.112 Gm, Sodium 1934 mg, Calcium 294 mg, Potassium 895.6 mg, Iron 3.695 mg

SERVES 6 TO 8

6 slices bread cut into cubes
1 lb. sliced mushrooms, sautéed in butter and drained
1 lb. cooked bacon or 6 slices ham or Canadian bacon
4 ozs. grated cheddar cheese
2 cups milk combined with 4 beaten eggs, ½ tsp. salt, 1 tsp. dry mustard (or 1 Tbsp. mustard)
No-stick cooking spray

1. Preheat oven to 350°F.
2. Spray a 9" x 13" baking dish with no-stick cooking spray.
3. Spread the bread into the bottom of the baking dish.
4. Top with mushrooms, then bacon (or ham), and lastly the cheese.
5. Pour mixture of milk, eggs, salt and mustard over the cheese.
6. Bake in preheated oven for 35 minutes.

[DARRIN & MICHELLE DAYKIN, AND JOSHUA & EMMI]

SCRAMBLED EGG & CHEESE

Nutrition Facts per serving: Calories 285.5, Protein 16.1 Gm, Carbs 3.285 Gm, Fat 22.86 Gm, Cholesterol 463.4 mg, Dietary Fiber 0.133 Gm, Sugar 0.287 Gm, Sodium 287.7 mg, Calcium 164.1 mg, Potassium 192.3 mg, Iron 1.621 mg

SERVES 4

8 eggs
2 to 3 Tbsp. butter
4 Tbsp. evaporated milk
⅓ cup shredded cheddar cheese
2 to 3 scallions, finely chopped (optional)
Freshly ground black pepper, to taste

1. In a small bowl, beat together eggs and milk.
2. In a saucepan, melt butter over Medium heat.
3. Add eggs to saucepan; cook until the mixture begins to set on the bottom and around the edges of the pan. Continue cooking 2 to 3 minutes. Using a rubber spatula, stir frequently scraping the bottom and sides of pan until the eggs are nearly cooked through.
4. Add scallions (if desired) and cheese. Toss over Medium heat for a couple of minutes until the cheese is melted and the eggs are thoroughly cooked through.
5. Sprinkle with freshly ground pepper.
6. Serve immediately with toast.

[DEAN & JENNIFER SCOTT, AND LAUREN, HANNAH & JONATHAN]

OVERNIGHT CARAMEL FRENCH TOAST

Nutrition Facts per serving: Calories 288, Protein 7.579 Gm, Carbs 56.37 Gm, Fat 3.774 Gm, Cholesterol 75.17 mg,
Dietary Fiber 0.636 Gm, Sugar 37.59 Gm, Sodium 297.1 mg, Calcium 227.8 mg, Potassium 315.9 mg, Iron 1.889 mg

1. Pour maple syrup into a 13" x 9" baking dish coated with cooking spray.
2. Arrange bread slices evenly over syrup.
3. Combine milk and the next 4 ingredients in a large bowl, stirring with a whisk.
4. Pour egg mixture over bread slices.
5. Cover, and refrigerate for about 8 hours, or overnight.
6. Preheat oven to 350°F.
7. Combine sugar and cinnamon; sprinkle evenly over bread.
8. Bake in preheated oven uncovered for 1 to 1-½ hours, or until golden.
9. Let stand for 5 minutes before serving.

NOTE:
It is nice to add finely grated lemon or orange zest to the egg mixture. Also, you can serve this with icing sugar sprinkled through a sieve on top, and garnished with berries.

[FRANS VANDENDRIES & SUZANNE SCHEUNEMAN, AND EMMA & LIORA VANDENDRIES]

SERVES 4 TO 6

1 cup maple syrup
No-stick cooking spray
Approx. 6 slices soft
   white bread
2-½ cups 1% milk
1 Tbsp. flour
1-½ tsp. vanilla extract
¼ tsp. salt
2 lg. eggs
2 Tbsp. sugar
1 tsp. cinnamon

APPLE BRAN MUFFINS

Nutrition Facts per serving: Calories 110, Protein 3.219 Gm, Carbs 18.61 Gm, Fat 3.29 Gm, Cholesterol 8.875 mg,
Dietary Fiber 2.542 Gm, Sugar 8.97 Gm, Sodium 130.7 mg, Calcium 38.11 mg, Potassium 220 mg, Iron 1.632 mg

1. Preheat oven to 350°F.
2. Toss flour, bran, salt, baking soda and nutmeg together with a fork.
3. Stir in orange rind, apples, raisins and nuts.
4. Pour juice of 1 orange into a 2 cup measuring cup; add buttermilk to make 2 cups.
5. Add juice/buttermilk mixture to egg, molasses and oil; stir thoroughly.
6. With a few swift strokes, stir liquid ingredients into dry ingredients.
7. Pour into greased muffin tins to two-thirds full.
8. Bake in preheated oven for 25 minutes.

[STEPHEN & DEBRA McTAGGART, AND SARAH, AMELIA & MATTHEW]

MAKES 24

2 cups whole wheat flour
1-½ cups wheat bran,
   or oat bran
½ tsp. salt
1-¼ tsp. baking soda
½ tsp. nutmeg
1 Tbsp. grated orange rind
1 cup peeled, chopped apple
½ cup raisins
½ cup chopped nuts,
   or sunflower seeds
Juice of 1 orange
Scant 2 cups buttermilk
   (or sour milk)
1 egg, beaten
½ cup molasses
2 Tbsp. vegetable oil

MACADAMIA NUT MUFFINS

Nutrition Facts per serving: Calories 444.7, Protein 4.957 Gm, Carbs 32.92 Gm, Fat 34.62 Gm, Cholesterol 120.5 mg,
Dietary Fiber 2.384 Gm, Sugar 1.729 Gm, Sodium 289.5 mg, Calcium 93.73 mg, Potassium 301.3 mg, Iron 1.571 mg

SERVES 6 TO 8

½ cup (1 stick) unsalted
  butter, softened
1 cup firmly packed
  brown sugar
3 eggs
¾ tsp. almond extract
½ tsp. vanilla extract
1 cup plus 2 Tbsp.
  bread flour
1-¼ tsp. baking powder
½ tsp. salt
¼ cup whipping cream
½ cup whole macadamia nuts
1 cup coarsely chopped
  macadamia nuts (careful
  not to chop too small or
  they disappear)

1. Preheat oven to 350°F.

2. With an electric beater, mix together the butter, brown sugar, eggs, vanilla and almond extracts, flour, baking powder, salt and whipping cream.

3. Fold nuts into mixture.

4. Pour into cupcake liners or greased muffin tins. (One nut can be placed on top of each muffin for decoration before baking.)

5. Bake in preheated oven for 25 minutes or until a toothpick inserted in the centre comes out clean.

[DWIGHT & SHANNON PANTON, AND DYLAN & FRASIER]

Macadamia Nut Muffins

BROWN SUGAR BACON

Nutrition Facts per serving: Calories 538, Protein 26.67 Gm, Carbs 35.67 Gm, Fat 31.07 Gm, Cholesterol 88.93 mg, Dietary Fiber 0 Gm, Sugar 0 Gm, Sodium 1707 mg, Calcium 31.17 mg, Potassium 127 mg, Iron 0.698 mg

SERVES 6 TO 8

1 lb. bacon slices (40% less fat or centre-cut)
1 cup dark brown sugar

1. Preheat oven to 350°F.

2. Line a baking sheet with parchment paper.

3. Roll bacon in sugar, until coated.

4. Bake in preheated oven for 15 minutes, turning once. Watch carefully to avoid burning.

5. Place bacon on wire cooling rack and do not overlap (otherwise the bacon will stick together). Let cool before serving.

[DARRIN & MICHELLE DAYKIN, AND JOSHUA & EMMI]

BUTTERMILK BANANA PANCAKES

Nutrition Facts per serving: Calories 382.5, Protein 9.412 Gm, Carbs 58.18 Gm, Fat 13.75 Gm, Cholesterol 85.2 mg, Dietary Fiber 7.002 Gm, Sugar 16.14 Gm, Sodium 629.6 mg, Calcium 201.2 mg, Potassium 736.6 mg, Iron 2.827 mg

SERVES 4 TO 5

2 eggs
¼ cup vegetable oil or melted butter
2 cups buttermilk
1 Tbsp. sugar
2 tsp. baking powder
½ tsp. baking soda
½ tsp. salt
1 cup all purpose flour
¾ cup self-rising cornmeal
2 to 3 ripe bananas, mashed

1. In a large mixing bowl, beat eggs.

2. Add the vegetable oil and buttermilk; beat until smooth.

3. Add sugar, baking powder, soda, salt, flour and cornmeal; mix thoroughly.

4. Stir in the mashed bananas.

5. For each pancake, pour about ¼ cup batter onto a hot, lightly greased griddle or large frying pan.

6. Turn pancakes when tops are covered with bubbles, and cook the other side.

7. Serve with syrup or hot jam.

[GREGORY & TERRI MERREN, AND JOSH & ZACHARY]

YUM-YUM SOUR CREAM COFFEE CAKE

Nutrition Facts per serving: Calories 452.4, Protein 3.401 Gm, Carbs 46.91 Gm, Fat 29.09 Gm, Cholesterol 95.07 mg,
Dietary Fiber 0.709 Gm, Sugar 2.683 Gm, Sodium 329.5 mg, Calcium 86.16 mg, Potassium 210.5 mg, Iron 1.947 mg

SERVES 12 TO 14

½ cup butter and/or
  margarine, softened
1 cup sugar
2 eggs
1 tsp. baking powder
1 tsp. baking soda
½ tsp. vanilla
2 cups flour
1 cup sour cream

Filling:
½ cup margarine, softened
1 cup sugar
1 cup chopped pecans
  (or walnuts)
2 tsp. cinnamon

1. Preheat oven to 325°F.

2. In a mixing bowl, cream the butter, sugar, eggs and vanilla.

3. In a separate bowl, combine flour, baking powder and baking soda; add to the creamed mixture.

4. Fold in sour cream.

5. In a separate bowl, combine all the filling ingredients; mix well.

6. Pour half the flour/creamed mixture into a greased 13" x 9" x 2" pan (or Bundt pan).

7. Spread half the filling over the flour/creamed mixture.

8. Add the remaining flour/creamed mixture; top with the remaining filling.

9. Bake in preheated oven for 40 minutes.

[CAREN WIGHT, AND JUSTIN & ERIC]

Yum-Yum Sour Cream Coffee Cake

CAYMAN LIMEADE

Nutrition Facts per quart: Calories 596.4, Protein 0.27 Gm, Carbs 155.6 Gm, Fat 0.062 Gm, Cholesterol 0 mg,
Dietary Fiber 0 Gm, Sugar 145.7 Gm, Sodium 2.865 mg, Calcium 7.025 mg, Potassium 70 mg, Iron 0.109 mg

1. Squeeze enough limes, and pass through a sieve, to make ½ cup of lime juice.

2. Pour lime juice into a 2-¼ quart pitcher, and add the sugar.

3. Add about 7 cups of water, or enough to fill the pitcher.

4. Stir the mixture vigorously, until the sugar has dissolved.

5. Refrigerate until cold.

[BILLY & LOLLI REID]

MAKES 2-¼ QUARTS

½ cup freshly squeezed lime juice (or more, to taste)
1-½ cups white sugar

NOTE:

It is best to use the local Cayman key limes (small and yellow). Purchased limes can be substituted, but the flavour is not quite as good.

HONEY NUT GRANOLA

Nutrition Facts per serving: Calories 320.5, Protein 8.954 Gm, Carbs 44.94 Gm, Fat 12.63 Gm, Cholesterol 16.4 mg,
Dietary Fiber 4.944 Gm, Sugar 10.37 Gm, Sodium 66.71 mg, Calcium 41.06 mg, Potassium 277 mg, Iron 2.761 mg

1. Preheat oven to 325°F.

2. Mix the first 9 ingredients together, and spread into a 9" x 13" baking pan.

3. Bake in preheated oven for 20 to 25 minutes.

4. Add 1 cup dried fruit; mix thoroughly.

5. Serve over yogurt or cereal.

NOTE:
This is also great on its own for breakfast, as a snack, or served over ice cream. Cool before storing in the refrigerator.

[ROD & PENNY MCDOWALL, AND JAMIE & JESSICA]

SERVES 16 TO 20

5 cups uncooked rolled oats
⅔ cup honey
½ cup wheat germ
2 tsp. vanilla extract
1 cup sunflower seeds or other nuts
⅔ cup brown sugar
⅔ cup melted butter
1 tsp. cinnamon
1 tsp. allspice
1 cup (your choice) dried fruit

Clockwise from top left: Baguettes including French Baguettes (page 56), Herb Scones (page 66), Sour Cream Dinner Rolls (page 57),
Pumpkin Walnut Bread (page 69), Whole Wheat Buttermilk Bread (page 68), Banana Bread (page 59), Scones (page 58),
Corn Bread Muffins, in the centre (page 57)

BREADS

QUICK BREADS

CORNBREAD

MUFFINS

YEAST BREADS AND ROLLS

SCONES

FRENCH BAGUETTES

Nutrition Facts per loaf: Calories 957.1, Protein 27.72 Gm, Carbs 201.2 Gm, Fat 2.69 Gm, Cholesterol 0 mg, Dietary Fiber 7.27 Gm, Sugar 12.84 Gm, Sodium 1076 mg, Calcium 51.98 mg, Potassium 374.3 mg, Iron 10.81

MAKES 2 LOAVES

1-½ cups water, warm
1 Tbsp. honey or sugar
2-½ tsp. instant bread yeast
4 cups flour, of any type
1 tsp. salt

TIP:
Spritz the oven several times with water in the first few minutes of baking (this is the secret).

1. Put the water in a large mixing bowl, and add the honey (or sugar); stir with a wooden spoon, until dissolved.

2. Add the yeast; stir until dissolved.

3. Let the yeast stand for 5 minutes. Stir in the flour and salt (if the dough is too sticky, add a little more flour).

4. Knead until the dough is smooth; place dough in a greased bowl, cover with a damp cloth and put in a warm place, until the dough doubles in bulk (about 40 minutes).

5. Turn it out onto a floured board, punch it down and return it to the bowl; cover and allow it again to double in bulk.

6. When it has doubled, turn it onto the floured board, divide the dough in half, and form the halves into baguettes.

7. Roll them flat, fold them lengthwise, and seal them.

8. Place the baguettes on a greased cookie sheet or in couches (if you have them), seam side down; allow them to rest for 10 minutes.

9. Score the top of each baguette with a knife, and place in a 450°F oven.

10. Bake until they are golden and sound hollow when tapped, about 20 minutes.

[TERRY & SUSAN WATLING, AND TOM, LYDIA, JULIA & HOLLY]

"I learned to make these baguettes from Mme. Clergeon, of Berd'huis, France, when I stayed in her home on foreign exchange in high school. They're simple and wonderful, and very versatile. This recipe figured prominently in my Education 14 final curriculum project, in which I wrote about teaching people to cook."
- Terry Watling

SHAMROCK ROLLS *(Continued from previous page)*

6. Shape into a ball, and place in a lightly greased bowl, turning once to grease the surface.

7. Cover and let rise in a warm place until double in size, about 1 hour.

8. Punch down, and shape into a ball; cover, and let rest for 10 minutes.

9. Cut the ball into fourths, then cut each fourth into 6 wedges. Form the wedges into smooth little balls.

10. Place balls of dough on greased baking sheet (leave room for rising).

11. To form leaves, snip balls almost to the centre in 3 places. Then snip at midpoint in edge of each leaf.

12. Let rolls rise on a greased baking sheet until almost double in size, about 1 hour; bake at 400°F for about 10 to 12 minutes.

[ARTHUR & KAREN HUNTER]

Shamrock Rolls

FIVE SEED BREAD
(USING A BREAD MACHINE)

Nutrition Facts per loaf: Calories 2364, Protein 73.38 Gm, Carbs 399.8 Gm, Fat 53.73 Gm, Cholesterol 0 mg,
Dietary Fiber 19.32 Gm, Sugar 10.34 Gm, Sodium 3258 mg, Calcium 293.6 mg, Potassium 2086 mg, Iron 34.04 mg

MAKES 1 FAMILY LOAF

1 (¼ oz.) pkg. active dry
 yeast
1-¼ cups plus 2 Tbsp.
 warm water (80°F/27°C)
2 tsp. sugar
1-½ tsp. salt
2 Tbsp. lecithin granules
 or olive oil
1-½ cups high grade flour
1-½ cups wholemeal flour
¼ cup each of sunflower,
 pumpkin, poppy, and raw or
 toasted sesame seed
2 Tbsp. linseed or flax seeds

1. Put ingredients in a 1.5 lb. (750 g) capacity bread machine, in the order specified by the manufacturer.

2. Set to Normal/White cycle; loaf size 1.5 lb., medium crust, and START.

[TONY & KAREN ATTENBOROUGH, AND CLAIRE,
HAMISH & MATTHEW]

ZUCCHINI BREAD

Nutrition Facts per serving: Calories 697.1, Protein 9.78 Gm, Carbs 81.72 Gm, Fat 38.34 Gm, Cholesterol 79.88 mg,
Dietary Fiber 1.791 Gm, Sugar 1.559 Gm, Sodium 628.6 mg, Calcium 93.71 mg, Potassium 428.8 mg, Iron 3.517 mg

SERVES 8

3 eggs
2 cups sugar
1 cup vegetable oil (or
 substitute with apple sauce
 for low fat version)
1 Tbsp. vanilla
2 cups zucchini, coarsely
 grated, loosely packed
2 cups all purpose flour
1 Tbsp. cinnamon
2 tsp. baking soda
1 tsp. salt
¼ tsp. baking powder
1 cup chopped walnuts

1. Preheat oven to 350°F.

2. In a bowl, beat eggs until frothy. Beat in sugar, vegetable oil and vanilla. Beat until mixture is thick and lemon-coloured.

3. Stir in zucchini.

4. Combine flour, cinnamon, baking soda, salt and baking powder; stir in.

5. Fold in chopped walnuts.

6. Pour mixture into two greased and floured 8" x 4-½" x 3" loaf pans.

7. Bake loaves for 1 hour or until cake tester inserted in the centre comes out clean.

8. Let loaves cool in pans for 10 minutes.

9. Invert loaves onto a rack; let cool.

[PAUL PEENE & TONI PINKERTON, AND SAMANTHA,
DEREK & ANDREW]

CAYMAN CORN BREAD

Nutrition Facts per serving: Calories 388.9, Protein 6.245 Gm, Carbs 54.85 Gm, Fat 16.55 Gm, Cholesterol 60.45 mg,
Dietary Fiber 4.325 Gm, Sugar 0.265 Gm, Sodium 506.9 mg, Calcium 192.5 mg, Potassium 291 mg, Iron 1.947 mg

SERVES 12

1. Preheat oven to 350°F.

2. Sift the corn meal, flour, sugar, nutmeg, cinnamon and salt into a large bowl; mix well.

3. Add milk and egg; mix well.

4. Melt the butter in a microwave oven (about 1 minute or so) and then pour into the batter, stirring until smooth.

5. Mix in the vanilla.

6. Pour batter into a greased 13"x 9"x 2" baking pan or casserole dish. Bake until browned, or until a knife inserted in the centre comes out clean (about 1 hour).

1-½ cups corn meal
1-½ cups self-rising flour
1-½ cups sugar
2 sticks butter
½ tsp. salt
1 can evaporated milk
1 tsp. ground cinnamon
½ tsp. ground nutmeg
1 egg
1 Tbsp. vanilla extract

[BRYAN & JENNIFER HUNTER, AND CORY & DANIEL]

CAYMAN CUSTARD TOPPED CORNBREAD

Nutrition Facts per serving: Calories 491.3, Protein 4.025 Gm, Carbs 71.82 Gm, Fat 23.33 Gm, Cholesterol 0 mg,
Dietary Fiber 2.218 Gm, Sugar 0.17 Gm, Sodium 81.72 mg, Calcium 62.82 mg, Potassium 473.6 mg, Iron 3.315 mg

SERVES 20 TO 25

1. Preheat oven to 350°F.

2. In a large bowl, combine dry ingredients, then very slowly add coconut milk, mixing as it is added.

3. Pour into a greased or sprayed 14" x 10" x 2" pan, and bake about 2-½ hours. The centre should be jiggly when it is done.

2 cups cornmeal
2 cups all purpose flour
4 to 6 cups brown sugar
½ tsp. salt
10 cups fresh coconut milk,
  or 2 cans coconut milk
  with water to make 10 cups

It is not traditional to add extra spices to this recipe but, if desired, you could add 2 teaspoons grated nutmeg and 2 tablespoons vanilla extract.

NOTE:
If the coconut milk is added too fast, the mixture will become lumpy.
Also, do not try to short-cut by decreasing water. If liquid is too thick, the cornmeal will not settle to the bottom. This is a large cake, but can be successfully halved. If halved, bake until the edges are quite firm and the middle still jiggles slightly (about 1 to 1-½ hours).

[BRYAN & ANDREA BOTHWELL]

EASTER BUN

Nutrition Facts per loaf: Calories 4176, Protein 71.74 Gm, Carbs 820 Gm, Fat 75.94 Gm, Cholesterol 616.1 mg,
Dietary Fiber 24.46 Gm, Sugar 86.36 Gm, Sodium 2184 mg, Calcium 2118 mg, Potassium 3326, Iron 26.59 mg

MAKES 1 LOAF

3 cups all purpose flour
2 cups milk
2 cups brown sugar
3 tsp. baking powder
2 ozs. butter, melted
2 tsp. allspice
2 eggs, lightly beaten
2 cups mixed dried fruit

1. Sift flour, baking powder and allspice into a mixing bowl; stir until combined.

2. In a large bowl, combine sugar, milk, eggs and butter; stir well.

3. Stir flour mixture into egg mixture, ½ cup at a time, alternating with the mixed fruit.

4. Bake in a greased 9"x 5" loaf pan at 350°F for approximately 1-½ hours.

This recipe was selected from a collection of recipes submitted by members of
John Gray Memorial Church.

[LEONARD & CAROL ANN EBANKS]

Cayman Bun

NOTE:
A combination
of 2 (1.5 oz.) boxes
of raisins, drained and
chopped Maraschino
cherries, chopped pitted
dates, chopped dried
apricots, currants or
other fruit may be
used in this
bun.

CHEESY GARLIC BREAD

Nutrition Facts per serving: Calories 352.8, Protein 8.554 Gm, Carbs 17.52 Gm, Fat 28.26 Gm, Cholesterol 72 mg,
Dietary Fiber 1.202 Gm, Sugar 0.015 Gm, Sodium 647.8 mg, Calcium 182.5 mg, Potassium 52.1, Iron 1.343 mg

SERVES 4

1 med. loaf French bread,
  unsliced
½ cup butter or margarine,
  softened
2 cloves garlic, halved
1 tsp. dried parsley
½ cup grated Parmesan cheese

1. Preheat oven to 375°F.

2. Cut slices down the length of bread loaf at 1" intervals, without cutting all the way through.

3. Rub slices and top of loaf with cut sides of garlic halves; mince the garlic.

4. Combine butter, minced garlic, parsley and Parmesan in a small bowl.

5. Spread butter mixture between bread slices and on top of loaf.

6. Wrap bread in foil, leaving top partially uncovered.

7. Bake in preheated oven until heated through, about 15 minutes.

[MARGARET EBANKS, AND MEGAN]

POTATO AND CHEESE BREAD

Nutrition Facts per serving: Calories 290, Protein 8.924 Gm, Carbs 49.17 Gm, Fat 6.609 Gm, Cholesterol 2.469 mg,
Dietary Fiber 0.542 Gm, Sugar 0.607 Gm, Sodium 332.2 mg, Calcium 66.47 mg, Potassium 153, Iron 1.974 mg

SERVES 8

3-½ cups unbleached flour
1 tsp. salt
1-½ cups water, warm
1 tsp. sugar
2-½ tsp. dried yeast
3 Tbsp. olive oil
¼ cup grated Parmesan cheese
½ cup dried potato flakes,
  or 1 cup mashed potato
2 tsp. dried onion,
  or ¼ onion, finely chopped
1 tsp. dried garlic or 2 cloves
  garlic, finely chopped
1 Tbsp. dried parsley
1 tsp. dried basil

Method 1 - Oven baking

1. Sift the flour and salt into a bowl.

2. Activate the yeast with the sugar and warm water (see tip on dissolving yeast on page 68).

3. Add the yeast and water mix to the flour; gradually add the remaining ingredients, and mix well into a smooth dough. Add a little extra flour if the mix is too sticky, or a little extra water if it is too dry.

4. Place the dough on a floured surface, and knead for 10 minutes.

5. Cover the dough, and put in a warm place for 1 hour to allow the dough to rise.

6. Knead again for a few minutes; cover and allow 30 to 45 minutes for the dough to rise a second time.

7. Place in a rectangular floured loaf tin; bake in a preheated oven at 425°F for about 30 minutes. When cooked, the bread should sound hollow when tapped.

Method 2 - Bread Machine

1. Pour the olive oil into the container/pan of the bread machine.

2. Dissolve the salt and sugar in the warm water; add these to the pan.

3. Add the flour, grated cheese, potato, onion, garlic, parsley and basil. Lastly, add the yeast.

4. Use a bread machine setting suitable for whole wheat or French bread, i.e. one which gives longer kneading and rising time.

5. Set loaf size to 2 lbs.

[MIKE & ANNE McGRATH]

HERB SCONES

Nutrition Facts per serving: Calories 77.45, Protein 2.431 Gm, Carbs 14.64 Gm, Fat 0.898 Gm, Cholesterol 14.53 mg, Dietary Fiber 0.451 Gm, Sugar 0.657 Gm, Sodium 222.5 mg, Calcium 104.8 mg, Potassium 92.08 mg, Iron 1.377 mg

SERVES 12 TO 15

2 cups self-rising flour
1 tsp. baking powder
¼ cup margarine
1 Tbsp. sugar
1 Tbsp. finely chopped parsley
1 Tbsp. finely chopped chives
1 Tbsp. finely chopped rosemary
1 egg, lightly beaten
½ cup low fat milk,
   plus some for glazing
No-stick cooking spray

1. Preheat oven to 400°F.

2. Line baking tray with baking paper, or spray with no-stick cooking spray.

3. Sift flour, and add baking powder to bowl.

4. Add margarine by rubbing in with fingertips, until mix resembles fine bread crumbs.

5. Stir in sugar, parsley, chives and rosemary.

6. Stir in egg and milk, until mixture forms a ball.

7. Toss mixture onto a lightly floured board; knead until smooth.

8. Roll mixture to ½" thickness; cut into 2" to 3" rounds or squares.

9. Place scones close together on baking tray; brush tops with milk, to glaze.

10. Bake for 15 minutes until scones sound hollow when tapped.

[TONY & KAREN ATTENBOROUGH, AND CLAIRE, HAMISH & MATTHEW]

SPICY CORNBREAD

Nutrition Facts per serving: Calories 305.25, Protein 6.43 Gm, Carbs 46.5 Gm, Fat 10.69 Gm, Cholesterol 57.64 mg, Dietary Fiber 1.48 Gm, Sugar 12.91 Gm, Sodium 457.75 mg, Calcium 80.79 mg, Potassium 217.63 mg, Iron 1.61 mg

SERVES 8

½ Tbsp. butter
2 (8.5 oz.) pkgs. Jiffy
   corn muffin mix
1 Tbsp. chili powder
⅔ cup whole milk
2 lg. eggs, beaten
½ cup drained oil-packed
   sun-dried tomatoes,
   chopped (optional)

1. Preheat oven to 350°F.

2. Butter an 8" square baking pan.

3. In a large mixing bowl, whisk together the muffin mix and chili powder.

4. Add the egg and milk to the dry ingredients. With a mixing spoon, mix until well-blended.

5. Stir in the tomatoes (if desired).

6. Spread batter into the prepared pan.

7. Bake in preheated oven for about 30 minutes, or until golden brown.

8. Cool slightly before cutting into squares.

9. Serve with hot soup or stew.

SWEET HAWAIIAN BREAD
(WITH A BREAD MACHINE)

Nutrition Facts per serving: Calories 347.1, Protein 8.87 Gm, Carbs 60.57 Gm, Fat 7.671 Gm, Cholesterol 42.29 mg, Dietary Fiber 2.848 Gm, Sugar 11.73 Gm, Sodium 219.6 mg, Calcium 30.95 mg, Potassium 322.6 mg, Iron 2.439 mg

SERVES 8

¼ cup milk
1 egg, beaten
¼ cup butter, melted
½ cup crushed pineapple
   with juice
1 tsp. coconut extract
½ cup mashed bananas
   (1 lg. banana, very ripe)
⅓ cup white sugar
½ tsp. salt
3-½ cups bread flour
1-½ tsp. active dry yeast

1. Add the wet ingredients to the bread pan first, in the order given.

2. Mix dry ingredients (except yeast) in a large bowl, and add to the bread pan.

3. Make a small indentation on top of the dry ingredients (not so deep that it reaches the wet layer), and add the yeast to the indentation.

4. Bake on sweet bread cycle, light setting, or on Fruit and Nut cycle, light crust. Loaf size: 1-½ lb.

[BRYAN & JENNIFER HUNTER, AND CORY & DANIEL]

Sweet Hawaiian Bread

WHOLE WHEAT BUTTERMILK BREAD

Nutrition Facts per loaf: Calories 1469, Protein 40.61 Gm, Carbs 253.9 Gm, Fat 34.63 Gm, Cholesterol 111 mg,
Dietary Fiber 18.84 Gm, Sugar 36.72 Gm, Sodium 1245 mg, Calcium 253.7 mg, Potassium 990.9 mg, Iron 12.34 mg

MAKES 2 LOAVES

1 (¼ oz.) pkg. active dry yeast
2 Tbsp. sugar
½ cup warm water (105°F to 115 °F)
1 cup buttermilk
¼ cup vegetable oil
3 Tbsp. honey
1 lg. egg, lightly beaten
1-¾ cups whole wheat flour
1 tsp. salt
⅛ tsp. baking powder
2-¼ to 2-¾ cups bread flour

1. In a large bowl, dissolve yeast and sugar in warm water; let stand 5 minutes.

2. Add buttermilk and next 3 ingredients, stirring well.

3. Add whole wheat flour, salt and baking powder; with an electric mixer, beat at Medium speed for 3 minutes, or until smooth.

4. Gradually stir in enough bread flour to make a soft dough.

5. Turn dough out onto a floured surface, and knead until smooth and elastic (about 8 to 10 minutes).

6. Place dough in a well-greased bowl, turning to grease top.

7. Cover and let rise in a warm place (85°F), free from drafts, 1-½ hours or until doubled in bulk.

8. Punch dough down, and divide in half.

9. Roll each half into a 15" x 8" rectangle. Roll dough, jellyroll fashion, starting with narrow end; pinch seams and ends to seal.

10. Place loaves, seam side down in two greased 8-½" x 4-½" x 3" loaf pans.

11. Cover and let rise in a warm place, free from drafts, 1 hour or until doubled in bulk.

12. Bake at 350°F for 30 minutes or until loaves sound hollow when tapped.

13. Cover with aluminum foil for the last 10 minutes of baking to prevent excessive browning, if necessary.

14. Remove loaves from pans, and let cool on a wire rack.

[BRYAN & JENNIFER HUNTER, AND CORY & DANIEL]

TIP:
A thermometer helps to detect the proper temperature (105° to 115°) for the water when dissolving yeast. Water that is too hot will kill the yeast, while water that is too cool will slow the dough's rising.

PUMPKIN-WALNUT BREAD

Nutrition Facts per serving: Calories 223.1, Protein 4.682 Gm, Carbs 20.96 Gm, Fat 13.49 Gm, Cholesterol 62.93 mg,
Dietary Fiber 1.395 Gm, Sugar 0.932 Gm, Sodium 307 mg, Calcium 64.66 mg, Potassium 163.9 mg, Iron 1.477 mg

MAKES 1 LOAF
SERVES 12

2 cups all purpose flour
1 tsp. baking powder
1 tsp. baking soda
1 tsp. salt
½ tsp. ground ginger
½ tsp. ground cloves
½ tsp. ground cinnamon
¾ cup, plus 1 Tbsp. sugar
½ cup (1 stick) unsalted
   butter, room temperature
2 lg. eggs, room temperature
1-½ tsp. grated lemon peel
1 tsp. vanilla extract
½ cup sour cream
1 cup canned pure pumpkin
½ cup whole milk
1-½ cups chopped walnuts

1. Position rack in centre of oven; preheat to 325°F.

2. Butter a 9" x 5" x 3" metal loaf pan.

3. Sift first 7 ingredients into a medium bowl.

4. Using an electric mixer, beat butter in a large bowl, until light. Gradually beat in ¾ cup sugar.

5. Beat in eggs one at a time. Beat in pumpkin, lemon peel and vanilla.

6. Whisk sour cream and milk in a small bowl.

7. Beat flour and sour cream mixtures alternately into batter in two additions each; fold in nuts.

8. Transfer batter to pan; smooth top.

9. Sprinkle with 1 tablespoon sugar.

10. Bake bread until tester inserted into centre comes out clean, about 1 hour and 10 minutes.

11. Cool in pan 10 minutes.

12. Turn out onto rack; let cool.

[ARTHUR & KAREN HUNTER]

NOTE:
Pumpkin-Walnut
Bread can be made
two days ahead.
Wrap in foil;
store at room
temperature.

Gaspacho (page 76)

SOUPS & STEWS

MEAT/POULTRY

VEGETABLE

SANDWICHES

SEAFOOD

JAMAICAN-STYLE STEW BEEF

Nutrition Facts per serving: Calories 187.5, Protein 20.11 Gm, Carbs 15.39 Gm, Fat 7.74 Gm, Cholesterol 47.25 mg, Dietary Fiber 1.161 Gm, Sugar 2.757 Gm, Sodium 148.8 mg, Calcium 24.12 mg, Potassium 481.9 mg, Iron 2.13 mg

SERVES 8 TO 12

2 lb. beef for stewing
2 Tbsp. cooking oil
1 Tbsp. dried meat seasoning
2 cloves garlic, chopped
1 lg. onion, chopped
1 scotch bonnet or seasoning
   pepper, seeded and
   finely chopped (optional)
3 thyme sprigs
Salt and pepper, to taste
1 Tbsp. Kitchen Bouquet
   Browning and Seasoning
   Sauce or soy sauce
2 potatoes, peeled and diced
2 lg. carrots, peeled and diced

1. If not already done by the butcher, cut beef into small bite-size cubes (about 1" thick).

2. Wash meat and season with meat seasoning, chopped onion, garlic, scotch bonnet or seasoning pepper, soy or browning sauce, salt, pepper and thyme. Rub seasoning into the meat and set aside for 2 to 3 hours (the longer it seasons, the better it will taste).

3. Separate the meat from the onion, garlic and thyme; set onion and garlic aside, until ready for use. Also, set thyme aside.

4. In a large saucepan, brown the meat in hot oil for about 6 minutes, stirring frequently and adding a little water when necessary; remove meat from pan, and set aside.

5. Lower heat to Medium; brown the onions and garlic in pan drippings. When the onions are tender, add beef and thyme to the pan.

6. Add about a cup of water, cover and cook over Medium heat for about 30 minutes, or until the meat is tender. Add water when necessary, as this stew should finish with a nice brown gravy.

7. Add potatoes and carrots; simmer covered for another 20 minutes, until potatoes and carrots are fork tender. If desired, thicken the gravy (see tip below).

8. Serve with white rice.

[GARY & ROSE LINDSAY, AND TIA & TAMIKA]

TIPS FOR COOKING STEW:

Brown large quantities of meat in two batches, otherwise, meat will stew in its own juice, which prevents browning. When making a range-top stew, bring stew to a full boil so bubbles break all over the surface of the stew. Reduce heat and simmer so bubbles break just below the surface of the stew. Make sure the lid fits tightly. Loose-fitting lids allow heat and moisture to escape, which alters cooking time and liquid content. Size of vegetable and meat cubes affects the cooking time. Large pieces or cubes take longer to cook. To thicken stew, mix flour and water to a smooth paste by shaking or stirring together. Stir mixture into stew. Stir constantly all over the pan to prevent lumps. Stir gently to avoid breaking vegetable pieces.

CREAMY DHAL SOUP

Nutrition Facts per serving: Calories 98.21, Protein 4.735 Gm, Carbs 16.32 Gm, Fat 1.674 Gm, Cholesterol 2.086 mg, Dietary Fiber 1.953 Gm, Sugar 2.457 Gm, Sodium 19.6 mg, Calcium 46.35 mg, Potassium 187.7 mg, Iron 1.988 mg

1. Sauté the onion, ginger and garlic in the oil for a couple of minutes.

2. Add the spices, and cook for a further 2 minutes.

3. Add the lentils and carrots, and stir so they are coated in the spices.

4. Add the stock, and bring to a boil. Reduce heat and simmer for 30 minutes, or until the vegetables are really tender and the lentils are mushy.

5. Puree in a blender or mash with a potato masher for a thicker texture; season to taste.

6. Reheat the soup gently.

7. Serve with a dollop of cream or yogurt.

[MARK & AOIFE MATTHEWS, AND MICHAEL & LARA]

SERVES 12 TO 16

1 lg. onion, coarsely chopped
Approx. 1" piece fresh ginger, peeled and grated
2 cloves garlic, minced
1 Tbsp. vegetable oil
1 tsp. ground cumin
1 tsp. ground coriander
1 tsp. turmeric
2 carrots, peeled and coarsely chopped
Approx. 12 ozs. split red lentils
Approx. 6 cups vegetable or chicken stock
6 Tbsp. cream or yogurt, to serve

CARROT AND CORIANDER (CILANTRO) SOUP

Nutrition Facts per serving: Calories 94.98, Protein 1.873 Gm, Carbs 14.42 Gm, Fat 3.677 Gm, Cholesterol 0 mg, Dietary Fiber 2.922 Gm, Sugar 7.576 Gm, Sodium 67.03 mg, Calcium 48.32 mg, Potassium 487.3 mg, Iron 1.296 mg

1. In a skillet, sauté the onions and garlic together in the olive oil.

2. Add the carrots; stir until they are coated in the oil/garlic/onion mixture.

3. Add vegetable broth, and season with black pepper; bring to a boil.

4. Reduce heat; simmer for 20 minutes, or until carrots are tender.

5. Add cilantro, and stir.

6. Transfer mixture to a blender, and puree.

7. Return mixture to the pan to re-heat.

8. Garnish with cilantro leaves and a swirl of cream and/or croutons.

9. Serve immediately with warm, crusty French bread.

[ROGER & RACHAEL HANSON, AND THOMAS & MATTHEW]

SERVES 4

1 lb. carrots, peeled and sliced
2 sm. onions, diced
2 cloves garlic, chopped
2 cans or 1 carton low sodium vegetable broth
¼ cup chopped fresh cilantro
1 Tbsp. olive oil
Black pepper, to taste
Cream, fresh cilantro and croutons, to garnish (optional)

NOTE:
May be placed in the refrigerator or freezer to be served later.

HAM-AND-BEAN SOUP

Nutrition Facts per serving: Calories 333, Protein 32.98 Gm, Carbs 39.14 Gm, Fat 7.73 Gm, Cholesterol 46.03 mg, Dietary Fiber 22.74 Gm, Sugar 0.028 Gm, Sodium 1097 mg, Calcium 105.2 mg, Potassium 890.8 mg, Iron 3.382 mg

SERVES 6 TO 8

1 (16 oz.) pkg. dried
   Great Northern beans
3 cups chopped cooked ham
1 lg. sweet onion, diced
2 cloves garlic, minced
2 Tbsp. olive oil
1 ham bone (optional)
2 (32 oz.) containers
   chicken broth
½ tsp. dried crushed red pepper
   (Cayenne pepper is also nice in
   this soup)

1. Sort and wash beans.

2. Place beans in a large pot, add water 2" above beans and soak 8 hours; drain.

3. Sauté ham, onion and garlic in hot oil in a large pot over Medium heat for 5 minutes, or until onion is tender.

4. Add beans, ham bone (if desired), chicken broth and red pepper.

5. Bring to a boil, cover, reduce heat and simmer, stirring occasionally, 1-½ hours, or until beans are tender and soup has thickened.

6. Serve with corn bread (see page 63 for Cayman Corn Bread).

This is a good old Southern recipe from Virginia (a good way to use up leftover baked ham).

[QUATRO & PENNY HATCH, AND JASON, CAITLIN & TANNER]

Ham-and-Bean Soup, with Cayman Corn Bread (page 63)

CAYMAN STEW BEEF

Nutrition Facts per serving: Calories 258.8, Protein 24.89 Gm, Carbs 18.33 Gm, Fat 9.315 Gm, Cholesterol 56.7 mg,
Dietary Fiber 2.226 Gm, Sugar 4.039 Gm, Sodium 361.1 mg, Calcium 24.16 mg, Potassium 662.4 mg, Iron 2.757 mg

1. About 2 to 3 hours before cooking, season the beef with salt, black pepper, scotch bonnet pepper, celery, onion, bell pepper and garlic salt.

2. In a large pot, separate beef from onions, bell pepper and celery (as best you can); brown the beef in about 1 to 2 tablespoons hot vegetable oil (better if browned in two batches).

3. Add onions, bell pepper, celery, 4 cups water and the stewed tomatoes.

4. Cook covered over Medium heat, until tender (approximately 1 hour), stirring occasionally and adding water, if necessary.

5. About halfway through the cooking process, add potatoes and carrots. Cover and continue cooking for about 30 minutes.

6. Serve hot over white rice.

[HELEN & EDLIN MERREN]

SERVES 8 TO 10

2 family packs stew beef
1 tsp. garlic salt
1 tsp. salt
1 tsp. black pepper
1 white onion, sliced
1 bell pepper, sliced
1 stalk celery, chopped
½ scotch bonnet pepper
   (no seeds), chopped (optional)
   or 4 seasoning peppers,
   chopped (no seeds)
1 (14.5 oz.) can stewed tomatoes
1 to 2 Tbsp. vegetable oil
4 to 5 potatoes, peeled and
   cut into fourths
4 to 5 carrots, peeled and
   sliced

SENEGALESE PEANUT SOUP

Nutrition Facts per serving: Calories 399.5, Protein 17.83 Gm, Carbs 43.06 Gm, Fat 17.86 Gm, Cholesterol 0.75 mg,
Dietary Fiber 9.525 Gm, Sugar 8.544 Gm, Sodium 1188 mg, Calcium 105.5 mg, Potassium 676 mg, Iron 4.994 mg

1. In a blender or food processor, combine the chick peas, ½ cup of the broth and the peanut butter; puree.

2. In a large non-stick saucepan or Dutch oven, heat the oil.

3. Sauté the onions and gingerroot until the onions are soft (7 to 8 minutes).

4. Stir in the curry powder and cumin; sauté 1 minute longer.

5. Add remaining 2-½ cups of broth, tomatoes and chick pea mixture; simmer 5 minutes to blend the flavours.

6. Season with cayenne pepper, to taste.

7. Serve sprinkled with cilantro.

[LINDA DALTON-RILEY & DARREN RILEY,
AND BRITTANY & SYDNEY]

SERVES 4

1 (15 oz.) can chick peas, rinsed
   and drained
3 cups reduced-sodium
   chicken broth
3 Tbsp. creamy peanut butter
1 tsp. peanut oil
2 onions, chopped
1 (1") piece peeled
   gingerroot, minced
1-½ tsp. curry powder
½ tsp. ground cumin
1 (14.5 oz.) can diced tomatoes
¼ tsp. cayenne pepper, or
   to taste
Chopped cilantro (optional)

CAYMAN-STYLE STEW CONCH

Nutrition Facts per serving: Calories 773.3, Protein 22.02 Gm, Carbs 32.87 Gm, Fat 65.96 Gm, Cholesterol 46.28 mg, Dietary Fiber 2.934 Gm, Sugar 2.022 Gm, Sodium 402.3 mg, Calcium 71.73 mg, Potassium 1197 mg, Iron 8.31 mg

SERVES 6 TO 8

3 lbs. conch
1 green bell pepper, chopped
1 med. onion, chopped
4 cups coconut milk
Salt and black pepper,
    to taste
1 sm. scotch bonnet pepper,
    finely chopped (no seeds)
½ cup all purpose flour

1. Clean the conch; pick off any remaining skin and hard tips.

2. Pound the conch until about ¼"-thick.

3. Put about 2 teaspoons of salt into a large saucepan of water; bring to a boil.

4. To the boiling water, add conch; boil for 5 minutes.

5. Drain off the water, cool the conch and cut into bite-size pieces.

6. In a separate saucepan, combine chopped bell pepper, onion and coconut milk.

7. Add scotch bonnet, salt and pepper to taste; bring to a boil.

8. Add conch; simmer for 1 hour.

9. Combine flour, 2 tablespoons water and 1 teaspoon salt; mix until pasty.

10. Roll out onto a floured surface, and cut into small pieces of dough.

11. Add dough to coconut milk; simmer for 30 minutes, or until mixture thickens.

12. Serve with white rice.

[CHARLES SMATT & LYNN BODDEN, AND KAYLYN BODDEN]

GASPACHO

Nutrition Facts per serving: Calories 213.8, Protein 4.011 Gm, Carbs 20.83 Gm, Fat 14.26 Gm, Cholesterol 0 mg, Dietary Fiber 4.467 Gm, Sugar 12.78 Gm, Sodium 656.2 mg, Calcium 50.82 mg, Potassium 957.2 mg, Iron 2.336 mg

SERVES 6 TO 8

2 cucumbers, halved and
    seeded, but not peeled
3 red bell peppers, cored and
    seeded
8 plum tomatoes or 1 (48 oz.)
    can whole or diced tomatoes
2 red onions, chopped
6 cloves garlic, minced
1 (48 oz.) can tomato juice
½ cup white wine vinegar
1 Tbsp. salt
½ cup olive oil
1-½ tsp. freshly ground
    black pepper, to taste

1. Chop the cucumbers, bell peppers, tomatoes and red onions into 1" cubes.

2. Put vegetables separately into a food processor; pulse until coarsely chopped (DO NOT OVER-PROCESS).

3. Combine vegetables in a large bowl; add the garlic, tomato juice, vinegar, olive oil, salt and pepper.

4. Mix well, refrigerate for several hours or overnight, and serve chilled.

This Gaspacho recipe belonging to Daniel and Caitlyn Harrington's grandmother, Sara Jane Meisner of Ottawa, Canada, is an excellent substitute for salad on a hot summer day.

[SEAN & LIZ HARRINGTON, AND DANIEL & CAITLYN]

RATATOUILLE

Nutrition Facts per serving: Calories 96.81, Protein 1.96 Gm, Carbs 8.123 Gm, Fat 7.158 Gm, Cholesterol 0 mg, Dietary Fiber 2.433 Gm, Sugar 4.327 Gm, Sodium 312.8 mg, Calcium 46.59 mg, Potassium 404.4 mg, Iron 1.381 mg

1. Preheat oven to 350°F.

2. Sweat the sliced onion and garlic in approximately 2 tablespoons olive oil; add the tomatoes, and mash with a potato masher; cook over Medium heat for at least half an hour.

3. In a large bowl, pour about 2 to 3 tablespoons of olive oil. Add salt, pepper, oregano and basil.

4. To the olive oil mixture, add the chopped aubergine, courgettes and bell peppers; toss until vegetables are lightly covered in the oil.

5. Place in a baking tin; roast for half an hour.

6. Put all the ingredients, including ½ the parsley, in a serving bowl, and mix together. Top with the remainder of the parsley.

[FIONA & CARLOS PIMENTEL, AND EDWARD, ANNA, AMELIA & JAMIE]

SERVES 4 TO 6

1 aubergine (eggplant), coarsely chopped
2 courgettes (zucchini), coarsely chopped
1 green bell pepper, coarsely chopped
1 red bell pepper, coarsely chopped
1 onion, sliced
1 clove garlic, sliced
2 (14.5 oz.) cans of diced tomatoes
Olive oil
½ tsp. salt
½ tsp. black pepper
1 tsp. oregano
1 tsp. basil
1 handful fresh parsley, chopped

Tomatoes, onion and garlic cooking (Picture kindly submitted by Fiona Pimentel)

Ratatouille may be served hot, but is best if cooled overnight. The traditional French method of making this stew is to cook all the ingredients together on the stove. The result is a rather greasy slush. This version, introduced to the Pimentel family by an English chef, always receives great praise from French relatives. Vive l'entente cordiale.

Ratatouille

SALT BEEF AND BEANS

Nutrition Facts per serving: Calories 421.3, Protein 28.33 Gm, Carbs 39.18 Gm, Fat 18.11 Gm, Cholesterol 0 mg, Dietary Fiber 0.669 Gm, Sugar 0.553 Gm, Sodium 19.16 mg, Calcium 91.29 mg, Potassium 975 mg, Iron 9.376 mg

SERVES 6 TO 8

1 lb. salt beef
1 (approx. 16 oz.) pack small red beans
1 can coconut milk
3 cups water
1 sprig fresh basil (with10 to 12 leaves on it)
1 sweet bell pepper, finely chopped
1 med. onion, finely chopped
2 cloves garlic, finely chopped
1 scotch bonnet pepper, seeded and finely chopped (or left whole for less heat)

SEA PIE:

Caymanians traditionally enjoy dumplings or sea pie in their Salt Beef and Beans. To make sea pie, combine about 1 cup sifted flour and a pinch of salt with enough ice water to form a bread dough consistency; knead. Set aside in a bowl, covered with a kitchen towel, for several hours, so that it can sponge and become light. Roll out thin with a rolling pin. Stretch until very thin, and lay across top of beans towards the end of the cooking time. Cook for about 15 minutes before folding into the coconut mixture.

1. Soak the salt beef overnight (or boil it once), then discard the water to rid the salt beef of salt.

2. Soak the beans overnight or for a couple of hours; discard the water.

3. In a medium pot, boil the salt beef until almost tender. Drain off the water.

4. Meanwhile, in a separate pot, boil the beans until almost tender (do not pour off the bean water).

5. To the beans, add coconut milk, the 3 cups of water, salt beef, basil sprig, onion, bell pepper, garlic and scotch bonnet pepper.

6. Cook on the stove top over Medium heat for 30 to 45 minutes, or until slightly thickened. Remove the basil stem.

7. Serve with white rice, Fried Plantain (page 118), cole slaw and Cayman Corn Bread (page 63).

Salt Beef and Beans

This recipe was selected from a collection of recipes submitted by members of John Gray Memorial Church, supporters of Cayman Prep and High School.

[LEONARD & CAROL ANN EBANKS]

DEB'S THAI SOUP

Nutrition Facts per serving: Calories 251.5, Protein 10.6 Gm, Carbs 25.57 Gm, Fat 13.25 Gm, Cholesterol 25.73 mg,
Dietary Fiber 2.484 Gm, Sugar 3.882 Gm, Sodium 572.5 mg, Calcium 105 mg, Potassium 457.8 mg, Iron 1.929 mg

SERVES 12 TO 16

1. Fill about an 8 quart pot with approximately 3 cups chicken stock and 4-½ cups water; drop in the drumsticks (do not overfill - no more than 8 cups of liquid should be in the pot).

2. Add bouillon cubes; bring to a boil.

3. Add fish sauce; reduce heat.

4. Add celery, Irish potato, sweet potato, parsnips and leek; simmer for about 2 hours, or until thickened.

5. Remove the chicken bones and any unwanted parts. Tear off any chicken remaining on the bone, and put back in the pot.

6. In about 2 tablespoons of water, thoroughly mix together the cumin and curry; add to the pot.

7. Add sea salt (if desired), chili sauce, Thai Garlic and Chili Sauce, Mongolian Fire Oil, coconut milk and milk to the pot.

8. Add onion, acorn squash and fresh corn; simmer an additional 15 minutes.

9. Add Thai noodles; simmer 10 minutes.

10. Serve hot.

[STEPHEN & DEBRA MCTAGGART, AND SARAH,
AMELIA & MATTHEW]

4 to 5 chicken drumsticks
3 sm. chicken bouillon cubes
3 cups chicken stock
4-½ cups water
3 Tbsp. fish sauce
   (located in the Thai section)
2 to 3 celery stalks, chopped
1 med. Irish potato, cubed
1 sweet potato, cubed
1 to 2 sm. parsnips, cut
   into strips
1 leek, thinly sliced
1 Tbsp. ground cumin
3 to 4 tsp. curry powder
1 to 2 tsp. sea salt (optional)
3 tsp. chili sauce or oil, or
   to taste
1 can coconut milk
2 cups milk
1 lg. white onion, chopped
½ an acorn squash, chopped
1 to 2 ears of corn, scraped
   off the cob
Approx. 12 ozs. Thai noodles
7 ozs. Thai Garlic and
   Chili Sauce
6 to 7 shakes Mongolian
   Fire Oil

CHICKEN AND BEAN STEW

Nutrition Facts per serving: Calories 1583, Protein 135.2 Gm, Carbs 111.7 Gm, Fat 67.81 Gm, Cholesterol 226.8 mg, Dietary Fiber 53.43 Gm, Sugar 12.87 Gm, Sodium 1047 mg, Calcium 301 mg, Potassium 3379 mg, Iron 12.3 mg

SERVES 3 TO 4

1 (12 oz.) pack Great
   Northern (haricot) beans
2 Tbsp. olive oil
3 onions, coarsely chopped
3 lbs. boneless chicken breast
   fillets, cut into 1" cubes
1 (6 oz.) can tomato paste
4 cloves garlic, chopped
1 level tsp. chili powder
2 tsp. turmeric
1 tsp. coriander
1 tsp. salt

NOTE:
*This stew tastes
even better when served
the day after it
is made.*

1. Wash the beans in cold water, drain and place in a pressure cooker or large pot.

2. Add 2 pints water, and allow beans to soak for 1 hour.

3. Add 1 tablespoon olive oil (to reduce the foam), and cook on High pressure for 6 minutes. If not using a pressure cooker, but instead using a large pot, add 4 pints of water, and simmer without a lid for about 2 hours, until the beans are almost cooked.

4. Add the chicken and most of the onions; bring to a slow simmer.

5. Heat the remaining oil in a frying pan to Medium-High heat, add the spices and the remaining onions; fry gently for 3 to 4 minutes.

6. Reduce heat to Medium-Low, add the tomato paste and chopped garlic; continue cooking for 3 to 4 minutes to bring out the full flavour of the spices.

7. Add the sauce from the pan to the pressure cooker (or large pot), and continue cooking for a further 15 minutes, to allow the sauce to thicken, stirring frequently.

[MIKE & ANNE MCGRATH]

TIP:
*To cut a bell pepper without making a mess of seeds, first cut off the
bottom part. Then turn the pepper upside down and slice off the flat sides,
leaving the white flesh containing the seeds intact.
- Fiona Pimentel*

DEBBIE'S SUPER BOWL SANDWICH

Nutrition Facts per serving: Calories 1641, Protein 60.21 Gm, Carbs 10.6 Gm, Fat 157.4 Gm, Cholesterol 235.4 mg,
Dietary Fiber 0.233 Gm, Sugar 0.085 Gm, Sodium 1278 mg, Calcium 360.8 mg, Potassium 643.9 mg, Iron 5.53 mg

SERVES 4 TO 6

1 lg. loaf (about 8" wide x 12" long) uncut bread, such as Rye
1-½ lbs. thinly sliced roast beef from the deli
1 lg. white onion, sliced
1 (8 oz.) pack fresh mushrooms, sliced
½ of a 10 oz. block Sharp cheddar cheese
Approx. 16 ozs. mayonnaise (about ½ of a qt.-size jar)
1 (4 oz.) jar Horseradish
10 slices bacon
Black pepper and garlic salt, to taste
1 tsp. dried basil
½ tsp. dried oregano
Seasoning blends, such as Garlic & Herb and/or Nature's Seasons

1. Cut the top off the bread with the knife angled, so that it forms a long bowl. The sides need to be high to hold all the ingredients in.

2. Hollow the bread out. Reserve the long cut off section of the bread (which will be placed on top of the sandwich after it is filled).

3. In a mixing bowl, mix together mayonnaise with horseradish. Season with black pepper, basil, oregano and garlic salt (any seasoning is nice in this).

4. Spread a fairly thick layer of the mayonnaise mixture (about ½ of the mixture) in the bread bowl.

5. Cook bacon. Heavily season with black pepper; set aside.

6. Sauté onions in 1 tablespoon of the bacon drippings; season heavily with seasoning blend, to taste, while sautéing. Spread in the bread bowl.

7. Sauté mushrooms; season with seasoning blend, to taste, while sautéing. Spread in the bread bowl.

8. Microwave the block of cheddar; stir, and pour over the mushrooms.

9. Spread bacon on top of cheese (the bowl should be almost full now).

10. Season the beef with black pepper and garlic salt; sauté in a little oil. Toss it around quickly (do not cook for long, as it will get tough, but just long enough for the seasonings to get mixed in); spread on top of bacon (not flat but all bunched up).

11. Put a thick layer of mayonnaise mixture on again, and place the top piece of bread on. The sandwich should now be a massive mound.

12. Press down on sandwich, and wrap in tin foil; place in refrigerator overnight with something heavy on top to help flatten it.

13. When ready to serve, place the wrapped sandwich in the oven for about 30 minutes at 350°F.

NOTE:

It is preferable to use a wide loaf of bread for this sandwich - NOT a long French or Italian-style bread. With the other ingredients, the key is to heavily season! Use the horseradish to suit your taste, which means a lot of tasting. The stronger, the better, because it needs to stand out over all the other ingredients. Jerk sauce can be used as a substitute for the horseradish.

This recipe came from a friend, Debbie Punnewaert,
and makes a delicious and easy way to serve friends
at a casual gathering.

[BRYAN & JENNIFER HUNTER, AND CORY & DANIEL]

HAM AND BEAN SOUP SUPREME

Nutrition Facts per serving: Calories 195.2, Protein 11.9 Gm, Carbs 35.88 Gm, Fat 1.08 Gm, Cholesterol 0 mg,
Dietary Fiber 13.69 Gm, Sugar 2.732 Gm, Sodium 601.3 mg, Calcium 96.06 mg, Potassium 590.6 mg, Iron 3.27 mg

SERVES 15 TO 20

1 meaty ham bone and any
   leftover scraps
1 (16 oz.) can Pinto Beans
1 (16 oz.) can Black Beans
1 (16 oz.) can Blackeye Peas
1 (16 oz.) can Great Northern
   white beans (or navy beans)
1 (16 oz.) can Red Kidney Beans
1 can lentil soup
6 qts. water
2 med. onions, coarsely
   chopped
1 (28 oz.) can crushed tomatoes
2 cloves garlic, minced
Juice of 1 lemon
Pinch of dried ginger powder
2 celery stalks, split lengthwise
½ lb. Ditalini (pre-cooked)
   pasta (optional)
Salt and pepper, to taste

1. Place ham bone, meat scraps, celery stalks, garlic, ginger and onions in a large stock pot (a 10 quart pot works well).

2. Add approximately 6 quarts of water until the pot is about ¾ full.

3. Place the lid on the pot slightly off-centre to allow steam to escape.

4. Boil on Medium-High heat for 3 hours, adding enough water every ½ hour to keep the pot at ¾ full.

5. Remove the ham bone and take off the meat, cutting it into small bits; discard fat.

6. Put the lean meat back into the soup pot.

7. Drain the liquid from all the cans of beans; add beans to the pot.

8. Add lentil soup, crushed tomatoes and lemon juice; reduce heat to Medium.

9. In a separate pot, boil the pasta in water, until just tender; drain.

10. Add the pasta (if desired) to the soup pot; continue to cook on Medium heat for 30 minutes.

11. Add salt and pepper, to taste (although none is usually needed).

12. Reduce heat to simmer, until ready to serve.

NOTE:
This soup can be frozen, thawed and served at a later date.

[STEPHEN & DEBRA MCTAGGART, AND SARAH,
AMELIA & MATTHEW]

BLACK BEAN SOUP

Nutrition Facts per serving: Calories 421.3, Protein 25.6 Gm, Carbs 75.04 Gm, Fat 3.487 Gm, Cholesterol 0 mg,
Dietary Fiber 1.808 Gm, Sugar 2.15 Gm, Sodium 555.1 mg, Calcium 175.8 mg, Potassium 1868 mg, Iron 6.351 mg

SERVES 4

1 lb. dried Black Beans
2 qts. water
2 med. onions, finely chopped
1 bay leaf
2 green bell peppers, cut into strips
½ cup olive oil
1 tsp. dried oregano
4 cloves garlic, minced
¼ tsp. ground cumin
1 Tbsp. salt
½ tsp. black pepper
White rice, cooked
Chopped scallions, for garnish

1. Spread beans onto a flat surface; pick out broken beans and foreign particles.

2. Wash beans thoroughly, and soak overnight in 2 quarts of water.

3. Next day, pour beans and water into a 4 quart soup kettle; bring to a boil.

4. Cover, and cook over Medium heat.

5. Meanwhile, in a skillet, sauté onions and green peppers in olive oil, until light golden.

6. Add crushed oregano, bay leaf, cumin and garlic.

7. Add mixture to beans, stirring well.

8. Add salt and pepper; cook slowly over Low heat, covered, until beans are tender (at least 1 hour).

9. Serve over white rice, and top with chopped scallions.

[WAYNE & PATRICIA DaCOSTA, AND AARON & ASHLEY]

Black Bean Soup

CREAM OF CORN CHOWDER

Nutrition Facts per serving: Calories 375.8, Protein 7.506 Gm, Carbs 28.71 Gm, Fat 18.24 Gm, Cholesterol 54.53 mg,
Dietary Fiber 4.403 Gm, Sugar 3.3 Gm, Sodium 659.4 mg, Calcium 150.8 mg, Potassium 524.5 mg, Iron 6.431 mg

MAKES 4 CUPS

3 med. ears fresh corn,
  scraped off the cob
1 sm. onion, chopped
2 Tbsp. butter or margarine,
  melted
1 bay leaf
Pinch of dried rosemary
Pinch of dried thyme
3 cups chicken broth
Pinch of dried basil
Dash of black pepper
¼ cup chicken broth
2 Tbsp. diced pimiento,
  drained
½ cup whipping cream
Fresh rosemary sprigs
  (optional)

1. In a large saucepan, over Medium heat, sauté onion in butter, until tender.

2. Add 1 cup corn kernels, and ½ cup water; cook over Medium heat for 3 minutes, stirring frequently.

3. Tie bay leaf, dried whole rosemary and thyme in a cheesecloth bag.

4. Add spice bag, broth, basil and black pepper to sautéed mixture; stir.

5. Simmer uncovered, 45 minutes (add water, if necessary, halfway through the cooking process). Remove and discard spice bag.

6. Place corn mixture in an electric blender; add ¼ cup chicken broth; cover, and blend, until smooth.

7. Return mixture to skillet.

8. Stir in pimiento and remaining corn; bring to a boil (add ½ cup water, if needed).

9. Reduce heat and simmer, uncovered, for 20 minutes.

10. Stir in whipping cream; cook over Low heat, until thoroughly heated.

11. Garnish with fresh rosemary, if desired.

[GREGORY & TERRI MERREN, AND JOSH & ZACHARY]

CHUTNEY-CHEESE SANDWICHES

Nutrition Facts per sandwich: Calories 88, Protein 2.96 Gm, Carbs 11.08 Gm, Fat 3.6 Gm, Cholesterol 8.53 mg,
Dietary Fiber 0.57 Gm, Sugar 1.01 Gm, Sodium 149.33 mg, Calcium 57.06 mg, Potassium 91.2 mg, Iron 0.78 mg

MAKES 1-½ DOZEN

1 (3 oz.) pkg. cream cheese,
  softened
½ cup shredded sharp
  cheddar cheese
1 tsp. finely chopped onion
Dash Worcestershire sauce
1-½ dozen 2" white bread
  rounds
¼ cup chutney

1. Combine cream cheese, shredded cheddar cheese, onion, and Worcestershire sauce; beat with an electric mixer or rotary beater until light and fluffy.

2. Spread mixture on bread rounds, and top each with a small amount of chutney.

3. Chill before serving.

Nice as a snack, or can be served
as a light appetiser.

CARROT GINGER SOUP WITH COCONUT ROASTED SHRIMP

Nutrition Facts per serving: Calories 198.8, Protein 14.06 Gm, Carbs 11.84 Gm, Fat 11.26 Gm, Cholesterol 0.735 mg, Dietary Fiber 0.95 Gm, Sugar 3.392 Gm, Sodium 983.5 mg, Calcium 102.2 mg, Potassium 237.8 mg, Iron 0.8 mg

SERVES 6

Ingredients:

2 Tbsp. extra virgin olive oil
1 med. onion, coarsely chopped
4 lg. carrots (¾ lb.), peeled and chopped
1 Tbsp. finely grated ginger
½ tsp. crushed red pepper
3 cups low-sodium chicken broth
3 Tbsp. soy sauce
2 Tbsp. fresh lime juice
2 Tbsp. light brown sugar
1 Tbsp. smooth peanut butter
1 tsp. Asian sesame oil
1 cup skim milk
¼ cup light coconut milk
Salt and freshly ground black pepper, to taste
16 lg. shrimp, shelled
3 Tbsp. shredded coconut
Pinch of cayenne pepper

1. Heat 1 tablespoon of olive oil in a large saucepan; add onion, and cook over Medium heat until softened (about 4 minutes).

2. Add the carrots, ginger and crushed red pepper; cook for 6 minutes.

3. Add the broth, and bring to the boil; simmer until the carrots are very tender (about 15 to 20 minutes).

4. Remove from heat; stir in the soy sauce, lime juice, brown sugar, peanut butter and sesame oil.

5. In a blender, puree the soup until smooth.

6. Return soup to the saucepan; stir in the skim milk and coconut milk.

7. Season soup with salt and black pepper. Keep warm.

8. Heat the oven to 425°F.

9. Toss the shrimp with the coconut, cayenne pepper and the remaining 1 tablespoon of olive oil; season with salt and black pepper.

10. Spread the shrimp onto a parchment-lined baking sheet; roast for 8 minutes, or until they are pink.

11. Ladle the soup into warmed bowls, and garnish with the coconut shrimp.

[LINDA DALTON-RILEY & DARREN RILEY,
AND BRITTANY & SYDNEY]

Carrot Ginger Soup with Coconut Roasted Shrimp

Mykonos Greek Salad (page 89)

SALADS

DRESSINGS

SEAFOOD

POULTRY

PASTA

VEGETABLE

FRUIT/GREEN

MISCELLANEOUS

GELATIN

MOM E'S MIXED BEAN SALAD

Nutrition Facts per serving: Calories 173.43, Protein 6.58 Gm, Carbs 31.33 Gm, Fat 3.31 Gm, Cholesterol 0 mg, Dietary Fiber 0.75 Gm, Sugar 0.85 Gm, Sodium 209.64 mg, Calcium 2.53 mg, Potassium 500.00 mg, Iron 2.53 mg

SERVES 12 TO 16

2 cups fresh green beans, boiled until fork tender, about 15 minutes and drained (or 1 can of green beans, drained well)
1 (14.5 oz.) can Wax Beans
1 (15.5 oz.) can Red Kidney Beans
½ cup chopped green pepper
¾ cup sugar
⅔ cup cider vinegar
⅓ cup salad oil
1 tsp. pepper
1 tsp. salt

1. Drain all the beans well, and combine in a serving bowl.

2. Add chopped green pepper to beans.

3. Combine remaining ingredients, pour over the beans, and mix all together.

4. Let stand in refrigerator for 24 hours.

5. Drain off excess liquid before serving.

This 'old faithful' recipe belonging to Kaitlyn, Laura & Matthew Elphinstone's paternal grandmother is great for get-togethers or to take to a pot-luck lunch or supper.

[SCOTT & KATHRYN ELPHINSTONE, AND KAITLYN, LAURA & MATTHEW]

BLUE CHEESE DRESSING

Nutrition Facts: Calories 1522, Protein 48.47 Gm, Carbs 5.412 Gm, Fat 146.1 Gm, Cholesterol 167.7 mg, Dietary Fiber 0 Gm, Sugar 2.378 Gm, Sodium 3430 mg, Calcium 1202 mg, Potassium 605.7 mg, Iron 1.16 mg

MAKES ABOUT ½ CUP

8 ozs. blue cheese, crumbled
6 Tbsp. extra virgin olive oil
2 Tbsp. white wine vinegar
Salt and freshly ground black pepper, to taste

1. Put the crumbled cheese in a bowl, and crush with a fork.

2. Add 2 tablespoons of the olive oil, and mash until creamy, adding the remaining olive oil and the vinegar as you go (if the end result is too thick, beat in a little hot water until the mixture is loose and creamy).

3. Add salt and pepper (keeping in mind that the blue cheese is already quite salty).

4. Pour over wedges of iceberg lettuce, and serve.

NOTE:
This dressing will thicken on standing, so beat it again before serving (or add a little water to thin it down).

MYKONOS GREEK SALAD

Nutrition Facts per serving: Calories 301.5, Protein 5.105 Gm, Carbs 15.19 Gm, Fat 25.22 Gm, Cholesterol 16.64 mg,
Dietary Fiber 2.781 Gm, Sugar 6.388 Gm, Sodium 542.7 mg, Calcium 132.4 mg, Potassium 539.2 mg, Iron 1.599 mg

SERVES 12

1. In a large decorative salad bowl, place in the following order: lettuce, tomatoes, cucumbers, feta cheese and black olives.

2. In a salad dressing carafe, combine both vinegars, water, sugar and salad dressing mix; shake until well-blended.

3. Add olive oil; blend again.

4. Garnish with Calamata Olives, Peperoncinis and red onion (if desired).

[LISA MERREN]

1 lg. head Romaine lettuce, washed, torn into lg. bite-size pieces

1 head red leaf lettuce, washed, torn into lg. bite-size pieces

6 vine-ripened tomatoes, or 6 plum (or Roma) tomatoes, seeded, quartered, chopped into 1" pieces

3 med. cucumbers, seeded, quartered, chopped into 1" cubes

1 (8 oz.) pkg. feta cheese, crumbled

2 sm. cans pitted, sliced, black olives

12 Calamata Greek Olives

12 Greek Golden Peperoncinis

½ red onion, diced (optional)

Dressing:
¼ cup distilled white vinegar
¼ cup Balsamic vinegar
1 Tbsp. sugar
6 Tbsp. water
2 packs Zesty Italian Salad Dressing and Recipe Mix
1 cup olive oil

First, build the salad.

Secondly, toss.

Lastly, just before serving, add dressing; toss again.

TIP:

To prepare lettuce ahead of time and store for future use, wash the lettuce leaves, layer with paper towel. Roll the lettuce in the paper towel and place in a plastic bag, until dry. Unroll, re-layer with more dry paper towel. Place in refrigerator. Use as needed.

BREADALBANE SALAD

Nutrition Facts per serving: Calories 213.5, Protein 2.189 Gm, Carbs 7.494 Gm, Fat 20.25 Gm, Cholesterol 17.2 mg,
Dietary Fiber 0.752 Gm, Sugar 6.01 Gm, Sodium 118.6 mg, Calcium 29.76 mg, Potassium 85.42 mg, Iron 0.634 mg

SERVES 12 TO 16

Dressing:
1 cup mild olive oil
¼ cup red wine vinegar
¼ cup Mandarin orange juice
4 pieces Mandarin orange
3 Tbsp. honey
1 tsp. seasoned salt
¼ tsp. lemon pepper
1 tsp. paprika
1 tsp. Tabasco sauce
1 egg yolk

Salad:
A selection of favourite greens
1 sm. can Mandarin orange
   pieces
1 sm. onion, sliced
4 ozs. sliced almonds, toasted
1 sm. pkg. cherry tomatoes
1 lg. cucumber, sliced
2 Tbsp. butter
2 Tbsp. vegetable oil

1. Combine all of the Dressing ingredients, except the oil, in an electric blender, and blend thoroughly.

2. Slowly add oil while blender is running.

3. In a large bowl, mix together a selection of your favourite greens. Add Mandarin orange pieces, thinly sliced onion, cherry tomatoes and sliced cucumber.

4. In a frying pan, heat 2 tablespoons each of butter and vegetable oil. Add sliced almonds; stir continually, until almonds turn a light brown. Salt well, pour off fat, and cool on a paper towel.

5. Top the salad with the toasted almonds.

6. About 5 minutes before serving, pour dressing over the salad, and toss.

This recipe was a popular one at a restaurant I worked at from age 15 to 18. The restaurant was in an old home, in a little village one hour North of Toronto. All the city slickers would come there to eat because they thought it was so quaint. - Sandy Hew

[RICHARD & SANDY HEW, AND THOMPSON,
LAUREN & HARRISON]

VINAIGRETTE DRESSING

Nutrition Facts: Calories 715.8, Protein 0 Gm, Carbs 0.75 Gm, Fat 81 Gm, Cholesterol 0 mg,
Dietary Fiber 0 Gm, Sugar 0 Gm, Sodium 266.6 mg, Calcium 2.77 mg, Potassium 2.25 mg, Iron .039 mg

MAKES ABOUT ½ CUP

6 Tbsp. extra virgin olive oil
1 Tbsp. white wine vinegar
Salt and freshly ground
   black pepper, to taste

1. In a small bowl, mix together the oil, vinegar, salt and pepper until well-blended.

2. Beat with a fork or small whisk.

3. Serve over crisp salad greens.

Variations:

Dijon Vinaigrette: Add 1 teaspoon Dijon mustard, and beat well.

Vinaigrette with Lime: Use freshly squeezed lime juice instead of the vinegar.

Honey Vinaigrette: Add 1 tablespoon of honey (or more, to taste).

BROCCOLI SALAD

Nutrition Facts per serving: Calories 482.7, Protein 9.736 Gm, Carbs 37.65 Gm, Fat 37.15 Gm, Cholesterol 17.5 mg, Dietary Fiber 4.603 Gm, Sugar 22.69 Gm, Sodium 370.7 mg, Calcium 63.95 mg, Potassium 585.7 mg, Iron 1.87 mg

1. Prepare the dressing the day before serving. Refrigerate overnight.

2. Cut off the broccoli heads, and discard the stems.

3. Toss together the raisins, celery, grapes, peanuts, bacon and broccoli.

4. About 1 to 2 hours before serving, pour the dressing over the salad, and toss; let stand until time to serve so that the broccoli soaks up the dressing and softens a bit.

[TONY & CHRISTINE CLEAVER, AND ALEX, JORDYN & BETHANY]

SERVES 8

1 lg. pkg. fresh broccoli
1 cup raisins
1 cup chopped celery
1 lb. red seedless grapes
1 cup peanuts
6 strips crisply fried
   bacon, crumbled

Dressing (make the day before):
1 cup mayonnaise
⅓ cup sugar
1 Tbsp. vinegar

GREEN GODDESS DRESSING

Nutrition Facts per serving: Calories 1087, Protein 2.081 Gm, Carbs 2.174 Gm, Fat 128.7 Gm, Cholesterol 57.87 mg, Dietary Fiber 0.197 Gm, Sugar 0.122 Gm, Sodium 1035 mg, Calcium 40.96 mg, Potassium 109.1 mg, Iron 0.968 mg

1. Put mayonnaise in a food processor or blender.

2. Add all other ingredients, and blend, until smooth.

3. Serve immediately, or cover and refrigerate for up to 8 hours.

MAKES ABOUT 3 CUPS

1 to 2 cups mayonnaise
4 anchovy fillets
2 Tbsp. fresh tarragon
2 Tbsp. fresh parsley
2 Tbsp. fresh chives
1 Tbsp. lemon juice
3 Tbsp. vinegar
Salt and freshly ground black
   pepper, to taste

PAM'S CAESAR SALAD MIXTURE

Nutrition Facts per cup: Calories 557.4, Protein 4.414 Gm, Carbs 4.957 Gm, Fat 58.98 Gm, Cholesterol 111.4 mg, Dietary Fiber 0.124 Gm, Sugar 0.396 Gm, Sodium 1276 mg, Calcium 120.4 mg, Potassium 122.4 mg, Iron 0.975 mg

1. Put all ingredients in a bottle or jar with a tight-fitting lid.

2. Shake until well-blended.

3. Serve immediately over Romaine lettuce.

This easy and economical caesar mixture is from a dear friend of the Elphinstone family, Pam Hammond.

[SCOTT & KATHRYN ELPHINSTONE, AND KAITLYN, LAURA & MATTHEW]

MAKES ABOUT 1-½ CUPS

½ cup vegetable oil
2 cloves garlic, minced
2 Tbsp. fresh lemon juice
2 Tbsp. cider vinegar
1 Tbsp. Worcestershire sauce
½ tsp. dried mustard
2 Tbsp. Parmesan cheese
1 egg yolk, beaten
1 tsp. salt

CONCH SALAD

Nutrition Facts per serving: Calories 165, Protein 26.3 Gm, Carbs 11.1 Gm, Fat 1.3 Gm,
Cholesterol 62 mg, Dietary Fiber 1.9 Gm, Sugar 4.4 Gm, Sodium 173 mg

SERVES 3 TO 4

3 fresh conch, diced (frozen,
    if fresh is not available)
1 med. onion, diced
2 stalks celery, diced
3 plum tomatoes, diced
Fresh hot pepper(s) (bird
    pepper or scotch bonnet),
    to taste
½ cup fresh squeezed
    key lime juice
½ sm. green bell pepper, diced
Salt, to taste

1. Mix all ingredients together.

2. Serve on fresh lettuce leaves, with crackers.

[L A R R Y & S H E L L E Y L E O N A R D , A N D A L E X & N I C H O L A S]

Diced vegetables and conch

Conch Salad

CURRIED CHICKEN SALAD

Nutrition Facts per serving: Calories 535.2, Protein 34.15 Gm, Carbs 23.59 Gm, Fat 35 Gm, Cholesterol 79.11 mg,
Dietary Fiber 3.283 Gm, Sugar 10.28 Gm, Sodium 1535 mg, Calcium 78.31 mg, Potassium 715.3 mg, Iron 2.417 mg

1. Season the chicken with salt and pepper.

2. In a medium serving bowl, combine chicken, oranges, pineapple, peanuts and celery.

3. In a separate bowl, combine sour cream, Miracle Whip and curry powder; add to the chicken combination, and mix well.

4. Adjust seasonings, and serve between 2 slices of bread as a sandwich, or on a pile of salad greens.

This tasty recipe originated in the Cayman Islands. It belonged to Carol Ann Ebanks' aunt, the late Marion Parsons of Grand Cayman. Aunt Marrie, as she was affectionately called, was known for her outstanding culinary skills. Friends at John Gray Church will attest to this and talk about the tasty cakes which she used to bake!

[LEONARD & CAROL ANN EBANKS]

SERVES 6

2 lbs. cooked chicken, diced
1 (11 oz.) can Mandarin oranges, drained and chopped
1 (15.25 oz.) can crushed pineapple, drained
1 cup coarsely chopped peanuts
3 stalks celery, chopped
½ cup sour cream
¼ cup Miracle Whip
1 tsp. curry powder
Salt and pepper, to taste

TACO SALAD

Nutrition Facts per serving: Calories 517.1, Protein 47.49 Gm, Carbs 10.37 Gm, Fat 32.25 Gm, Cholesterol 112 mg,
Dietary Fiber 1.959 Gm, Sugar 2.985 Gm, Sodium 1101 mg, Calcium 1052 mg, Potassium 279.3 mg, Iron 1.314 mg

1. Place ground beef in a large frying pan; cook over Medium-High heat until evenly brown; drain.

2. Add taco seasoning mix, and prepare as directed on package; set aside to cool.

3. In a very large bowl, combine the lettuce, onions, bell pepper, cheese, beef, tomatoes and tortilla chips.

4. Add enough dressing to coat; mix well, and serve.

[BRENDA BRYCE]

SERVES 10

1 lb. lean ground beef
1 (1.25 ounce) pkg. taco seasoning mix
1 head iceberg lettuce - rinsed, dried, and shredded
1 onion, chopped
1 green bell pepper, chopped
3 cups shredded cheddar-Monterey Jack cheese blend
2 tomatoes, chopped
4 ozs. tortilla chips, crushed
¼ cup French or Catalina dressing

QUICK PASTA SALAD WITH SALSA

Nutrition Facts per serving: Calories 189.9, Protein 6.388 Gm, Carbs 38.9 Gm, Fat 1.02 Gm, Cholesterol 0 mg, Dietary Fiber 3.312 Gm, Sugar 4.244 Gm, Sodium 589.8 mg, Calcium 6.978 mg, Potassium 128.3 mg, Iron 1.49 mg

SERVES 4 TO 6

7ozs. pasta shapes
1 (14 oz.) jar salsa
1 (8 oz.) can sweet corn, drained
½ cucumber, diced

1. Cook pasta according to package; drain and rinse.

2. Tip into a large bowl; add salsa, and stir well.

3. Mix in sweet corn and diced cucumber.

4. Cover and chill.

5. Serve within 3 days.

This healthy but tasty recipe is from Matty and Amy Cooke's "Granny" who lives in England.

[CHRIS & CHRISSY COOKE, AND MATTY & AMY]

Quick Pasta Salad with Salsa Dressing

CAESAR SALAD DRESSING

Nutrition Facts: Calories 1128, Protein 12.93 Gm, Carbs 10.84 Gm, Fat 118 Gm, Cholesterol 222.3 mg, Dietary Fiber 0.846 Gm, Sugar 1.44 Gm, Sodium 823.6 mg, Calcium 190.4 mg, Potassium 233.7 mg, Iron 1.509 mg

MAKES 1 CUP

1 egg
1 to 2 anchovie fillets
3 cloves garlic
Juice of ½ lemon
1 tsp. Dijon mustard
1-½ tsp. Worcestershire sauce
1 to 1-½ Tbsp.
    Parmesan cheese
Vegetable oil

1. Put the first 7 ingredients in a small blender, then fill to double that amount with oil; blend well.

2. Serve on torn Romaine lettuce and thinly sliced fresh mushrooms.

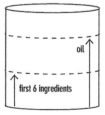

[LARRY & SHELLEY LEONARD, AND ALEX & NICHOLAS]

SUSHI-ROLL RICE SALAD

Nutrition Facts per serving: Calories 246.4, Protein 3.604 Gm, Carbs 26.66 Gm, Fat 14.53 Gm, Cholesterol 0 mg, Dietary Fiber 4.098 Gm, Sugar 2.552 Gm, Sodium 696.9 mg, Calcium 67.23 mg, Potassium 456.6 mg, Iron 2.014 mg

SERVES 4

1. Rinse rice in several changes of cold water in a bowl until water is almost clear; drain in a colander and let it rest in the colander for 30 minutes.

2. Bring rice and 1-¾ cups water to a boil in a 3 to 4 quart heavy saucepan; simmer, covered, for 2 minutes.

3. Remove from heat; let rice stand, covered, for 10 minutes (do not lift lid).

4. While rice is standing, bring vinegar, sugar and salt just to a boil in a very small saucepan, stirring constantly until sugar is dissolved; cool 2 minutes.

5. Spread rice in a large shallow baking pan; sprinkle with vinegar mixture, and toss with a wooden spoon.

6. Shave thin, lengthwise slices from carrot with a vegetable peeler; cut slices diagonally into ¼"-wide strips.

7. Whisk together wasabi, remaining 1-½ tablespoons water and oil in a bowl; add rice, carrot, cucumber, scallions, pickled ginger and sesame seeds, and toss gently.

8. Halve, pit and peel avocado. Cut crosswise into ¼"-thick slices.

9. Arrange 2 shiso leaves (if using) on each of 4 plates. Top with avocado and rice mixture, and sprinkle with nori strips.

[DON & TRACEY POTKINS, AND MEGHAN & SARAH]

Ingredients

1-½ cups short-grain sushi rice
1-¾ cups plus 1-½ Tbsp. water
¼ cup seasoned rice vinegar
1 Tbsp. sugar
1 tsp. salt
1 med. carrot
1-¼ tsp. wasabi paste (Japanese horseradish paste)
1-½ Tbsp. vegetable oil
½ lg. seedless cucumber (usually plastic-wrapped), peeled, halved lengthwise, cored, and chopped (1 cup)
3 scallions, thinly sliced diagonally
3 Tbsp. drained sliced Japanese pickled ginger, coarsely chopped
1 Tbsp. sesame seeds, toasted
1 firm-ripe California avocado
8 fresh shiso leaves (optional)
1 (6") square toasted nori, cut into very thin strips with scissors

NOTE:
This wonderful, light dish is excellent with cooked shrimp added in step 7.

TIPS:
To test an avocado for ripeness, cradle it in the palm of your hand, and squeeze gently. If it just gives to the pressure, it is perfect. To keep it from turning brown, add lime juice, lemon juice or vinegar at the very last minute before serving.

DEVILED EGGS

Nutrition Facts per serving: Calories 43.78, Protein 3.162 Gm, Carbs 1.598 Gm, Fat 2.666 Gm, Cholesterol 106.5 mg, Dietary Fiber 0.006 Gm, Sugar 0 Gm, Sodium 126 mg, Calcium 12.87 mg, Potassium 37.51 mg, Iron 0.317 mg

MAKES 12

6 hard-boiled eggs
¼ cup mayonnaise
1 tsp. white vinegar
1 tsp. prepared mustard
1 to 2 tsp. sweet pickle relish
⅔ tsp. salt, or to taste
Paprika (optional)

1. Halve the hard-cooked eggs lengthwise; remove yolks and mash with a fork.

2. Stir in mayonnaise, vinegar, mustard, relish and salt.

3. Stuff egg whites with yolk mixture.

4. Sprinkle with paprika, if desired.

AVOCADO SALAD

Nutrition Facts per serving: Calories 395.1, Protein 5.92 Gm, Carbs 2.737 Gm, Fat 42.15 Gm, Cholesterol 7.995 mg, Dietary Fiber 12.78 Gm, Sugar 1.133 Gm, Sodium 272 mg, Calcium 25.01 mg, Potassium 806.9 mg, Iron 1.19 mg

SERVES 4

6 very thin slices bacon
1 to 2 ripe avocados
1 Tbsp. olive oil, for sautéing
8 ozs. salad leaves (a mixture of
  soft, crisp and peppery)

Dressing:
⅓ cup extra virgin olive oil
1 Tbsp. cider vinegar or rice
  vinegar
1 clove garlic, crushed
1 tsp. Dijon mustard
Sea salt and freshly ground
  black pepper, to taste

1. In a frying pan, cook the bacon at Medium heat, until crisp but not too brown; remove, and drain on paper towels.

2. Combine all the Dressing ingredients in a salad bowl, and beat with a fork or small whisk.

3. When ready to serve, add the leaves. Using your hands, turn them in the Dressing.

4. Cut the avocados in half, and remove the seeds. Using a teaspoon, scoop out balls of avocado into the salad; toss gently.

5. Add the bacon, and serve immediately.

CHINESE SALAD DRESSING

Nutrition Facts: Calories 133.9, Protein 0.281 Gm, Carbs 1.866 Gm, Fat 14.22 Gm, Cholesterol 0 mg, Dietary Fiber 0.02 Gm, Sugar 0 Gm, Sodium 257.8 mg, Calcium 2.438 mg, Potassium 18.12 mg, Iron 0.176 mg

MAKES ABOUT ½ CUP

¼ cup oil
3 Tbsp. rice or white vinegar
1 Tbsp. soy sauce
1 tsp. sugar
1 tsp. fresh ginger
  root, finely grated
½ tsp. sesame oil or
1 tsp. toasted sesame seeds
⅛ tsp. pepper

1. Mix all the ingredients together.

2. Serve over fresh salad greens.

[TONY & CHRISTINE CLEAVER, AND ALEX, JORDYN & BETHANY]

ALMOND-CRUSTED GOAT CHEESE SALAD WITH RASPBERRY DRESSING

Nutrition Facts per serving: Calories 997.9, Protein 19.23 Gm, Carbs 46.79 Gm, Fat 84.26 Gm, Cholesterol 121.5 mg, Dietary Fiber 3.753 Gm, Sugar 28.26 Gm, Sodium 534.8 mg, Calcium 226.2 mg, Potassium 317.7 mg, Iron 4.994 mg

SERVES 4

⅔ cup frozen raspberries, thawed
½ cup sugar
¼ cup red wine vinegar
2 Tbsp. minced red onion
1 Tbsp. dry mustard
½ tsp. salt
½ tsp. lemon juice
1 cup olive oil
1 Tbsp. poppy seeds
2 (5 oz.) logs soft fresh goat cheese, each log cut into 4 round slices
1 lg. egg
1 Tbsp. water
½ cup all purpose flour
½ cup sliced almonds
2 tsp. butter, melted
6 ozs. mesclun mix (about 8 cups lightly packed)
Salt and pepper, to taste

1. Blend first 7 ingredients in food processor.
2. With processor running, gradually add oil.
3. Add poppy seeds, and blend 5 seconds.
4. Preheat oven to 350°F.
5. Pat each goat cheese slice to ½" thickness.
6. Whisk egg and 1 tablespoon water in small bowl, to blend.
7. Place flour in another small bowl.
8. Place almonds in a shallow dish.
9. Roll goat cheese slices in flour, then dip into egg mixture, then roll in almonds to coat, pressing gently to adhere.
10. Place cheese in glass baking dish; drizzle lightly with butter.
11. Sprinkle with salt and pepper.
12. Bake until almonds are lightly browned, about 10 minutes.
13. Divide mesclun among 4 plates.
14. Top each with 2 warm cheese slices; drizzle with dressing, and serve.

[DWIGHT & SHANNON PANTON, AND DYLAN & FRASIER]

Almond-Crusted Goat Cheese Salad with Raspberry Dressing

MANDARIN CHICKEN SALAD WITH SESAME DRESSING

Nutrition Facts per serving: Calories 1282, Protein 39.53 Gm, Carbs 124.9 Gm, Fat 80.61 Gm, Cholesterol 45 mg, Dietary Fiber 7.322 Gm, Sugar 42.49 Gm, Sodium 1452 mg, Calcium 296.7 mg, Potassium 1049 mg, Iron 7661 mg

SERVES 4

Sesame Dressing:
½ cup corn syrup
3 Tbsp. white vinegar
2 Tbsp. pineapple juice
4 tsp. granulated sugar
1 Tbsp. light brown sugar
1 Tbsp. rice wine vinegar
1 Tbsp. soy sauce
1 tsp. sesame oil
¼ tsp. ground mustard
¼ tsp. ground ginger
⅛ tsp. salt
⅛ tsp. paprika
1 dash garlic powder
1 dash ground black pepper
½ cup canola oil
½ tsp. sesame seeds

Mandarin Chicken Salad:
4 chicken breast fillets
1 head iceberg lettuce,
    chopped
4 cups red leaf lettuce,
    chopped
1-⅓ cup canned Mandarin
    orange segments
1 cup chow mein noodles
1 cup sliced almonds, roasted
Salt and pepper, to taste

1. Prepare dressing by combining all dressing ingredients, except canola oil and sesame seeds, in a blender on High speed.
2. Slowly add oil to mixture (to create an emulsion).
3. Add sesame seeds, and blend for just a couple of seconds.
4. Pour dressing into a cruet; chill until needed.
5. Rub each chicken fillet with oil; season each piece with salt and pepper.
6. Grill chicken on Medium-High heat, until done.
7. Chill breasts in the refrigerator.
8. When chicken is cold, build each salad, first by arranging about 4 cups of iceberg lettuce in the bottom of a large bowl, or on a plate.
9. Arrange a cup of red leaf lettuce on the iceberg lettuce.
10. Dice each breast into bite-sized pieces; sprinkle the pieces over the salad.
11. Arrange about ⅓ cup of Mandarin orange wedges on each salad.
12. Sprinkle about ¼ cup of chow mein noodles and ¼ cup of roasted sliced almonds on top of each salad.
13. Add desired amount of Sesame Dressing; serve.

[DON & TRACEY POTKINS, AND MEGHAN & SARAH]

Mandarin Chicken Salad

CREAMY ORANGE PINEAPPLE SALAD

Nutrition Facts per serving: Calories 215.4, Protein 8.701 Gm, Carbs 20.81 Gm, Fat 11.44 Gm, Cholesterol 40 mg, Dietary Fiber 0.264 Gm, Sugar 1.278 Gm, Sodium 45.58 mg, Calcium 44.41 mg, Potassium 281.5 mg, Iron 0.578 mg

1. Drain pineapple, reserving the juice.
2. Add enough water to the pineapple juice to make 1 cup of liquid; pour into a saucepan, and heat to boil.
3. Add boiling liquid to gelatin and cream cheese; beat with a rotary beater, until smooth.
4. Cool, stirring occasionally.
5. Whip the cream until soft peaks form.
6. Fold the cream, carrot and pineapple into the cooled gelatin mixture.
7. Pour into 1 large mold (or individual molds), and chill until firm.

[BRYAN & JENNIFER HUNTER, AND CORY & DANIEL]

SERVES 10

1 (8.5 oz.) can crushed pineapple
1 (3 oz.) pkg. orange flavoured gelatin
1 (3 oz.) pkg. cream cheese
1 cup (½ pint) whipping cream
1 carrot, grated (⅓ cup)

LAYERED SALAD

Nutrition Facts per serving: Calories 440.1, Protein 6.968 Gm, Carbs 11.53 Gm, Fat 42.66 Gm, Cholesterol 42.26 mg, Dietary Fiber 1.947 Gm, Sugar 2.581 Gm, Sodium 670.1 mg, Calcium 184.3 mg, Potassium 215.4, Iron 0.955 mg

1. Blanch peas in water for 1 or 2 minutes; drain.
2. Cool under cold water; drain dry.
3. Line the bottom of an 8" round salad bowl with lettuce (a glass bowl is nice because you can see the layers).
4. Layer in this order: bell pepper, celery, onion and peas.
5. Spread mayonnaise on top of the layers.
6. Sprinkle with sugar and grated cheese.
7. Refrigerate for 8 hours.
8. Before serving, garnish with bacon, tomato wedges, olives and egg slices.

This recipe is a favourite of Kathryn Elphinstone's sister, Janet Lennox, who likes to cook for casual gatherings at her cabin in Alberta, Canada.

[SCOTT & KATHRYN ELPHINSTONE, AND KAITLYN, LAURA & MATTHEW]

SERVES 12

1 (12 oz.) pkg. frozen peas
1 sm. head of lettuce, chopped/ shredded with a knife
1 lg. green or red bell pepper, chopped
1 med. Spanish onion (or 2 red onions), chopped
3 celery stalks, sliced
1-¾ cup mayonnaise
1 tsp. sugar
1 cup grated sharp cheddar cheese
8 slices bacon, cooked, drained and crumbled
Tomato wedges, black or green olives and hard-cooked egg slices, for garnish

Fettucini Alfredo (page 105)

PASTA

THE ULTIMATE SPAGHETTI & MEAT SAUCE

Nutrition Facts per serving: Calories 212.6, Protein 10.78 Gm, Carbs 14.94 Gm, Fat 12.57 Gm, Cholesterol 34.55 mg,
Dietary Fiber 2.496 Gm, Sugar 5.093 Gm, Sodium 617.2 mg, Calcium 48.37 mg, Potassium 439.3 mg, Iron 1.941 mg

SERVES 20

2 lbs. extra lean ground beef
½ lb. hot Italian sausage
  (casings removed)
2 ripe tomatoes, diced
1 celery stalk, diced
3 carrots, diced
1 (8 oz.) pack mushrooms, diced
  (divide into 3 containers)
2 med. onions, diced
  (divide into 3 containers)
1 clove garlic, chopped (divide
  into 3 portions)
1 (4 oz.) jar stuffed green olives
  (optional)
1 (14 oz.) jar of your favourite
  spaghetti sauce
1 (8 oz.) can tomato sauce
1 (12 oz.) can whole tomatoes,
  coarsely chopped
1 (12 oz.) can stewed tomatoes
  (seasoned with onions &
  garlic, or basil & oregano)
1 (6 oz.) can tomato paste
3 Tbsp. all purpose flour
4 Tbsp. olive oil or any
  cooking oil
2 Tbsp. Kitchen Bouquet
2 beef bouillon cubes,
  crumbled
¼ tsp. dried oregano
¼ tsp. dried basil
2 whole bay leaves
Salt and black pepper, to taste

1. Mix the 2 meats together.

2. Place a very large frying pan with 2 tablespoons oil on Medium heat.

3. Place a very large cooking pot with 2 tablespoons oil on Medium heat; cover.

4. In both the pan and the pot, add 1 portion of onions and mushrooms each. After 3 or 4 minutes, add 1 portion of garlic to both the pan and the pot.

5. When mushrooms are soft, add meats to frying pan, and add bottled spaghetti sauce to pot.

6. **Frying Pan**: Brown meat evenly. Add Kitchen Bouquet, beef bouillon cubes, ½ of oregano, ½ of basil, and all of the flour. STIR OFTEN.

7. **Pot**: Add 1 can each of canned tomato sauce, whole and stewed tomatoes, and tomato paste (stir often while adding the remainder of ingredients).

8. Add the remainder of the oregano and basil, fresh tomatoes, bay leaves and browned meat from the frying pan; cover and simmer for 15 to 20 minutes.

9. Add carrots, celery and remaining onions, garlic, mushrooms and green olives (if desired). If using olives, do not add much salt, as the olives are salty.

10. Cover and simmer on Low heat about ¼ to ½ hour. The sauce will become thicker, and tastes better the longer it cooks.

11. Remove bay leaves, and serve hot over spaghetti noodles.

NOTE:
This beautiful spaghetti dish, belonging to a close friend of the Merren family, Dennis Mastry, is enjoyed mostly by adults, but children love it too. It is nice with a green salad and Italian garlic bread.

[GREGORY & TERRI MERREN, AND JOSH & ZACHARY]

PASTA WITH BACON

Nutrition Facts per serving: Calories 539.7, Protein 18.63 Gm, Carbs 78.8 Gm, Fat 16.43 Gm, Cholesterol 39.86 mg, Dietary Fiber 5.628 Gm, Sugar 2.981 Gm, Sodium 1033 mg, Calcium 75.23 mg, Potassium 878.9 mg, Iron 5.125 mg

1. In a large frying pan, fry the bacon; set aside, and pour off most of the grease, leaving only about a tablespoon in the pan.

2. To the pan, add minced garlic, green pepper slivers, celery, onion and bay leaf; fry until the onion is transparent.

3. Add bacon and the jar of spaghetti sauce; simmer until heated through. Remove bay leaf.

4. Pour sauce over cooked pasta spirals, and toss.

5. Serve hot.

[BILL & DONNA SULLIVAN, AND MICHAEL]

SERVES 6

1 lb. bacon, cut into small pieces
1 lg. clove garlic, minced
1 sm. sweet green bell
  pepper, julienned
1 stalk celery, sliced
1 med. onion, chopped
Bay leaf
1 (25 oz.) jar spaghetti sauce
1 (1 lb.) box pasta spirals,
  cooked as directed on box

QUICK CHEESY RAVIOLI CASSEROLE

Nutrition Facts per serving: Calories 306.4, Protein 26.53 Gm, Carbs 4.656 Gm, Fat 19.93 Gm, Cholesterol 55.2 mg, Dietary Fiber 0 Gm, Sugar 0.429 Gm, Sodium 1123 mg, Calcium 858.6 mg, Potassium 139.7 mg, Iron 0.719 mg

1. Cook the ravioli according to the package directions.

2. Combine the Marinara Sauce and Pesto Sauce with the sour cream.

3. Spread the ravioli into the bottom of a 9" x 9" (or similar) microwave-proof casserole dish.

4. Pour the Marinara/Pesto/sour cream mixture over the ravioli.

5. Top first with the cheddar cheese and then with the Parmesan cheese.

6. Place in the microwave, and cook on High for 2 to 3 minutes, or until the cheese has melted.

7. Serve with a green salad and crisp garlic bread.

[EDLIN & HELEN MERREN]

SERVES 6 TO 8

2 (9 oz.) pkgs. Buitoni (or
  DiGiorno) Four
  Cheese Ravioli
1 (15 oz.) pkg. Buitoni (or
  DiGiorno) Marinara Sauce
1 (7 oz.) pkg. Buitoni (or
  DiGiorno) Pesto with Basil
1 cup sour cream
1 cup grated cheddar cheese
¼ cup Parmesan cheese

OLD FASHIONED MACARONI & CHEESE

Nutrition Facts per serving: Calories 347.5, Protein 17.22 Gm, Carbs 26.99 Gm, Fat 18.81 Gm, Cholesterol 118.9 mg, Dietary Fiber 1.565 Gm, Sugar 4.552 Gm, Sodium 534.6 mg, Calcium 357.7 mg, Potassium 195.2 mg, Iron 1.928 mg

SERVES 6 TO 8

2 cups milk
3 Tbsp. margarine, melted
2 Tbsp. all purpose flour
½ tsp. salt
½ tsp. pepper
3 eggs, beaten
5 cups cooked elbow macaroni
2-½ cups (10 ozs.) shredded cheddar cheese
¾ cup fresh bread crumbs or cracker crumbs

1. Preheat oven to 350°F.
2. Combine first 6 ingredients in a bowl; using a wire whisk, beat until smooth.
3. Layer half of the cooked macaroni in the bottom of a greased 9" square baking dish.
4. Sprinkle with 1-²⁄₃ cups cheese, and layer remaining macaroni on top.
5. Pour milk mixture over macaroni (completely covering the macaroni).
6. Sprinkle with bread crumbs.
7. Bake, uncovered, for 50 minutes.
8. Sprinkle with the remaining cheese; bake 5 minutes longer, or until set.

[GREGORY & TERRI MERREN, AND JOSH & ZACHARY]

SLOW COOKER LASAGNA

Nutrition Facts per serving: Calories 952.7, Protein 55.93 Gm, Carbs 66.51 Gm, Fat 50.03 Gm, Cholesterol 140.4 mg, Dietary Fiber 1.493 Gm, Sugar 8.154 Gm, Sodium 1295 mg, Calcium 824.1 mg, Potassium 1625 mg, Iron 4.633 mg

SERVES 4

1 lb. ground beef
1 tsp. dried Italian seasoning
1 (26 oz.) jar spaghetti sauce Garden Chunky-style (or your favorite homemade)
⅓ cup water
8 lasagna noodles (UNCOOKED)
1 (4.5 oz.) jar mushrooms
1 (15 oz.) carton ricotta cheese
2 cups shredded part skim milk
Approx. 2 cups Mozzarella cheese

1. Cook beef and Italian seasoning in a large skillet over Medium heat, stirring until beef crumbles; drain.
2. Combine spaghetti sauce and water in a small bowl.
3. Place 4 uncooked noodles in the bottom of a lightly greased 5 quart electric slow cooker.
4. Layer with ½ each of beef mixture, spaghetti sauce mixture and mushrooms.
5. Spread ricotta cheese over mushrooms. Sprinkle with ½ the Mozzarella cheese. Layer with remaining noodles, meat, sauce mixture, mushrooms and Mozzarella cheese.
6. Cover, and cook on High setting for 1 hour; reduce heat and cook on Low setting for 5 hours.

[RICK & KIM MCTAGGART, AND JONATHAN, KATELEE & NICHOLAS]

FETTUCINI ALFREDO

Nutrition Facts per serving: Calories 494.3, Protein 11.5 Gm, Carbs 13.82 Gm, Fat 44.55 Gm, Cholesterol 142.1 mg,
Dietary Fiber 0.693 Gm, Sugar 3.056 Gm, Sodium 622.2 mg, Calcium 173.6 mg, Potassium 299.1 mg, Iron 1.527 mg

SERVES 6

3 slices of processed
    ham, coarsely chopped
1 (8 oz.) box fettucini
4 slices bacon
1 onion, chopped
1 (8 oz.) pkg. cream cheese
1-½ cups whipping cream
    or half and half
1 Tbsp. all purpose flour
2 Tbsp. butter or margarine
¼ tsp. salt
½ tsp. freshly ground pepper
3 to 4 Tbsp. shredded
    Parmesan cheese
1 tsp. dried basil
1 tsp. dried oregano

1. Cook and drain fettucini as directed on box.

2. In a skillet, fry the bacon. When cool, crumble and set aside.

3. In a saucepan, melt butter over Medium-High heat.

4. Mix whipping cream, flour and salt, until smooth. Stir into butter and add cream cheese; whisk until heated through and smooth.

5. Stir in Parmesan cheese, ground pepper, basil and oregano.

6. In 1 tablespoon of reserved bacon grease, sauté onions, until translucent; add ham and toss over Medium heat for approximately 2 minutes.

7. In a large mixing bowl, mix together fettucini and cheese/milk mixture. Toss in ham, onion and bacon.

8. Transfer to a serving bowl; serve warm with crusty bread.

[ROBERT & PAULA EBANKS, AND ASHLEIGH]

BAHAMIAN MACARONI & CHEESE

Nutrition Facts per serving: Calories 308.3, Protein 14.95 Gm, Carbs 26.69 Gm, Fat 14.39 Gm, Cholesterol 183.5 mg,
Dietary Fiber 1.44 Gm, Sugar 1.466 Gm, Sodium 700.2 mg, Calcium 420.7 mg, Potassium 297.7 mg, Iron 1.616 mg

SERVES 10 TO 12

16 ozs. elbow macaroni
1 lb. cheddar cheese, grated
2 onions, finely chopped
1 green bell pepper, finely
    chopped
2 cans evaporated milk
8 eggs, beaten
Salt and hot pepper (such as
    cayenne), to taste

1. Cook macaroni according to package directions; drain. Add cheese, onions, bell pepper, milk and half of the eggs. Season with salt and pepper, to taste.

2. Cook on Low heat until the cheese is melted.

3. Pour into a greased 9" x 13" casserole, and pour the remaining eggs over the top.

4. Bake at 375°F until golden brown.

This is a favourite Bahamian family recipe, which
was very kindly sent by a cousin, De'Ann D'Arville, to the Leonard family. Their family
connection to the Bahamas comes from Jennie Stewart who is the maternal grandmother of
Cayman Prep and High School students, Alex and Nicholas Leonard,
and their first cousin, Megan Green.

[LARRY & SHELLEY LEONARD, AND ALEX & NICHOLAS]

CHICKEN AND BOW TIE PASTA

Nutrition Facts per serving: Calories 583.3, Protein 39.3 Gm, Carbs 43.8 Gm, Fat 25.71 Gm, Cholesterol 175 mg,
Dietary Fiber 1.059 Gm, Sugar 2.963 Gm, Sodium 394 mg, Calcium 137.9 mg, Potassium 605.9 mg, Iron 3.051 mg

SERVES 4

8 oz. bow tie pasta
2 cloves garlic, minced
2 Tbsp. olive oil
1 lb. skinless, boneless chicken
   breasts, cut into bite-size strips
1 tsp. dried basil, crushed
$\frac{1}{8}$ tsp. crushed red pepper
¾ cup chicken broth
½ cup oil-packed
   sundried tomatoes, drained
   and cut into thin strips
¼ cup dry, white wine
½ cup whipping cream
¼ cup grated Parmesan cheese

1. Cook pasta according to package directions; drain.

2. Meanwhile, in a large skillet, cook the garlic in hot oil over Medium-High heat for 30 seconds.

3. Add chicken, basil and crushed red pepper. Cook and stir for 4 minutes, or until browned.

4. Add chicken broth, tomatoes and white wine; bring to a boil. Reduce heat.

5. Simmer uncovered for about 10 minutes, or until chicken is tender.

6. Stir in whipping cream and Parmesan cheese. Simmer 2 minutes.

7. Stir pasta into chicken mixture. Heat through.

8. Pass additional Parmesan cheese, if desired.

[TONY & CHRISTINE CLEAVER , AND ALEX , JORDYN & BETHANY]

BAKED LASAGNA

Nutrition Facts per serving: Calories 471.7, Protein 36.81 Gm, Carbs 38.29 Gm, Fat 17.69 Gm, Cholesterol 109.5 mg,
Dietary Fiber 3.217 Gm, Sugar 9.556 Gm, Sodium 1147 mg, Calcium 616.8 mg, Potassium 416.3, Iron 3.9 mg

SERVES 8

1-½ lbs. ground beef
½ cup chopped onion
1 clove garlic, minced
1 (16 oz.) can diced tomatoes
1 (8 oz.) can tomato sauce
1 (6 oz.) can tomato paste
2 tsp. dried basil, crushed
2 tsp. salt, divided
½ tsp. black pepper
1 tsp. dried oregano
1 (8 oz.) pkg. lasagna noodles
   (or approx. 10 to 12 noodles)
1 Tbsp. olive oil
2 eggs, beaten
2-½ cups ricotta cheese
¾ cup grated Parmesan cheese
1 lb. Mozzarella cheese, thinly
   sliced, or 2 to 3 (8 oz.) pkgs.
   shredded Mozzarella cheese

1. Preheat oven to 375°F.

2. Cook meat, onion and garlic, until meat is browned; drain off fat.

3. Stir in the undrained tomatoes, tomato sauce, tomato paste, basil and 1 teaspoon salt; cover and simmer 15 minutes, stirring frequently.

4. Boil noodles in salted water with the olive oil added, until tender; drain.

5. Mix together eggs, ricotta, oregano, ½ cup Parmesan cheese, 1 teaspoon salt and ½ teaspoon black pepper.

6. In a 13" x 9" x 2" baking dish, layer half of the noodles, then half of the meat sauce, then half of the ricotta and finally half of the Mozzarella cheese. Repeat layers.

7. Top with the remaining Parmesan cheese.

8. Bake uncovered for 30 to 35 minutes, or until heated through and brown on top.

GREEK-STYLE MACARONI PASTA

Nutrition Facts per serving: Calories 261, Protein 6.989 Gm, Carbs 37.81 Gm, Fat 9.343 Gm, Cholesterol 8.319 mg,
Dietary Fiber 1.966 Gm, Sugar 7.671 Gm, Sodium 872.7 mg, Calcium 75.17 mg, Potassium 99.99 mg, Iron 1.988 mg

SERVES 4 TO 6

1 cup uncooked Ready Cut macaroni
1 can black olives, drained
1 sm. bottle sliced green pimiento olives, drained
1 (3.75 oz.) jar cocktail onions, drained
1 (6 oz.) jar artichoke hearts, with juice
1 (14.5 oz.) can diced tomatoes, with basil, garlic & oregano
½ of a (4 oz.) pkg. Feta cheese crumbles, with basil, kalamata olive & sun dried tomato
3 Tbsp. red wine vinegar salad dressing
Salt and black pepper, to taste

1. Cook macaroni according to the package instructions; drain.

2. Place macaroni in a large mixing bowl.

3. Add all the other ingredients to the macaroni; toss together until well-blended.

4. Serve cold or warm as a compliment to any meat dish, or hot on a bed of lettuce leaves, with garlic bread.

[ROBERT & PAULA EBANKS, AND ASHLEIGH]

Greek-style Macaroni Pasta

PENNE CONTADINA

Nutrition Facts per serving: Calories 1122, Protein 59.66 Gm, Carbs 37.98 Gm, Fat 81.57 Gm, Cholesterol 349.4 mg,
Dietary Fiber 2.906 Gm, Sugar 9.156 Gm, Sodium 1146 mg, Calcium 230.2 mg, Potassium 962.4 mg, Iron 3.681 mg

SERVES 6

1-½ to 2 lbs. boneless chicken
   breasts, cut into cubes
10 ozs. fresh mushrooms, wiped
   clean, and sliced
1 qt. heavy cream
1 (15 oz.) can tomato sauce
3 leaves of fresh
   basil, chopped
1 oz. chopped onion
1 oz. grated Parmesan cheese
1 (1 lb.) box penne pasta
1 tsp. olive oil

1. In a large saucepan, sauté onions in olive oil.

2. Add chicken to onion; sauté until golden brown.

3. Add tomato sauce; bring to a boil, and boil 5 minutes.

4. Add cream, and let cook for another 3 minutes; reduce heat to Low.

5. Cook penne pasta in a large pot of boiling salted water; drain.

6. Add the chicken mixture to the cooked pasta, along with mushrooms, basil and Parmesan cheese.

7. Mix thoroughly, and stir over Low heat for approximately 5 minutes, or until heated through.

8. Serve warm.

[CELICEA MYLES & KAI-LEIGH HAUGHTON, AND
TREVOR & NICOLO TUMMINGS]

PAPA'S PENNE PESTO PASTA

Nutrition Facts per serving: Calories 711.1, Protein 21.16 Gm, Carbs 47.43 Gm, Fat 51.1 Gm, Cholesterol 17.86 mg,
Dietary Fiber 12.14 Gm, Sugar 4.141 Gm, Sodium 936.5 mg, Calcium 829.6 mg, Potassium 994.7, Iron 11.84 mg

SERVES 6

1 (1 lb.) box penne pasta
¾ cup mayonnaise
2 cups fresh basil leaves
3 to 4 cloves garlic
½ tsp. black pepper
½ tsp. salt
1 (10 oz.) pkg. frozen spinach,
   thawed and squeezed dry
½ cup olive oil
1 handful of pine nuts,
   toasted (optional)
½ cup grated Parmesan cheese
½ cup grated Mozzarella cheese

1. In a large pot, cook pasta in boiling water as instructed on box. Drain, and set aside.

2. In an electric blender or food processor, blend mayonnaise, basil, garlic, salt, pepper, spinach and pine nuts (if desired) until fairly smooth.

3. While blending, slowly add olive oil.

4. Add blended pesto mixture to the hot pasta. Stir in Parmesan cheese and the Mozzarella cheese. Toss over Medium heat for about 2 minutes, or until heated through.

5. Serve with a green salad, and crusty bread.

[GREGORY & TERRI MERREN, AND JOSH & ZACHARY]

STUFFED SHELLS

*Nutrition Facts per serving: Calories 404.7, Protein 23.34 Gm, Carbs 36.03 Gm, Fat 18.29 Gm, Cholesterol 78.18 mg,
Dietary Fiber 1.445 Gm, Sugar 1.924 Gm, Sodium 591.2 mg, Calcium 470.9 mg, Potassium 346.1 mg, Iron 3.126 mg*

SERVES 10 TO 12

1 (26 oz.) jar spaghetti sauce
1 (12 oz.) box jumbo shells
1 (10 oz.) pkg. frozen chopped spinach, thawed and squeezed dry
3 cloves garlic, peeled
¾ lb. ground beef or ground pork
½ tsp. salt
½ tsp. black pepper
1 tsp. oregano
1 cup fresh parsley, chopped
1 cup Italian bread crumbs
2 eggs, beaten
3 cloves garlic, minced
2 cups Italian cheese blend, divided in 2
1 cup cottage cheese
3 Tbsp. Parmesan cheese, grated
Approx. 2 Tbsp. olive oil

1. Preheat oven to 375°F.

2. Cook the jumbo shells according to package directions; let cool.

3. Season the meat with salt, pepper and oregano.

4. Cook the 3 whole garlic cloves in olive oil until lightly browned. Discard garlic.

5. Brown the meat, breaking it into small pieces; drain, and let cool.

6. Combine eggs, spinach, parsley, bread crumbs, minced garlic, 1 cup Italian cheese blend and other cheeses. Season with a little salt.

7. Add meat to the spinach mixture; mix well.

8. Stuff shells with the meat/spinach mixture.

9. Spread 1 cup spaghetti sauce in the bottom of a large oven-proof casserole.

10. Place stuffed shells side by side, seam side up, in the sauce.

11. Pour the remaining sauce over the top, and sprinkle with the remaining 1 cup Italian cheese blend.

12. Bake in preheated oven uncovered for 35 minutes.

[C A R L E N E A L E X A N D E R - K A Y , A N D L I A M K A Y &
C R I S T I N A L E X A N D E R]

Stuffed Shells

Fresh Garden Vegetables

VEGETABLES & SIDES

MARINATED TOMATOES

Nutrition Facts per serving: Calories 77.03, Protein 1.297 Gm, Carbs 6.945 Gm, Fat 5.663 Gm, Cholesterol 0 mg, Dietary Fiber 1.721 Gm, Sugar 3.896 Gm, Sodium 10.6 mg, Calcium 12.16 mg, Potassium 294.7 mg, Iron 0.855 mg

SERVES 4 TO 6

1 (8 oz.) pack fresh mushrooms, wiped clean and sliced
3 Tbsp. scallions, chopped
5 lg. vine ripe tomatoes, sliced
Lettuce

Marinade:
1 tsp. curry powder
1 tsp. white sugar
½ cup salad oil
¼ cup vinegar
1 clove garlic, chopped
1 Tbsp. parsley, minced
Salt and pepper, to taste

1. Combine all marinade ingredients in a jar; shake well.
2. Pour marinade over sliced tomatoes, mushrooms and scallions.
3. Marinate tomatoes for several hours.
4. Arrange on a bed of lettuce in a large platter or on individual plates.

NOTE:
Marinated Tomatoes are great with barbecued chicken, steak or pork.

[DAVID & MELANIE KHOURI, AND JESSICA]

CARROT SOUFFLÉ

Nutrition Facts per serving: Calories 386.3, Protein 3.934 Gm, Carbs 49.83 Gm, Fat 19.17 Gm, Cholesterol 126.5 mg, Dietary Fiber 2.122 Gm, Sugar 3.08 Gm, Sodium 261.7 mg, Calcium 111.2 mg, Potassium 270 mg, Iron 1.335 mg

SERVES 8

1-½ lb. pkged. baby carrots
¾ cup butter (1-½ sticks)
3 lg. eggs
¼ cup all purpose flour
½ Tbsp. baking powder
1-½ cups sugar
⅛ tsp. ground cinnamon

1. Cook baby carrots in boiling water to cover for 15 minutes, or until tender; drain.
2. Position knife blade in food processor bowl; add carrot, butter and remaining ingredients and process until smooth, stopping once to scrape down the sides.
3. Spoon into a lightly greased 1-½ quart soufflé or baking dish.
4. Bake at 350°F for 1 hour, or until set and lightly browned.
5. Serve immediately.

[BRYAN & JENNIFER HUNTER, AND CORY & DANIEL]

EASY CORN CASSEROLE

Nutrition Facts per serving: Calories 599.8, Protein 9.922 Gm, Carbs 48.66 Gm, Fat 42.6 Gm, Cholesterol 175.8 mg, Dietary Fiber 1.208 Gm, Sugar 1.875 Gm, Sodium 908.4 mg, Calcium 123.4 mg, Potassium 263.6 mg, Iron 1.581 mg

SERVES 8

1 (approx. 8 oz.) can whole kernel corn, undrained
1 (8.75 oz.)can cream style corn
1 box cornbread/muffin mix
1 stick butter
1 cup sour cream
1 egg, beaten

1. Preheat oven to 350°F.
2. Mix all ingredients together.
3. Pour into an oven-proof (approximately 11" x 7") casserole dish.
4. Bake uncovered in preheated oven for 45 minutes.

[ROD & PENNY McDOWALL, AND JAMIE & JESSICA]

BAKED ZUCCHINI

Nutrition Facts per serving: Calories 125.3, Protein 10.77 Gm, Carbs 5.692 Gm, Fat 6.825 Gm, Cholesterol 22.94 mg,
Dietary Fiber 1.462 Gm, Sugar 2.53 Gm, Sodium 263.5 mg, Calcium 288.1 mg, Potassium 321.7 mg, Iron 0.519 mg

1. Cut zucchini into ¼" (or slightly thicker) rounds.

2. Spray bottom of an 8" x 8" microwave-safe baking dish with cooking spray.

3. Put in a single layer of zucchini, sprinkle lightly with salt, pepper and top with Mozzarella cheese.

4. Repeat with second and third layers of zucchini, salt, pepper and cheese.

5. Sprinkle oregano over the top and then a generous layer of bread crumbs.

6. Sprinkle Parmesan cheese over the bread crumbs.

7. Cover, and microwave at Level 7 for 7 minutes*.

8. Let stand covered for 5 minutes before serving.

*This is based on a 1,300 watt microwave oven with automatic turntable. Do not add water - the zucchini and/or yellow squash has quite enough water in it naturally.

[D A V I D   R .   M Y E R S ,   A N D   G A B R I E L L E]

SERVES 4 TO 6

1-½ lbs. (3 to 4 med.) zucchini or yellow squash or a combination thereof
Butter-flavoured no-stick cooking spray
1 (8 oz.) pkg. grated Mozzarella cheese
Salt or salt substitute
Freshly ground black pepper (optional)
Oregano (dried)
Italian-favoured bread crumbs
Grated Parmesan cheese

ROSEMARY AND GARLIC ROASTED VEGGIES

Nutrition Facts per serving: Calories 125.3, Protein 2.303 Gm, Carbs 18.78 Gm, Fat 5.183 Gm, Cholesterol 0 mg,
Dietary Fiber 2.768 Gm, Sugar 8.138 Gm, Sodium 9.506 mg, Calcium 59 mg, Potassium 430.7 mg, Iron 1.694 mg

1. Preheat oven to 400°F.

2. Cut the potatoes and mushrooms into bite-size pieces.

3. In a large bowl, toss the potatoes, mushrooms, onion, bell pepper, garlic and fresh rosemary in the olive oil. Place in a baking tray, and cover with aluminum foil.

4. Bake covered in preheated oven for 45 minutes.

5. To brown, remove foil, then place under a broiler for a further 5 minutes.

[A D R I A N   &   K A T H Y   B A R N E T T ,   A N D   R Y A N   &   M A T T H E W]

SERVES 4 TO 6

1 lb. potatoes
½ lb. fresh mushrooms
1 med. onion, chopped
1 sm. green bell pepper, chopped
3 cloves garlic, chopped
1 handful of fresh rosemary, chopped
2 Tbsp. (approx.) olive oil

GRILLED PORTABELLO MUSHROOMS

Nutrition Facts per serving: Calories 190.7, Protein 12.7 Gm, Carbs 8.517 Gm, Fat 11.95 Gm, Cholesterol 15 mg, Dietary Fiber 0.675 Gm, Sugar 5.223 Gm, Sodium 1492 mg, Calcium 359.6 mg, Potassium 181.9 mg, Iron 0.783 mg

SERVES 4

1 pack Portabello mushrooms, wiped clean w/damp paper towel
1 lg. ripe tomato, sliced
Mozzarella cheese, sliced
Parsley, to garnish

Marinade:
¼ cup soy sauce
¼ cup Balsamic vinegar (red)
2 Tbsp. olive oil
3 cloves garlic, chopped

1. Combine marinade ingredients in a jar; shake well.
2. Pour marinade over mushrooms.
3. Marinate for several hours.
4. Grill mushrooms 3 to 5 minutes each side.
5. Place mushrooms on centre of serving plates.
6. Place Mozzarella slice on each mushroom.
7. Place a slice of tomato on top of Mozzarella; sprinkle with parsley.
8. Serve immediately.

[DAVID & MELANIE KHOURI, AND JESSICA]

FRIED OKRA

Nutrition Facts per serving: Calories 565.4, Protein 3.591 Gm, Carbs 20.56 Gm, Fat 54.99 Gm, Cholesterol 0 mg, Dietary Fiber 1.975 Gm, Sugar 0.265 Gm, Sodium 731.4 mg, Calcium 141.3 mg, Potassium 19.38 mg, Iron 1.985 mg

SERVES 4

1 lb. fresh okra
Self-rising flour
Vegetable oil
Salt

1. Wash okra well.
2. Drain and cut off tips and stem ends.
3. Cut into ½" slices and place in a large bowl.
4. Sprinkle a little water over okra, and toss. The okra needs to be damp for the flour to adhere.
5. Sift the flour over the okra, tossing to coat well.
6. Lift okra in batches with hands or a slotted spoon, allowing excess flour to fall back into the bowl and setting okra on a plate.
7. Deep-fry in hot oil (375°F) until browned. Do not crowd okra in the pan or it will turn mushy and not brown properly.
8. Transfer to a colander; drain. Do not drain on paper towels, as paper towels make the okra soggy.

[GREGORY & TERRI MERREN, AND JOSH & ZACHARY]

PINK POTATO SALAD

Nutrition Facts per serving: Calories 373, Protein 1.929 Gm, Carbs 11.3 Gm, Fat 38.4954.99 Gm, Cholesterol 16 mg,
Dietary Fiber 2.057 Gm, Sugar 2.584 Gm, Sodium 415.2 mg, Calcium 12.41 mg, Potassium 266.9 mg, Iron 1.02 mg

1. In a medium pot, boil the potatoes until just tender (about 10 minutes - do not over-cook); drain immediately, and run cold water over them. Allow to cool.

2. Season the potatoes with salt and pepper.

3. In a bowl, combine the bell pepper, onion, seasoning peppers, beets, peas and mayonnaise. Mix thoroughly, then add to the potatoes (this prevents too much stirring of the potatoes, so they do not get mushy). If desired, add some beet juice to make the potato salad pinker in colour.

4. Cover and place in the refrigerator for at least 1 hour (this allows the flavours to soak into the potatoes).

[DEAN & JENNIFER SCOTT, AND LAUREN, HANNAH & JONATHAN]

SERVES 10 TO 12

About 8 to 10 Idaho potatoes, peeled and cut into 1" cubes
¼ onion, finely chopped
1 med. green bell pepper, finely chopped
Seasoning peppers, seeded and finely chopped, to taste (optional)
1 (9.25 oz.) can sliced beets (partially drained and chopped)
1 (8.5 oz.) can sweet peas (drained)
2 cups mayonnaise, or to taste
Salt and black pepper, to taste

BREADFRUIT SALAD

Nutrition Facts per serving: Calories 80.54, Protein 2.296 Gm, Carbs 18.19 Gm, Fat 1.117 Gm, Cholesterol 0.375 mg,
Dietary Fiber 6.819 Gm, Sugar 1.575 Gm, Sodium 163.8 mg, Calcium 22.18 mg, Potassium 338.5 mg, Iron 0.82 mg

1. Peel the breadfruit with a knife to remove skin and outer layer of flesh. Cut into large slices and remove the core. Cut the remaining flesh into 1" cubes.

2. In a pot on the stove top, boil breadfruit in salted water for 25 minutes, or until tender; drain and let cool for about 15 minutes.

3. Meanwhile, in a food processor, grind the onion and seasoning/scotch bonnet peppers together.

4. In a mixing bowl, combine mayonnaise, vinegar, sweet peas, ground onions and peppers. Season with black pepper, Season All and salt. Add breadfruit, and toss in the mayonnaise mixture until well-coated.

5. Transfer to a serving bowl, and garnish with julienned red and green sweet bell peppers.

6. Serve with fish, crab backs or turtle.

[SHELLY MILLER-SMITH, AND CHELSEA & AMY SMITH]

SERVES 10

1 full/fit breadfruit
½ sm. onion
6 seasoning peppers, seeded
1 sm. scotch bonnet pepper, seeded
2 Tbsp. vinegar
¾ cup mayonnaise
1 (8.5 oz.) can sweet green peas
1 Tbsp. black pepper
½ Tbsp. Season All
½ Tbsp. salt
¼ red bell pepper, for garnish
¼ green bell pepper, for garnish

NOTE:
You can also add chopped celery, sweet relish and sliced hard-boiled eggs.

BAKED ASPARAGUS

Nutrition Facts per serving: Calories 54.68, Protein 1.888 Gm, Carbs 1.627 Gm, Fat 4.53 Gm, Cholesterol 2.8 mg, Dietary Fiber 0.164 Gm, Sugar 1.259 Gm, Sodium 128.3 mg, Calcium 51.25 mg, Potassium 31.22 mg, Iron 0.144 mg

SERVES 8

2 packs of fresh asparagus, rinsed in water and the tough ends snapped off
2 Tbsp. olive oil (or more, to taste)
2 Tbsp. balsamic vinegar (or more, to taste)
Garlic & Herb seasoning
Freshly grated Parmesan cheese

1. Preheat oven to 375°F.
2. Toss asparagus with olive oil and balsamic vinegar, to coat.
3. Sprinkle with Garlic & Herb seasoning.
4. Arrange asparagus in a single layer on a cookie sheet.
5. Bake in preheated oven until fork tender (about 15 minutes).
6. Sprinkle with Parmesan cheese; bake another 5 minutes until melted.

"This tasty recipe comes from our cousin, Victoria deWildt, who loves to entertain." - the Hunter family

[BRYAN & JENNIFER HUNTER, AND CORY & DANIEL]

SPINACH CASSEROLE

Nutrition Facts per serving: Calories 592.5, Protein 18.12 Gm, Carbs 19.48 Gm, Fat 51.3 Gm, Cholesterol 139.7 mg, Dietary Fiber 5.371 Gm, Sugar 3.593 Gm, Sodium 785.2 mg, Calcium 514.2 mg, Potassium 763.5 mg, Iron 3.802 mg

SERVES 6 TO 8

2 (1-¾ lb.) bags frozen whole leaf spinach, cooked and drained
2 (8 oz.) pkgs. cream cheese, softened
2 cups sour cream
1 (14.5 oz.) can whole tomatoes, drained and halved
1 (6 oz.) jar artichoke hearts, drained (optional)
½ cup grated Parmesan cheese or 1 cup shredded Parmesan cheese
3 Tbsp. butter or margarine

1. Preheat oven to 325°F.
2. Place drained spinach in the bottom of a small baking/casserole dish.
3. Place the tomatoes and artichoke hearts (if desired) over the spinach.
4. In a small bowl, combine cream cheese and sour cream; spread over the tomatoes.
5. Sprinkle the Parmesan cheese on top completely covering the cream cheese topping.
6. Dot pieces of the butter or margarine on top of the cheese; cover loosely with foil.
7. Bake in preheated oven for 25 to 30 minutes, or until golden brown on top.
8. Remove foil for last 5 minutes of cooking to allow butter and cheese to change colour; watch carefully to avoid burning.

Great with barbecue chicken, ribs, steak, baked ham or roast beef.

[SUZAN MERREN]

ASPARAGUS WITH TOMATO VINAIGRETTE

Nutrition Facts per serving: Calories 114.6, Protein 4.917 Gm, Carbs 6.828 Gm, Fat 8.55 Gm, Cholesterol 53.25 mg, Dietary Fiber 2.415 Gm, Sugar 2.959 Gm, Sodium 31.48 mg, Calcium 33.4 mg, Potassium 293 mg, Iron 1.258 mg

SERVES 4

1 lb. lg. asparagus spears, trimmed
¼ cup plus 2 Tbsp. olive oil
¼ cup red wine vinegar
1 sm. tomato, finely chopped
¼ green bell pepper, finely chopped
1 scallion, finely chopped
1 Tbsp. chopped parsley
1 hard-boiled egg, finely chopped

1. Cook asparagus in a large pot of boiling, salted water for about 5 minutes, or until just tender; drain.

2. Refresh under cold running water; drain thoroughly.

3. Arrange asparagus on a large platter; cover and refrigerate until cold.

4. Whisk oil and vinegar, to blend, in a small bowl.

5. Add tomato, bell pepper, scallion and parsley; season with salt and pepper (can be prepared 3 hours ahead, but let stand at room temperature before serving).

6. Spoon half of the vinaigrette over asparagus, and garnish with egg.

7. Pass remaining dressing separately.

[LARRY & SHELLEY LEONARD, AND ALEX & NICHOLAS]

Asparagus with Tomato Vinaigrette

FRIED PLANTAIN

Nutrition Facts per serving: Calories 114.7, Protein 0.583 Gm, Carbs 14.28 Gm, Fat 6.978 Gm, Cholesterol 0 mg, Dietary Fiber 1.03 Gm, Sugar 0 Gm, Sodium 1.75 mg, Calcium 1.25 mg, Potassium 223.3 mg, Iron 0.268 mg

SERVES 6 TO 8

2 lg. ripe plantains, peeled (see note below)
¼ cup vegetable oil

1. Cut the plantains on a diagonal into ¼"-thick pieces.
2. In a large frying pan over Medium-High heat, fry the plantains for about 2 minutes on each side, or until golden brown (keeping a close eye on them to prevent them from burning).
3. Serve immediately.

NOTE:
To select ripe plantains, squeeze the fruit firmly but gently. If it has no "give" and feels hard then the fruit is not ripe. Ripe plantains will also have black, or mostly black, skins. Fried plantain is a frequent side dish used in the Caribbean region. It goes well with just about everything, especially local and seafood dishes.

Fried Plantain and Cheesy Baked Tomatoes

CHEESY BAKED TOMATOES

Nutrition Facts per serving: Calories 80.77, Protein 6.78 Gm, Carbs 3.667 Gm, Fat 4.549 Gm, Cholesterol 12.79 mg, Dietary Fiber 0.835 Gm, Sugar 1.737 Gm, Sodium 314.4 mg, Calcium 195.6 mg, Potassium 157.8 mg, Iron 0.421 mg

SERVES 6

3 lg. ripe tomatoes
Salt and black pepper, to taste
Garlic powder, to taste
Season All, to taste
Parmesan cheese, grated
Mozzarella cheese, grated

1. Preheat oven to 350°F.
2. Cut each tomato in half. Place side-by-side, cut-side up, in a baking tin.
3. Season with salt, pepper, garlic powder and Season All.
4. Top with Parmesan and Mozzarella cheeses.
5. Bake in preheated oven for 30 minutes, or until tops are golden brown.

NOTE:
Cheesy Baked Tomatoes are great with grilled steak or chicken.

[GREGORY & TERRI MERREN, AND JOSH & ZACHARY]

BACON, PEPPER AND PARMESAN PILAFF

Nutrition Facts per serving: Calories 620.9, Protein 22.7 Gm, Carbs 60.08 Gm, Fat 31.31 Gm, Cholesterol 61.49 mg, Dietary Fiber 1.32 Gm, Sugar 1.866 Gm, Sodium 911.7 mg, Calcium 233.5 mg, Potassium 390.3 mg, Iron 4.116 mg

SERVES 4

1 Tbsp. olive oil
1 oz. butter
1 lg. onion, coarsely chopped
1 pack of about 10 smoked, rindless back bacon rashers, coarsely chopped
10 ozs. mixed grain rice
1-¼ pint chicken stock, fresh or cube
1 bunch chopped fresh tarragon
1 yellow bell pepper, seeded and finely chopped
1 green bell pepper, seeded and finely chopped
Salt and freshly ground black pepper, to taste
2 ozs. grated Parmesan cheese

1. Heat the oil and butter in a heavy-based saucepan, and fry the onion and bacon gently, until the onion is transparent.

2. Add the rice, and fry for a further 2 to 3 minutes.

3. Pour on the stock; cover and simmer gently for 30 minutes.

4. Add tarragon and bell peppers, cook for a further 10 minutes.

5. Season well with salt and freshly ground black pepper, and stir in the Parmesan.

6. Serve with a crisp green salad.

[CLYDE & HELEN ALLEN, AND JAMES & CHARLES]

CHEESY SCALLOPED POTATOES

Nutrition Facts per serving: Calories 620.9, Protein 22.7 Gm, Carbs 60.08 Gm, Fat 31.31 Gm, Cholesterol 61.49 mg, Dietary Fiber 1.32 Gm, Sugar 1.866 Gm, Sodium 911.7 mg, Calcium 233.5 mg, Potassium 390.3 mg, Iron 4.116 mg

SERVES 8

2-½ lbs. lg. red potatoes
3 Tbsp. butter
⅓ cup scallions, chopped
⅓ cup red bell pepper, chopped
1 clove garlic, minced
¼ tsp. cayenne pepper
1 pint whipping cream
¾ cup milk
¾ tsp. salt
¼ tsp. freshly ground pepper
1 cup shredded Swiss cheese
¼ cup grated Parmesan cheese

1. Peel potatoes and cut into ⅛"-thick slices; set aside.

2. Melt butter in a Dutch oven over Medium-High heat; add scallions and next 3 ingredients.

3. Cook 2 minutes, stirring constantly.

4. Add whipping cream and next 3 ingredients, stirring mixture well.

5. Add potato slices; bring to a boil over Medium heat; cook 15 minutes or until potato slices are tender, stirring gently.

6. Spoon into a lightly greased large casserole dish (11" x 7"), and sprinkle with cheeses.

7. Bake at 350°F for 45 minutes, or until bubbly and golden.

8. Let stand 15 minutes before serving.

[BRYAN & JENNIFER HUNTER, AND CORY & DANIEL]

FRIED RICE

Nutrition Facts per serving: Calories 256.7, Protein 5.042 Gm, Carbs 38.16 Gm, Fat 8.906 Gm, Cholesterol 7.796 mg, Dietary Fiber 0.711 Gm, Sugar 0.692 Gm, Sodium 83.15 mg, Calcium 23.41 mg, Potassium 99.83 mg, Iron 2.178 mg

SERVES 4

2 Tbsp. oil
1 cup long-grain rice
2-½ cups chicken
    (or beef) stock
Salt and pepper, to taste

1. Heat the oil in a wok (or saucepan) to Medium-High.

2. Add the rice, and stir-fry until the grains are lightly browned and transparent.

3. Turn off the heat; gradually pour in the stock, taking care not to scald your hand in the burst of steam which rises when the stock hits the hot surface of the wok (or saucepan).

4. Bring to a boil, reduce the heat, and season with salt and pepper.

5. Cover, and simmer for 15 minutes, or until the rice has absorbed all the stock.

6. Fluff up the grains with a fork, and serve.

Variations:

1. Add chopped onion, seeded and chopped red and green bell peppers, diced carrots and celery, chopped chiles or crushed garlic when frying the rice. Frozen peas, corn or other frozen mixed vegetables may also be added. Stir them into the rice 5 minutes before the end of the cooking time. Chopped nuts or herbs may also be added after the rice is cooked.

2. For "special fried rice," when the rice has finished cooking, stir in 2 eggs (which have been scrambled into small pieces in a separate pan), finely diced cooked **smoked** sausage, small cooked shrimp and some soy sauce (to taste).

SWEET RED CABBAGE

Nutrition Facts per serving: Calories 144.8, Protein 2.774 Gm, Carbs 28.36 Gm, Fat 3.407 Gm, Cholesterol 5.076 mg, Dietary Fiber 2.537 Gm, Sugar 14.38 Gm, Sodium 640.2 mg, Calcium 47.48 mg, Potassium 289.1 mg, Iron 0.779 mg

SERVES 5 TO 6

4 cups shredded red cabbage
2 cups cubed, unpeeled apple
2 Tbsp. bacon drippings, or
    cooking oil
¼ cup packed brown sugar
¼ cup vinegar
¼ cup water
1-¼ tsp. salt
Dash black pepper

1. Heat bacon drippings (or oil) in a saucepan.

2. Stir in brown sugar, vinegar, water, salt and pepper.

3. Add red cabbage and apple, stirring to coat.

4. Cover, and cook over Medium-Low heat, stirring occasionally,

5. For crisp cabbage, cook 15 minutes. For tender cabbage, cook for approximately 30 to 45 minutes, adding a little water, if necessary.

SWEET POTATO CASSEROLE

Nutrition Facts per serving: Calories 488.3, Protein 3.492 Gm, Carbs 41.14 Gm, Fat 35.88 Gm, Cholesterol 33.96 mg, Dietary Fiber 1.393 Gm, Sugar 1.234 Gm, Sodium 655.1 mg, Calcium 71.23 mg, Potassium 233.1 mg, Iron 1.451 mg

1. Preheat oven to 350°F.

2. In a large bowl, mash sweet potatoes with a potato masher.

3. Add all remaining ingredients to the sweet potatoes, and mix to custard consistency.

4. Pour into two (9" x 13") casserole dishes, or one very large casserole (if using a large casserole dish, the cooking time will be longer). Place in the refrigerator to harden a bit (this makes spreading the topping much easier).

Topping:

1. Mix all ingredients together.

2. Spoon topping over sweet potatoes.

3. Bake uncovered in preheated oven 35 to 45 minutes, or until browned and bubbling (it will be dangerously hot).

This yummy American recipe belongs to Laura Hinds, a good friend of many parents and children at Cayman Prep and High School. These sweet potatoes are a must on Thanksgiving or Christmas day!

[TONY & CHRISTINE CLEAVER, AND ALEX, JORDYN & BETHANY]

SERVES 16 TO 20

5 (15 oz.) cans sweet potatoes/yams, drained
3 sticks margarine, softened
1 lg. can evaporated milk
1-½ cups sugar
3 eggs, beaten
1-½ tsp. salt
2 tsp. cinnamon

Topping:
3 sticks of margarine, softened
1 cup flour
1 box brown sugar
2 cups pecans, chopped

BROWN & WILD RICE

Nutrition Facts per serving: Calories 94.96, Protein 2.093 Gm, Carbs 17.34 Gm, Fat 1.968 Gm, Cholesterol 3.883 mg, Dietary Fiber 0.369 Gm, Sugar 0.163 Gm, Sodium 284.9 mg, Calcium 11.01 mg, Potassium 69.9 mg, Iron 0.425 mg

1. In a 3 quart saucepan, bring first 3 ingredients to a boil, stirring to melt butter and dissolve salt.

2. Add rice; stir constantly, while continuing to boil for 2 minutes.

3. Reduce heat and simmer (covered tightly).

4. Cook for 50 minutes, or a bit more. All water should be absorbed.

5. Remove from heat. Set pan cover slightly ajar.

6. Let stand for 10 minutes before serving.

[DAVID R. MYERS, AND GABRIELLE]

SERVES 6 TO 8

3 cups water
1 tsp. salt (or salt substitute)
1 Tbsp. butter
¾ cup brown rice
¼ cup wild rice

Grilled Barbecued Chicken (page 144) and Deviled Eggs (page 96)

POULTRY

CHICKEN & VEGETABLE STIR FRY

Nutrition Facts per serving: Calories 621.4, Protein 59.68 Gm, Carbs 76.63 Gm, Fat 8.079 Gm, Cholesterol 146.5 mg,
Dietary Fiber 5.607 Gm, Sugar 28.92 Gm, Sodium 703 mg, Calcium 60.13 mg, Potassium 1001 mg, Iron 3.419 mg

SERVES 4

4 boneless chicken breasts,
  cubed and seasoned with
  salt and black pepper,
  to taste
1 tsp. peanut oil
½ white onion, julienned
½ red onion, julienned
½ green bell pepper, julienned
1 (8 oz.) can sliced water
  chestnuts
6 to 8 fresh mushrooms, sliced
1 carrot, peeled, sliced into ¼"
  rounds
1 zucchini, sliced into ⅓"
  diagonals and cut in half

Stir Fry Sauce:
⅓ cup corn starch
½ cup Karo Light Corn Syrup
2 cups chicken broth
½ cup soy sauce
2 Tbsp. cider vinegar
1 Tbsp. minced garlic
1 tsp. grated fresh ginger
½ tsp. cayenne pepper

1. In a small saucepan, boil the carrots in salted water, until slightly tender; drain.

2. Heat oil in a wok (or a heavy pot may be used) to Medium-High. Brown chicken, then move to the outer edges of the wok.

3. To the centre of the wok, add the vegetables, cook for about 2 to 3 minutes, tossing occasionally. Stir in the chicken from the outer edges of the wok; steam.

4. Prepare Stir Fry Sauce by combining all ingredients in a 1-quart jar with a tight-fitting lid; shake well.

5. Pour into the wok, and mix thoroughly with the chicken and vegetables; cook on Medium-High heat for about 2 to 3 minutes, or until sauce thickens.

6. Serve over white rice or Fried Rice (page 120).

1. Brown chicken, add vegetables, and toss.

2. Steam the vegetables and chicken.

3. Pour in the sauce.

4. Cook until sauce thickens.

HEARTY CHICKEN BAKE

Nutrition Facts per serving: Calories 571.2, Protein 56.95 Gm, Carbs 42.43 Gm, Fat 20.64 Gm, Cholesterol 74.46 mg,
Dietary Fiber 10.14 Gm, Sugar 1.35 Gm, Sodium 1242 mg, Calcium 505 mg, Potassium 1737 mg, Iron 6.92 mg

1. Preheat oven to 375°F.
2. Combine mashed potatoes, ½ cup cheese and ½ can french fried onions; mix well. Spread up sides of a greased 1-½ quart casserole to form a shell.
3. Combine cooked chicken, mixed veggies, soup, milk and seasonings.
4. Pour into potato shell.
5. Bake uncovered in preheated oven for 30 minutes.
6. Top with remaining cheese and onions.
7. Bake an additional 3 to 5 minutes, until golden brown.
8. Let stand 5 minutes before serving.

[CHRIS & CHERYL KELLETT, AND BRITTNEY & BRAYDON]

SERVES 4 TO 6

3 cups hot mashed potatoes
1 cup shredded cheddar cheese
1 can (2.8 oz.) french fried onions
1-½ cups cubed cooked chicken
1 (10 oz.) pkg. frozen mixed veggies (thawed and drained)
1 (10-¾ oz.) can Cream of Chicken soup
¼ cup milk
½ tsp. ground mustard
¼ tsp. garlic powder
¼ tsp. black pepper

TIP:
The hot potatoes can be mashed with a little milk to make them fluffier.

BAKED CURRY CHICKEN BREASTS WITH ORANGE CRANBERRY SAUCE

Nutrition Facts per serving: Calories 226.5, Protein 13.91 Gm, Carbs 33.46 Gm, Fat 5.05 Gm, Cholesterol 36.02 mg,
Dietary Fiber 2.697 Gm, Sugar 24.79 Gm, Sodium 100.1 mg, Calcium 42.81 mg, Potassium 351.5 mg, Iron 1.571 mg

1. Preheat oven to 350°F.
2. Combine curry, paprika, rosemary, salt and pepper.
3. Dredge chicken breasts in seasoning, and arrange in a shallow baking dish.
4. Brush breasts lightly with a small amount of olive oil.
5. Bake 30 minutes in preheated oven, or until done.

Sauce:
1. Combine orange juice, ginger, honey and cranberries in a small saucepan.
2. Gently heat over Medium heat until cranberries are soft, but not mushy.
3. Stir in enough cornstarch mixture to create a slightly thickened sauce.
4. Add sliced orange, and heat through.
5. Divide sauce between chicken breasts to serve.

[KEVIN & LYNE LLOYD, AND JESSICA, MORGAN & RYAN]

SERVES 4

1-½ to 2 tsp. curry powder
½ tsp. paprika
1 tsp. ground rosemary
Dash of salt and pepper (or season to taste)
4 (6 oz.) boneless chicken breasts
Olive oil
¾ cup fresh orange juice
2 Tbsp. ginger, freshly grated
4 Tbsp. honey
1 cup cranberries
1 orange, peeled, pith removed and thinly sliced
2 tsp. cornstarch, dissolved in small amount of water

HONEY CHICKEN

Nutrition Facts per serving: Calories 372.6, Protein 25.83 Gm, Carbs 4.94 Gm, Fat 28 Gm, Cholesterol 56.7 mg,
Dietary Fiber 0.445 Gm, Sugar 3.721 Gm, Sodium 427.9 mg, Calcium 11.78 mg, Potassium 277.3 mg, Iron 1.356 mg

SERVES 4

1 lb. boneless chicken
Chutney

Marinade:
¼ cup oil
2-½ tsp. curry powder
2-½ tsp. honey
1-½ Tbsp. lemon juice
½ tsp. turmeric
2 tsp. garlic salt

1. Mix the marinade ingredients well.
2. Place chicken pieces in a large Ziplock bag, and pour marinade over chicken.
3. Marinate chicken for a minimum of 4 hours, or longer. Turn and shake occasionally. Marinade can be refrigerated, but turn and shake before placing in refrigerator.

To bake:
1. Preheat oven to 350°F.
2. Place chicken pieces in baking dish (Pyrex, if possible) with marinade, skin side down.
3. Place foil over the baking dish and puncture with a few holes to allow steam to vent. Bake for 45 minutes. Turn and baste with marinade; cover and bake a further 15 minutes.
4. Turn and baste again with marinade; spread each piece with 1 teaspoon chutney.
5. Bake uncovered for a further 30 minutes, or until done. Serve hot.

[ROBIN & LANA JARVIS, AND ANDREW & AARON]

EASY CHICKEN ENCHILADAS

Nutrition Facts per serving: Calories 660, Protein 48.5 Gm, Carbs 14.11 Gm, Fat 43.15 Gm, Cholesterol 189.7 mg,
Dietary Fiber 0.463 Gm, Sugar 0.996 Gm, Sodium 1935 mg, Calcium 489 mg, Potassium 372 mg, Iron 3.752 mg

SERVES 3 TO 4

1 pkg. flour tortillas
1-½ lbs. boneless chicken,
   cooked and cut into
   bite-size pieces
1 (3 oz.) pkg. cream cheese
¼ cup picante salsa
1 cup cheddar cheese, grated
1 sm. onion, finely chopped
½ to 1 tsp. cumin
Sour cream,
   for thinning (optional)

1. Preheat oven to 350°F.
2. Sauté onion in frying pan.
3. Add chicken, cream cheese, salsa, cheese and cumin; cook over Medium heat until cheese is melted and bubbly (may be thinned with a bit of sour cream).
4. Place about 2 tablespoons of mixture into individual flour tortillas, and roll the tortillas around mixture.
5. Line the tortillas side-by-side, seam side down, on a baking sheet; top with additional cheddar cheese, and bake for 15 minutes. Top with a dollop of sour cream, if desired, before serving.

[TONY & CHRISTINE CLEAVER, AND ALEX, JORDYN & BETHANY]

CHICKEN, DATE AND APRICOT TAGINE

Nutrition Facts per serving: Calories 638.9, Protein 40.38 Gm, Carbs 66.09 Gm, Fat 24.3 Gm, Cholesterol 116.4 mg,
Dietary Fiber 9.684 Gm, Sugar 21.19 Gm, Sodium 676.9 mg, Calcium 103.8 mg, Potassium 937.7 mg, Iron 4.819 mg

SERVES 4

1. Rub the chicken thighs with the garam masala.

2. Heat the oil in a deep frying pan; add chicken, and brown on both sides.

3. Add onion and the next 5 ingredients (onion through garlic); cook for 4 minutes.

4. Add broth, dates, apricots, lemon and salt. Bring to a boil; cover and simmer for 1 hour, or until chicken is cooked through and tender. While simmering, turn the chicken pieces over from time to time. (If desired, thicken gravy with cornstarch mixed with a little water.)

5. Serve over couscous (or white rice).

8 chicken thighs (with bone in
   and skinned)
1 Tbsp. olive oil
1 Tbsp. ground garam masala
1 cup chopped onion
1 tsp. ground cumin
½ tsp. ground ginger
½ tsp. ground cinnamon
⅛ tsp. red pepper
2 cloves garlic, minced
1-½ cups fat-free chicken broth
⅓ cup whole pitted dates,
   chopped in quarters
⅓ cup dried apricots, chopped
   in quarters
⅓ cup lemon sections, peeled
   and chopped
½ tsp. salt
3 cups hot couscous
   (or white rice)

NOTE:

Garam Masala is a mixture of dry, ground spices and is used in Indian cooking.
Look for it in the Indian food section of large supermarkets.

[LINDA DALTON-RILEY & DARREN RILEY,
AND BRITTANY & SYDNEY]

BAKED HONEY-CURRIED CHICKEN

Nutrition Facts per serving: Calories 535.6, Protein 76.69 Gm, Carbs 3.994 Gm, Fat 21.59 Gm, Cholesterol 233 mg,
Dietary Fiber 0.537 Gm, Sugar 1.455 Gm, Sodium 521.1 mg, Calcium 48.55 mg, Potassium 665.5 mg, Iron 3.009 mg

SERVES 4 TO 6

1. Preheat oven to 350°F.

2. In a greased shallow lasagna dish, arrange the chicken in a single layer, skin-side down.

3. Combine the butter, honey, mustard, curry powder and cayenne pepper; stir until well-blended.

4. Pour butter/honey mixture over chicken. (Cover and refrigerate if preparing ahead.)

5. Bake uncovered in preheated oven for 20 minutes.

6. Baste once, and turn chicken over.

7. Bake another 20 minutes after basting.

3 lbs. chicken breasts
   (with skin or without)
⅓ cup melted butter
⅓ cup liquid honey
¼ cup Dijon or deli-style
   mustard
4 tsp. curry powder
Pinch of cayenne pepper

Kids love this one. An option is to use boneless chicken cut
into small cubes.

[KEVIN & LYNE LLOYD , AND JESSICA, MORGAN & RYAN]

CHICKEN CACCIATORE

Nutrition Facts per serving: Calories 294.6, Protein 31.43 Gm, Carbs 12.19 Gm, Fat 12.8 Gm, Cholesterol 85.31 mg, Dietary Fiber 1.944 Gm, Sugar 3.905 Gm, Sodium 870.9 mg, Calcium 53.91 mg, Potassium 431.4 mg, Iron 2.005 mg

SERVES 6

1 (28 oz.) can crushed tomatoes
2 packs fresh button
   mushrooms, sliced
1 (8 oz.) can tomato sauce
1 Tbsp. oregano
2 tsp. salt, or to taste
2 bay leaves
Black pepper, to taste
2-½ cups chicken broth
¼ cup oil
½ tsp. dried crushed red pepper
4 split chicken breasts
4 chicken legs/thighs
2 sm. (or 1 med.) onion, chopped
4 lg. cloves garlic, minced
Flour, for dredging

1. Season the chicken pieces with salt and pepper, then dust them with flour.

2. Sear the chicken in hot oil to seal in the juices.

3. Remove chicken; set aside.

4. Sauté the onions and garlic in pan drippings, until onions are translucent (be careful not to burn the garlic).

5. Add mushrooms, and add a dab of butter; cook down until soft.

6. Add crushed tomato and tomato sauce; cook down for 5 to 6 minutes.

7. Add broth, oregano, bay leaves and crushed red pepper.

8. Bring to a boil; add the chicken, cover and cook down for about 20 minutes.

9. Remove bay leaves, and serve hot over linguini or white rice.

[DON & JENNIE STEWART]

1. Sear chicken in hot oil.

2. Add mushrooms to sautéed onions and garlic.

3. Add tomatoes, broth and seasonings; bring to a boil, and add chicken.

Chicken Cacciatore

ROAST CHICKEN

Nutrition Facts per serving: Calories 216.6, Protein 19.38 Gm, Carbs 2.326 Gm, Fat 14.52 Gm, Cholesterol 82.69 mg, Dietary Fiber 1.124 Gm, Sugar 0.464 Gm, Sodium 367 mg, Calcium 21.31 mg, Potassium 261 mg, Iron 1.106 mg

1. Preheat oven to 350°F.

2. Remove giblets from inside the chicken. To clean, run cold water into body cavity of chicken several times. Also clean the outside of the chicken under running cold water. Pat chicken dry with paper towels. Place in a roasting pan.

3. If desired, for a bit more spiciness, cut a scotch bonnet pepper in half, and remove the stem and seeds. Rub chicken all over with the inside of both halves of the pepper. After rubbing the chicken with the pepper, either dice the pepper and place it inside the chicken cavity (which will make the gravy spicier), or discard it.

4. Lift the skin, and stuff several small cubes of butter between the skin and the chicken, then rub the chicken all over with the remaining butter.

5. Season the chicken with salt, pepper, Season All and finely chopped seasoning (or scotch bonnet) pepper, if desired. Rub seasonings into chicken.

6. In a small bowl, season the onion, bell pepper and celery with a little salt and black pepper. Spread onions, bell pepper and celery on the top and bottom, as well as around and on the inside of the chicken.

7. Cover tightly with aluminum foil but try to prevent it from touching the chicken.

8. Bake for 1-½ to 2 hours. Uncover and bake a further 15 minutes, or until brown.

9. Move chicken to a platter. Let stand for a few minutes before carving.

Gravy:

1. Scrape the bottom and sides of the roasting pan to loosen the brown bits and then pour off all the contents of the roasting pan into a medium saucepan.

2. Add about 2 tablespoons of water to the drippings in the saucepan and bring to a gentle boil. At this point the gravy can be thickened, if desired, by mixing 1 teaspoon of flour with 2 to 4 tablespoons of cold water to form a paste, and then stirring this into the saucepan continuously until the gravy is smooth and thickened. Serve the gravy over the chicken, stuffing and rice or potato.

[ROBERT & PAULA EBANKS, AND ASHLEIGH]

SERVES 8 TO 10

1 (3 to 4 lb.) whole
   broiler-fryer chicken
1 med. onion, chopped
1 green bell pepper, chopped
1 stalk celery, chopped
Salt, black pepper
   and Season All, to taste
1 scotch bonnet or seasoning
   pepper (seeds removed),
   finely chopped (optional)
½ stick butter

TIPS:
Try to avoid handling scotch bonnet pepper with your fingers! Instead, use a knife and fork to remove seeds and dice the pepper. It is also always important to wash your hands frequently when handling raw chicken.

CHICKEN MARBELLA

Nutrition Facts per serving: Calories 453.6, Protein 26.56 Gm, Carbs 28.7 Gm, Fat 24.98 Gm, Cholesterol 56.7 mg, Dietary Fiber 2.211 Gm, Sugar 6.091 Gm, Sodium 603.8 mg, Calcium 68.29 mg, Potassium 479.4 mg, Iron 2.658 mg

SERVES 12

3 lbs. boneless chicken breasts (or a combination of breasts and thighs)
1 head garlic, chopped
¼ cup dried oregano
Coarse salt and freshly ground black pepper, to taste
½ cup red wine vinegar
½ cup olive oil
1 cup pitted prunes
½ cup Spanish green olives
½ cup capers, with a bit of juice
6 bay leaves
1 cup brown sugar
1 cup white wine
¼ cup Italian parsley or fresh cilantro, finely chopped

1. In a bowl, combine chicken, garlic, oregano, salt, pepper, vinegar, olive oil, prunes, olives, capers and juice, and bay leaves; cover and let marinate, refrigerated, overnight (24 hours is really good).

2. Preheat oven to 350°F.

3. Arrange chicken in a single layer in 1 or 2 large, shallow baking pans, and spoon marinade over it evenly.

4. Sprinkle chicken with brown sugar, and pour white wine around it.

5. Bake in preheated oven for 50 minutes to 1 hour, basting frequently with pan juices. Chicken is done when the thickest part, when pricked with a fork, yields clear yellow (rather than pink) juices.

6. With a slotted spoon, transfer chicken, prunes, olives and capers to a serving platter.

7. Moisten with a few spoonfuls of pan juices, and sprinkle generously with parsley or cilantro.

8. Pass the remaining pan juices in a gravy boat.

This recipe is a Canadian favourite of Cayman Prep and High School teacher, Brenda Bryce, and her Ontario cousin, Lori Reaman. It is best served with white rice and a nice French bread.

[BRENDA BRYCE]

CURRIED CHICKEN CASSEROLE

Nutrition Facts per serving: Calories 300.3, Protein 21.16 Gm, Carbs 22.93 Gm, Fat 13.72 Gm, Cholesterol 43.9 mg,
Dietary Fiber 0.835 Gm, Sugar 0.436 Gm, Sodium 1360 mg, Calcium 52.59 mg, Potassium 335.5 mg, Iron 1.922 mg

SERVES 10

6 to 8 boneless chicken breasts
2 cans Cream of Chicken soup
2 Tbsp. curry powder (more, if
   you like it strong)
½ green bell pepper, chopped
½ med. onion, chopped
1 stalk celery, chopped
1 cup bread crumbs
2 cups mayonnaise or sour
   cream, or 1 cup of each
Salt and black pepper, to taste

1. Preheat oven to 350°F.

2. Steam chicken in a sauce pot with bell peppers, onion and celery; add salt and pepper, to taste.

3. When chicken is tender, cut into chunks and place in a 9" x 12" casserole.

4. Mix mayonnaise, sour cream, soup and curry powder together in a bowl, until well-blended; stir in the vegetables strained from the sauce pot.

5. Pour mixture evenly over chicken in the casserole dish.

6. Sprinkle bread crumbs all over the mixture.

7. Bake uncovered in preheated oven for about 30 minutes, or until bubbly and lightly browned.

8. Serve with white rice or mashed potato, your favourite vegetable, fried or baked plantain, and a salad.

[EDLIN & HELEN MERREN]

CREAMY CHICKEN AND BOW TIES

Nutrition Facts per serving: Calories 492, Protein 28.93 Gm, Carbs 26.88 Gm, Fat 28.28 Gm, Cholesterol 99.34 mg,
Dietary Fiber 1.984 Gm, Sugar 2.146 Gm, Sodium 1792 mg, Calcium 375.8 mg, Potassium 426.9 mg, Iron 1.966 mg

SERVES 4 TO 5

1 qt. water
4 skinned and boned
   chicken breasts, cut
   into bite-size pieces
8 ozs. uncooked bow
   tie pasta
1 cup chicken broth
½ cup chopped celery
½ cup chopped onion
1 (10-¾ oz.) can Cream of
   Mushroom soup
1 (8 oz.) pkg. cheddar cheese,
   cubed or grated
Salt and pepper (optional)

1. Bring water to a boil.

2. Add chicken; cook 10 to 12 minutes, or until done.

3. Remove chicken from water with a slotted spoon.

4. Add pasta to water; cook 10 minutes. Drain, and keep warm.

5. Heat ¼ cup broth over Medium-High heat in pot.

6. Add celery and onion; cook 5 minutes, or until tender.

7. Stir in chicken, soup, cheese and remaining ¾ cup chicken broth, stirring until cheese is melted.

8. Toss with pasta. Season with a little salt and pepper, if desired.

9. Serve immediately.

[QUATRO & PENNY HATCH, AND JASON, CAITLIN & TANNER]

CHICKEN PAPRIKA

Nutrition Facts per serving: Calories 1812, Protein 188.3 Gm, Carbs 8.202 Gm, Fat 108.9 Gm, Cholesterol 774.6 mg, Dietary Fiber 0.307 Gm, Sugar 0.906 Gm, Sodium 1334 mg, Calcium 200.2 mg, Potassium 1671 mg, Iron 12.43 mg

SERVES 4 TO 5

Chicken parts (2 packs thighs, or 1 pack thighs and 1 pack legs, or a mixture of thighs, legs and boneless breasts), washed and skinned
Salt, pepper, cayenne pepper and garlic powder, to taste
5 Tbsp. butter
1 onion, sliced
1 carrot, sliced
8 ozs. mushrooms, sliced
2 Tbsp. paprika (Hungarian sweet paprika is very good)
3 Tbsp. flour
1 Tbsp. ketchup
½ tsp. salt
¼ tsp. pepper
2 cups chicken broth (made using chicken bouillon cubes)
½ cup white wine
½ cup sour cream
3 Tbsp. grated Parmesan cheese

1. Sprinkle each piece of chicken generously with salt, pepper, cayenne pepper and garlic powder.

2. Heat 3 tablespoons butter in a large frying pan (or electric frying pan) and brown chicken on both sides; remove chicken.

3. Add 1 tablespoon butter to same pan. Add onion and carrot, and cook slowly for 5 to 10 minutes.

4. Add paprika, and cook another 3 minutes.

5. Stir in flour, ketchup, salt and pepper.

6. Gradually add broth and wine, and cook over Low heat, stirring until thickened and boiling; simmer for 15 minutes.

7. Put chicken back in the pan, and simmer until cooked, turning the chicken over from time to time (about 1 hour and 15 minutes), and adding water if the sauce gets too thick. About 30 minutes before the end of cooking time, add mushrooms.

8. Remove cooked chicken to a casserole dish. Add sour cream and 1 tablespoon Parmesan cheese to sauce in pan; spoon it over the chicken.

9. Sprinkle with remaining Parmesan cheese before serving.

10. Serve with egg noodles.

[BILLY & LOLLI REID]

TIPS FOR ROASTING POULTRY:
Use a shallow roasting pan. Deep, old-fashioned roasters may slow the cooking time.
Place bird on a roasting rack so it does not stew in its own juice. A rack also helps to distribute heat more evenly.
Use cooking times for whole poultry only as guidelines. Factors that affect cooking time are:
Stuffing - *Unstuffed birds cook more quickly than stuffed birds.*
Meatiness - *Meaty birds cook more slowly than bony birds.*
Temperature - *Refrigerated birds cook more slowly than birds at room temperature.*
Poultry is extremely perishable. Do not keep it at room temperature for any period of time.

GREEN CHICKEN ENCHILADAS

Nutrition Facts per serving: Calories 878.9, Protein 94.73 Gm, Carbs 24.66 Gm, Fat 44.33 Gm, Cholesterol 244.8 mg, Dietary Fiber 0.743 Gm, Sugar 2.6 Gm, Sodium 1776 mg, Calcium 486.6 mg, Potassium 865.3 mg, Iron 4.221 mg

SERVES 6

1 (10 oz.) can Las Palmas
   Green Enchilada Sauce
8 chicken breast halves,
   cooked and cubed
2 cans Cream of Chicken soup
1 cup sour cream
1 sm. can green
   chiles, diced
1 to 2 cups shredded
   cheddar cheese
½ of a (15 oz.) can black
   olives, sliced in half (optional)
Large flour tortillas

1. Preheat oven to 350°F.

2. Mix together the cooked chicken and Green Enchilada Sauce.

3. Spread the mixture into a tortilla. Roll the tortilla, then cut it in half; place in a large casserole.

4. Repeat Step 2 until the casserole is full of the rolled tortillas placed side by side.

5. Combine the Cream of Chicken soup, sour cream and green chiles.

6. Pour the soup/sour cream mixture over the tortillas; top with shredded cheese and chopped olives.

7. Bake uncovered in preheated oven for 45 minutes. Keep a close eye on it for the last 10 minutes to ensure that the cheese does not burn.

8. Serve hot.

[STEPHEN & DEBRA MCTAGGART , AND SARAH, AMELIA & MATTHEW]

Green Chicken Enchiladas

CHICKEN A LA KING

Nutrition Facts per serving: Calories 404.9, Protein 21.18 Gm, Carbs 10.1 Gm, Fat 31.28 Gm, Cholesterol 98.85 mg,
Dietary Fiber 0.609 Gm, Sugar 1.726 Gm, Sodium 2118 mg, Calcium 76.92 mg, Potassium 655.6 mg, Iron 2.298 mg

SERVES 8

2 cups chopped cooked chicken
½ cup (1 stick) butter
1 (8 oz.) pkg. fresh mushrooms,
   cleaned and sliced
3 scallions, sliced
⅓ cup all purpose flour
½ tsp. salt
½ tsp. ground black pepper
1 (14.5 oz.) can chicken broth
1 cup heavy whipping cream
1 (2 oz.) jar diced pimientos,
   drained
Hot, cooked rice

1. In a large saucepan, melt butter over Medium heat.

2. Add mushrooms and scallions; cook 5 minutes, stirring occasionally.

3. Stir in flour, salt and pepper; cook 2 minutes, stirring constantly.

4. Gradually stir in chicken broth and cream, stirring constantly; cook 5 minutes, or until slightly thickened.

5. Add chicken and pimientos; cook 5 to 8 minutes, or until thickened and bubbly.

6. Serve over hot, cooked rice.

NOTE:
Children love this simple, tasty recipe.

Chicken a la King

ALMOND CHICKEN

Nutrition Facts per serving: Calories 466.2, Protein 46.97 Gm, Carbs 13.99 Gm, Fat 25.41 Gm, Cholesterol 104 mg,
Dietary Fiber 4.703 Gm, Sugar 3.292 Gm, Sodium 714.3 mg, Calcium 135.9 mg, Potassium 827.5 mg, Iron 3.1 mg

SERVES 4 TO 6

3 to 4 chicken breasts, diced
3 Tbsp. oil
4 water chestnuts, chopped
    and drained
2 cups chopped celery
1 cup fresh mushrooms,
    cleaned and diced
1 cup chopped onion
1 (6 oz.) pkg. slivered almonds
1 to 2 Tbsp. dry white wine
3 Tbsp. soy sauce
½ cup water
Salt and black pepper, to taste
½ tsp. minced garlic
1 Tbsp. cornstarch

1. Sprinkle chicken with wine, salt and pepper; set aside.

2. Toss together mushrooms, celery, onion and water chestnuts; set aside.

3. In a frying pan over Medium heat, brown almonds in 1 tablespoon oil for 2 minutes, stirring constantly; remove from pan.

4. Add 1 tablespoon of oil to pan; heat to Medium, add garlic, and brown slightly.

5. Add chicken to pan; cook over Medium heat, until brown (about 2 minutes).

6. Remove chicken and garlic from pan; set aside.

7. Add 1 tablespoon oil. Increase heat to High, and add vegetables; stir-fry for 3 minutes.

8. Reduce heat to Medium, and return chicken and garlic to pan.

9. In a small container, mix together the cornstarch and water; add soy sauce. Pour over chicken, and stir.

10. Cover, and cook for 3 minutes.

11. Sprinkle with almonds, and serve over white rice.

[JIM & JANICE GILLIES, AND STEPHANIE, JAMES & AMY]

CHICKEN IN MUSHROOM SAUCE

Nutrition Facts per serving: Calories 550.8, Protein 61.03 Gm, Carbs 6.321 Gm, Fat 29.88 Gm, Cholesterol 184.3 mg,
Dietary Fiber 0.344 Gm, Sugar 0.237 Gm, Sodium 609.9 mg, Calcium 98.77 mg, Potassium 633.9 mg, Iron 2.539 mg

SERVES 4 TO 6

4 to 6 boneless chicken breasts,
    cut in halves (if desired)
2 to 3 Tbsp. margarine
Salt and black pepper, to taste
1 tsp. paprika
1 pack fresh mushrooms, sliced
2 tsp. chives, chopped
1 (10 oz.) can Cream of
    Mushroom soup
1 pint whipping cream

1. Season the chicken with salt and pepper.

2. In a hot skillet, brown the chicken in the margarine.

3. Add paprika, mushrooms, chives, Cream of Mushroom soup and whipping cream.

4. Stir well; simmer for 20 minutes.

5. Serve hot over white or yellow rice.

[CHRIS & CHERYL KELLETT, AND BRITTNEY & BRAYDON]

GRILLED BARBECUED CHICKEN

Nutrition Facts per serving: Calories 309.6, Protein 30.63 Gm, Carbs 6.351 Gm, Fat 17.42 Gm, Cholesterol 121.7 mg, Dietary Fiber 0.086 Gm, Sugar 2.083 Gm, Sodium 292.1 mg, Calcium 26.26 mg, Potassium 331 mg, Iron 2.149 mg

SERVES 12

2 family packs chicken parts
¼ cup finely chopped onion
1 clove garlic, minced
2 Tbsp. cooking oil
¾ cup ketchup
⅓ cup vinegar
1 Tbsp. Worcestershire sauce
2 tsp. brown sugar
1 tsp. celery seed
1 tsp. dry mustard
½ tsp. salt
¼ tsp. pepper

1. Prepare sauce (see method below); set aside. Season chicken pieces with salt and pepper, to taste.
2. On the grill, place chicken pieces, bone-side down, over Medium heat.
3. Grill chicken for 25 minutes, or until bone-side is well-browned; turn over.
4. Grill 20 to 25 minutes more, or until chicken is tender.
5. Brush chicken often with sauce during the last 10 minutes of grilling, using all of the sauce.

Sauce:

1. In a saucepan, cook chopped onion and minced garlic in cooking oil, until onion is tender, but not brown; drain off the oil.
2. Stir in the ketchup, vinegar, Worcestershire sauce, brown sugar, celery seed, dry mustard, salt and pepper; bring to a boil.
3. Reduce heat, and simmer sauce uncovered for 10 minutes, stirring once or twice during the cooking process.

CLASSY CHICKEN

Nutrition Facts per serving: Calories 609.7, Protein 32.62 Gm, Carbs 60.67 Gm, Fat 26.4 Gm, Cholesterol 72.89 mg, Dietary Fiber 6.302 Gm, Sugar 17.65 Gm, Sodium 1536 mg, Calcium 235.3 mg, Potassium 92.5 mg, Iron 3.524 mg

SERVES 4 TO 6

3 to 4 boneless chicken breasts
3 Tbsp. vegetable oil
1 (approx. 10 oz.) pkg. frozen asparagus or broccoli (fresh is better)
1 (10 oz.) can Cream of Chicken soup
½ cup mayonnaise
1 tsp. curry powder
1 tsp. lemon juice
Salt and black pepper, to taste
1 cup grated cheddar cheese

1. Preheat oven to 375°F.
2. Cut chicken into 2" x 4" pieces, and season with salt and pepper.
3. In a large saucepan, sauté chicken in oil over Medium heat, until white and opaque, about 6 minutes; drain.
4. In a pot of water, boil asparagus (or broccoli), until tender crisp.
5. Drain and arrange in the bottom of a buttered 7" diameter casserole.
6. Place chicken on top of asparagus (or broccoli).
7. Mix soup, mayonnaise, curry and lemon juice together, and pour over chicken.
8. Sprinkle cheddar cheese over the top; bake for 30 to 35 minutes.
9. Serve with white rice and a green salad or vegetable.

[JIM & JANICE GILLIES, AND STEPHANIE, JAMES & AMY]

CHICKEN WITH GREEN OLIVES

Nutrition Facts per serving: Calories 525.8, Protein 57.75 Gm, Carbs 8.93 Gm, Fat 26.05 Gm, Cholesterol 172.9 mg,
Dietary Fiber 4.262 Gm, Sugar 4.747 Gm, Sodium 1240 mg, Calcium 79.66 mg, Potassium 1098 mg, Iron 3.565 mg

1. Preheat oven to 350°F.

2. Season chicken with salt and pepper.

3. In a frying pan over Medium-High heat, brown chicken on both sides in oil and butter; set aside.

4. Sauté onion and garlic; add bell peppers and mushrooms; cook for a few minutes.

5. Add tomatoes; season well with salt and pepper. Cook for about 1 to 2 minutes.

6. Transfer the vegetable mixture to a casserole; place the chicken on the bed of vegetables.

7. Add wine to the frying pan, and bring to a boil; pour over the chicken.

8. Cover, and bake in preheated oven for 50 minutes.

9. Add olives, mix lightly, then pour in the cream.

10. Re-cover the casserole and bake for a further 10 to 20 minutes.

11. Adjust seasonings, and serve over hot fettucini.

SERVES 4 TO 6

4 boneless chicken breasts
2 Tbsp. olive oil
2 Tbsp. butter
1 lg. onion, finely chopped
2 cloves garlic, crushed
1 red and 1 yellow bell pepper, seeded and cut into lg. pieces
3 cups quartered mushrooms
2 sm. tomatoes, chopped
⅔ cup dry white wine
1 cup pitted green olives, sliced
4 to 6 Tbsp. heavy cream
Salt and black pepper, to taste

1. Season chicken with salt and pepper.

2. Brown the chicken in oil and butter.

3. Sauté vegetables.

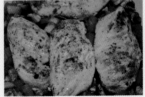

4. Add wine, and bake.

Chicken with Green Olives

CHICKEN DIVAN

Nutrition Facts per serving: Calories 612.8, Protein 40.04 Gm, Carbs 17.48 Gm, Fat 44.48 Gm, Cholesterol 125.2 mg, Dietary Fiber 4.348 Gm, Sugar 2.327 Gm, Sodium 751.4 mg, Calcium 110.6 mg, Potassium 567.6 mg, Iron 3.369 mg

SERVES 6

2 lbs. boneless
 chicken breasts
1 pack frozen chopped
 broccoli
1 can Cream of Chicken soup
1 cup mayonnaise or plain
 yogurt
4 Tbsp. curry powder
Bread crumbs, for topping
½ stick butter, cut into
 several square pieces
1 lime
1 onion, coarsely chopped
1 stalk celery, coarsely chopped
Salt and black pepper, to taste

1. In a large pot of water, gently boil the chicken with onion, celery, salt and pepper for approximately 30 minutes, or until cooked through.

2. Preheat oven to 350°F.

3. Allow the chicken to cool, then break into bite-size pieces. Discard vegetables.

4. Lightly grease a 9" x 9" casserole dish.

5. Cook broccoli as directed on package.

6. Mix together soup, mayonnaise, curry powder and juice of 1 lime.

7. Arrange broccoli on the bottom of the dish, top the broccoli with the chicken, then pour soup/mayonnaise mixture on top of the chicken.

8. Top with breadcrumbs, and bake for 30 minutes, or until heated through.

9. If desired, while still hot, dot butter over the casserole.

10. Serve hot over white rice.

[WILLIAM & SHARON WALMSLEY, AND KIRSTEN, EMMA, JONATHAN & KATHERINE]

CHICKEN & DUMPLINGS

Nutrition Facts per serving: Calories 387.5, Protein 24.57 Gm, Carbs 43.74 Gm, Fat 12.07 Gm, Cholesterol 41.57 mg, Dietary Fiber 2.462 Gm, Sugar 5.643 Gm, Sodium 1585 mg, Calcium 125.2 mg, Potassium 709.1 mg, Iron 2.844 mg

SERVES 6 TO 8

1 store bought roasted chicken
 (or homemade)
3 carrots, sliced
1 (8.5 oz.) can sweet
 peas, drained
About 6 cups chicken broth
2 cups Bisquick
⅔ cup milk

"Chicken n' Dumplins, sweet peas and carrots, apple pie and a glass of milk ... now that's a nice dinner!" - Orlando Bonar, great-grandfather of Jonathan, Katelee and Nicholas McTaggart.

1. Carve the chicken, and remove the meat from the legs and wings. Set chicken meat aside. Discard the skin.

2. Place the remaining carcass in a pot filled with the broth; bring to a boil.

3. Lower the heat; simmer for about 45 minutes. Remove bones from pot, and discard.

4. To the pot, add 2 to 3 cups of water, the carrots and sweet peas; bring to a boil.

5. In a medium bowl, combine Bisquick and milk until a soft dough forms. Drop by spoonfuls into the boiling stew; cook for about 2 minutes.

6. Add the reserved chicken meat, reduce heat, cover and simmer for a further 15 minutes. Serve hot.

[RICK & KIM MCTAGGART, AND JONATHAN, KATELEE & NICHOLAS]

Trinidadian Chicken Pelau

Nutrition Facts per serving: Calories 490.3, Protein 23.7 Gm, Carbs 40.51 Gm, Fat 25.63 Gm, Cholesterol 92.51 mg, Dietary Fiber 1.216 Gm, Sugar 5.565 Gm, Sodium 1005 mg, Calcium 49.74 mg, Potassium 440.5 mg, Iron 3.059 mg

SERVES 10 TO 12

2 whole chickens, cut up
2 tsp. salt
1 tsp. black pepper
4 seasoning peppers, seeded and chopped
4 cloves garlic, crushed
2 onions, grated
2 blades of chive
2 Tbsp. Worcestershire sauce
Piece of ginger, minced (optional)
1 can pigeon peas, drained
3 Tbsp. oil
2 Tbsp. sugar (brown or white)
2 cups rice
4 cups hot water combined with 4 small or 2 large chicken bouillon cubes
4 Tbsp. raisins
12 stuffed olives, sliced
1 scotch bonnet pepper
Lime juice

1. Wash chicken with lime juice, and then season with next 8 ingredients. Set aside for approximately 1 hour to allow the chicken to absorb flavour.

2. Heat oil in a large frying pan. When hot, sprinkle with sugar. Stir quickly and well so as to prevent sugar from sticking and becoming caramelised.

3. When sugar begins to bubble, add chicken pieces, without the seasoning, and coat well until nicely brown. A little browning sauce may be added if a darker colour is preferred.

4. Add the rice and continue to stir well, turning over the chicken and rice until both have become an even golden brown colour, adjusting the heat to make sure that no sticking occurs.

5. Add the pigeon peas, raisins, olives and seasoning from the chicken; cook for 15 minutes on Medium to Low heat. Melt chicken stock cubes in water, and add to the pan. Raise the heat, and bring to a quick boil.

6. Place scotch bonnet carefully on top of the chicken and rice mixture, reduce heat, cover, and cook on a very Low heat for 40 to 45 minutes, or until the rice is cooked. Do not stir while cooking, and avoid removing the cover. The pelau is ready when the rice is cooked, and all the water has been absorbed. If when the rice is cooked it still seems "sappy," then remove the cover at the end for a little while, to help it to become more dry.

7. Remove the hot pepper, and place the rice in a big dish to cool. Very important - do not cut or allow the hot pepper to burst!

NOTE:
Serves a "big lime." In Trinidad, a "big lime" means a big group of people.

Variation: Pork or beef can be used instead of chicken. Peas and carrots can be used instead of pigeon peas.

[VANDA FERNANDEZ]

Ackee and Saltfish (page 150), Scotch Bonnet Pickled Pepper Sauce (page 201) and boiled green bananas

SEAFOOD

PRAWNS WITH MUSTARD & CORIANDER

Nutrition Facts per serving: Calories 650.6, Protein 9.202 Gm, Carbs 94.29 Gm, Fat 25.91 Gm, Cholesterol 28.84 mg, Dietary Fiber 1.165 Gm, Sugar 0.463 Gm, Sodium 1072 mg, Calcium 168.9 mg, Potassium 189.2 mg, Iron 2.006 mg

SERVES 4

1 oz. butter
2 tsp. sesame oil
2 sticks celery, chopped
1 clove garlic, chopped
1 lb. fresh prawns, peeled
3 Tbsp. fish stock
3 tsp. Dijon mustard
2 Tbsp. medium dry sherry
1.5 level Tbsp. cornstarch
5 fl. oz. carton double cream
Fresh ground black pepper
1 to 2 Tbsp. fresh
    coriander leaves, chopped

1. Heat the butter and oil in a large sauté pan.

2. Add the celery, garlic and prawns; stir fry for one minute.

3. Add the fish stock, mustard and sherry.

4. Blend the cornstarch with about two tablespoons of water, and stir in.

5. Bring to a boil.

6. Add the cream and black pepper.

7. Sprinkle the chopped coriander over the top.

8. Serve immediately with long grain and wild rice, and a mixed green salad.

[GARRY & DINAH GREEN, AND KEELAN]

ACKEE AND SALTFISH

Nutrition Facts per serving: Calories 439.6, Protein 27.21 Gm, Carbs 6.23 Gm, Fat 33.86 Gm, Cholesterol 54.93 mg, Dietary Fiber 1.002 Gm, Sugar 4.168 Gm, Sodium 1350 mg, Calcium 78.9 mg, Potassium 996.3 mg, Iron 2.163 mg

SERVES 6

1 lb. saltfish (codfish)
4 to 6 slices bacon, chopped
24 ackees (or 2 tins canned
    ackees)
1 lg. onion, chopped
Salt and pepper, to taste
3 tomatoes, diced
1 stalk scallion, chopped
1 Tbsp. oil

NOTE:
To make this recipe easier to prepare, saltfish can be purchased in local supermarkets without the skin on.

1. Soak codfish in water to cover overnight; remove the skin while it is soaking, as a lot of salt is in the skin. Alternatively, soak for 30 to 40 minutes, place in fresh cold water, bring to a boil, drain and repeat.

2. Flake fish, and set aside.

3. Fry the bacon in a large pan, and set aside. Reserve bacon drippings in the pan.

4. Prepare ackees for cooking by removing seeds and pink lining. Boil for 20 minutes in salted water; drain. If using canned ackees, just drain and stir into sauté mixture.

5. Sauté onions, tomatoes and scallion in the reserved bacon drippings. Add seasoning, bacon and ackees; sauté for approximately 5 minutes.

6. Add flaked saltfish to mixture; sauté briefly so the flavours can blend.

7. Serve with white rice and boiled green bananas.

[CELICEA MYLES & KAI-LEIGH HAUGHTON, AND
TREVOR & NICOLO TUMMINGS]

CAYMAN-STYLE FISH

Nutrition Facts per serving: Calories 117.1, Protein 16.9 Gm, Carbs 9.59 Gm, Fat 1.987 Gm, Cholesterol 28.05 mg,
Dietary Fiber 1.432 Gm, Sugar 3.602 Gm, Sodium 758.5 mg, Calcium 36.66 mg, Potassium 425 mg, Iron 1.073 mg

SERVES 4 TO 6

1 lg. whole fish (such as snapper, mahi mahi or wahoo), cleaned, de-boned and filleted
½ lg. onion, chopped
½ green bell pepper, chopped
1 scotch bonnet pepper, seeded and coarsely chopped
1 scotch bonnet pepper, seeded and finely chopped (optional)
1 lg. tomato, diced
Salt, pepper and garlic powder, to taste
2 Tbsp. Pickapeppa Sauce
¼ cup salsa
¼ cup ketchup
Juice from 2 limes

1. Season the fish with salt and pepper. Cut small slits in fish, and stuff with coarsely chopped scotch bonnet pepper (if desired). Marinate with the juice from 1 lime for at least 30 minutes.

2. In a frying pan over Medium-High heat, sauté onions and bell peppers in a little oil until onions are translucent. Add finely chopped scotch bonnet pepper and tomatoes. Cook a further 5 minutes.

3. Add Pickapeppa Sauce, ketchup, salsa, garlic powder and the juice from 1 lime. Cook until heated through.

4. Place the fish in a large baking dish/casserole, and top with the tomato mixture.

5. Bake covered on 350°F for approximately 45 minutes, testing the fish after 30 minutes, as cooking times may vary. When almost done, push the tomato mixture off the top of the fish to the sides, place back in oven uncovered, and bake about 10 to 15 minutes to slightly brown the top and cook through.

6. Serve immediately with white rice, green salad and Fried Plantain (page 118).

[THE B. HUNTER & G. MERREN FAMILIES]

Cayman-Style Snapper

Fresh fish and chopped vegetables

Finely chopped scotch bonnet pepper and diced tomatoes

Fish topped with sauce - ready for baking

TASTY FISH PATTIES

Nutrition Facts per serving: Calories 78.47, Protein 14.89 Gm, Carbs 10.17 Gm, Fat 2.642 Gm, Cholesterol 53.25 mg, Dietary Fiber 0.445 Gm, Sugar 0.648 Gm, Sodium 430.4 mg, Calcium 15.07 mg, Potassium 182.4 mg, Iron 2.219 mg

SERVES 4

1-½ cups cornflake cereal
1 tsp. vegetable oil
1 (6 oz.) can tuna or salmon,
   drained and mashed
½ cup mashed potato
   (or sweet potato)
1 egg (or 2 egg whites)
3 Tbsp. mayonnaise
1 tsp. Worcestershire sauce
1 tsp. onion salt (or ¼ white
   onion, finely chopped)
¼ tsp. dried oregano
¼ tsp. dried dill
Pinch of black pepper
No-stick cooking
   spray, optional

1. Preheat oven to 350°F.

2. Line a baking sheet with parchment paper (or spray with cooking spray).

3. Seal cornflakes in a large Ziplock bag, and crush with a rolling pin to the size of rolled oats. Put in a bowl, mix in oil with a fork; set aside.

4. Mix all the other ingredients with a fork. Shape into ½"-thick patties and coat them in the cornflakes.

5. Place on a baking sheet; bake for 25 minutes, until lightly browned.

[TONY & KAREN ATTENBOROUGH, AND CLAIRE, HAMISH & MATTHEW]

SALMON WITH SWEET PEPPERS, MUSHROOMS & PASTA IN A WHITE SAUCE

Nutrition Facts per serving: Calories 578.7, Protein 50.46 Gm, Carbs 46.88 Gm, Fat 21.12 Gm, Cholesterol 111.4 mg, Dietary Fiber 4.126 Gm, Sugar 7.343 Gm, Sodium 788.7 mg, Calcium 375.9 mg, Potassium 1238 mg, Iron 3.571 mg

SERVES 2 TO 4

1 lb. fresh fillet of salmon,
   skinned and cut into 1" pieces
6 ozs. penne or other tube pasta
Salt and pepper, to taste
1 Tbsp. olive oil
3 lg. cloves garlic, peeled
   and chopped
3 lg. scallions, cut diagonally
1 med. onion, roughly chopped
2 Tbsp. fresh basil, chopped
10 mushrooms, halved with
   stems on
½ orange sweet pepper, chopped
1 chicken bouillon cube
12 fl. ozs. 2% milk
2 ozs. grated Parmesan cheese
Cornstarch, to thicken
Chopped fresh parsley, basil
   and scallion, to garnish

1. Season the salmon with salt and pepper.

2. In a frying pan, gently fry the garlic in the olive oil over Medium heat.

3. Add salmon, and sear until cooked, 3 to 4 minutes (be careful not to break salmon).

4. Remove salmon pieces, leaving garlic and any small flakes of salmon in pan.

5. Add chopped onion and scallion to pan; cook over Medium heat until golden brown.

6. Add chopped basil, mushrooms and sweet pepper; season with salt and pepper. Cook 3 to 4 minutes. Crumble stock cube into pan, and stir.

7. Remove pan from heat, and gradually stir in milk. Add Parmesan cheese; return to pan, and simmer gently, stirring constantly until cheese starts to melt. Thicken sauce with cornstarch to a creamy texture.

8. Cook pasta in boiling water, until done; drain, and add to sauce, stirring to coat.

9. Add salmon back to pan, and reheat gently.

10. Garnish with parsley, scallion and basil; serve warm.

[HUGH & ANN MURPHY, AND SEAN, DANIEL & LAURA]

SEA BASS IN CORN HUSKS

Nutrition Facts per serving: Calories 535.1, Protein 16.11 Gm, Carbs 70.84 Gm, Fat 28.08 Gm, Cholesterol 77.04 mg, Dietary Fiber 5.204 Gm, Sugar 16.2 Gm, Sodium 68.67 mg, Calcium 57.18 mg, Potassium 229 mg, Iron 1.257 mg

SERVES 4

8 pcs. fresh corn in husks
4 (4 oz.) Sea Bass fillets
½ cup unsalted butter, softened
2 Tbsp. tomato paste
2 Tbsp. chopped fresh basil
Salt and black pepper, to taste

1. Husk corn. Use the larger, outer husks to wrap the fish for best coverage.

2. Soak the husks and 8 pieces of cotton string in hot water for 10 minutes.

3. Mix softened butter, tomato paste and basil well.

4. Season the Sea Bass with salt and pepper generously.

5. Place 2 soaked corn husks on work surface, one on top of the other - two layers will keep the fish from burning (use more husks if the ones being used are not large enough to cover the width of the fish). Centre the fish fillet in the cradle of the husk(s).

6. Spread 1-½ tablespoons of butter mixture onto the fish.

7. Place another husk on top of the fish, and tuck into the bottom husk. Make pouch as gap-free as possible. Secure both ends of the packet with the string.

8. Place the packets on the barbecue grill; cook over Medium heat for 10 minutes per inch of thickness. They will poach and steam in the packet, so they must not be turned over.

9. To serve, present fish in the grilled corn husks. Remove 1 knot and pull back the top husk for a nice presentation.

[RICHARD & SANDY HEW, AND THOMPSON,
LAUREN & HARRISON]

Sea Bass in Corn Husks

SEA BASS WITH INDIAN SPICES

Nutrition Facts per serving: Calories 205.1, Protein 15.62 Gm, Carbs 9.974 Gm, Fat 11.49 Gm, Cholesterol 54 mg,
Dietary Fiber 1.32 Gm, Sugar 0.128 Gm, Sodium 100.2 mg, Calcium 88.57 mg, Potassium 690.2 mg, Iron 3.305 mg

SERVES 4

4 skinless Sea Bass fillets
 (about 6 oz. & 1" thick)
Olive oil
Cilantro sprigs (optional)
Lime wedges (optional)

Marinade:
2 Tbsp. extra-virgin olive oil
2 tsp. fresh lemon juice
1 tsp. fresh ginger, grated
½ tsp. garlic, minced
½ tsp. turmeric
½ tsp. chili powder
½ tsp. ground cumin
½ tsp. kosher salt
¼ tsp. freshly ground
 black pepper
¼ tsp. cayenne

1. In a small bowl, whisk together the marinade ingredients.

2. Brush the bass fillets all over with the marinade.

3. Cover with plastic wrap, and refrigerate for at least 30 minutes to 1 hour.

4. Remove the fillets from the marinade, and lightly brush or spray with olive oil.

5. Grill over direct High heat until the flesh is opaque throughout, 5 to 7 minutes, turning once halfway through grilling time.

6. Remove from the grill. Garnish with cilantro sprigs and lime wedges, if desired.

7. Serve with jasmine or white rice.

[KEVIN & LYNE LLOYD, AND JESSICA, MORGAN & RYAN]

CURRIED SHRIMP

Nutrition Facts per serving: Calories 274.2, Protein 11.49 Gm, Carbs 51.31 Gm, Fat 3.159 Gm, Cholesterol 50.74 mg,
Dietary Fiber 6.885 Gm, Sugar 28.72 Gm, Sodium 943.8 mg, Calcium 94.2 mg, Potassium 220.2 mg, Iron 3.174 mg

SERVES 4 TO 6

3 to 4 lbs. shrimp, peeled
 and de-veined
4 tsp. curry powder
1-½ tsp. ground cumin
1-½ lg. onions, finely
 chopped
7 cloves garlic, minced
1 sprig fresh thyme
3 whole scallions, crushed
1 lg. potato, diced into fine cubes
1 to 2 plum tomatoes, diced
1 to 2 cups water, as needed
 (start with 1 cup)
2 tsp. salt, divided
Black pepper, to taste
1 green scotch bonnet,
 chopped and seeded
1 Tbsp. vegetable oil

1. Season shrimp with 1 teaspoon curry powder, 1 teaspoon of the salt and a little black pepper; let sit until ready to cook.

2. Heat vegetable oil in a large frying pan; add chopped onions, and cook down until tender.

3. Add garlic, scotch bonnet, thyme, scallions and tomatoes. Sauté a few minutes; add cumin, the remaining curry, salt and pepper mixed with 1 cup water.

4. Bring to a simmer, and add the potato. Stir, cover and let simmer for a few minutes (more water may be added if it gets too dry).

5. When sauce is to the desired thickness, simmer on Low for about 10 minutes.

6. Remove the scallions and thyme sprig, add shrimp, and continue cooking for 3 to 5 minutes.

7. Serve over white rice, with a green vegetable.

[DAVID & MELANIE KHOURI, AND JESSICA]

SEARED PEPPER-CRUSTED TUNA

Nutrition Facts per serving: Calories 471.8, Protein 52.13 Gm, Carbs 9.097 Gm, Fat 25.71 Gm, Cholesterol 30.8 mg,
Dietary Fiber 8.948 Gm, Sugar 1.567 Gm, Sodium 659.2 mg, Calcium 69.21 mg, Potassium 904.3 mg, Iron 3.509 mg

SERVES 4

4 medium-size tuna steaks
Fresh peppercorns
1 pkg. fresh cherry/grape
   tomatoes, diced
1 lg. cucumber, diced
1 green bell pepper, diced
1 red bell pepper, diced
Bunch of fresh cilantro, chopped
3 to 4 fresh limes
1 ripe avocado, diced (optional)
Olive oil

1. Smother the tuna steaks in lime juice.

2. Fold large dessert spoonful of peppercorns into a paper towel or clean cloth, and crush them with the meat masher/mallet; put to one side.

3. In a medium bowl, combine diced tomatoes, cucumber, peppers and avocado.

4. Squeeze lime juice all over the vegetables; season with salt and pepper.

5. Add chopped cilantro to the vegetable and lime mixture, and combine all together into a salsa.

6. Fire up the hot (flat) plate on the barbecue grill until red hot. Splash on a good dollop of olive oil.

7. Quickly take the fresh tuna and dunk into the crushed peppercorns, coating both sides.

8. With the flat plate smoking hot, throw the tuna steaks on and sear them for a couple of minutes on each side (the trick is to have a great seared outside with a pink, but warm middle).

9. Serve with piping hot Sauté Potatoes (page 127) and the salsa.

[GRAHAM & JANE PECK, AND REBECCA & MICHAEL]

TESTING FISH FOR DONENESS
Insert fork tines into a fish at a 45-degree angle. Twist the fork gently.
If fish resists flaking and is still translucent, it is not done. If it flakes
apart easily and is milky white, it is done. A dry and mealy texture
indicates that the fish is over-cooked.

LOBSTER THERMIDOR

Nutrition Facts per serving: Calories 575.3, Protein 51.63 Gm, Carbs 16.9 Gm, Fat 31.14 Gm, Cholesterol 218.6 mg, Dietary Fiber 0.454 Gm, Sugar 0.993 Gm, Sodium 778.8 mg, Calcium 350.4 mg, Potassium 221.4 mg, Iron 3.451 mg

4 boiled lobster tails
1 Tbsp. butter, for sautéing
4 Tbsp. butter, for white sauce
4 Tbsp. flour
½ cup cream
½ cup half & half
1 cup grated Parmesan cheese
4 Tbsp. sherry
Salt, to taste
1 cup fresh sliced mushrooms
1 Tbsp. chopped chives
Paprika, to sprinkle on top

For a nice presentation, wash and clean the lobster shells, and serve the lobster inside them. About half of a green bell pepper can be sliced and also used in this recipe.

1. Preheat oven to 375°F.
2. In a saucepan, sauté mushrooms and chives in 1 tablespoon butter; remove from pan.
3. Melt 4 tablespoons butter in pan, and stir in flour. Add cream, half & half, salt, mushrooms and chives; heat until thick.
4. Add sherry; taste and adjust seasoning. Remove from heat.
5. Remove meat from tails, and cut into chunks; add to sauce.
6. Place lobster in an oven-proof dish (Pyrex or French). Sprinkle cheese, then paprika on top.
7. Bake in preheated oven for about 20 minutes, or until slightly brown on top.
8. Serve with white rice or potatoes.

[DON & JENNIE STEWART]

FISH FILLETS WITH SPINACH

Nutrition Facts per serving: Calories 344.5, Protein 31.55 Gm, Carbs 9.039 Gm, Fat 19.26 Gm, Cholesterol 122.8 mg, Dietary Fiber 1.985 Gm, Sugar 4.583 Gm, Sodium 1067 mg, Calcium 397.6.4 mg, Potassium 539 mg, Iron 2.398 mg

2 Tbsp. butter
2 Tbsp. all purpose flour
1 tsp. instant chicken bouillon
Dash of nutmeg, cayenne pepper and white pepper
1 cup milk
⅔ cup shredded sharp cheddar
1 (10 oz.) pack frozen chopped spinach, thawed and drained
1 Tbsp. lime juice
1 lb. fish fillets, cut into serving pieces (tilapia or sole)
½ tsp. salt
2 Tbsp. Parmesan cheese
Paprika

1. Heat butter over Low heat, until melted; stir in flour, bouillon, nutmeg and seasonings.
2. Cook over Low heat until smooth and bubbly; add milk, and stir constantly, until thickened. Add cheese.
3. Place spinach in an ungreased dish, sprinkle with lime juice.
4. Arrange fish on spinach, sprinkle with salt; spread sauce over fish and spinach.
5. Bake uncovered at 350°F for 20 to 25 minutes, or until fish flakes easily; sprinkle with Parmesan and paprika (can be prepared early in the day, refrigerated, then heated in oven 40 minutes or 30 minutes, if using sole).

[MICHAEL & JENNIFER GODFREY]

KEDGEREE

Nutrition Facts per serving: Calories 602.2, Protein 37.93 Gm, Carbs 19.27 Gm, Fat 41.16 Gm, Cholesterol 394 mg,
Dietary Fiber 0.309 Gm, Sugar 1.573 Gm, Sodium 1296 mg, Calcium 140 mg, Potassium 642.1 mg, Iron 3.272 mg

1. Preheat oven to 375°F.

2. Poach haddock (or trout) in milk dotted with unsalted butter and a good grind of black pepper in a shallow glass dish in the oven for approximately 20 minutes; let cool.

3. Remove fish, and flake, removing any skin and bones.

4. Fry the onions gently in the butter, and add the curry; stir gently for about 4 minutes.

5. Stir in all the other ingredients; heat through for about 5 minutes.

6. Mound on an oval plate, sprinkle with parsley, and enjoy!

NOTE:

Kedgeree, a favourite recipe of the late Rev. John R. Gray, is a great brunch or supper dish.
For those who like a little heat, finely chopped scotch bonnet pepper can be added, as well as
Scotch Bonnet Pickled Pepper Sauce (page 201).

[TONY & MARY MELLIN, AND A. J. MCKENZIE]

SERVES 4

1 lb. smoked haddock
   or smoked trout
Milk, to poach
2 ozs. unsalted butter
1 sm. onion, finely chopped
8 ozs. long grain rice, cooked
4 hardboiled eggs, chopped
1 tsp. curry powder
Parsley (or scallions), finely
   chopped, to taste
2 Tbsp. lemon juice, or to taste
4 to 6 ozs. butter
Black pepper, to taste

Kedgeree

LUXURY FISH PIE

Nutrition Facts per serving: Calories 795.5, Protein 44.75 Gm, Carbs 61.58 Gm, Fat 41.44 Gm, Cholesterol 280.9 mg, Dietary Fiber 3.454 Gm, Sugar 8.343 Gm, Sodium 798.9 mg, Calcium 247.8 mg, Potassium 1693 mg, Iron 2.529 mg

SERVES 4 TO 6

2 lbs. cod or haddock
20 ozs. milk
2-½ ozs. all purpose flour
½ lb. shrimp (not too lg.),
    cooked, peeled and de-veined
3 hard-boiled eggs, roughly
    chopped
1-½ Tbsp. capers (small ones
    are best)
3 Tbsp. parsley, finely chopped
2 Tbsp. lemon juice, or to taste
4 to 6 ozs. butter
Salt and freshly ground
    black pepper, to taste

Topping:
3 lbs. potatoes, boiled
1-½ ozs. butter
1 (8 oz.) container sour cream

1. Preheat oven to 400°F.
2. Arrange fish in a glass baking dish, and season with salt and pepper.
3. Pour ½ the milk over the fish, and dot with about 2 ounces of butter.
4. Bake for about 15 to 20 minutes; drain off liquid, and reserve.
5. Remove fish, and flake in fairly large pieces, removing any skin and bones.
6. Make a sauce by melting the remaining butter, stirring in the flour and gradually adding the combined remaining milk and reserved liquid, seasoning to taste with salt and pepper.
7. Mix in the fish, shrimp, eggs, capers, parsley and lemon juice. Adjust seasonings.
8. Pour into a buttered casserole dish.

Topping:
1. Mash the potatoes, and combine with butter and sour cream.
2. Cover the fish mixture with the mashed potato.
3. Bake at 400°F for about 30 minutes, until browned.

[TONY & MARY MELLIN, AND A.J. MCKENZIE]

EASY COCONUT SHRIMP

Nutrition Facts per serving: Calories 140.7, Protein 10.11 Gm, Carbs 14.62 Gm, Fat 4.346 Gm, Cholesterol 97.43 mg, Dietary Fiber 0.778 Gm, Sugar 4.376 Gm, Sodium 283.1 mg, Calcium 35.54 mg, Potassium 123.1 mg, Iron 1.68 mg

SERVES 5

Approximately 25 cooked
    jumbo shrimp, peeled
    and de-veined
1 cup pkgd. grated
    coconut flakes
1 cup flour
2 tsp. sugar
1 tsp. salt
Oil, for frying

Egg wash:
2 eggs, beaten
    combined with
    ¼ cup milk

1. In a skillet, heat oil over Medium heat.
2. In a shallow bowl, combine flour, sugar and salt. Place coconut flakes in another shallow bowl, and the egg wash in a third shallow bowl.
3. Dip each shrimp first in the flour mixture, shaking off the excess, then in the egg wash, then finally in the coconut.
4. Cook shrimp until golden brown, about 1 minute per side. Drain on paper towels. Serve with a sweet and spicy sauce, like Jack's Jezebel Sauce (page 195).

[LESLIE METCALF]

PRAWNS IN GINGER SAUCE

Nutrition Facts per serving: Calories 205.3, Protein 21.31 Gm, Carbs 7.085 Gm, Fat 10.26 Gm, Cholesterol 220.4 mg,
Dietary Fiber 0.346 Gm, Sugar 0.155 Gm, Sodium 1181 mg, Calcium 95.29 mg, Potassium 354.3, Iron 2.226 mg

1. Peel the prawns, and discard the shells.

2. Pat the prawns dry with kitchen paper, and combine them with the salt, corn flour and 1 teaspoon sesame oil.

3. Heat a wok or large frying pan; add the oil, prawns and ginger.

4. Stir fry for 30 seconds.

5. Add the sauce ingredients; continue to cook for 2 minutes.

6. Serve at once.

[RICHARD & MEELIN VERNON, AND ELLIOT, LAUREN & YASMIN]

SERVES 4

1 lb. fresh uncooked prawns
3 Tbsp. fresh ginger,
 finely chopped
Fresh coriander (to garnish)
1 tsp. salt
1 tsp. corn flour
1 tsp. sesame oil
1-½ Tbsp. groundnut or
 peanut oil

Sauce:
2 Tbsp. chinese rice wine
 or dry sherry
1 Tbsp. light soy sauce
1 Tbsp. water
½ tsp. salt
1 tsp. sugar
2 Tbsp. finely chopped coriander
2 Tbsp. sesame oil

Quick Thai Supper (Photo kindly submitted by Fiona Pimentel)

QUICK THAI SUPPER

Nutrition Facts per serving: Calories 257.5, Protein 40.71 Gm, Carbs 7.144 Gm, Fat 7.7 Gm, Cholesterol 440.8 mg,
Dietary Fiber 1.35 Gm, Sugar 1.369 Gm, Sodium 1070 mg, Calcium 155 mg, Potassium 564.1, Iron 2.917 mg

1. Marinate prawns for 15 minutes in the soy sauce, Five Spice, ginger and garlic.

2. In the sesame oil over Medium heat, stir-fry the peppers and onion with the prawns for 5 minutes.

3. Garnish with coriander, and serve with Jasmine rice or oriental noodles.

[CARLOS & FIONA PIMENTEL, AND EDWARD, ANNA, AMELIA & JAMIE]

SERVES 4 TO 5

1 to 2 lbs. king prawns
1 green bell pepper, chopped
2 cloves garlic, finely chopped
1 sm. onion, chopped
1 piece fresh ginger,
 finely chopped
1 Tbsp. finely chopped fresh
 coriander (cilantro), to garnish
Approx. ½ cup soy sauce
¼ tsp. Five Spice powder
Sesame oil

MIXED GRILL OF SHRIMP, SAUSAGE AND MUSHROOMS

Nutrition Facts per serving: Calories 329.1, Protein 19.66 Gm, Carbs 11.47 Gm, Fat 23.28 Gm, Cholesterol 80.77 mg, Dietary Fiber 1.072 Gm, Sugar 3.807 Gm, Sodium 780.5 mg, Calcium 36.62 mg, Potassium 249.9 mg, Iron 2.305 mg

SERVES 6 TO 8

¾ cup olive oil
2 Tbsp. (packed) fresh
   thyme leaves, or
   1 Tbsp. dried
2 lg. cloves garlic, minced
½ tsp. dried crushed
   red pepper
32 lg. uncooked shrimp,
   peeled and de-veined
32 button mushrooms,
   stems trimmed
6 to 8 skewers
1-½ lbs. andouille sausage,
   or other spicy smoked fully
   cooked sausage, cut into
   ¾"-thick rounds

1. Blend olive oil, thyme, minced garlic and crushed red pepper in processor for 1 minute.

2. Pour mixture into large bowl; add shrimp, and let stand for 1 hour at room temperature.

3. Remove shrimp from marinade; reserve marinade.

4. Thread 1 mushroom horizontally on 1 skewer. Hold 1 andouille piece in curve of 1 shrimp; thread together on skewer, sliding next to mushroom.

5. Repeat, alternating a total of 4 to 5 mushrooms, 4 to 5 shrimp and 4 to 5 andouille pieces on each skewer (can be prepared one day ahead, covered and chilled until ready to cook).

6. Prepare the barbecue grill (Medium-High heat).

7. Bring reserved marinade to a boil in a small heavy saucepan.

8. Arrange skewers on grill; brush with marinade.

9. Grill until shrimp are cooked through, turning occasionally, and basting with marinade (about 8 minutes).

10. Transfer to plates, and serve.

[LARRY & SHELLEY LEONARD, AND ALEX & NICHOLAS]

Mixed Grill of Shrimp, Sausage and Mushrooms

COCONUT TUNA TARTARE WITH AVOCADO MOUSSE

Nutrition Facts per serving: Calories 224.3, Protein 17.67 Gm, Carbs 3.716 Gm, Fat 16.56 Gm, Cholesterol 17.01 mg, Dietary Fiber 7.313 Gm, Sugar 1.105 Gm, Sodium 364 mg, Calcium 42.78 mg, Potassium 542.2 mg, Iron 1.733 mg

SERVES 8

1 lb. sushi grade tuna, cut into ¼" dice
5 Tbsp. grated coconut, toasted
1 tsp. soy sauce
2 Tbsp. fresh lime juice
1 tsp. rice wine vinegar
4 Tbsp. toasted almond slivers, chopped
4 Tbsp. currants
1 Tbsp. vegetable oil
1 tsp. minced fresh ginger
½ tsp. minced garlic
½ tsp. sesame oil
2 ripe avocados
⅛ tsp. cayenne pepper
¼ tsp. ground cumin
⅛ tsp. paprika
1 Tbsp. olive oil
Salt and freshly ground black pepper, to taste

1. In a medium stainless mixing bowl, combine the diced tuna, coconut, soy sauce, 1 tablespoon of the lime juice, rice wine vinegar, almonds, currants, vegetable oil, ginger, garlic and sesame oil.

2. Toss well, and season with salt and pepper; cover and refrigerate until ready to serve.

3. Peel and halve the avocados and remove the pits. Give them a rough chop, and place them in a small stainless mixing bowl.

4. Add the remaining lime juice, cayenne, cumin, paprika and olive oil.

5. Mash the seasoned avocado with a sturdy whisk until creamy in texture; season with salt and pepper.

6. Divide the avocado mixture equally into the bottom of 8 martini glasses.

7. Separate the tuna into 8 equal portions, and spoon on top of the avocado.

[LINDA DALTON-RILEY & DARREN RILEY,
AND BRITTANY & SYDNEY RILEY]

CAYMAN TURTLE STEW

Nutrition Facts per serving: Calories 382.3, Protein 76.2 Gm, Carbs 11.22 Gm, Fat 2.185 Gm, Cholesterol 189 mg, Dietary Fiber 2.781 Gm, Sugar 3.87 Gm, Sodium 991.3 mg, Calcium 468.3 mg, Potassium 1152 mg, Iron 6.045 mg

SERVES 6 TO 10

5 lbs. turtle meat
2 med. onions, chopped
12 seasoning peppers,
    seeded and diced
1 scotch bonnet pepper,
    seeded and diced
2 tsp. salt, garlic salt or Season All
    (or any combination of these)
2 tsp. black pepper
Vinegar

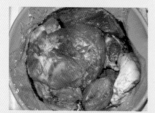

Turtle meat

Turtle, with seasoning

Turtle Stew

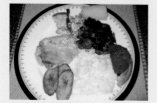

Turtle Stew, dished

1. Place the turtle fin into a large pot of boiling water; let it soak for a few minutes. Remove the fin, allow it to cool slightly, and then remove all of the outer shell with a knife. If the fin does not peel easily, soak it again in the hot water.

2. Wash the turtle fin, turtle meat, turtle bone and liver in water and vinegar; drain.

3. Cut the meat and fin into bite-size chunks. If using the liver, it must be cooked when it is fresh (and not after it has been frozen for any length of time). The membrane covering the liver should be removed and the liver can then be cut into chunks, or it can be added to the stew as a whole piece so that it is easier to separate at the end of cooking and served only to those who have a preference for it.

4. Place the turtle parts into a large heavy pot; season with dry seasonings, onions and peppers. Fry over Medium-High heat until bubbly and the stew yields water.

5. Reduce heat to Low, and simmer covered for at least 2 hours (do not add water).

6. About 30 minutes before the end of cooking, slide the pot cover to one side to allow the stew to darken.

7. Serve hot with white rice, boiled breadfruit or cassava and Fried Plantain (pg. 118).

[SHELLY MILLER-SMITH, AND CHELSEA & AMY SMITH]

NOTE:

Turtle Stew is a national dish of the Cayman Islands. Turtles were at one time very plentiful in our waters and therefore provided an easy and available source of food for the Caymanian people. Since those early days, most of our food is now imported from other countries but Caymanians still enjoy the old tradition of eating turtle meat which is farmed locally at the world's only Turtle Farm. The recipes for Turtle Stew differ from family to family. Some like to add water whilst others do not. Some like to add more lean meat to the stew and prefer not to add the liver (which can give the stew a stronger, more distinct flavour). Turtle Stew is not an easy recipe to put into writing, but with a great deal of effort, Shelly Miller-Smith has assisted us enormously in our attempt to do so. With a certain amount of intuition (which seems to be embedded in the Caymanian-born cooks), one CAN get it right!

Photos kindly submitted by Shelly Miller-Smith

BAKED CAYMAN CRAB

Nutrition Facts per serving: Calories 167.6, Protein 24.7 Gm, Carbs 5.025 Gm, Fat 4.828 Gm, Cholesterol 139.2 mg,
Dietary Fiber 0.489 Gm, Sugar 0.778 Gm, Sodium 721.4 mg, Calcium 66.29 mg, Potassium 202.4 mg, Iron 1.362 mg

SERVES 8 TO 10

3 lbs. local Cayman crab
  (picked and pre-cooked
  on purchase)
1 med. onion
1 green bell pepper
6 seasoning peppers, seeded
1 scotch bonnet pepper,
  seeded
2 slices white bread
2 Tbsp. squeezable margarine
4 Tbsp. stick butter
  or margarine cut into several
  small squares
Salt and pepper, to taste
8 slices bacon
Bread crumbs, for topping

1. Preheat oven to 350°F.

2. In a food processor, chop onion, bell pepper, scotch bonnet and seasoning peppers.

3. Place crab in a large bowl, and mix in chopped seasoning; add salt and pepper and squeezable margarine, and mix thoroughly.

4. Break 2 slices of bread, and mix in with the crab mixture (bread gives it body).

5. In a baking dish, place 4 slices of raw bacon, put crab on top of bacon, then 4 more slices of bacon. Top with bread crumbs.

6. Dot the surface evenly with the butter.

7. Bake in preheated oven covered for 30 to 45 minutes, then uncover for about 15 minutes. Keep in mind that the crab is pre-cooked, so you are just baking it to allow the seasonings to soak in. Over-cooking the crab would dry it out.

8. Serve with mashed potato or white rice, rolls, bread kind and plantain. A nice drink to serve with this dish would be Lemonade or Cayman Limeade (page 53).

[DEAN & JENNIFER SCOTT, AND LAUREN, HANNAH & JONATHAN]

Braised Pork Loin with Port and Prunes (page 171)

MEATS

BEEF

PORK

LAMB

STEAK DIANNE

Nutrition Facts per serving: Calories 1452, Protein 83.12 Gm, Carbs 57.09 Gm, Fat 98.64 Gm, Cholesterol 336.9 mg, Dietary Fiber 2.211 Gm, Sugar 44.59 Gm, Sodium 1162 mg, Calcium 134.6 mg, Potassium 2404 mg, Iron 9.907 mg

1 (12 oz.) Top Sirloin steak
2 tsp. lemon pepper
1 tsp. fresh parsley, chopped
2 Tbsp. olive oil
6 ozs. sliced fresh mushrooms
2 Tbsp. chopped shallots
2 Tbsp. brandy
½ cup whipping cream
2 tsp. Worcestershire sauce

1. Heat 1 tablespoon olive oil in a skillet over Medium heat. Add mushrooms and shallots; cook for 3 minutes, remove and set aside.

2. Season Top Sirloin with lemon pepper.

3. Heat 1 tablespoon olive oil in a skillet over Medium heat. Add the steak, and cook 8 to 12 minutes, turning occasionally, for medium rare to medium doneness.

4. Remove the steak, and keep warm.

5. Add brandy to the skillet, and deglaze.

6. Stir in the cream and Worcestershire sauce. Add mushroom mixture, and cook. Check for thickness, and adjust seasonings.

7. Add steak, turning to coat with the sauce for 30 seconds.

8. Pour desired amount of remaining sauce over steak; sprinkle with parsley and serve.

[COPPER FALLS STEAKHOUSE]
- SEE ADVERTISEMENT ON PAGE 249 -

Photo kindly submitted by Copper Falls Steakhouse

Steak Dianne

BOBOTIE

Nutrition Facts per serving: Calories 430.5, Protein 63.11 Gm, Carbs 10.71 Gm, Fat 15.12 Gm, Cholesterol 117.2 mg,
Dietary Fiber 0.839 Gm, Sugar 1.972 Gm, Sodium 555.6 mg, Calcium 95.61 mg, Potassium 566.1 mg, Iron 2.42 mg

SERVES 8

1 lb. minced (ground) beef
2 thick slices white bread
1 cup milk
1 Tbsp. butter
3 onions, chopped
2 bay leaves
4 Tbsp. parsley, chopped
2 Tbsp. curry powder (or paste)
1 tsp. sugar
Salt, to taste
Juice from 1 lemon
3 eggs
1 cup beef stock

1. Preheat oven to 350°F.

2. Soak the bread in some of the milk. Squeeze until dry, retaining the milk.

3. In a large saucepan, fry the chopped onions in butter; add curry and fry another minute.

4. Add the meat, sugar, salt and lemon juice.

5. Beat the eggs.

6. Mixing in 1 spoonful at a time, add half the eggs to the meat mixture.

7. Whisk the other half of the eggs into the milk.

8. Mix the soaked bread into the meat mixture thoroughly; add stock.

9. Spread the meat mixture into a buttered oven-proof dish.

10. Pour the egg mixture over meat mixture, and add 2 bay leaves.

11. Cook uncovered in preheated oven for 30 to 40 minutes, or until set.

12. Remove from oven, and decorate with chopped parsley.

13. Serve with yellow rice.

[ROBIN & LANA JARVIS, AND ANDREW & AARON]

Bobotie is a favourite recipe of the Jarvis family and can be cooked many ways. Andrew and Aaron Jarvis' paternal grandmother cooked this dish for their father when he was growing up in South Africa. It is a very popular dish there.

TIPS FOR COOKING PORK:
Roast meat at a constant 325°F oven temperature.
Most 5 to 8 lb. Shoulder Picnic Roasts should be cooked approximately 3 to 4 hours.
3 to 5 lb. Shoulder Arm and Boneless Shoulder Blade Boston Roasts should cook for about 2 to 3 hours.
4 to 6 lb. Rib Crown Roasts should cook for 2-3/4 to 3-1/2 hours.
3 to 4 lb. Loin Blade Roasts should cook for 2-1/4 to 2-3/4 hours.
3 to 5 lb. Loin Centre Loin and Loin Centre Rib Roasts should cook for 1-3/4 to 2-1/2 hours.
2 to 4 lb. Boneless Loin Top Loin Roasts (double) should cook for 1-1/4 to 2 hours.
2 to 4 lb. Smoked Shoulder Roll and Boneless Loin Top Loin Roasts should cook 1-1/4 to 2 hours.
A 12 to 16 lb. Leg (fresh ham) should cook for 5 to 6 hours.
Half a leg (about 5 to 8 lbs.) should cook
3-1/4 to 4-3/4 hours.

EASY SWISS PORK

Nutrition Facts per serving: Calories 209.5, Protein 19.49 Gm, Carbs 1.174 Gm, Fat 13.79 Gm, Cholesterol 78.91 mg, Dietary Fiber 0.029 Gm, Sugar 0.702 Gm, Sodium 283.6 mg, Calcium 177.6 mg, Potassium 281 mg, Iron 1.031 mg

SERVES 8 TO 10

1-½ lbs. pork tenderloin
(cut into 1" medallions)
2 med. onions,
finely chopped
4 ozs. grated Parmesan cheese
½ pint double cream
About 1 oz. butter
Salt and freshly ground
black pepper, to taste

1. Preheat oven to 400°F (or gas mark 6).

2. Season the meat with salt and pepper.

3. Lightly butter a deep 3 pint oven-proof dish.

4. Arrange layers of meat, finely chopped onions and Parmesan cheese (2 layers - meat, onion, cheese, meat, onion, cheese.)

5. Bake in the preheated oven for 50 minutes.

6. Add the double cream; bake for a further 15 minutes, until golden brown.

7. Serve with rice and a fresh green salad.

[CHRIS & OLIVIA SUTTON, AND LAURENCE & TOBY]

SMOKY BARBECUE RIBS
IN A SLOW COOKER

Nutrition Facts per serving: Calories 1037, Protein 51.51 Gm, Carbs 17.89 Gm, Fat 82.45 Gm, Cholesterol 185.3 mg, Dietary Fiber 0.236 Gm, Sugar 2.053 Gm, Sodium 595.6 mg, Calcium 42.77 mg, Potassium 1001 mg, Iron 3.807 mg

SERVES 6

2 Tbsp. balsamic vinegar
1 Tbsp. Dijon-style mustard
1 Tbsp. Worcestershire sauce
2 Tbsp. brown sugar
1 Tbsp. soy sauce
¼ tsp. crumbled dry red
pepper flakes
1 tsp. fresh grated ginger root
½ tsp. Liquid Smoke
1 cup chili sauce (mild, not hot)
¼ cup chopped scallions
4 lbs. spare ribs cut into
individual ribs

This recipe belongs to Daniel and Caitlyn Harrington's "Granny," Sara Jane Meisner, of Ottawa, Canada

1. In a medium bowl, combine all the ingredients except the ribs.

2. Dip each rib in the sauce, or brush sauce on both sides of the ribs.

3. Place the coated ribs in a Slow Cooker; pour remaining sauce over the ribs.

4. Cover, and cook on Low for 5 to 6 hours, or until the meat is tender.

5. Remove the ribs from the sauce; keep warm.

6. Pour the sauce into a medium saucepan. Skim the fat off the top.

7. Mix 2 tablespoons cornstarch in ½ cup cold water; add to sauce slowly, and bring to a boil.

8. Cook on Medium heat until the sauce is thickened (add more cornstarch, if necessary).

9. Serve the sauce in a gravy boat with the ribs and white rice.

[SEAN & LIZ HARRINGTON, AND DANIEL & CAITLYN]

MEATBALLS WITH GRAVY

Nutrition Facts per serving: Calories 295.9, Protein 18.1 Gm, Carbs 15.07 Gm, Fat 18.2 Gm, Cholesterol 113.3 mg,
Dietary Fiber 1.185 Gm, Sugar 2.04 Gm, Sodium 631 mg, Calcium 54.48 mg, Potassium 505.1 mg, Iron 2.908 mg

SERVES 4 TO 6

1 lb. ground beef
2 eggs, beaten
1 onion, chopped (divided in 2)
¼ tsp. finely chopped scotch
   bonnet pepper (optional)
2 Tbsp. finely chopped celery
½ tsp. dried thyme
½ tsp. garlic powder
1 tsp. Season All
½ tsp. salt
¼ tsp. black pepper
½ cup bread crumbs
1 stalk celery, coarsely chopped
1 whole scotch bonnet pepper
¼ green bell pepper,
   coarsely chopped
1 (8 oz.) can tomato sauce
¼ cup ketchup
1 Tbsp. sugar
1-½ cups water
2 Tbsp. vegetable oil

1. In a large mixing bowl, season the ground beef with thyme, garlic powder, Season All, salt and pepper.

2. Add finely chopped scotch bonnet pepper, finely chopped celery, ½ of the onion and beaten eggs. Add bread crumbs, and mix thoroughly.

3. Form the meat into approximately 2" balls.

4. In a large saucepan over Medium-High heat, brown the meatballs in the oil 4 to 5 minutes, turning occasionally to brown all around; remove from oil, and set aside. Discard oil.

5. Add the remainder of the onion, coarsely chopped celery, bell pepper, whole scotch bonnet pepper and a dash of salt. Add water, and bring to a boil.

6. Stir in tomato sauce, ketchup and sugar, reduce heat, and simmer 2 to 3 minutes.

7. Add meatballs; simmer 15 minutes. Remove scotch bonnet pepper.

8. Serve over white rice or mashed potato, with a green vegetable.

NOTE:

As a healthy alternative, the meatballs can be placed on a baking sheet, and baked at 375°F for 30 minutes, and turned over after 15 minutes to brown both sides.

Meatballs and Gravy

BEEF WITH STAR ANISE

Nutrition Facts per serving: Calories 444.3, Protein 48.16 Gm, Carbs 10.66 Gm, Fat 22.28 Gm, Cholesterol 130.4 mg,
Dietary Fiber 1.226 Gm, Sugar 0.23 Gm, Sodium 660.6 mg, Calcium 36.24 mg, Potassium 645.7 mg, Iron 6.27 mg

SERVES 4 TO 6

2 lbs. braising or beef chuck steak, cut into 1" cubes
2 lg. onions, chopped
2 heaping Tbsp. brown sugar
2 Tbsp. sunflower oil or olive oil
2 Tbsp. soy sauce
½ tsp. garlic salt
2 cloves garlic, crushed
1 (10-¾ oz.) can tomato puree
1-½ cups of water
1 beef bouillon cube
2 star anise pods

TIP:
Star Anise are somewhat large star-shaped pods that can be found bottled in the dry spice section of the supermarket.

1. Prepare ingredients.
2. Preheat oven to 375°F.
3. Heat oil in a large frying pan over Medium-High heat, and sauté crushed garlic and onion for a few minutes.
4. Add meat to the frying pan, and garlic salt. Brown the meat on both sides.
5. Transfer meat, onions and garlic to a covered oven-proof casserole dish.
6. To the residue in the frying pan, add the remaining ingredients except the star anise pods. Stir frequently and bring to a boil. Pour this over the meat mixture.
7. Place the star anise pods on top.
8. Cover with lid, and cook in preheated oven for 1 to 1-½ hours.
9. Discard the star anise pods at the end of cooking.
10. Serve with new potatoes, egg noodles, or rice and green vegetables.

[CLYDE & HELEN ALLEN, AND JAMES & CHARLES]

BURGER PATTIES

Nutrition Facts per serving: Calories 149.7, Protein 16.15 Gm, Carbs 2.797 Gm, Fat 7.703 Gm, Cholesterol 58.07 mg,
Dietary Fiber 0.084 Gm, Sugar 0 Gm, Sodium 327.4 mg, Calcium 23.97 mg, Potassium 175.7 mg, Iron 1.417 mg

SERVES 6 TO 8

1 lb. minced turkey, or minced beef
¼ tsp. allspice, ground
¼ tsp. bay leaf, ground
¼ tsp. savory
½ tsp. basil leaves
½ tsp. black pepper, ground
½ tsp. garlic powder
½ tsp. onion powder
½ tsp. tarragon
½ tsp. dried thyme
1 tsp. rubbed sage
1 tsp. salt (or salt substitute)
⅓ cup Quick Oats (as used for oatmeal)

1. Preheat oven to 350°F.
2. In a mixing bowl, thoroughly combine all ingredients. Divide into 8 equal portions.
3. Using an ice cream scoop (or similar), fill each scoop with meat mixture and turn out onto a sheet of waxed paper; flatten to about ³/₈" thick.
4. Place patties on an open rack (trivet) on a baking sheet or oven-proof dish (so that the fat can drain away).
5. Bake for 20 minutes (do not over-cook, as they will become dry).
6. Serve at once. These can be refrigerated or frozen for later use. Frozen patties can be quickly re-heated in a microwave oven but be careful not to over-heat, or they become tough.

[DAVID R. MYERS, AND GABRIELLE]

BRAISED PORK LOIN WITH PORT AND PRUNES

Nutrition Facts per serving: Calories 582.9, Protein 52.99 Gm, Carbs 18.6 Gm, Fat 30.2 Gm, Cholesterol 176 mg, Dietary Fiber 2.877 Gm, Sugar 9.722 Gm, Sodium 450.6 mg, Calcium 62.31 mg, Potassium 1093 mg, Iron 3.044 mg

SERVES 8

Spice rub:
1-½ tsp. black pepper
1 tsp. salt
1 tsp. dry mustard
1 tsp. dried sage
½ tsp. dried thyme
1 (3-¼ pound) boneless
   pork loin roast

Remaining ingredients:
1 Tbsp. olive oil
2 cups sliced onion
1 cup finely chopped leek
1 cup finely chopped carrot
1 cup port or other sweet
   red wine
¾ cup fat-free, less sodium
   chicken broth
1 cup pitted prunes (about
   20 prunes)
2 bay leaves

1. Preheat the oven to 325°F.

2. To prepare the spice rub, combine first 5 ingredients.

3. Trim the fat from the pork, and rub surface of roast with spice rub; secure with string, if necessary.

4. Heat the oil in a large Dutch oven over Medium-High heat. Add pork, cook for 8 minutes, browning on all sides. Remove pork from pan.

5. Add onion, leek and carrot; cover, reduce heat, and cook for 5 minutes, stirring frequently.

6. Stir in the wine and broth, scraping the pan to loosen browned bits.

7. Return pork to pan, and add prunes and bay leaves; bring to a boil.

8. Cover, and bake for 1-½ hours, or until pork is tender; discard bay leaves.

9. Place pork on a platter, cover with foil.

10. Remove 6 prunes with a slotted spoon; place prunes in a food processor or blender, and process, until smooth.

11. Stir pureed prunes into port mixture.

12. Serve sauce over pork, with white rice or potato, and vegetables.

[LINDA DALTON-RILEY & DARREN RILEY,
AND BRITTANY & SYDNEY]

HAM & RED GRAVY

Nutrition Facts per serving: Calories 234.4, Protein 11.49 Gm, Carbs 12.99 Gm, Fat 16.19 Gm, Cholesterol 27.26 mg, Dietary Fiber 1.507 Gm, Sugar 2.37 Gm, Sodium 720.6 mg, Calcium 16.56 mg, Potassium 189.1 mg, Iron 1.577 mg

SERVES 4

½ lb. leftover ham, thinly sliced
    or pre-cooked sliced ham
1 sm. onion, sliced
½ green bell pepper, chopped
¼ cup flour, for dredging
¼ tsp. garlic powder
½ tsp. black pepper
1 ripe tomato, diced
1 cup water
½ tsp. flour
1 tsp. cornstarch
3 to 4 Tbsp. ketchup, or
    more to taste
3 to 4 Tbsp. vegetable oil,
    for browning the ham

1. Season the ham with garlic powder and black pepper.

2. Very slightly dredge the ham in flour.

3. In a frying pan over Medium-High heat, starting with about 1 tablespoon of oil and adding more when necessary, brown the ham in batches; remove from pan.

4. Sauté the onion, bell pepper and tomato in pan drippings until onions are translucent (add a little water, if necessary).   Lower heat to Medium.

5. Combine 1 cup water with flour and cornstarch; add to pan and cook over Medium heat for about 5 minutes, or until thickened.   Stir in ketchup.

6. Place ham back in the frying pan with the gravy, and cook for about 2 minutes or until heated through.   Add water to thin the sauce, and more ketchup, if desired.

7. Serve with white rice and Fried Plantain (page 118).

[DERVYN & HIO SCOTT]

BASIC OVEN MEATBALLS

Nutrition Facts per serving: Calories 609.17, Protein 48.46 Gm, Carbs 14.44 Gm, Fat 38.51 Gm, Cholesterol 237.5 mg, Dietary Fiber 0.836 Gm, Sugar 2.7 Gm, Sodium 463.5 mg, Calcium 96.7 mg, Potassium 765.16 mg, Iron 5.46 mg

MAKES 6 DOZEN

3 eggs, beaten
¾ cup milk
3 cups soft bread crumbs
    (4-½ slices bread)
½ cup finely chopped onion
1 tsp. salt and seasoned pepper
3 lbs. ground sirloin

1. Preheat oven to 375°F.

2. In a large mixing bowl, combine beaten eggs, milk, bread crumbs, chopped onion, salt and seasoned pepper; add meat, and mix well.

3. Shape into 6 dozen 1" balls.

4. Bake meatballs in two baking pans in preheated oven for 25 minutes. Turn over halfway through the cooking time to brown both sides.

5. Remove from pans; cool. Use desired amount of meatballs to make Stroganoff Meatballs (see page 181) and freeze the remaining meatballs for later use.

[BILLY & LOLLI REID]

ENGLISH SHEPHERD'S PIE

Nutrition Facts per serving: Calories 474.7, Protein 26.22 Gm, Carbs 35.92 Gm, Fat 25.27 Gm, Cholesterol 81.93 mg,
Dietary Fiber 3.563 Gm, Sugar 1.033 Gm, Sodium 857.9 mg, Calcium 274.6 mg, Potassium 1154 mg, Iron 3.297 mg

SERVES 6 TO 8

5 lg. potatoes, cut into chunks
Salt and pepper, to taste
2 Tbsp. butter or margarine
A little milk
1 lb. lean ground beef
1 lg. tomato, chopped
6 mushrooms, sliced
2 Tbsp. chopped parsley
1 Tbsp. tomato paste
Worcestershire sauce
1 cup brown gravy
   (recipe page 200)
1 (10 oz.) pkg. frozen
   mixed vegetables
1 cup grated cheddar cheese

1. Cook potatoes in boiling water to cover for 30 minutes, or until tender; drain.

2. Mash potatoes with a potato masher. Stir in enough milk and melted butter to make mixture light and fluffy; season to taste with salt and pepper.

3. Preheat oven to 400°F.

4. Sauté beef until browned, stirring often to break up any lumps. Season with salt and pepper.

5. Add tomatoes, parsley, mushrooms, tomato paste, Worcestershire sauce and gravy; stir to mix.

6. Add mixed vegetables, and cook for about 5 minutes.

7. Line the bottom of a buttered baking dish with a layer of mashed potato. Add the meat mixture, then cover with the remaining mashed potato.

8. Sprinkle top with grated cheese.

9. In the preheated oven, bake for about 30 minutes, or until the potato topping is browned and the Shepherd's Pie is thoroughly heated through.

10. Serve immediately.

[BRIAN & DOROTHY WILSON, AND JERROD & BRIANNA]

SWISS STEAK

Nutrition Facts per serving: Calories 422.6, Protein 45.83 Gm, Carbs 10.17 Gm, Fat 20.93 Gm, Cholesterol 102.3 mg,
Dietary Fiber 1.697 Gm, Sugar 4.409 Gm, Sodium 532.3 mg, Calcium 33.83 mg, Potassium 1264 mg, Iron 6.656 mg

SERVES 4 TO 6

8 slices bacon
¼ cup bacon drippings
2 lbs. ½"-thick beef round
    steak or beef tenderloin
    (sliced into about 8 pcs.)
½ cup dry white wine
2 cups fresh mushrooms, sliced
4 fresh tomatoes, cut into wedges
½ cup chopped shallots
2 tsp. dried leaf tarragon
¼ cup snipped parsley
½ tsp. salt
½ to 1 tsp. black pepper
1 tsp. Season All

1. Preheat oven to 325°F.

2. Rub salt, pepper and Season All into the beef.

3. In a large oven-proof skillet, cook bacon over Medium-High heat for 8 to 9 minutes, or until crisp, turning once. Drain on paper towels.

4. Reserve ¼ cup bacon drippings. Crumble bacon, and set aside.

5. Cut meat into serving pieces. Slash off fat edges.

6. Cook meat in reserved drippings over Medium heat for 20 to 25 minutes, or until lightly browned, turning once. Do not drain.

7. Pour wine over meat. Top with mushrooms, tomatoes and shallots; sprinkle with tarragon.

8. Cover and bake in preheated oven for 1-¾ to 2 hours, or until tender.

9. Spoon pan juices over meat and vegetables once or twice during cooking.

10. Top with crumbled bacon and snipped parsley.

11. Serve with pan juices over fettucini.

[GREGORY & TERRI MERREN, AND JOSH & ZACHARY]

INDONESIAN COCONUT BEEF

Nutrition Facts per serving: Calories 310.6, Protein 12.5 Gm, Carbs 22.72 Gm, Fat 19.92 Gm, Cholesterol 16.36 mg,
Dietary Fiber 5.419 Gm, Sugar 1.529 Gm, Sodium 914.3 mg, Calcium 103.1 mg, Potassium 495.3 mg, Iron 2.027 mg

SERVES 4

1-½ lbs. boneless sirloin
    steak, trimmed
3 Tbsp. corn oil
1 lg. spanish (red) onion, sliced
1 clove garlic, crushed
1 tsp. ground ginger
1 tsp. ground cumin
1 tsp. ground coriander
1 tsp. chili powder
⅔ cup shredded coconut
2 tsp. light brown sugar
1 Tbsp. lemon juice
1-¼ cup beef stock
1-½ chopped small red hot
    pepper (optional)

1. Cut steak into ½"-thick strips.

2. Heat oil in saucepan; add onion slices and garlic. Fry, stirring, until brown.

3. Add beef, and fry, stirring, until brown.

4. Add spices to beef, and cook 2 minutes.

5. Add shredded coconut, brown sugar, lemon juice and beef stock; stir well.

6. Simmer gently, uncovered, for 35 to 45 minutes, stirring occasionally (more towards the end as the liquid starts to thicken and dry). Add water during the cooking process, if necessary.

7. Garnish with slivers of bell pepper, green chiles and small slices of onion, if desired.

[RAY & JACQUI FARRINGTON, AND KYLE]

LEG OF LAMB WITH BUTTER AND HERBS

Nutrition Facts per serving: Calories 913.57, Protein 56.14 Gm, Carbs 6.12 Gm, Fat 72.37 Gm, Cholesterol 242.57 mg, Dietary Fiber 0.290 Gm, Sugar 4.33 Gm, Sodium 756.71 mg, Calcium 64.12 mg, Potassium 835.29 mg, Iron 6.07 mg

1. Preheat oven to 375°F.

2. In a mixing bowl, mix together the chopped herbs, butter and garlic.

3. Add salt and black pepper; mix well.

4. Cut small holes in the leg in several places with a skewer, and rub the herb butter all over the meat (this will allow the butter to run into the lamb leg during cooking).

5. Wrap the leg loosely in aluminum foil, allowing a bit of space to let air circulate, then fold the edges, and seal well.

6. Place in a large roasting pan, and cook for 2 hours in the centre shelf of the preheated oven.

7. Open out the foil, and cook it for a further 30 minutes, or until browned on the outside (the lamb should be slightly pink on the inside, but if you prefer it well done, cook it a little longer before opening out the foil).

Gravy:

1. Empty the juices from the foil into the roasting pan, then tilt the pan slightly; spoon off most of the fat into a bowl and discard, leaving the juices in the pan.

2. Place the pan over Medium heat on the stove top and, when the juices start to bubble, sprinkle in the flour and, using a wooden spoon, work it into a smooth paste; cook for a minute or so, to brown.

3. Pour in the wine, and let it bubble.

4. Gradually add the stock, to make a thin gravy.

5. Season to taste with salt and pepper.

[ANDREW & AMANDA MILLER, AND ROMILLY & JAMES]

SERVES 6 TO 8

1 (4 to 5 lb.) leg lamb
1-½ ozs. butter, at room temperature
1 tsp. finely chopped fresh rosemary
2 Tbsp. chopped fresh mint
2 Tbsp. chopped fresh curly parsley
1 tsp. chopped fresh thyme
1 clove garlic, crushed
1 tsp. salt
Freshly ground black pepper, to taste

Gravy:
1 tsp. all purpose flour
3 fl. ozs. dry white or red wine
10 fl. ozs. vegetable stock
Salt and freshly ground black pepper, to taste

NOTE:
It is also nice to cook the lamb on the grill after the 2 hours of baking. Remove from foil and cook directly over Medium heat for 20 to 30 minutes, turning occasionally.

PORK BABY BACK RIBS

Nutrition Facts per serving: Calories 536.4, Protein 22.57 Gm, Carbs 27.88 Gm, Fat 35.61 Gm, Cholesterol 79.91 mg,
Dietary Fiber 0.513 Gm, Sugar 21.6 Gm, Sodium 1057 mg, Calcium 18.99 mg, Potassium 544.1 mg, Iron 2.112 mg

SERVES 6

4 racks pork baby back ribs, cut into 3 or 4-bone sections
2 Tbsp. garlic powder
½ bottle Kraft Spicy Honey Barbecue Sauce (or your favorite sauce)
2 Tbsp. soy sauce
2 Tbsp. honey
Tabasco sauce and black pepper, to taste

1. Combine barbecue sauce with soy sauce, honey, Tabasco and black pepper; set aside.

2. Put ribs in a large pot, and add water to just cover.

3. Add garlic powder to the water.

4. Bring water to boiling; add ribs, reduce to simmer, and cook for 1 hour; drain. Keep an eye on the pot to make sure it does not boil over.

5. Arrange ribs in a baking dish. Generously spread half the sauce over 1 side of the ribs. Turn ribs over, and coat the other side with the remainder of the sauce.

6. Place rack on top shelf in oven, and broil ribs to desired tenderness, basting once on each side, turning halfway through (or place on barbecue grill over High heat, turning once and basting halfway through).

[LARRY & SHELLEY LEONARD, AND ALEX & NICHOLAS]

MAMAW SUE'S ROAST BEEF

Nutrition Facts per serving: Calories 922, Protein 59.25 Gm, Carbs 27.37 Gm, Fat 62.48 Gm, Cholesterol 209.2 mg,
Dietary Fiber 3.305 Gm, Sugar 6.489 Gm, Sodium 1080 mg, Calcium 68.87 mg, Potassium 1607 mg, Iron

SERVES 6 TO 8

1 (3 to 4 lb.) chuck or rump roast
1 tsp. salt
1 tsp. black pepper
1 tsp. garlic powder (or to taste)
1 med. green bell pepper, chopped
3 to 4 sm. onions, quartered
1 packet Lipton Onion Soup Mix (dry)
1 (10-¾ oz.) can Cream of Mushroom soup, plus ½ soup can of water
3 to 4 carrots, peeled and cut into fourths
3 to 4 Idaho potatoes, peeled and cut in half

1. Preheat oven to 350°F.

2. Place the roast in a large baking pan; season with salt, black pepper and garlic powder.

3. On top of the roast, add soup, plus water and the dry packet of Lipton Onion Soup Mix.

4. Cover and cook at least 1-½ hours.

5. Remove pan from oven. To the gravy in the pan, add onions, bell pepper, carrots and potatoes.

6. Cover and cook 30 minutes.

7. Uncover and cook a further 5 to 10 minutes in order to 'roast' the vegetables and brown the top of the beef.

[GREGORY & TERRI MERREN, AND JOSH & ZACHARY]

ROAST PORK

Nutrition Facts per serving: Calories 1337, Protein 69.99 Gm, Carbs 3.76 Gm, Fat 114.7 Gm, Cholesterol 191.9 mg,
Dietary Fiber 0.862 Gm, Sugar 1.017 Gm, Sodium 3648 mg, Calcium 36.3 mg, Potassium 1215 mg, Iron 3.964 mg

SERVES 6

1 (2 to 3 lb.) boneless pork roast
1 Tbsp. vegetable oil
1sm. scotch bonnet pepper,
  (seeds removed) diced (optional)
1 med. scotch bonnet pepper
  (seeds removed), finely
  chopped, (optional)
1 med. onion, coarsely chopped
1 med. bell pepper, coarsely
  chopped
2 stalks celery, coarsely chopped
Salt and black pepper, to taste
1 tsp. Season All

1. Season the roast with finely chopped scotch bonnet, and cut small slits into the surface of the roast, and stuff with diced scotch bonnet (if desired).

2. In a small bowl, combine black pepper, salt and Season All. Rub the roast with the combined seasonings. Let stand for 2 to 4 hours (the longer it seasons, the better it will taste).

3. On the stove top in a large oven-proof pot, over High heat, sear the roast in the oil for approximately 8 minutes, turning to brown on all sides. Remove from pot.

4. Add onion, bell pepper, celery and chopped scotch bonnet (if using). Season with salt and pepper, to taste. Add about ½ cup water, and cook over Medium heat for 5 minutes, tossing occasionally in the pan drippings, scraping any bits from the bottom of the pot.

5. Return roast to pot, and add a little water to the bottom of the pot. Tightly cover, and bake in oven preheated to 325°F for about 1-½ hours, or until tender, basting 1 or 2 times during the cooking process.

6. Uncover, and bake for a further 15 minutes, to brown.

7. Let stand for at least 15 minutes before carving.

Sauce:
Remove the roast
from the pot; set aside.
Return the pot with the
drippings to the stove top,
and add the necessary
water to the desired
consistency.
To thicken the sauce, in
a small container mix
together about 1 Tbsp.
cornstarch with a little
water, and stir into the
sauce; season to taste with
salt and pepper.
Heat over Medium
heat until
thickened.

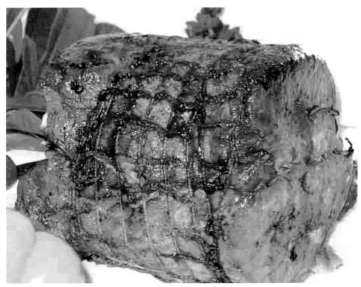

Roast Pork

CAYMANIAN BEEF PATTIES

Nutrition Facts per serving: Calories 206.5, Protein 4.554 Gm, Carbs 16.67 Gm, Fat 13.92 Gm, Cholesterol 13.73 mg, Dietary Fiber 0.595 Gm, Sugar 0.284 Gm, Sodium 400.3 mg, Calcium 58.11 mg, Potassium 139.9 mg, Iron 2.179 mg

MAKES 16

Pastry:
2 cups all purpose flour
1 Tbsp. curry powder
2 Tbsp. sugar
½ tsp. salt
1 tsp. baking powder
¾ cup Crisco shortening
Cold water

Meat filling:
1 pkg. lean ground sirloin or ground round (over 1 lb.)
1 onion, finely chopped
3 scallions, finely chopped
1 clove garlic, crushed
2 to 3 sprigs fresh thyme
1 russet or Idaho potato, finely diced
1 scotch bonnet pepper, finely chopped, seeds removed
1 tsp. salt
½ tsp. freshly ground pepper
1 Tbsp. hot (spicy) Jamaican curry powder
1 tsp. cayenne pepper (or more for very spicy patties)
2 Tbsp. oyster or hoisin sauce
3 Tbsp. Pickapeppa sauce
1 tsp. scotch bonnet sauce (optional, for added spice)
Canola oil

Egg wash:
1 lg. egg, beaten with 1 tsp. water

NOTE:
Many people prefer homemade patties due to the pastry.

Pastry (make 2 batches):
1. Sift the dry ingredients into a large bowl, and mix together with a spoon.
2. Use a pastry blender or two knives to cut the Crisco into the dry ingredients, until it resembles coarse crumbs.
3. Add about 5 tablespoons of ice cold water, and mix it in with a fork until the mixture binds together (you may need to add a little more water until the mixture forms a soft dough that binds and pulls away from the side of the bowl).
4. Use hands to form the mixture into a ball but DO NOT HANDLE the mixture too much, as it will make it tough.
5. Refrigerate the pastry while preparing the meat filling.

Meat Filling:
1. In a large frying pan over Medium heat, sauté onion, garlic, scallions and scotch bonnet pepper in a little canola oil.
2. Add beef, and use the back of a spoon or a potato masher to break up the lumps while browning the meat.
3. Add the remaining ingredients and about ¼ cup water; cook covered for about 20 minutes over Low heat. Keep stirring the mixture and, if it starts to get too dry, add a little more water.
4. Cook until potato is tender and the mixture is fairly dry. Let cool, and discard the thyme.
5. Remove dough from the refrigerator. If it is very cold (and hard), let it sit at room temperature for about 15 minutes before handling.
6. Roll out the dough onto a floured surface using a rolling pin.
7. Use a 6" diameter saucer to cut circles in the dough (cut smaller circles to make cocktail patties).
8. Place meat filling in the centre of each circle, moisten the edges with water, and then fold over, enclosing the meat filling; crimp the edges of the dough together with a fork to seal the patty.
9. Arrange patties in a single layer on an ungreased baking sheet. Brush with egg wash, and bake at 400°F for about 25 to 30 minutes, or until slightly browned.

[BRYAN & JENNIFER HUNTER, AND CORY & DANIEL]

KID FRIENDLY

CAKE

COOKIES/BROWNIES/ BARS

BEVERAGES

FRUIT

FROZEN

MISCELLANEOUS

PIES

FRUIT WHIP

Nutrition Facts per serving: Calories 303.7, Protein 4.399 Gm, Carbs 41.74 Gm, Fat 13.84 Gm, Cholesterol 32.93 mg, Dietary Fiber 0.191 Gm, Sugar 7.605 Gm, Sodium 113.1 mg, Calcium 131.7 mg, Potassium 349.8 mg, Iron 4.791 mg

SERVES 12

1 (8 oz.) pkg. cream cheese
1 can sweetened
  condensed milk
1 (8 oz.) container Cool Whip
1 (15 oz.) can fruit cocktail,
  drained
1 (15 oz.) can Mandarin oranges,
  drained
1 (15 oz.) can chunked
  pineapples, drained
Any fruits or nuts desired
About 1 cup mini-
  marshmallows (optional)

1. With electric mixer, beat cream cheese and milk, until smooth.

2. Add Cool Whip.

3. Fold in fruit, nuts and mini-marshmallows (if desired).

4. Chill and serve in an attractive bowl.

[WILLIAM & SHARON WALMSLEY, AND KIRSTEN, EMMA, JONATHAN & KATHERINE]

EASY APPLE SAUCE CAKE

Nutrition Facts per serving: Calories 195.7, Protein 1.78 Gm, Carbs 36.77 Gm, Fat 4.861 Gm, Cholesterol 1.467 mg, Dietary Fiber 0.128 Gm, Sugar 1.754 Gm, Sodium 274.1 mg, Calcium 58.07 mg, Potassium 48.18 mg, Iron 0.697 mg

SERVES 12

1 box yellow cake mix
½ cup apple sauce
Confectioners' sugar

1. Prepare cake mix as directed on box.

2. Pour cake mix into prepared pan or pans, as suggested in box directions.

3. Pour or spoon apple sauce over cake batter (divide evenly as needed for pans used).

4. Bake at 350°F, adding 5 additional minutes to box directed times.

5. Sprinkle with confectioners' sugar after letting cool slightly.

[TROY & JEWEL STUDENHOFFT, AND CALLHAN & GUNNAR]

NO BAKE CHOCOLATE SLICE

Nutrition Facts: Calories 513.7, Protein 6.006 Gm, Carbs 72.18 Gm, Fat 24.26 Gm, Cholesterol 41.03 mg, Dietary Fiber 2.208 Gm, Sugar 27.21 Gm, Sodium 413.1 mg, Calcium 115.3 mg, Potassium 283.9 mg, Iron 1.737 mg

SERVES 6 TO 8

¾ cup condensed milk
4 ozs. butter, melted
½ cup cocoa powder
1 cup dry coconut flakes
1 cup dried fruit
  (e.g. sultanas, cranberries, etc.)
9 ozs. graham crackers, finely
  crumbled (approx. 2 packets
  from a 14.4 oz. box)
Chocolate icing (optional)

1. Mix all the ingredients together thoroughly, except for the chocolate icing.

2. Press into the base of a 9" round non-stick baking pan (or pan of similar size).

3. Refrigerate until firm (at least 2 hours).

4. Ice with chocolate icing, if desired. Cut into squares.

[TONY & KAREN ATTENBOROUGH, AND CLAIRE, HAMISH & MATTHEW]

PIGS-IN-BLANKETS

Nutrition Facts per serving: Calories 48.33, Protein 0.83 Gm, Carbs 10.33 Gm, Fat 0.17 Gm, Cholesterol 0 mg,
Dietary Fiber 0.0.37 Gm, Sugar 0 Gm, Sodium 483.3 mg, Calcium 3.33 mg, Potassium 130.83, Iron 0.06 mg

1. Preheat oven as directed on the crescent roll (or biscuit) dough package.

2. Separate the dough where perforated. Cut each piece into thirds.

3. Wrap dough around each sausage, leaving ends of sausages showing, pressing dough together well so that it does not come apart while baking.

4. Place on a baking sheet, and bake for the length of time indicated on crescent roll (or biscuit) dough package, or until brown.

SERVES 4 TO 6

1 lg. pkg. Pillsbury crescent roll dough (or biscuit dough)
1 (16 oz.) pack Lit'l Smokies smoked sausages

NOTE:
These are nice dipped in mustard, and kids love them!

Pigs-in-Blankets

APPLE DIP

Nutrition Facts per serving: Calories 319.4, Protein 4.332 Gm, Carbs 32.52 Gm, Fat 19.96 Gm, Cholesterol 62.69 mg,
Dietary Fiber 0.015 Gm, Sugar 5.25 Gm, Sodium 180.9 mg, Calcium 70.14 mg, Potassium 166.7, Iron 1.236 mg

1. In a medium mixing bowl, combine softened cream cheese, brown sugar and vanilla. Mix until well-blended.

2. Peel and cut apples into wedges.

3. Transfer dip to a serving bowl surrounded by apple wedges.

SERVES 4

1 (8 oz.) pkg. cream cheese, softened
1 Tbsp. vanilla extract
½ cup brown sugar
Apple wedges, for dipping

CARI'S DELICIOUS DATE FINGERS

Nutrition Facts per serving: Calories 243.6, Protein 0.877 Gm, Carbs 19.31 Gm, Fat 18.97 Gm, Cholesterol 60.35 mg, Dietary Fiber 0.842 Gm, Sugar 7.281 Gm, Sodium 213.5 mg, Calcium 21.47 mg, Potassium 125.4 mg, Iron 0.453 mg

MAKES ABOUT 20

2 sticks butter
1 cup brown sugar
2 (8 oz.) pkgs. chopped dates
1 egg, beaten
1 tsp. vanilla extract
1 packet of tea biscuits
　(Marie's), crushed
Desiccated coconut (optional)

1. In a saucepan, melt butter and sugar.

2. Add chopped dates, and bring to boil, stirring to prevent the mixture sticking.

3. Remove from the stove top, and add the egg together with vanilla extract.

4. Add the packet of crushed biscuits, and mix well (more biscuits can be added to make the fingers more crunchy).

5. Spread the mixture onto a greased baking tray.

6. Place in the refrigerator until cool.

7. Cut into fingers, and roll in desiccated coconut, if desired.

[MIKE & LAUREN NELSON, AND MARC & CARI]

SAND CAKE

Nutrition Facts per serving: Calories 364.4, Protein 4.416 Gm, Carbs 52.4 Gm, Fat 17.08 Gm, Cholesterol 19.95 mg, Dietary Fiber 0.649 Gm, Sugar 21.9 Gm, Sodium 261.5 mg, Calcium 63.38 mg, Potassium 104.3 mg, Iron 1.318 mg

SERVES 6 TO 8

1 (12 oz.) box Nilla Wafers
1 (8 oz.) container Cool Whip
2 (3 oz.) pkgs. cream cheese,
　softened
1 (4 oz.) pkg. vanilla or chocolate
　instant pudding mix (lemon
　is good too)
1-½ cups milk
1 tsp. vanilla extract
Candy shells for decorating
　(available at most candy stores)

1. To make the sand, crush the Nilla Wafers with a potato masher, or in a food processor.

2. With a mixer, combine the Cool Whip, cream cheese, pudding mix, milk and vanilla.

3. Layer a fifth of the crumbs in the bottom of a large, clean sand pail.

4. Top with a third of the pudding mixture, then a layer of crumbs; continue layering, ending with the crumbs.

5. Cover and refrigerate for at least 30 minutes.

6. Decorate with the candy shells.

[DARRIN & MICHELLE DAYKIN, AND JOSHUA & EMMI]

FRUIT DIP

Nutrition Facts: Calories 467.7, Protein 5.889 Gm, Carbs 57.78 Gm, Fat 24.24 Gm, Cholesterol 51.39 mg,
Dietary Fiber 0.248 Gm, Sugar 5.863 Gm, Sodium 805.4 mg, Calcium 217 mg, Potassium 332.7 mg, Iron 0.236 mg

1. Mix all the ingredients together.

2. Pour into an attractive bowl; chill in the refrigerator.

3. Serve with fresh, sliced fruit.

[TONY & CHRISTINE CLEAVER, AND ALEX, JORDYN & BETHANY]

Fruit Dip

MAKES 1-1/2 CUPS

1 (3.3 oz.) pkg. vanilla instant
   pudding
8 ozs. sour cream
1/4 cup orange juice
1 tsp. vanilla extract
1/2 cup milk

NOTE:
This is an excellent way to get children to eat fruit. They can have fun helping to prepare it too.

EASY KEY LIME PIE

Nutrition Facts per serving: Calories 259.1, Protein 6.252 Gm, Carbs 45.06 Gm, Fat 6.895 Gm, Cholesterol 26 mg,
Dietary Fiber 0.025 Gm, Sugar 0.272 Gm, Sodium 103 mg, Calcium 220 mg, Potassium 318.8 mg, Iron 0.188 mg

1. Blend the first 3 ingredients together, and pour into the piecrust.

2. Place in the refrigerator for a few hours, until set.

NOTE:
The above ingredients (without the piecrust) can also be combined to make a nice pudding.

[EDLIN & HELEN MERREN]

SERVES 6 TO 8

1 cup lime juice (fresh
   squeezed or bottled can
   be used)
2 cans sweetened
   condensed milk
1 (8 oz.) container Cool Whip
1 graham cracker piecrust

DIRT CAKE

Nutrition Facts per serving: Calories 713.6, Protein 7.886 Gm, Carbs 70.43 Gm, Fat 45.83 Gm, Cholesterol 68.16 mg, Dietary Fiber 1.035 Gm, Sugar 31.27 Gm, Sodium 931.7 mg, Calcium 197.5 mg, Potassium 339.4 mg, Iron 1.793 mg

SERVES 6 TO 8

1 lg. pkg. Oreo cookies,
   finely crushed (reserve
   1 cup for topping)
½ cup butter, melted
1 (8 oz.) pkg. cream cheese
¼ cup confectioners' sugar
1 (12 oz.) container Cool Whip
2 sm. pkgs. (7 ozs. total)
   INSTANT chocolate pudding
3-½ cups milk
Gummy worms
Additional Cool Whip (optional)

1. Mix together (all except one cup) crushed Oreo cookies and butter.

2. Press into serving dish (see note below); chill.

3. With an electric mixer, beat together the cream cheese, confectioners' sugar and Cool Whip; spread over cookies.

4. Mix the chocolate powdered pudding mix with the 3-½ cups milk. Whip until thick in texture (about 2 minutes); pour over the cheese layer.

5. Top with additional Cool Whip, if desired.

6. Sprinkle with remaining crushed Oreos.

7. Decorate with gummy worms.

NOTE:
Looks great when made in a clay pot with silk flowers and "gummy" worms coming out of the dirt! Enjoy!

[STEPHEN & DEBRA MCTAGGART, AND SARAH, AMELIA & MATTHEW]

EASY PEANUT BUTTER COOKIES

Nutrition Facts per serving: Calories 83.11, Protein 2.887 Gm, Carbs 6.697 Gm, Fat 5.542 Gm, Cholesterol 8.875 mg, Dietary Fiber 0.673 Gm, Sugar 0.8 Gm, Sodium 55.42 mg, Calcium 8.5648 mg, Potassium 95.04 mg, Iron 0.295 mg

MAKES 24

1 cup peanut butter
1 egg
½ cup of sugar

1. Preheat oven to 325°F.

2. Mix all the ingredients together.

3. Drop small spoonfuls onto a baking sheet.

4. Bake for 12 minutes.

[JEFF & MICHELLE BOUCHER, AND MICHAEL & JENNA]

BANANA MILKSHAKE

Nutrition Facts per serving: Calories 386.1, Protein 15.78 Gm, Carbs 69.52 Gm, Fat 4.904 Gm, Cholesterol 68.18 mg,
Dietary Fiber 5.62 Gm, Sugar 39.8 Gm, Sodium 204.4 mg, Calcium 458.8 mg, Potassium 1273 mg, Iron 0.832 mg

1. Peel and roughly chop the bananas; place in a blender.

2. Add milk and vanilla ice cream; blend 15 to 20 seconds, or until smooth.

3. Pour into tall glasses, and serve.

[ANDREW & AMANDA MILLER, AND ROMILLY & JAMES]

SERVES 2

2 med. fresh, ripe bananas
1 pint milk
2 scoops vanilla ice cream

Banana and Strawberry Milkshakes

STRAWBERRY MILKSHAKE

Nutrition Facts per serving: Calories 233.3, Protein 10.4 Gm, Carbs 35.71 Gm, Fat 6.299 Gm, Cholesterol 23.23 mg,
Dietary Fiber 1.855 Gm, Sugar 27.32 Gm, Sodium 157.2 mg, Calcium 371.5 mg, Potassium 652.6 mg, Iron 0.579 mg

1. Wash the strawberries and remove the stems; cut in half and place in a blender.

2. Add milk and strawberry ice cream; blend 15 to 20 seconds, or until smooth.

3. Pour into tall glasses, and serve.

[ANDREW & AMANDA MILLER, AND ROMILLY & JAMES]

SERVES 2

Approx. 6-½ ozs.
  fresh strawberries
1 pint milk
2 scoops strawberry ice cream

MOCK SUSHI - A CHILDREN'S TREAT

Nutrition Facts per serving: Calories 651.9, Protein 7.825 Gm, Carbs 161.2 Gm, Fat 0.672 Gm, Cholesterol 0 mg,
Dietary Fiber 1.206 Gm, Sugar 74.21 Gm, Sodium 285.2 mg, Calcium 34.9 mg, Potassium 50.64 mg, Iron 3.44 mg

SERVES 6 TO 8

¼ cup margarine
4 cups mini-marshmallows
6 cups crispy rice cereal
20 to 25 gummy worms
1 to 2 boxes of fruit leather
    OR 1 to 2 boxes of
    Fruit Roll-ups

1. Grease a 12" x 7" baking sheet.

2. Melt margarine in a microwaveable bowl for 30 seconds, or until melted.

3. Add marshmallows; stir until coated.

4. Microwave marshmallows for 1 minute, or until melted.

5. Add crispy rice cereal; toss until evenly coated.

6. Turn the baking sheet so that the shorter ends are at the top and the bottom.

7. Press the marshmallow mixture onto the sheet, distributing it evenly.

8. Starting at one side, an inch or so up from the lower edge, place gummy worms atop the mixture end-to-end in a horizontal line.

9. Roll the lower edge of the marshmallow mixture over the gummy worms.

10. Stop and cut the log away from the rest of the main mixture.

11. Use the same method to form more logs.

12. If using fruit leather, slice each log into 1" thick "sushi-type" rolls, and wrap them individually with a strip of the fruit leather. If using the sheets of fruit roll-ups, roll the "sushi roll" in the fruit roll-up and then slice the "roll" into 1"-thick slices of "sushi".

[DON & TRACEY POTKINS, AND MEGHAN & SARAH]

MARC'S OREO COOKIE PIE

Nutrition Facts per serving: Calories 818.4, Protein 7.878 Gm, Carbs 113.9 Gm, Fat 38.3 Gm, Cholesterol 26.4 mg, Dietary Fiber 1.26 Gm, Sugar 78.5 Gm, Sodium 1176 mg, Calcium 138.8 mg, Potassium 287.3 mg, Iron 2.349 mg

SERVES 10

1 lb. Oreo cookies, crushed
2 sm. boxes (or 1 lg.) vanilla/ french vanilla instant pudding
1 (8 oz.) pkg. cream cheese (whipped is easier to use)
½ cup confectioners' sugar
3 cups milk
1 (12 oz.) container Cool Whip

1. Put five-sixths of the cookies into the bottom of a 9" x 13" pan.

2. Combine pudding and milk; add cream cheese and sugar, and mix well.

3. Pour over crushed cookies.

4. Spread Cool Whip over pudding layer.

5. Top with remaining crushed cookies.

6. Refrigerate until ready to serve.

[MIKE & LAUREN NELSON, AND MARC & CARI]

ICE CREAM TODAY

Nutrition Facts per serving: Calories 23.68, Protein 1.044 Gm, Carbs 4.704 Gm, Fat 0.055 Gm, Cholesterol 0.551 mg, Dietary Fiber 0 Gm, Sugar 4.381 Gm, Sodium 15.8 mg, Calcium 37.78 mg, Potassium 50.81 mg, Iron 0.014 mg

SERVES 3 TO 6

1 gallon-size Ziplock bag
1 pint-size Ziplock bag
Ice
6 Tbsp. rock salt
½ cup milk
1 Tbsp. granulated sugar
¼ tsp. vanilla extract

1. Fill gallon-size Ziplock bag halfway full with ice.

2. Add rock salt, and seal bag.

3. Pour milk, vanilla and sugar into pint-size Ziplock bag; seal it.

4. Place the small bag inside the large bag, and seal again carefully.

5. Shake until mixture becomes thick (about 5 minutes).

6. Remove small bag.

7. Wipe off salt. Rinse under water before opening, and enjoy.

[RICK & KIM MCTAGGART, AND JONATHAN, KATELEE & NICHOLAS]

Apple-Orange Cranberry Sauce (page 200), and Apricot Sauce (page 196)

ACCOMPANIMENTS, ETC.

AWESOME BARBECUE SAUCE

Nutrition Facts per serving: Calories 127.3, Protein 12.8 Gm, Carbs 11.52 Gm, Fat 3.737 Gm, Cholesterol 0.567 mg,
Dietary Fiber 0.557 Gm, Sugar 0.161 Gm, Sodium 414.2 mg, Calcium 24.63 mg, Potassium 248.5 mg, Iron 0.905 mg

SERVES 4

2 Tbsp. vegetable oil
1 clove garlic, chopped
1 lg. onion, finely chopped
5 fl. ozs. tomato puree
3 Tbsp. lemon juice
½ tsp. salt
¼ tsp. black pepper
½ tsp. dried sage
4 Tbsp. soft brown sugar
4 fl. ozs. beef stock
4 Tbsp. Worcestershire sauce
2 tsp. dry mustard

1. Cook onion and garlic in oil for about 3 minutes, until translucent, not brown.

2. Add tomato puree, lemon juice, salt, pepper, sage, sugar, beef stock, Worcestershire sauce and mustard to the mixture in the frying pan, and stir well.

3. Simmer over Low heat for about 10 minutes, stirring frequently.

NOTE:
This sauce can be served over pork spare ribs and chicken.
Before basting chicken or burgers on the grill with this sauce,
cook it about 20 more minutes in the pan.

[TONY & BRIDGET PITCAIRN, AND SOPHIE]

BÉARNAISE SAUCE

Nutrition Facts per serving: Calories 254, Protein 3.687 Gm, Carbs 1.408 Gm, Fat 25.59 Gm, Cholesterol 168.6 mg,
Dietary Fiber 0.055 Gm, Sugar 0.144 Gm, Sodium 279.6 mg, Calcium 35.18 mg, Potassium 95.16 mg, Iron 0.584 mg

SERVES 8

4 scallions, chopped
2 Tbsp. vinegar
6 Tbsp. white wine
2 Tbsp. chopped fresh tarragon
2 tsp. Worcestershire sauce
4 egg yolks
1 cup butter, melted

1. In a saucepan over Medium heat, combine first 5 ingredients; cook down a little, and set aside to cool.

2. Pour into a blender, and mix.

3. With the blender on High, add egg yolks (best if at room temperature). Slowly add melted butter.

4. Return to saucepan, and cook, stirring constantly, over very Low heat, until thick.

NOTE:
This sauce is great on any red meat. It can be made before guests arrive and left in
the pan until ready to serve. Tastes just as good served at room temperature.

CRANBERRY AND PEAR CHUTNEY

Nutrition Facts per serving: Calories 194.8, Protein 0.754 Gm, Carbs 50.2 Gm, Fat 0.474 Gm, Cholesterol 0 mg,
Dietary Fiber 4.6 Gm, Sugar 13.54 Gm, Sodium 11.81 mg, Calcium 39.78 mg, Potassium 298 mg, Iron 0.945 mg

1. Combine cranberries and sugar in a saucepan.

2. Cook over Medium-Low heat until berries release their juice (about 8 minutes).

3. Place pears in a medium bowl; toss with lemon juice.

4. Add orange juice and raisins to cranberries.

5. Raise heat to Medium-High; stir occasionally, adding pears when mixture begins to bubble.

6. Cook, stirring until mixture thickens, and pears turn red and are cooked through (about 10 minutes).

7. Transfer to a bowl; let cool. Refrigerate up to 24 hours.

[LESLIE METCALF]

SERVES 6 TO 8

3 cups fresh cranberries
1 cup sugar
3 firm pears, peeled,
  cored and diced into ½" cubes
1 Tbsp. fresh lemon juice
½ cup fresh orange juice
¼ cup golden raisins

TERIYAKI MARINADE

Nutrition Facts: Calories 102.3, Protein 0.976 Gm, Carbs 22.59 Gm, Fat 1.959 Gm, Cholesterol 0 mg,
Dietary Fiber 1.473 Gm, Sugar 0.099 Gm, Sodium 9.879 mg, Calcium 27.03 mg, Potassium 216.2 mg, Iron 1.031 mg

1. In a small mixing bowl, combine all ingredients.

2. Refrigerate until ready to use.

3. Marinate either salmon, steak or chicken for at least 2 hours before grilling on the barbecue.

[BRENDA BRYCE]

MAKES ABOUT 1 CUP

½ cup tamari or light soy sauce
2 Tbsp. granulated sugar
2 Tbsp. finely grated fresh
  ginger root
2 Tbsp. lemon juice
1 Tbsp. vegetable oil
2 lg. cloves garlic, minced

JACK'S JEZEBEL SAUCE

Nutrition Facts: Calories 2223, Protein 17.08 Gm, Carbs 522.4 Gm, Fat 17.45 Gm, Cholesterol 0 mg,
Dietary Fiber 6.804 Gm, Sugar 374.4 Gm, Sodium 259 mg, Calcium 545 mg, Potassium 1565 mg, Iron 16.89 mg

1. Mix all ingredients together, and place in a decorative serving bowl.

2. Serve with ham, lamb, shrimp or veal (can also be served as an appetizer with corn chips).

This recipe originated with the father of a very close friend of the Merren family, Anne
Davis Hasson, who lived many years in the Cayman Islands.

[GREGORY & TERRI MERREN, AND JOSH & ZACHARY]

MAKES ABOUT 3 CUPS

1 (12 oz.) jar pineapple
  preserves
1 (12 oz.) jar apple jelly
1 (6 oz.) jar horseradish
2 ozs. dry mustard
1 tsp. coarse ground pepper

MARINADE FOR PORK TENDERLOIN

Nutrition Facts per cup: Calories 290.9, Protein 3.754 Gm, Carbs 44.51 Gm, Fat 10.22 Gm, Cholesterol 10.13 mg,
Dietary Fiber 0.12 Gm, Sugar 34.4 Gm, Sodium 4422 mg, Calcium 57.99 mg, Potassium 185 mg, Iron 2.053 mg

MAKES ABOUT ½ CUP

2 Tbsp. honey
4 Tbsp. hoisin sauce
4 Tbsp. soy sauce
4 tsp. red wine vinegar
¼ tsp. Five-Spice powder

1. Combine marinade ingredients, and pour over pork tenderloin.

2. Marinate for several hours, or overnight, before cooking.

[TONY & CHRISTINE CLEAVER, AND ALEX, JORDYN & BETHANY]

HOMEMADE TARTAR SAUCE

Nutrition Facts per cup: Calories 1686, Protein 0.718 Gm, Carbs 23.4 Gm, Fat 192.4 Gm, Cholesterol 80 mg,
Dietary Fiber 0.224 Gm, Sugar 0.362 Gm, Sodium 1614 mg, Calcium 15.08 mg, Potassium 90 mg, Iron 1.616 mg

MAKES ABOUT 1 CUP

1 cup mayonnaise
¼ cup sweet pickle
  relish, drained
1 Tbsp. finely chopped onion
1 Tbsp. snipped parsley
1 Tbsp. chopped pimiento
1 tsp. lemon juice

1. In a bowl, combine mayonnaise, pickle relish, onion, parsley, pimiento, and lemon juice.

2. Cover and chill for several hours.

3. Serve with fried fish, Conch Fritters (page 31) or Codfish Fritters (page 32).

[GREGORY & TERRI MERREN, AND JOSH & ZACHARY]

APRICOT SAUCE

Nutrition Facts: Calories 308.5, Protein 3.307 Gm, Carbs 72.14 Gm, Fat 0.4 Gm, Cholesterol 0 mg,
Dietary Fiber 8 Gm, Sugar 44 Gm, Sodium 14.01 mg, Calcium 53.96 mg, Potassium 1290 mg, Iron 4.888 mg

MAKES 1-½ CUPS

1 packet dried apricots
Water
Port wine, to taste
About 1 Tbsp. dark brown
  sugar (the VERY dark, like
  Muscovado sugar)

1. Put whole packet of apricots in a saucepan, and just cover with water.

2. Simmer, until soft.

3. Add dark brown sugar.

4. Put in blender; blend until a thick puree consistency.

5. Add Port wine.

6. Serve hot with Christmas (or Thanksgiving) turkey, or serve cold with ham.

"A VERY easy recipe, which was fool-proof, even in Malawi...!
Any red wine can be substituted, but it does not taste as good as Port. Of course,
wine could be left out altogether, but it does add that certain something ...
especially if made the day before."
- Catharine Boyd-Moss

[GRAHAM & CATHARINE BOYD-MOSS, AND EMMA & RACHEL]

HOLLANDAISE SAUCE

Nutrition Facts per serving: Calories 985.1, Protein 14.82 Gm, Carbs 12.94 Gm, Fat 102.3 Gm, Cholesterol 674.5 mg,
Dietary Fiber 1 Gm, Sugar 2.7 Gm, Sodium 1344 mg, Calcium 144.4 mg, Potassium 308 mg, Iron 2.393 mg

1. Place egg yolks in an electric blender. Add lemon juice, and blend.

2. Add salt and, if desired, Tabasco sauce. Slowly add butter, while the blender is running.

3. Pour mixture into a saucepan; cook over Low heat, stirring constantly, until thick.

MAKES ABOUT ¾ CUP

2 egg yolks (at room
temperature)
Juice of 1 lg. lemon
Pinch of salt
2 drops Tabasco
sauce (optional)
½ cup butter, melted

MUSHROOM GRAVY

Nutrition Facts per cup: Calories 910.4, Protein 10.61 Gm, Carbs 23.03 Gm, Fat 88.81 Gm, Cholesterol 278.4 mg,
Dietary Fiber 3.175 Gm, Sugar 10.75 Gm, Sodium 728.4 mg, Calcium 181.9 mg, Potassium 1069 mg, Iron 3.34 mg

1. Sauté mushrooms in butter; set aside.

2. Combine milk, flour and whipping cream; add to mushrooms.

3. Cook over Low heat, stirring constantly, until sauce thickens.

4. Add sherry, paprika, salt and pepper, just before serving.

5. Serve over baked chicken and rice, or mashed potato.

MAKES 2 CUPS

1 lb. fresh mushrooms, sliced
½ cup butter, melted
½ cup milk
2 Tbsp. all purpose flour
1 cup whipping cream
1 Tbsp. cooking sherry
Paprika
Salt and pepper, to taste

RED PEPPER JELLY

Nutrition Facts per pint: Calories 1906, Protein 1.667 Gm, Carbs 493.1 Gm, Fat 0.143 Gm, Cholesterol 0 mg,
Dietary Fiber 1.926 Gm, Sugar 423.1 Gm, Sodium 9.496 mg, Calcium 21.58 mg, Potassium 344.7 mg, Iron 1.417 mg

1. Chop scotch bonnet and bell peppers in a food processor or electric blender.

2. In a large saucepan, combine the sugar and vinegar; cook over Medium heat until the sugar is dissolved.

3. Stir in the peppers, and bring to a rapid boil. Boil for 3 minutes, stirring frequently to prevent sticking.

4. Add the pectin; boil for 1 minute. Remove from heat, and let stand for 5 minutes.

5. Ladle into hot, sterilised jars, filling to $1/8$" from top.

6. Seal, and let stand without disturbing for 24 hours.

MAKES 3 PINTS

6-½ cups granulated sugar
1-½ cups apple cider vinegar
2 red bell peppers, seeded
2 scotch bonnet peppers,
seeded
1 (6 oz.) bottle liquid pectin,
or 2 (3 oz.) pkgs.

[DON & JENNIE STEWART]

SAUSAGE GRAVY

Nutrition Facts per serving: Calories 230.7, Protein 12.89 Gm, Carbs 6.669 Gm, Fat 16.56 Gm, Cholesterol 44.84 mg,
Dietary Fiber 0.183 Gm, Sugar 4.135 Gm, Sodium 712.1 mg, Calcium 94.08 mg, Potassium 298.9 mg, Iron 0.915 mg

SERVES 3 TO 4

½ lb. pork sausage
2 Tbsp. all purpose flour
⅔ to 1 cup milk
¼ to ½ tsp. black pepper

This gravy is popular in the southern United States and is nice served over open breakfast biscuits/scones.

1. Cook sausage in a large heavy frying pan, until browned, stirring to crumble.

2. Remove from frying pan with a slotted spoon; drain well.

3. Reserve 2 tablespoons of the drippings in the frying pan (if not enough drippings were rendered, add 2 tablespoons of either bacon grease or vegetable oil).

4. Add flour to drippings, stirring until smooth.

5. Cook over Medium heat for 1 minute, stirring constantly.

6. Gradually add ⅔ cup milk, stirring constantly until smooth and thickened. Add remaining ⅓ cup milk, if a thinner gravy is desired.

7. Stir in pepper and sausage; cook until hot, stirring constantly.

MARINARA SAUCE

Nutrition Facts: Calories 309.3, Protein 18.28 Gm, Carbs 70.06 Gm, Fat 1.615 Gm, Cholesterol 0 mg,
Dietary Fiber 15.92 Gm, Sugar 16.3 Gm, Sodium 2951 mg, Calcium 174.2 mg, Potassium 3009 mg, Iron 17.89 mg

MAKES ABOUT 4 CUPS

2 cloves garlic, chopped
1 lg. onion, chopped
1 (14.5 oz.) can whole
  peeled tomatoes
½ of the (14.5 oz.) tomato can
  filled with water
1 (6 oz.) can tomato paste
1 (8 oz.) can tomato sauce
1 tsp. dried parsley
1 tsp. dried oregano
1 tsp. dried basil
½ tsp. salt
½ tsp. black pepper

1. Sauté onion and garlic in 2 teaspoons of water.

2. Toss in tomato products.

3. Mash up whole tomatoes with a fork or slice with a knife.

4. Add water; bring to a boil.

5. Reduce heat and simmer about 30 minutes.

6. Add spices and toss.

7. Serve over pasta.

[SCOTT & KATHRYN ELPHINSTONE, AND KAITLYN, LAURA & MATTHEW]

TIPS FOR MARINATING MEATS:
Do not save marinades once they have been used on meats. Cover and refrigerate extra marinade which was not poured over meat. Most marinades keep for up to 1 week. Marinated meat may cook a little more quickly than usual guidelines indicate. Less-tender cuts, such as beef round steak and beef flank steak, require 18 to 24 hours of marinating for maximum tenderness. Beef steaks, such as rib eyes, are already tender and will absorb desired marinade flavour in about 8 hours.

GUAVA JAM

Nutrition Facts per cup: Calories 950.4, Protein 1.968 Gm, Carbs 242.5 Gm, Fat 1.44 Gm, Cholesterol 0 mg,
Dietary Fiber 14.4 Gm, Sugar 14.4 Gm, Sodium 102.5 mg, Calcium 241.7 mg, Potassium 1446 mg, Iron 4.947 mg

1. Cut the guavas into big chunks.

2. In a saucepan over Medium heat, dissolve the sugar in the water.

3. Add guava, and cook down until thickened, stirring constantly.

4. Remove from burner, and let cool.

5. Blend in an electric blender, until smooth.

[DON & JENNIE STEWART]

MAKES 2 TO 3 CUPS

8 lg. ripe guavas, peeled and
  seeds removed
4 cups water
3 cups sugar (or more for a
  sweeter taste)

NOTE:
*To remove the
seed from a
guava, cut in
half and scoop
the seed out with
a spoon.*

Guava Jam

ASIAN DIPPING SAUCE

Nutrition Facts: Calories 286, Protein 0.806 Gm, Carbs 10.91 Gm, Fat 27.24 Gm, Cholesterol 0 mg,
Dietary Fiber 0.11 Gm, Sugar 5.903 Gm, Sodium 562.3 mg, Calcium 19.96 mg, Potassium 24.87 mg, Iron 0.375 mg

1. Combine all ingredients in a bowl.

2. Serve with Crispy Wontons (page 36).

NOTE:
This dip will keep indefinitely if stored in the refrigerator.

[LARRY & SHELLEY LEONARD, AND ALEX & NICHOLAS]

MAKES ABOUT 1 CUP

½ cup low sodium soy sauce
2 Tbsp. dark sesame oil
2 Tbsp. rice vinegar
1 tsp. chili oil
1 tsp. honey
½ cup bottled water

EASY BARBECUE SAUCE

Nutrition Facts: Calories 324.4, Protein 0.942 Gm, Carbs 31.58 Gm, Fat 23.24 Gm, Cholesterol 62.13 mg,
Dietary Fiber 0.468 Gm, Sugar 8.611 Gm, Sodium 2466 mg, Calcium 61.25 mg, Potassium 471 mg, Iron 1.774 mg

MAKES 1-½ CUPS

½ cup water
¼ cup vinegar
¼ cup butter or margarine
2 Tbsp. sugar
2 Tbsp. Worcestershire sauce
1 Tbsp. prepared mustard
1-½ tsp. salt
½ tsp. black pepper
¼ tsp. red pepper
1 thick slice of lemon
1 thick slice of onion
½ cup ketchup
1 drop of liquid smoke

1. In a heavy medium saucepan, combine all ingredients EXCEPT KETCHUP; bring to a boil.
2. Reduce heat and simmer, partially covered, for 20 minutes. Stir frequently.
3. Remove from heat; discard lemon and onion slices, and stir in ketchup.
4. Brush over chicken or ribs when grilling.

BROWN GRAVY

Nutrition Facts: Calories 224.3, Protein 3.682 Gm, Carbs 29.27 Gm, Fat 9.525 Gm, Cholesterol 0 mg,
Dietary Fiber 3.423 Gm, Sugar 6.105 Gm, Sodium 1949 mg, Calcium 51.17 mg, Potassium 321.1 mg, Iron 1.572 mg

MAKES ABOUT 1-½ CUPS

1 cup chopped onion
2 tsp. cooking oil
2 Tbsp. all purpose flour
1 cup water
2 tsp. beef bouillon powder
1 tsp. Worcestershire sauce
Salt and pepper, to taste

1. In a frying pan, sauté onion in cooking oil for about 4 minutes, until soft.
2. Sprinkle the flour over the onion mixture; mix well and cook for 2 minutes.
3. Add water and stir over Medium-High heat, until boiling and thickened.
4. Add bouillon powder, Worcestershire sauce, salt and pepper. Mix well, and cook through.

[BRIAN & DOROTHY WILSON, AND JERROD & BRIANNA]

APPLE-ORANGE CRANBERRY SAUCE

Nutrition Facts per serving: Calories 277.9, Protein 0.588 Gm, Carbs 71.78 Gm, Fat 0.412 Gm, Cholesterol 0 mg,
Dietary Fiber 4.624 Gm, Sugar 5.463 Gm, Sodium 27.2 mg, Calcium 73.64 mg, Potassium 325.5, Iron 1.527 mg

MAKES 3-½ TO 4 CUPS

½ orange
2 cups water
1 apple, peeled, cored and diced into small pieces
1 (12 oz.) can whole cranberries
1 cup sugar
1 tsp. cinnamon
½ tsp. ground cloves

1. Squeeze juice from orange; set juice aside.
2. Dice orange rind into small pieces; boil in the water for 10 minutes; discard water.
3. In a saucepan, add orange juice, orange rind, apple, cranberries, sugar, cinnamon and cloves; simmer for 25 minutes. To thin the sauce, you can add more orange juice, if desired.
4. Serve at room temperature.

[DWIGHT & SHANNON PANTON, AND DYLAN & FRASIER]

TRINIDADIAN HOT PEPPER SAUCE

Nutrition Facts per serving: Calories 8.635, Protein 0.219 Gm, Carbs 2.146 Gm, Fat 0.041 Gm, Cholesterol 0 mg, Dietary Fiber 0.34 Gm, Sugar 1.153 Gm, Sodium 204.7 mg, Calcium 4.802 mg, Potassium 38.24 mg, Iron 0.139 mg

1. Combine all ingredients in an electric blender.

2. If desired, dice mango, pommescythere or pawpaw into small squares, and add after blending.

3. Place in a screw-top jar, and keep in the refrigerator.

[VANDA FERNANDEZ]

SERVES 32

12 scotch bonnet peppers,
   (seeds and stems removed)
4 to 5 cloves garlic
3 med. onions
½ cup vinegar
   or lime juice
   or half of each
2 to 3 tsp. salt
2 tsp. mustard (optional)
Mango or pommescythere
   (June plums) or green
   pawpaw

SCOTCH BONNET PICKLED PEPPER SAUCE

Nutrition Facts per serving: Calories 10.14, Protein 0.426 Gm, Carbs 2.402 Gm, Fat 0.044 Gm, Cholesterol 0 mg, Dietary Fiber 0.44 Gm, Sugar 0.654 Gm, Sodium 2.331 mg, Calcium 4.753 mg, Potassium 69.62 mg, Iron 0.245 mg

1. Place peppers, onions (or shallots) and carrots into the jar, alternating by first placing a couple of peppers, then onions, then carrots, until the jar is nearly full.

2. Pour in the vinegar, filling the jar and covering all the vegetables.

3. Screw on the top, and place in a cool place for 2 to 3 days, so the flavours will blend together.

4. Keep in the refrigerator for future use (can be stored and used for up to a couple of months).

FILLS ABOUT AN 8 TO 10 OUNCE JAR

6 to 8 assorted coloured scotch
   bonnet peppers (stems
   removed)
2 shallots, sliced
   or ¼ white onion, sliced
3 slices raw, peeled cho-cho
1-½ carrots, peeled and
   julienned
⅔ cup white vinegar
1 screw top jar

TIPS FOR GRAVY:
Add butter, margarine or bacon drippings to pan drippings if there are not enough pan drippings for gravy. To prevent lumps in gravy, shake 1 to 2 tablespoons of all purpose flour and 2 to 4 tablespoons of cold water or broth together until flour dissolves completely and mixture is smooth. Whisk flour mixture into pan drippings. Stir gravy constantly, scraping up browned bits from the bottom of the pan. If gravy is too thick, add more water or broth. Bring gravy back to a boil, stirring constantly. If gravy is too thin, shake together more flour and water or broth. Add to gravy. Bring gravy back to a boil, stirring constantly. If fat separates from gravy, there is too much fat in proportion to flour. To adjust proportion, shake together more flour and broth, then cook the gravy again.

NOTE:
Scotch Bonnet Pickled Pepper Sauce is great spooned over fried, steamed or grilled fish, and is very popular in Jamaica and the Cayman Islands. Be careful, as it is very hot!

Left, Butterfinger Banana Cake (page 224), right, Easy Keylime Pie (page 187) and center, Zabaglione with Strawberries (page 226)

DESSERTS

BANANA SPLIT CAKE

Nutrition Facts per serving: Calories 914.8, Protein 8.472 Gm, Carbs 113.4 Gm, Fat 50.66 Gm, Cholesterol 158.9 mg,
Dietary Fiber 3.317 Gm, Sugar 16.71 Gm, Sodium 707.3 mg, Calcium 105.4 mg, Potassium 755.3 mg, Iron 3.631 mg

SERVES 12 TO 16

Crust:
1-½ sticks melted butter
3 cups graham cracker crumbs

Filling:
2 sticks butter, softened
2 cups confectioners' sugar
2 eggs
1 tsp. vanilla
7 bananas
Juice from 2 lemons
1 lg. can crushed pineapple,
   well-drained

1 pint whipping cream
Approx. ½ cup chopped nuts

Crust:

1. Combine crumbs and butter.
2. Press on bottom and sides of a 9" x 13" pan.

Filling:

1. Place 2 sticks softened butter, sugar, eggs and vanilla in a bowl; beat 5 minutes with an electric mixer.
2. Spread filling over crust.
3. Slice bananas, and dip in bowl with lemon juice.
4. Cover filling with sliced bananas.
5. Cover bananas with crushed pineapple.
6. Whip the cream using an electric mixer; spread over pineapple. Decorate with nuts.

[PAUL PEENE & TONI PINKERTON, AND SAMANTHA, DEREK & ANDREW]

CHOCOLATE CHIP PIE

Nutrition Facts per serving: Calories 524.8, Protein 9.351 Gm, Carbs 72.11 Gm, Fat 25.29 Gm, Cholesterol 61.64 mg,
Dietary Fiber 0.82 Gm, Sugar 24.49 Gm, Sodium 223.1 mg, Calcium 69.7 mg, Potassium 317.1 mg, Iron 2.798 mg

SERVES 6 TO 8

1 unbaked 9" pie shell
2 lg. eggs
½ cup all purpose flour
½ cup granulated sugar
½ cup packed brown sugar
¾ cup (1-½ sticks)
   butter, softened
1 cup (6 oz.) semi-sweet
   chocolate morsels
1 cup chopped nuts
Sweetened whipped
   cream or vanilla ice cream

1. Preheat oven to 325°F.
2. Beat eggs in a large mixing bowl on High speed until foamy.
3. Beat in flour, granulated sugar and brown sugar.
4. Beat in butter.
5. Stir in morsels and nuts.
6. Spoon mixture into pie shell.
7. Bake in preheated oven for 55 to 60 minutes, or until fork inserted halfway between outside edge and centre comes out clean.
8. Cool on a wire rack.
9. Serve warm with whipped cream or vanilla ice cream.

[EDLIN & HELEN MERREN]

ULTIMATE TRIPLE LAYER CHEESECAKE

Nutrition Facts per serving: Calories 251.4, Protein 4.689 Gm, Carbs 27.42 Gm, Fat 14.12 Gm, Cholesterol 58.98 mg,
Dietary Fiber 0.897 Gm, Sugar 10.96 Gm, Sodium 220.7 mg, Calcium 42.53 mg, Potassium 115.8 mg, Iron 1.094 mg

SERVES 12 TO 16

Chocolate Crumb Crust:
1 cup chocolate cookie crumbs
3 Tbsp. sugar
3 Tbsp. vegetable oil,
   or melted margarine

Filling:
3 (8 oz.) pkgs. reduced-fat
   cream cheese, softened
³/₄ cup Splenda Granular
3 eggs
¼ cup reduced-fat sour cream
2 Tbsp. all purpose flour
1-½ tsp. vanilla extract
¼ tsp. salt
½ cup butterscotch baking chips
½ cup semi-sweet chocolate chips
½ cup white chocolate chips

Triple Drizzle (optional):
1 Tbsp. each of butterscotch
   chips, chocolate chips, white
   chips, combined with 1-½ tsp.
   Crisco shortening and melted
   in the microwave

Crust:

1. Preheat oven to 350°F.

2. Mix crumbs, sugar and margarine (or oil) together. Press on bottom and sides of an 8" or 9" cheesecake pan.

3. Bake for 7 to 8 minutes.

4. Let cool.

Filling:

1. Place the cream cheese and Splenda in a large mixing bowl; beat on Medium speed, until smooth.

2. Add the eggs, sour cream, flour, vanilla extract and salt; blend well.

3. Place the chips in 3 separate microwave-safe bowls and cook on High for 1 minute. Stir immediately (while hot), until smooth.

4. Stir 1-¹/₃ cups of batter into the melted butterscotch chips, until well-blended. Pour over the crust.

5. Stir 1-¹/₃ cups of batter into the melted chocolate chips, until well-blended. Pour over the butterscotch layer.

6. Stir the remaining batter into the melted white chips, until well-blended. Pour over the chocolate layer.

7. Bake for 55 to 60 minutes on 350°F, until almost set in the centre.

8. Remove from the oven to a wire rack, and immediately loosen the cake from the sides of the pan.

9. Cool completely before serving.

10. If desired, pour Triple Drizzle over the top before serving.

[CY & CHERYL ELLIOTT, AND JADA]

LEMON POUND CAKE WITH MIXED BERRIES

Nutrition Facts per serving: Calories 309.5, Protein 6.003 Gm, Carbs 53.81 Gm, Fat 7.798 Gm, Cholesterol 92.16 mg, Dietary Fiber 2.776 Gm, Sugar 13.68 Gm, Sodium 148.1 mg, Calcium 107.5 mg, Potassium 229.4 mg, Iron 1.434 mg

SERVES 8

Cake:
No-stick cooking spray
2 tsp. all purpose flour
1 cup all purpose flour
¼ tsp. baking powder
²/₃ cup sugar
¹/₃ cup butter, softened
2 lg. egg whites
1 lg. egg
1 tsp. grated lemon rind
1 tsp. lemon extract
¼ cup vanilla low-fat yogurt

Topping:
1 cup sliced strawberries
½ cup fresh blueberries
  or blackberries
1 (10 oz.) pkg. frozen
  raspberries in light syrup,
  thawed and undrained
1 cup vanilla low-fat yogurt

1. Preheat oven to 350°F.

2. Coat an 8" x 4" loaf pan with cooking spray; dust with 2 teaspoons flour.

3. Lightly spoon 1 cup flour into a dry measuring cup; level with a knife.

4. Combine 1 cup flour and baking powder, stirring with a whisk; set aside.

5. Place sugar and butter in a large bowl; beat with a mixer at High speed, until fluffy (about 2 minutes).

6. Add egg whites and egg, beating well after each addition.

7. Beat in rind and extract.

8. Add flour mixture and ¼ cup yogurt alternately to sugar mixture, beginning and ending with flour mixture; mix well after each addition.

9. Spoon batter into prepared pan.

10. Bake for 45 minutes, or until a toothpick inserted in centre comes out clean.

11. Cool in pan for 10 minutes on a wire rack; remove from pan.

12. Cool completely on wire rack.

Lemon Pound Cake with Mixed Berries

Topping:

1. Combine berries, tossing well.

2. Cut cake into 8 slices, and top each slice with ¼ cup berry mixture and 2 tablespoons yogurt.

[WAYNE & PATRICIA DaCOSTA, AND AARON & ASHLEY]

CORDON BLEU CAKE

Nutrition Facts per serving: Calories 855.5, Protein 11.18 Gm, Carbs 95.73 Gm, Fat 49.38 Gm, Cholesterol 92.64 mg,
Dietary Fiber 0.067 Gm, Sugar 27.71 Gm, Sodium 1380 mg, Calcium 152 mg, Potassium 357.9 mg, Iron 4.282 mg

SERVES 10

7 ozs. butter, softened
   (or margarine)
½ cup (4 oz.) castor (extra
   fine granulated) sugar
7 ozs. cream cheese
1 lg. egg
1 tsp. lemon juice
½ tsp. cinnamon
6 Tbsp. brandy
6 Tbsp. milk
30 Nice biscuits (or 30
   Pepperidge Farm Bordeaux
   biscuits)
Candied (glace) cherries,
   to decorate, or 1 Cadbury
   Flake bar
4 Tbsp. caster sugar
4 Tbsp. water
2 Tbsp. cocoa
4 ozs. plain chocolate
2 Tbsp. butter
¼ cup sliced (flaked) almonds,
   for decorating

NOTE:

Nice biscuits are a well-known brand of plain, sweet, oblong-shaped biscuits in the U.K. In this recipe, they can be substituted with Pepperidge Farm Bordeaux biscuits, if necessary.

1. Using an electric mixer, cream the butter and sugar together until light and fluffy, stopping to scrape down the sides of the bowl.

2. Add the cream cheese, egg, lemon juice and cinnamon; mix together well.

3. Mix the brandy and milk together in another large bowl.

4. Lay out a large piece of foil on a flat surface.

5. Dip the biscuits in the brandy mixture for a few seconds and lay them on the foil in a single layer (3 biscuits wide x 5 biscuits lengthwise).

6. Spread a thin layer of the cheesy mixture on top of the biscuits.

7. Dip the remaining biscuits in the brandy mix, and lay them on top of the spread.

8. Spread the remainder of the cheesy mixture in a thick long line down the centre row of the biscuits. Now place a row of cherries along the top of the cheesy mixture (or omit the cherries, and sprinkle with a crumbled Flake bar instead).

9. Pull up the foil gently along both long sides of the cake so that the foil comes together and overlaps at the top. The object is to bring the long biscuit sides of the cake together at the top, so that the cake now forms a long triangular log shape.

10. Place the cake (enclosed in foil) in a large shallow pan, and refrigerate for several hours or overnight, so that the cake can harden and keep its shape. If necessary, after the cake has hardened, mould it some more to form a nice log shape with the cheesy centre being fully enclosed by the biscuits.

11. Next day, in a saucepan, boil the sugar, water, cocoa and chocolate for 2 minutes.

12. Remove from heat, and beat in butter; cool slightly.

13. Remove the foil from the cake, and place on a serving dish.

14. Pour enough melted chocolate over the cake to give it a nice coating. You can reserve the remaining melted chocolate, and place in a gravy boat to serve alongside the cake.

15. Decorate top of cake with a row of cherries, if desired. Sprinkle cake with flaked almonds. Refrigerate and serve chilled.

[CLYDE & HELEN ALLEN, AND JAMES & CHARLES]

THE ULTIMATE NANAIMO BAR

Nutrition Facts per serving: Calories 382.3, Protein 3.368 Gm, Carbs 41.64 Gm, Fat 23.88 Gm, Cholesterol 56.02 mg, Dietary Fiber 1.687 Gm, Sugar 31.21 Gm, Sodium 259.9 mg, Calcium 56.39 mg, Potassium 150.7 mg, Iron 0.906 mg

SERVES 6 TO 8

Bottom Layer:
½ cup unsalted butter
   (European-style cultured)
¼ cup sugar
5 Tbsp. cocoa
1 egg, beaten
1-¾ cup graham wafer crumbs
½ cup finely chopped
   almonds (optional)
1 cup coconut flakes

Second Layer:
½ cup unsalted butter
2 Tbsp. and 2 tsp. cream
2 Tbsp. vanilla custard powder
2 cups icing sugar

Third Layer:
6 ozs. semi-sweet chocolate
   (either squares or chocolate
   morsals)
4 Tbsp. unsalted butter

Bottom Layer:

1. Melt first 3 ingredients in the top of a double boiler.

2. Add egg, and stir continuously to cook and thicken.

3. Remove from heat.

4. Stir in crumbs, coconut and nuts.

5. Press firmly into an ungreased 8" x 8" pan (or 9" round pan).

6. Refrigerate.

Second Layer:

1. Cream butter, cream, custard powder and icing sugar together well.

2. Beat until light.

3. Spread over the bottom layer.

4. Refrigerate.

Third Layer:

1. Melt chocolate and butter over Low heat; let cool.

2. When cool, but still liquid, pour over second layer, and chill in the refrigerator.

3. Prior to cutting into the bars, remove pan from refrigerator. This is best done at room temperature to avoid cracking the chocolate third layer.

[ANDREW & MARY FALCONER, AND LUKA & EVAN]

"This recipe originates from the city of Nanaimo, British Columbia on Vancouver Island in Canada. According to local folklore, about 35 years ago, a Nanaimo housewife entered her recipe for chocolate squares in a magazine contest. She chose to dub the entry after her hometown "Nanaimo Bars". Her recipe won a prize, thereby publicizing Nanaimo as much as her cooking. Most Canadians have had the pleasure of tasting these wonderful treats and I personally serve it at most functions - always a crowd favourite, especially in the Cayman Islands!"

- Mary Falconer

GRANDMA'S LEMON DRIZZLE CAKE

Nutrition Facts per serving: Calories 528.6, Protein 10.72 Gm, Carbs 82.32 Gm, Fat 17.73 Gm, Cholesterol 71 mg,
Dietary Fiber 10.7 Gm, Sugar 1.863 Gm, Sodium 1291 mg, Calcium 357.4 mg, Potassium 304.3 mg, Iron 4.11 mg

SERVES 8

1 cup all purpose flour
2 flat tsp. baking powder
1 cup sugar
8 ozs. margarine or butter, softened
4 lg. eggs
Rinds from 2 firm skin lemons, washed and fine-grated
Juice from 2 lemons - (4 tsp. for cake, and the remaining juice for the drizzle)
4 ozs. granulated sugar, for drizzle

1. Preheat oven to 350°F.

2. Grease the bottoms and sides of an 8" round cake pan, and line with wax paper or parchment paper. Lightly grease the paper.

3. Sieve flour and baking powder into a large bowl. To this, add sugar, margarine and 4 eggs.

4. Add lemon juice to the mixture, then add the grated lemon rind.

5. Beat with a wooden spoon for about 3 to 4 minutes, or until mixture is smooth; pour into the cake pan.

6. Bake in preheated oven for approximately 40 minutes. Cake is done when a toothpick inserted in the centre comes out clean.

7. When cooked, turn out onto a wire rack and leave upside down.

8. Cool for 5 minutes.

Drizzle:

1. Put remaining lemon juice into a small microwave-safe bowl, and heat for 30 to 40 seconds.

2. Add 4 ounces granulated sugar to lemon juice, and mix.

3. Remove greased paper from cake, and turn upright onto a serving plate while still very hot.

4. Spoon mix onto top of cake, letting mixture run down the sides.

5. Cover with a food net, and leave to harden 8 to 12 hours (or overnight).

[RICHARD & MEELIN VERNON, AND ELLIOT, LAUREN & YASMIN]

DAD'S BOILED FRUIT CAKE

Nutrition Facts per serving: Calories 552.9, Protein 23.72 Gm, Carbs 51.36 Gm, Fat 20.23 Gm, Cholesterol 113.6 mg, Dietary Fiber 0.985 Gm, Sugar 0.577 Gm, Sodium 1124 mg, Calcium 61.3 mg, Potassium 199.2 mg, Iron 2.129 mg

SERVES 10

1 lb. mixed dried fruit
3 eggs
12 ozs. all purpose flour
1 tsp. baking powder
9 ozs. sugar
8 ozs. butter
1 tsp. vanilla extract
½ tsp. almond extract
Glazed cherries or
   nuts, to garnish

1. Preheat oven to 300°F.

2. Line a baking tin with wax paper.

3. In a saucepan, cover fruit with water.

4. Bring to a boil, and boil for 5 minutes; strain.

5. Cut butter into strained fruit.

6. Beat together eggs, sugar, vanilla and almond extracts; add to fruit.

7. Fold in flour and baking powder.

8. Pour into the tin, and smooth top with a knife.

9. Top with cherries and/or nuts.

10. Bake for 30 minutes, and then reduce heat to 280°F. Continue to cook for approximately 1-½ hours, or until skewer or knife inserted in the centre comes out clean.

[TONY & KAREN ATTENBOROUGH, AND CLAIRE, HAMISH & MATTHEW]

Dad's Boiled Fruit Cake

COFFEE-TOFFEE PIE

Nutrition Facts per serving: Calories 530.8, Protein 5.356 Gm, Carbs 29.31 Gm, Fat 45.42 Gm, Cholesterol 165.8 mg,
Dietary Fiber 1.627 Gm, Sugar 13.98 Gm, Sodium 241.2 mg, Calcium 71.99 mg, Potassium 187.9 mg, Iron 1.232 mg

SERVES 8

Pastry Shell:

1. Preheat oven to 375°F.

2. In a medium bowl, combine piecrust mix, brown sugar, walnuts, grated chocolate and vanilla extract.

3. Turn into a well-greased 9" pie plate; press firmly against bottom and side of pie plate.

4. Bake for 11 minutes.

5. Cool on a wire rack.

Filling:

1. In a small bowl, with an electric mixer at Medium speed, beat the butter until it is creamy. Gradually add granulated sugar, beating until light.

2. Blend in cool melted chocolate and 2 teaspoons instant coffee.

3. Add 1 egg; beat for 5 minutes. Add remaining egg; beat for 5 minutes longer.

4. Turn filling into baked pie shell; cover and refrigerate overnight.

Topping (to be made the next day):

1. In a large bowl, combine cream with 2 tablespoons instant coffee and the confectioners' sugar. Cover and refrigerate for 1 hour.

2. Beat cream mixture, until stiff.

3. Decorate pie with the topping. If desired, garnish with chocolate curls.

4. Refrigerate pie at least 2 hours before serving.

[PAUL PEENE & TONI PINKERTON, AND
SAMANTHA, DEREK & ANDREW]

Pastry Shell:
½ pkg. piecrust mix
¼ cup light brown sugar,
    firmly packed
¾ cup finely chopped walnuts
1 sq. unsweetened
    chocolate, grated
1 tsp. vanilla extract

Filling:
½ cup soft butter
    or margarine
¾ cup granulated sugar
1 sq. unsweetened chocolate,
    melted and cooled
2 tsp. instant coffee
2 eggs

Topping:
2 cups heavy cream
2 Tbsp. instant coffee
½ cup confectioners' sugar
Chocolate curls

PECAN ICE CREAM

Nutrition Facts per serving: Calories 255.38, Protein 2.56 Gm, Carbs 28.69 Gm, Fat 15.33 Gm, Cholesterol 38.44 mg, Dietary Fiber 0.74 Gm, Sugar 0.42 Gm, Sodium 129.81 mg, Calcium 51.31 mg, Potassium 128.31 mg, Iron 0.84 mg

1 cup flour
1 cup chopped pecans
1 cup brown sugar
1 cup melted butter
Caramel syrup, for topping
Vanilla ice cream,
    thawed a little so that it can
    spread easily

1. Preheat oven to 350°F.
2. Combine the first 4 ingredients; mix thoroughly. Spread onto a cookie sheet and bake in preheated oven until golden brown
3. Place half the mixture into a 9" x 13" pan.
4. Drizzle the top with caramel syrup.
5. Press vanilla ice cream over pecan mixture about 1" thick.
6. Spread the remainder of the pecan mixture over the ice cream; drizzle with more caramel syrup.
7. Press down and freeze until firm.

[RUSSELL & SHEENA BUNTON, AND MADISON & QUINCEY]

APPLE FLAN

Nutrition Facts per serving: Calories 332, Protein 5.755 Gm, Carbs 61.73 Gm, Fat 7.53 Gm, Cholesterol 52.17 mg, Dietary Fiber 5.967 Gm, Sugar 23.22 Gm, Sodium 445.5 mg, Calcium 161.4 mg, Potassium 102 mg, Iron 1.62 mg

6 ozs. self-rising flour
1 oz. confectioners' sugar
1 egg
Pinch salt
2 Tbsp. water, to mix
2 lg. apples
½ oz. all purpose flour
2 ozs. castor or
    granulated sugar
¼ tsp. ground cloves
¼ pint double cream
Rind of 1 orange

1. Preheat oven to 425°F.
2. Make a sweet short-crust pastry by combining self-rising flour, salt, confectioners' sugar, egg and water.
3. Roll out the pastry on a floured surface; evenly line a 9" flan ring or quiche dish with the pastry.
4. Prick the base of pastry in about 5 places with a fork.
5. Peel and slice the apples to about the thickness of a quarter.
6. Make the filling by beating together all purpose flour, castor sugar, ground cloves and double cream.
7. Spread the apples in the base of the flan; spread the cream mixture over the top.
8. Grate the whole rind of 1 orange directly over the flan; bake for about 30 minutes.
9. Serve warm or cold - never hot because it will disintegrate.

[PEARSE & ALISON MURPHY, AND GRACE, AOIFE & SARAH]

BANANA PUDDING

Nutrition Facts per serving: Calories 261.8, Protein 5.166 Gm, Carbs 48.98 Gm, Fat 5.874 Gm, Cholesterol 70.43 mg, Dietary Fiber 1.363 Gm, Sugar 17.44 Gm, Sodium 131.2 mg, Calcium 85 mg, Potassium 329.5 mg, Iron 1.398 mg

SERVES 12

⅓ cup all purpose flour
¾ cup sugar, divided
Dash salt
½ tsp. vanilla extract
3 eggs, separated
2 cups milk
Approx. ¾ of a (12 oz.) box Nilla Wafers
6 lg. ripe bananas, sliced into ¼" rounds

1. Preheat oven to 350°F.

2. Mix together flour, salt and ½ cup of the sugar in the top of a double boiler.

3. Add egg yolks and milk to the dry ingredients; mix well.

4. Cook uncovered over boiling water for 10 to 12 minutes, or until thickened, stirring constantly to avoid lumpiness.

5. When thickened, remove from heat, and stir in the vanilla extract.

6. Cover the bottom of a 2 quart baking dish with Nilla Wafers, and prop wafers all around the sides of the baking dish.

7. Top the wafers with the sliced bananas.

8. Spread the pudding over the bananas.

9. With an electric mixer on High speed, beat egg whites until soft peaks form.

10. Gradually add the remaining ¼ cup sugar, beating until stiff peaks form.

11. Spoon over pudding; spread evenly to cover entire surface, using back of spoon or a rubber spatula to fluff up the meringue.

12. Bake 15 to 20 minutes, or until lightly browned.

[LISA MERREN]

Banana Pudding

213

KEY LIME PIE

Nutrition Facts per serving: Calories 365.4, Protein 7.384 Gm, Carbs 58.97 Gm, Fat 12.73 Gm, Cholesterol 68.51 mg, Dietary Fiber 2.335 Gm, Sugar 4.983 Gm, Sodium 318.2 mg, Calcium 152.5 mg, Potassium 308.3, Iron 2.011 mg

SERVES 10

Graham Cracker Crust:
1-¼ cups graham cracker crumbs (about 11 graham crackers)
2 Tbsp. sugar
4 Tbsp. melted butter

Filling:
6 to 8 limes, preferably key limes
1 (14 oz.) can sweetened condensed milk
2 lg. eggs, separated
Fresh strawberries, sliced (or whole raspberries), for garnish (optional)

NOTE:
To save on time, a purchased graham cracker piecrust will work with this recipe.

Crust:

1. Preheat oven to 375°F.

2. With a fork, mix together in a bowl graham cracker crumbs, sugar and butter.

3. Turn mixture into a 9" pie plate or tart pan; using hands, press mixture to the bottom and up the side of the pie plate.

4. Bake in preheated oven for 10 minutes.

5. Cool on a wire rack.

Key Lime Pie

Filling:

1. Grate 2 teaspoons of peel from the limes; squeeze ½ cup juice.

2. In a medium bowl, with a wire whisk or fork, combine condensed milk with lime peel and juice; add egg yolks, and stir until mixture thickens.

3. In a small bowl, with a mixer at High speed, beat egg whites until stiff peaks form when beaters are lifted.

4. With rubber spatula or wire whisk, gently fold egg whites into lime mixture.

5. Pour filling into cooled piecrust; smooth top.

6. Bake on 375°F for 15 to 20 minutes, just until filling is firm.

7. Cool on a wire rack, then refrigerate 3 hours, or until well-chilled.

8. Garnish with strawberries or raspberries, if desired.

[BRYAN & JENNIFER HUNTER, AND CORY & DANIEL]

14-KARAT CAKE

Nutrition Facts per serving: Calories 569.7, Protein 6.126 Gm, Carbs 61.44 Gm, Fat 34.32 Gm, Cholesterol 71 mg,
Dietary Fiber 2.052 Gm, Sugar 5.288 Gm, Sodium 385.7 mg, Calcium 116.1 mg, Potassium 418.3, Iron 2.778 mg

SERVES 10 TO 12

2 cups all purpose flour
2 cups sugar
2 tsp. baking powder
1-½ cups oil
1-½ tsp. baking soda
4 eggs
1 tsp. salt
2 cups grated raw carrots
2 Tbsp. cinnamon
8-½ ozs. crushed
    pineapple (drained)
½ cup chopped walnuts

Frosting:
½ cup butter or margarine
1 (8 oz.) pkg. cream cheese
1 tsp. vanilla extract
1 cup confectioners' sugar
2 Tbsp. milk or
    whipping cream

1. Preheat oven to 350°F.

2. Sift together flour, baking powder, baking soda, salt and cinnamon.

3. Add sugar, oil and eggs; mix well.

4. Add grated carrots, drained pineapple and nuts.

5. Grease and flour either two 8" round cake pans (or a Bundt cake pan).

6. Pour even amounts of mixture into each pan (or all of the mixture into the Bundt cake pan).

7. Bake in preheated oven for 55 minutes to 1 hour if using two round cake pans. Bake for 1 hour and 20 minutes if using a Bundt cake pan.

8. Let cool before frosting.

Frosting:

1. With an electric mixer, cream together the butter and cream cheese; add vanilla, and mix.

2. Beat in sifted confectioners' sugar.

3. Add about 2 tablespoons milk or whipping cream, and mix well.

4. Spread over the entire cake, before serving.

[RAY & JACQUI FARRINGTON, AND KYLE]

CHRISTMAS CHOCOLATE BARK

Nutrition Facts per serving: Calories 128, Protein 3.6 Gm, Carbs 16.7 Gm, Fat 6.4 Gm,
Cholesterol 6 mg, Dietary Fiber 2.1 Gm, Sugar 13 Gm, Sodium 33

SERVES 6 TO 8

2 ozs. slivered almonds
¾ cup dried cranberries
14 ozs. white chocolate

1. Preheat oven to 350°F.

2. Toast almonds in preheated oven for approximately 7 to 9 minutes; let cool.

3. Melt white chocolate in a double boiler over Medium-Low heat.

4. When chocolate is smooth, remove from heat; add almonds and cranberries.

5. Spread out onto waxed paper, and cover; refrigerate for 2 hours.

6. Break into pieces, and serve.

[RICHARD & SANDY HEW, AND THOMPSON,
LAUREN & HARRISON]

STICKY TOFFEE PUDDING

Nutrition Facts per serving: Calories 603.2, Protein 3.885 Gm, Carbs 79.09 Gm, Fat 32.33 Gm, Cholesterol 119.9 mg,
Dietary Fiber 3.728 Gm, Sugar 35.31 Gm, Sodium 404.2 mg, Calcium 126.4 mg, Potassium 603.5 mg, Iron 2.239 mg

SERVES 10

Pudding:
4 ozs. butter
½ cup brown sugar
1 egg
4 tsp. vanilla extract
1 cup all purpose flour
1 tsp. baking soda
1 tsp. baking powder
¼ tsp. salt
2 cups chopped dates
¼ cup molasses
1-¼ cup boiling water
Butter, for greasing ramekins

Treacle Sauce:
4 ozs. melted butter
1 cup brown sugar
¼ cup treacle (or water)
1-½ cups heavy cream

Pudding:

1. Preheat oven to 325°F.

2. Butter (well) ten 1 cup ramekins (or soufflé dishes).

3. Sift together flour, baking powder and baking soda.

4. Cream butter, salt and brown sugar.

5. Add egg, vanilla and ¼ cup of the flour mixture to creamed butter; mix until smooth.

6. Add the remaining flour mixture.

7. Add chopped dates, molasses and boiling water, stirring to combine.

8. Divide batter evenly between the ramekins (or soufflé dishes).

9. Place ramekins on a baking sheet; bake in preheated oven for 20 minutes.

10. Lower the temperature to 300°F, and bake for an additional 30 minutes (or until toothpick or skewer inserted in the centre of cakes comes out clean).

11. Cool slightly.

Treacle Sauce:

1. Combine brown sugar and treacle in a small saucepan over Medium-High heat.

2. Stir constantly and bring mixture to a boil for 1 minute (be careful not to burn the mixture).

3. Add the melted butter; stir to combine. Boil for 1 minute.

4. Stir in heavy cream; bring to a boil.

5. Reduce heat, and simmer the sauce for 15 minutes, stirring occasionally.

6. Cool slightly.

7. Spread the warm mixture evenly over Sticky Toffee Pudding. Serve warm.

[GORDON & LANA ROWELL, AND MADELEINE & MATTHEW]

FRESH APPLE CAKE

Nutrition Facts per serving: Calories 762.5, Protein 7.032 Gm, Carbs 85.45 Gm, Fat 45.74 Gm, Cholesterol 63.9 mg,
Dietary Fiber 2.121 Gm, Sugar 10.9 Gm, Sodium 197.8 mg, Calcium 58.45 mg, Potassium 329.2 mg, Iron 3.073 mg

SERVES 8 TO 10

3 cups all purpose flour
2 cups sugar
1-½ tsp. salt
1 tsp. baking soda
½ tsp. cinnamon
½ tsp. ground cloves
1-½ cups vegetable oil
3 eggs, beaten
⅔ cup coconut flakes (optional)
½ cup chopped pecans
   or walnuts
3 lg. apples, peeled and
   chopped into small pieces
Confectioners' sugar (optional)

1. Preheat oven to 325°F, and grease a Bundt cake pan.

2. In a large bowl, mix the first six ingredients together.

3. In a separate mixing bowl, blend eggs and oil.

4. Add the dry ingredients to the egg mixture.

5. Add coconut (if desired), nuts and apples; mix thoroughly.

6. Pour mixture into the greased Bundt pan, and bake in preheated oven for 1 hour and 10 minutes.

7. Cool for 30 minutes before inverting onto cake plate.

8. Dust the top with confectioners' sugar, if desired.

This recipe was selected from a collection of recipes submitted by members of John Gray Memorial Church, supporters of Cayman Prep and High School.

[LEONARD & CAROL ANN EBANKS]

Fresh Apple Cake

BANANA FLAMBÉ

Nutrition Facts per serving: Calories 359, Protein 6.275 Gm, Carbs 52.14 Gm, Fat 14.16 Gm, Cholesterol 61.57 mg,
Dietary Fiber 0.499 Gm, Sugar 1.433 Gm, Sodium 276.9 mg, Calcium 79.82 mg, Potassium 223.9 mg, Iron 1.71 mg

SERVES 4 TO 6

4 bananas (not too ripe) peeled and cut in half lengthwise, and then cut crosswise in 1" pcs.
2 Tbsp. brown sugar
2 Tbsp. Cognac
2 Tbsp. butter
2 Tbsp. granulated sugar
2 Tbsp. Tia Maria
Juice of 1 lemon
Juice of 2 oranges
Cinnamon
Vanilla ice cream

1. Place banana slices, brown sugar, Cognac and lemon juice in a bowl; marinate 15 minutes.

2. Meanwhile, heat butter and granulated sugar together; cook until mixture caramelizes and is golden brown.

3. Pour in orange juice; mix well.

4. Continue cooking for 2 to 3 minutes over Medium heat, stirring constantly.

5. Add bananas along with marinade to the orange mixture.

6. Pour in Tia Maria, and flambé. Continue cooking over High heat for 1minute.

7. Serve with a scoop of vanilla ice cream.

8. Garnish with sprinkled cinnamon.

[DAVID & MELANIE KHOURI, AND JESSICA]

BUTTERSCOTCH PIE

Nutrition Facts per serving: Calories 314.6, Protein 7.421 Gm, Carbs 53.21 Gm, Fat 8.078 Gm, Cholesterol 74.45 mg,
Dietary Fiber 2.507 Gm, Sugar 20.43 Gm, Sodium 128.9 mg, Calcium 208.1 mg, Potassium 641.9 mg, Iron 0.857 mg

SERVES 6 TO 8

2 eggs
1 cup brown sugar
1 cup milk
5 Tbsp. all purpose flour
2 Tbsp. butter
1 tsp. vanilla
3 Tbsp. water
9" frozen piecrust

1. Prepare piecrust as directed on package.

2. Combine dry ingredients in a medium saucepan.

3. Add remaining ingredients except vanilla and butter; cook over Medium heat stirring constantly, until it thickens and bubbles. Remove from heat, and stir in vanilla and butter.

4. Pour into baked piecrust. Add meringue, if desired.

5. Refrigerate for 4 hours, and serve chilled.

Meringue:

1. With an electric mixer on High speed, beat 3 egg whites until soft peaks form.

2. Gradually add ¼ cup sugar, beating until stiff peaks form.

3. Spread meringue over pie filling, carefully pushing the meringue to the pastry edge to seal well and prevent shrinking.

4. Bake at 425°F until meringue is golden brown (for about 10 minutes).

This recipe originated with Kate Sauber's grandmother, Louise Voss, who travelled to the U.S. from Scotland as a very young child. She claimed this was a traditional Scottish pie recipe.

[JAMES & KATE SAUBER, AND ANNE]

CASSAVA HEAVY CAKE

Nutrition Facts per serving: Calories 318.4, Protein 2.106 Gm, Carbs 48.63 Gm, Fat 14.7 Gm, Cholesterol 20.71mg, Dietary Fiber 4.374 Gm, Sugar 4.262 Gm, Sodium 366.1 mg, Calcium 53.62 mg, Potassium 470 mg, Iron 1.938 mg

1. Boil coconut milk with sugar, butter and spices for about 15 minutes. This should produce 8 cups of liquid. Reserve ½ cup of this liquid, and mix the remainder of it with the cassava, until combined.

2. Place the cassava mixture into a greased rectangular baking pan.

3. Bake at 400°F for about 30 minutes.

4. Reduce heat to 350°F, and bake for approximately another 2 hours.

5. Meanwhile, add 1 tablespoon butter to the reserved liquid; simmer it on the stove until it reaches a syrup consistency. Use this syrup to periodically baste the top of the heavy cake with a pastry brush while it is baking. This will give the top of the cake a rich glossy colour.

SERVES 15

6 cups grated cassava (frozen)
3 cans coconut milk (add
    1 can of water to milk)
4-½ cups sugar
1 tsp. salt
1 Tbsp. cinnamon
1 tsp. ground cloves
1 tsp. ground allspice
1 stick butter or margarine

TIP:
Frozen grated cassava can be purchased at the supermarket although it is not always available.

NOTE:
"This recipe was given to me by a family friend, Mrs. Laurel Watler, who is an excellent cook." - Karen Hunter

[ARTHUR & KAREN HUNTER]

Cassava Heavy Cake

AUNT KATHY'S CHOCOLATE CAKE

Nutrition Facts per serving: Calories 691.1, Protein 6.892 Gm, Carbs 92.21 Gm, Fat 36.08 Gm, Cholesterol 59.49 mg, Dietary Fiber 0.311 Gm, Sugar 0 Gm, Sodium 1217 mg, Calcium 162.7 mg, Potassium 336.3, Iron 3.632 mg

SERVES 6 TO 8

1 box of chocolate cake mix
1 sm. box chocolate
   instant pudding
¼ cup water
½ cup melted butter
1-½ cups sour cream
6 ozs. chocolate chips
Confectioners'
   sugar, for topping

1. Preheat oven to 350°F.

2. Mix all the ingredients together, and pour into a greased Bundt pan.

3. Bake 50 minutes.

4. Dust the top with confectioners' sugar.

[TONY & CHRISTINE CLEAVER, AND ALEX, JORDYN & BETHANY]

Aunt Kathy's Chocolate Cake

OUR FAVOURITE ICE CREAM

Nutrition Facts per serving: Calories 348.1, Protein 6.661 Gm, Carbs 42.33 Gm, Fat 17.66 Gm, Cholesterol 66.75 mg, Dietary Fiber 0 Gm, Sugar 0.833 Gm, Sodium 108.5 mg, Calcium 236.3 mg, Potassium 306.8 mg, Iron 0.155 mg

SERVES 4 TO 6

1 tin sweetened condensed milk
½ pint double cream (heavy
   cream or whipping cream
   may be used as alternatives)
2 tsp. instant coffee granules
   (or strong espresso coffee)

This easy ice cream recipe was until now a secret one ... known only to parishioners, friends and family of the congregation at St. Peter's Church, Harrogate, England

1. Whip up the cream with an electric mixer.

2. Add condensed milk, and whip again.

3. Dissolve coffee in as little hot water as possible; let cool.

4. Whip coffee into cream mixture, and pour into a freezer-proof dish, ready for serving.

5. Freeze for at least 10 hours.

6. Remove from freezer, and place in refrigerator about 20 minutes before serving.

[TONY & BRIDGET PITCAIRN, AND SOPHIE]

PUMPKIN DUMP CAKE

Nutrition Facts per serving: Calories 425.7, Protein 6.1 Gm, Carbs 56.96 Gm, Fat 20.52 Gm, Cholesterol 93.03 mg,
Dietary Fiber 2.17 Gm, Sugar 2.806 Gm, Sodium 485 mg, Calcium 136.6 mg, Potassium 281.7 mg, Iron 2.109 mg

SERVES 12

1 (15 oz.) can pumpkin
1 (12 oz.) can evaporated milk
4 eggs
1 cup sugar
1 tsp. ground nutmeg
1 tsp. ground ginger
1 tsp. ground cloves
2 tsp. ground cinnamon
½ tsp. salt
1 pkg. yellow cake mix
1 stick butter, melted
1 cup chopped pecans

1. Preheat oven to 350°F.

2. Grease and flour a 9" x 13" pan.

3. In a large bowl, stir together the pumpkin, sugar, salt, nutmeg, ginger, cloves and cinnamon.

4. Stir in the milk, then beat in the eggs one at a time; pour pumpkin mixture into the prepared pan.

5. Sprinkle the yellow cake mix over the pumpkin mixture, then sprinkle on the pecans.

6. Drizzle melted butter all over the top.

7. Bake in preheated oven for 55 minutes, or until the edges are lightly brown.

8. Allow to cool before serving.

[R E X & K I M M I L L E R , A N D K A Y L A , C O R E Y & H A L L E]

APPLE DUMP CAKE

Nutrition Facts per serving: Calories 306.5, Protein 1.39 Gm, Carbs 5.317 Gm, Fat 32.32 Gm, Cholesterol 62.13 mg,
Dietary Fiber 0.891 Gm, Sugar 0.579 Gm, Sodium 245.2 mg, Calcium 16.31 mg, Potassium 67.99, Iron 0.518

SERVES 10 TO 12

2 tsp. cinnamon
2 (16.5 oz.) cans
  apple pie filling (not
  sliced apples)
1 pkg. spice or
  caramel cake mix
1-½ cups oleo or
  butter, melted
1-½ cups pecans

1. Preheat oven to 350°F.

2. Spread pie filling in a 9" x 12" baking tin or casserole dish.

3. Sprinkle cinnamon all over filling.

4. Sprinkle cake mix evenly over cinnamon.

5. Place pecans evenly over cake mix.

6. Pour melted butter all over cake mix (DO NOT STIR ANYTHING).

7. Bake in preheated oven for about 30 to 45 minutes, or until lightly browned.

8. Serve hot, topped with Cool Whip or vanilla ice cream.

[E D L I N & H E L E N M E R R E N]

FRUIT-FILLED LAYERED ANGEL DESSERT

Nutrition Facts per serving: Calories 273, Protein 5.507 Gm, Carbs 52.21 Gm, Fat 5.111 Gm, Cholesterol 0.735 mg,
Dietary Fiber 0.662 Gm, Sugar 7.165 Gm, Sodium 443 mg, Calcium 105.6 mg, Potassium 217.3 mg, Iron 0.322 mg

SERVES 12

1 pkg. white angel food cake
  mix
1 (3-½ oz.) pkg. vanilla or
  lemon instant pudding and
  pie filling
2 cups skim milk
1 (8 oz.) container whipped
  topping with real cream,
  thawed
1 pint strawberries, cut into
  halves or fourths
1 kiwi fruit, peeled

NOTE:
1 cup
strawberries,
cut into
halves, can be
substituted
for the kiwi
fruit, if
desired.

1. Bake and cool cake as directed on package.

2. Trim brown crust from cake, and discard.

3. Tear cake into about 1" pieces.

4. Prepare pudding and pie filling as directed on package for pudding (except use skim milk).

5. Fold in 2 cups whipped topping (reserve remaining whipped topping for garnish).

6. Place one-half of the cake pieces in a 3 quart glass serving bowl.

7. Top with one-third of the pudding mixture, one-half of the strawberries, one-third of the cake pieces and one-third of the pudding mixture.

8. Slice the kiwi fruit, and cut each slice into halves.

9. Place the slices against the side of the bowl.

10. Top with remaining cake pieces, pudding mixture and strawberries.

11. Refrigerate until chilled (at least 4 hours).

12. Garnish with remaining whipped topping.

[DON & JENNIE STEWART]

Fruit-filled Layered Angel Dessert

RHUBARB-STRAWBERRY CRISP

Nutrition Facts per serving: Calories 336.6, Protein 2.929 Gm, Carbs 47.69 Gm, Fat 15.77 Gm, Cholesterol 41.42 mg, Dietary Fiber 2.024 Gm, Sugar 2.963 Gm, Sodium 169.7 mg, Calcium 76.08 mg, Potassium 307.2 mg, Iron 1.762 mg

1. Place cut-up rhubarb and strawberries into a greased 9" square pan.

2. Sprinkle with the lemon juice and ¼ cup of brown sugar.

3. Mix flour, margarine and brown sugar together. Add the cinnamon, and stir the mixture until crumbly adding more flour, if necessary.

4. Sprinkle over the rhubarb mixture.

5. Bake at 350°F for 30 minutes, or until the topping is browned and the fruit is bubbling through.

6. Serve warm with cream or ice cream.

This recipe was submitted by Daniel and Caitlyn Harrington's grandmother, Sara Jane Meisner of Ottawa, Canada. Frozen cut-up rhubarb may be used if fresh is not available. Also, rhubarb is seasonal and therefore unavailable at times, but blueberries and/or blackberries can be used as substitutes in this dish. It may need to cook longer if frozen fruit is used.

[SEAN & LIZ HARRINGTON, AND DANIEL & CAITLYN]

SERVES 6

2 cups cut-up rhubarb
 (or blueberries)
1 cup of cut-up fresh strawberries
1 Tbsp. lemon juice
1 cup all purpose flour
½ cup brown sugar
1 tsp. cinnamon
½ cup softened butter
 or margarine
¼ cup brown sugar

DUTCH DAINTIES

Nutrition Facts per serving: Calories 224.5, Protein 2.723 Gm, Carbs 37.53 Gm, Fat 7.648 Gm, Cholesterol 42.16 mg, Dietary Fiber 0.824 Gm, Sugar 4.505 Gm, Sodium 76.47 mg, Calcium 31.22 mg, Potassium 163.7 mg, Iron 1.181 mg

1. Preheat oven to 350°F.

2. Cream butter and sugar.

3. Add 1 egg plus one egg yolk; mix in flour.

4. Place approximately 1 tablespoon of the mixture into 16 greased cupcake pans; press flat with floured fingers.

5. Beat the egg white, until stiff.

6. Mix in the brown sugar and vanilla; add in all other ingredients.

7. Place approximately 1 tablespoon of second mixture on top of base mixture.

8. Bake for 17 minutes in preheated oven; let cool before removing from baking tin.

This cherished recipe was passed down to Sandy Hew by her mother, whose own mother passed it down to her. It originated in Alberta, Canada.

[RICHARD & SANDY HEW, AND THOMPSON,
LAUREN & HARRISON]

MAKES 16

½ cup butter, softened
¾ cup sugar
1-½ cups all purpose flour
2 eggs (1 of the eggs separated)
1 cup brown sugar
¼ cup dates, finely chopped
¼ cup cherries, halved
¼ cup raisins
¼ cup walnuts
1 tsp. vanilla

Cherries can be substituted with dried cranberries. Dates can be omitted and extra raisins added.

EASY FESTIVE FUDGE

Nutrition Facts per serving: Calories 311.1, Protein 7.759 Gm, Carbs 36.16 Gm, Fat 16.97 Gm, Cholesterol 14.44 mg,
Dietary Fiber 1.248 Gm, Sugar 17.77 Gm, Sodium 78.08 mg, Calcium 178.3 mg, Potassium 294.2 mg, Iron 1.073 mg

SERVES 12 TO 16

3 cups (1-½ pkgs.) milk
   chocolate chips
Dash salt
1-½ tsp. vanilla extract
½ to 1 cup chopped
   nuts (optional)
1 can sweetened
   condensed milk

Microwave method:

1. Line an 8" x 9" square pan with wax paper.

2. In a medium microwave-safe bowl, stir together chocolate chips, sweetened condensed milk and salt.

3. Microwave on High for 1 minute. Stir until smooth. If necessary, microwave an additional 15 seconds at a time, stirring after each heating, until the chips are melted and the mixture is smooth.

4. Stir in vanilla and nuts.

5. Spread evenly in prepared pan.

6. Refrigerate 2 hours, or until firm.

7. Turn fudge onto cutting board. Peel off paper and cut into squares.

8. Store covered in refrigerator.

Conventional method:

1. Stir together chocolate chips, condensed milk and salt in a heavy saucepan.

2. Cook over Low heat, until chocolate is melted and smooth.

3. Remove from heat.

4. Repeat steps 4 through 8 above.

[EDLIN & HELEN MERREN]

BUTTERFINGER BANANA CAKE

Nutrition Facts per serving: Calories 302.2, Protein 3.015 Gm, Carbs 62.08 Gm, Fat 5.818 Gm, Cholesterol 1.1 mg,
Dietary Fiber 0.677 Gm, Sugar 2.215 Gm, Sodium 287.1 mg, Calcium 47.16 mg, Potassium 139 mg, Iron 0.626 mg

SERVES 12 TO 16

1 box yellow cake mix
2 med. mashed
   ripe bananas
3 Butterfinger candy
   bars, crumbled
1 (16 oz.) container white
   frosting, prepared

1. Preheat oven to 350°F.

2. Grease and flour a 13" x 9" baking pan.

3. Prepare cake mix batter according to package directions; stir in bananas and ¾ cup crumbled Butterfinger bars. Pour into the prepared pan.

4. Bake 40 to 50 minutes, or until a toothpick inserted in the centre comes out clean.

5. Frost, and sprinkle with remaining crumbled Butterfinger.

[REX & KIM MILLER, AND KAYLA, COREY & HALLE]

CHOCOLATE OAT BARS

Nutrition Facts per serving: Calories 240.9, Protein 3.046 Gm, Carbs 24.4 Gm, Fat 15.55 Gm, Cholesterol 33.13 mg, Dietary Fiber 0.445 Gm, Sugar 5.758 Gm, Sodium 200.7 mg, Calcium 23.73 mg, Potassium 118.2 mg, Iron 1.113 mg

MAKES 15

Butter, for greasing baking pan
1 cup butter
½ cup superfine sugar
2 Tbsp. maple syrup or honey
3 cups oats
½ tsp. salt
4 oz. semisweet chocolate
   or chocolate chips

1. Preheat the oven to 350°F.

2. Grease a 9" x 13" baking pan with butter.

3. Put the 1 cup butter, sugar and maple syrup or honey into a large saucepan, and melt over Low heat.

4. Remove the pan from heat. Add the oats and salt to the butter mixture; mix everything together well.

5. Tip the mixture into the baking pan, and press it down firmly. Bake for 20 to 30 minutes, until golden brown.

6. Let the bars cool slightly, then cut them into squares. Once they have cooled completely, remove them from the baking sheet.

7. Break the chocolate into a bowl, and stand it over a saucepan of water.

8. Heat the saucepan of water until it simmers. Stir the chocolate as it melts and forms a smooth chocolate sauce.

9. Dip one end of each piece of oat bar into the melted chocolate. Place them on a wire rack until the chocolate sets.

[LINDA DALTON-RILEY & DARREN RILEY,
AND BRITTANY & SYDNEY]

Chocolate Oat Bars

ZABAGLIONE WITH STRAWBERRIES

Nutrition Facts per serving: Calories 223.4, Protein 5.516 Gm, Carbs 21.4 Gm, Fat 9.578 Gm, Cholesterol 180.1 mg,
Dietary Fiber 1.534 Gm, Sugar 9.263 Gm, Sodium 60.45 mg, Calcium 51.84 mg, Potassium 262.2 mg, Iron 1.142 mg

SERVES 6 TO 8

1 to 1-½ lbs. fresh
   ripe strawberries
1 Tbsp. sugar, plus
   more to taste
2 tsp. freshly squeezed lemon
   juice, plus more to taste

Zabaglione/Sabayon:
6 egg yolks
1 cup sweet Marsala wine
   or port, sherry, or Madeira
⅓ cup sugar, plus more
   to taste
Drops of freshly squeezed
   lemon juice (optional)

Whipped Cream
   (for glazed version):
½ cup heavy cream
1 tsp. sugar

NOTE:
*If it is desired
to serve the zabaglione
warm, make it at the
last minute. If it is
desired to glaze the
sabayon under the
broiler, or make it
ahead of time to serve
chilled, have a large
bowl (larger than the
one in which the sauce
was whipped) partly
filled with ice cubes
ready for use.*

Prepare the strawberries:

1. About an hour before serving the dessert, rinse the strawberries (stems on) and drain them on paper towels.

2. Slice off the stems, and halve or quarter the strawberries lengthwise, depending on size, and place in a bowl.

3. Sprinkle over the sugar and the lemon juice.

4. Fold gently together to blend well (add more sugar or lemon juice, if needed); set aside.

Whip the zabaglione/sabayon:

1. Whisk to blend the yolks, Marsala and sugar in a stainless steel bowl. Rest the bowl over a saucepan of very hot water. Heat the saucepan of water until it simmers.

2. Whisk constantly for 4 to 5 minutes or more to cook the sauce, until it has the consistency of lightly whipped cream with soft peaks. Clear the bottom of the bowl constantly with the whisk so that the eggs do not scramble and get lumpy; adjust heat as needed.

3. Taste the sauce. The sabayon should never get so hot that you cannot stick a very clean finger in it. Whisk in drops of lemon juice or more sugar, if desired.

4. When thick, foamy and tripled in volume, remove from heat. Serve hot as is, moderately warm, or cool.

Serve:

1. Spoon a portion of the strawberries (about ½ cup or more) into about 6 goblets or glasses.

2. Top the strawberries with ⅓ to ½ cup warm or cool sabayon, or put the sauce in first, then the strawberries (can be topped with Cool Whip, if desired).

(Continued on following page)

(Continued from previous page)

VARIATION to Zabaglione with Strawberries (Glazed version):

1. Cool the sabayon to room temperature, and turn on the broiler.

2. Whip the cream and sugar until soft peaks form; fold the cream into the sabayon with a rubber spatula.

3. Spread strawberries in a baking dish in one layer, or in individual gratin dishes.

4. Spoon the sauce over the berries so they are completely covered; set the dish under the broiler, 5 to 6 inches from the heat.

5. With the door open, keeping a close eye on the dish, broil for 1 to 2 minutes, turning as needed to glaze evenly, until the top is nicely browned and slightly crusted. Serve immediately.

[DON & TRACEY POTKINS, AND MEGHAN & SARAH]

BANANA CAKE WITH CHOCOLATE CHIPS

Nutrition Facts per serving: Calories 279.6, Protein 4.035 Gm, Carbs 45.38 Gm, Fat 9.41 Gm, Cholesterol 50.1 mg, Dietary Fiber 1.23 Gm, Sugar 6.356 Gm, Sodium 299.2 mg, Calcium 58.02 mg, Potassium 227.6 mg, Iron 1.731 mg

SERVES 8 TO 10

2 cups all purpose flour
1 tsp. baking powder
1 tsp. baking soda
½ tsp. salt
1 cup sugar
2 eggs (or ½ cup egg substitute)
¼ cup softened butter
  or margarine
1 cup mashed ripe bananas
  (about 3 bananas)
½ cup low fat sour cream
1 tsp. vanilla
½ cup mini chocolate chips
No-stick cooking spray

1. Preheat oven to 350°F. Spray a 9" x 13" baking pan (or a large loaf tin) with no-stick cooking spray.

2. In a medium bowl, combine flour, baking powder, baking soda and salt; set aside.

3. In a large bowl, with an electric mixer, beat sugar, eggs and butter on Medium speed.

4. Add bananas, sour cream and vanilla; beat until smooth.

5. Gradually add flour mixture to banana mixture, beating well after each addition (the batter will be thick).

6. Fold the chocolate chips into the flour/banana mixture.

7. Spoon into pan, and spread evenly.

8. Bake in preheated oven for 25 to 28 minutes, or until a skewer or toothpick inserted in the centre comes out clean.

9. Cool on a wire rack.

[TONY & KAREN ATTENBOROUGH, AND CLAIRE,
HAMISH & MATTHEW]

HOT CHOCOLATE LAVA CAKES

Nutrition Facts per serving: Calories 544.1, Protein 7.59 Gm, Carbs 65.67 Gm, Fat 30.71 Gm, Cholesterol 258.3 mg, Dietary Fiber 2.227 Gm, Sugar 51.36 Gm, Sodium 211.9 mg, Calcium 42.88 mg, Potassium 61.34 mg, Iron 2.02 mg

SERVES 8

1-½ sticks butter
7 ozs. bittersweet chocolate, chopped, or 7 ozs. chocolate chips
2 Tbsp. Baileys or Amaretto liqueur
4 lg. eggs plus 4 lg. egg yolks
¾ cup all purpose flour
1-½ cups confectioners' sugar
8 tsp. butter, for preparing the dessert molds
8 tsp. granulated sugar, for preparing the dessert molds
Vanilla ice cream
Blueberries and strawberries (optional)

NOTE:
These cannot be made a day ahead but can be prepared the day they are to be served and left on the counter until just after dinner. Since they cook so quickly, they can be popped into the oven just before it is time to serve dessert.

1. Preheat oven to 350°F.

2. Butter 8 cupcake-size muffin/dessert molds with a diameter of about 2-½" (5 to 6 ounce ramekins work well also). Sprinkle each mold with granulated sugar.

3. In the top of a double boiler, melt the butter and chocolate; add the liqueur.

4. Remove the double boiler from the heat, and add the eggs and egg yolks.

5. Using a wire whisk, temper the yolks and chocolate while whisking to combine (the mixture will be very thick).

6. In a mixing bowl, sift together the flour and confectioners' sugar; stir into the chocolate mixture.

7. Spoon about ½ cup of the mixture into each of the dessert molds.

8. Place the molds onto a cookie sheet, and transfer to the preheated oven.

9. Bake for 8 to 10 minutes, or until the cakes are set on the outside and soft in the middle.

10. Remove the cakes from the molds by placing a cutting board or cookie sheet on top, and flipping them over.

11. Serve hot with a scoop of vanilla ice cream, together with whole blueberries and finely diced strawberries, if desired.

This wonderfully delicious dessert is very popular with several Cayman Prep families. It originated with Jennifer Hunter, who passed it on to her friend and relative, Shannon Panton, who in turn served it to the Leonard family, who shared it with the Hew family, who submitted it for inclusion in the Prep for Success cookbook, so that others may enjoy it too!

[RICHARD & SANDY HEW, AND THOMPSON, LAUREN & HARRISON]

CHRISTMAS COOKIES

Nutrition Facts per serving: Calories 145.4, Protein 1.506 Gm, Carbs 11.26 Gm, Fat 10.82 Gm, Cholesterol 20.71 mg, Dietary Fiber 0.594 Gm, Sugar 0.37 Gm, Sodium 78.46 mg, Calcium 5.421 mg, Potassium 31.31 mg, Iron 0.526 mg

MAKES ABOUT 24

2 cups all purpose flour
½ cup confectioners' sugar
1 cup melted butter
1 cup crushed pecans

1. Mix butter, sugar and nuts, then slowly add flour.

2. Form into 1-½" balls or crescents, and place on a baking pan.

3. Bake at 350°F for approximately 20 minutes; let cool.

4. Sprinkle with confectioners' sugar.

[STEPHEN & DEBRA MCTAGGART, AND SARAH, AMELIA & MATTHEW]

Christmas Cookies (photo kindly submitted by Kim McTaggart)

STRAWBERRY PRETZEL JELLO

Nutrition Facts per serving: Calories 468.9, Protein 4.83 Gm, Carbs 56.59 Gm, Fat 25.82 Gm, Cholesterol 25.08 mg, Dietary Fiber 1.013 Gm, Sugar 46.17 Gm, Sodium 464.5 mg, Calcium 27.17 mg, Potassium 56.55 mg, Iron 1.454 mg

SERVES 10 TO 12

2 cups crushed pretzels
¼ cup sugar
1-½ sticks margarine, melted
1 (8 oz.) pkg. cream cheese, softened
1 cup sugar
2 cups Cool Whip
2 (10 oz.) pkgs. frozen strawberries (do not thaw)
2 (3 oz.) pkgs. strawberry (or cherry) jello
2 cups water
No-stick cooking spray.

1. Preheat oven to 350°F. Spray a 9" x 13" baking pan with cooking spray.

2. Combine pretzels, ¼ cup sugar and margarine; spread into the baking pan.

3. Bake in preheated oven for 10 minutes; let cool.

4. In a large bowl, combine cream cheese, 1 cup sugar and Cool Whip; spread over pretzel mixture.

5. In a saucepan, bring water to boil; add jello, and mix well. Remove from heat.

6. Add frozen strawberries to the jello mixture, and stir until it begins to thicken; spread over the cream cheese layer.

7. Refrigerate, until chilled. Top with a dollop of Cool Whip, and serve chilled.

[CAREN WIGHT, AND JUSTIN & ERIC]

RICE PUDDING

Nutrition Facts per serving: Calories 343.2, Protein 5.076 Gm, Carbs 63.09 Gm, Fat 8.206 Gm, Cholesterol 77.09 mg, Dietary Fiber 0.663 Gm, Sugar 8.12 Gm, Sodium 126.4 mg, Calcium 109.9 mg, Potassium 333 mg, Iron 1.905 mg

SERVES 10 TO 12

4 cups water
1 cup rice
1 stick margarine
4 eggs, separated (reserve whites for meringue)
1 can evaporated milk
2 Tbsp. vanilla extract
1 Tbsp. pineapple or strawberry extract
1 cup raisins
2 cups sugar

Meringue:
4 egg whites
2 Tbsp. sugar

1. In a large pot, bring water to boil. Reduce heat to Medium, add rice and cook for 10 to 12 minutes, or until about halfway done. A little salt may be added to the water, if desired.

2. In a small bowl, beat the egg yolks.

3. One tablespoon at a time, add the hot rice mixture to the egg yolks until the yolks are the same temperature as the rice mixture. This will prevent the yolks from hard-boiling or curdling during the cooking process.

4. Add the warm yolks to the pot of partially cooked rice. Mix thoroughly.

5. Add margarine, evaporated milk, vanilla extract, pineapple (or strawberry) extract, raisins and sugar to the pot; cook for about 25 to 30 minutes, or until thick, stirring frequently to prevent lumping, and especially in the last 5 minutes of cooking to prevent burning.

6. Place rice mixture in a 3 quart (9" x 13") casserole dish; top with meringue.

7. Bake at 350°F for approximately 10 minutes, or until meringue is lightly browned on top.

Rice Pudding

Meringue:

1. With an electric mixer on High speed, beat egg whites until soft peaks form.

2. Gradually add the sugar, beating until stiff peaks form.

[LESLIE & MICHELE EBANKS, AND JESSICA & KALEB]

LITTLE CAYMAN

Nutrition Facts per serving: Calories 765, Protein 11.6 Gm, Carbs 66.8 Gm, Fat 52.9 Gm,
Cholesterol 469 mg, Dietary Fiber 2.3 Gm, Sugar 55.4 Gm, Sodium 134 mg

SERVES 8

Banana custard:
1 vanilla bean
1 qt. heavy cream
10 egg yolks, lightly beaten
7 ozs. sugar
3 ripe bananas
1 Tbsp. banana
   liqueur (optional)

Meringue Island:
4 egg whites
1 cup sugar
1 tsp. vanilla extract

Toasted pecans, for topping

Banana custard:

1. In a medium saucepan, bring cream and vanilla bean to a near boil. Remove from heat; very slowly add hot cream to yolks while whisking to avoid curdling.

2. Return mixture to Medium heat, stirring constantly until slightly thickened and the mixture coats the back of a wooden spoon. Remove from the heat, strain and chill.

3. Just before serving, puree bananas with the custard and liqueur, until smooth.

4. Place in individual serving bowls, and top with Meringue Island and toasted pecans.

Meringue Island:

1. In the bowl of an electric mixer, stir together egg whites and sugar. Set over a saucepan with simmering water; stir constantly until the mixture is hot to the touch.

2. Remove from the heat, place bowl in mixer and beat on High speed until the mixture has tripled in volume and forms stiff, glossy peaks. Add vanilla.

3. Spoon meringue over custard and, using a blow torch or the broiler, brown slightly.

4. Sprinkle with toasted pecans, and serve.

NOTE:
The bananas should not be added until just before serving since they can cause the custard to turn brown if added too early.

[THE BRASSERIE RESTAURANT]
- SEE ADVERTISEMENT ON PAGE 250 -

COOKING TERMS

Bake - To cook by dry heat, either covered or uncovered, in an oven or oven-type appliance.

Baste - To moisten meat or other foods with pan drippings, fruit juice or a sauce. Prevents drying of food surface and adds flavour.

Beat - To make a mixture smooth by introducing air with a brisk over and over motion using an egg beater or electric mixer.

Blanch - To preheat in boiling water or steam. Helps loosen skins of fruits, vegetables or nuts; also used to prepare food for canning, freezing or drying.

Blend - To combine two or more ingredients thoroughly.

Boil - To heat a liquid until bubbles continuously break on the surface.

Braise - To cook slowly in a small amount of liquid in a covered pan.

Bread - To coat with flour, then dip into slightly diluted beaten egg or milk, and finally coat with bread, cereal or cracker crumbs.

Broil - To cook by direct heat, under a broiler or over hot coals.

Caramelize - To melt sugar, or foods containing sugar, slowly over low heat without burning, until it melts and becomes brown in colour.

Chop - To cut food into small pieces with a knife.

Clarify - To make a liquid (stock, broth, butter) clear by skimming away or filtering out fat or other impurities.

Coat - To cover food evenly with flour, crumbs or batter.

Coddle - To cook food slowly in water just below the boiling point.

Compote - Fruit stewed or cooked in syrup, usually served as a dessert.

Cool - To let food stand at room temperature until it is no longer warm to the touch.

Cream - To make a fat, such as butter, soft and smooth by beating with a spoon or mixer. Also, to combine a fat with sugar until mixture is light and fluffy.

Cube - To cut a solid food into cubes of about $\frac{1}{2}$ inch or more.

Cut in - To mix evenly a solid fat into dry ingredients (e.g. shortening and flour) by chopping with two knives or a pastry blender.

Dice - To make small cubes of $\frac{1}{8}$ to $\frac{1}{4}$ inch.

Dredge - To cover or coat food with flour or a similar fine, dry substance.

Dust - To sprinkle lightly with flour or sugar.

Fillet - A piece of meat, poultry or fish without bones.

Flake - To break food into small pieces, usually with a fork.

Flute - To make decorative indentations around edge of pastries, fruits or vegetables.

Fold - To combine two ingredients. Using a spoon or rubber spatula, go down through the mixture on the far side of the bowl, bring the spoon across the bottom of the bowl and up the near side, turn the mixture over on the top. Turn bowl slightly and repeat until mixture is blended.

Fry - To cook in hot fat; pan-fry or sauté in a small amount of fat, deep-fat fry in deep layer of fat that covers the food.

Glaze - To coat with a smooth mixture to give food a glossy appearance.

Grate - To rub food against a grater to form small particles.

Grill - To cook on a rack over hot coals or other direct heat.

Grind - To reduce to particles in a grinder, blender or food processor.

Julienne - To cut meat, vegetables or fruit into long match-like strips.

Knead - To manipulate with a pressing motion accompanied by folding and stretching. For yeast bread: fold dough toward you, push dough away using the heel of your hand. Rotate $\frac{1}{4}$ turn and repeat. For tea biscuits: kneading process is much less vigorous and requires less time.

Marinate - To let food stand in a seasoned sauce called a **marinade** to tenderize and increase flavour.

Mince - To cut or chop into very small pieces, but smaller than diced.

Mix - To combine ingredients until evenly distributed.

Panbroil - To cook uncovered on a hot surface removing fat as it accumulates.

Parboil - To cook food in a boiling liquid until partially done. Cooking is usually completed by another method.

Pare - To remove outer covering of fruit or vegetable with a knife.

Peel - To strip off or pull away outer covering of fruit or vegetable.

Poach - To cook slowly in simmering liquid such as water or milk.

Puree - To put food through a sieve, blender or processor to produce the thick pulp or paste with juice.

Reduce - To rapidly boil down the volume of a liquid to concentrate flavour.

Roast - To cook meat in an uncovered pan by dry heat in an oven.

Sauté - To brown or cook in a small amount of fat (see **fry**).

Scald - To heat milk to just below the boiling point, when tiny bubbles appear around the edge of the pan; to dip certain foods briefly into boiling water (see **blanch**).

Score - To make shallow slits into the surface of a food in a diamond or rectangular pattern.

Sear - To brown and seal surface of meat quickly with intense heat.

Shred - To cut into long, thin strips with a knife or shredder.

Simmer - To cook in liquid just below boiling point; bubbles form slowly and burst before reaching surface.

Sliver - To cut into long thin pieces with a knife; e.g. almonds, or pimiento.

Steam - To cook in a covered container above boiling water.

Steep - To let stand for a few minutes in water that has just been boiled to enhance flavour and colour.

Stew - To simmer slowly in liquid deep enough to cover.

Stir - To mix ingredients in a circular motion until blended with uniform consistency.

Stir fry - To cook in a frying pan or wok over high heat in a small amount of fat, tossing or stirring constantly.

Toast - To brown with dry heat in an oven or toaster.

Whip - To beat rapidly with a wire whisk, beater or mixer to incorporate air to lighten and increase volume.

Bakers in Tubingen, Germany, 1900, the late Mr. and Mrs. Giesel, Great-Great-Grandparents of Hamish, Claire & Matthew Attenborough

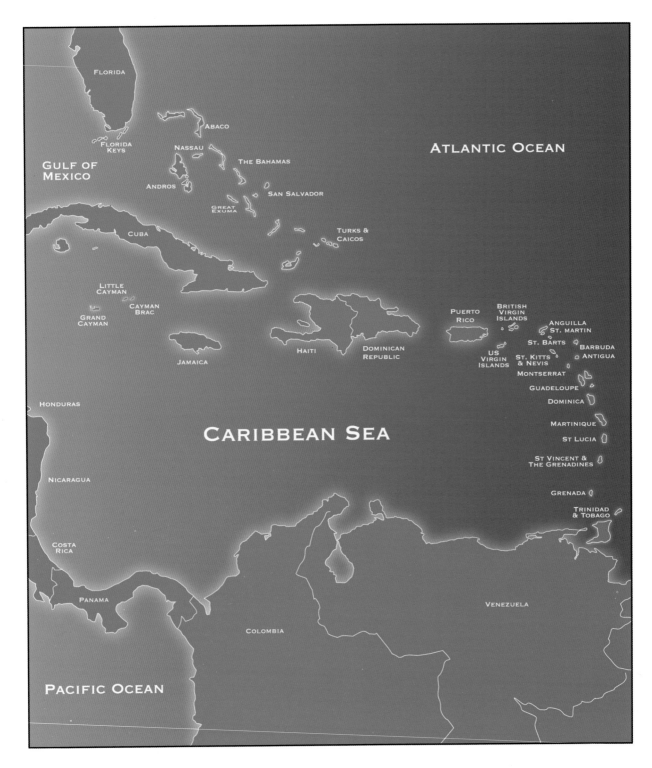

FLORIDA

ATLANTIC OCEAN

FLORIDA KEYS

GULF OF MEXICO

ABACO

NASSAU

THE BAHAMAS

ANDROS

SAN SALVADOR

GREAT EXUMA

CUBA

TURKS & CAICOS

LITTLE CAYMAN

CAYMAN BRAC

GRAND CAYMAN

PUERTO RICO

BRITISH VIRGIN ISLANDS

ANGUILLA
ST. MARTIN

ST. BARTS

BARBUDA

JAMAICA

HAITI

DOMINICAN REPUBLIC

US VIRGIN ISLANDS

ST. KITTS & NEVIS

ANTIGUA

MONTSERRAT

GUADELOUPE

DOMINICA

HONDURAS

CARIBBEAN SEA

MARTINIQUE

ST LUCIA

ST VINCENT & THE GRENADINES

NICARAGUA

GRENADA

TRINIDAD & TOBAGO

COSTA RICA

PANAMA

VENEZUELA

COLOMBIA

PACIFIC OCEAN